The City in American Cinema

The City in American Cinema

Film and Postindustrial Culture

Edited by
Johan Andersson and Lawrence Webb

BLOOMSBURY ACADEMIC

LONDON • NEW YORK • OXFORD • NEW DELHI • SYDNEY

BLOOMSBURY ACADEMIC
Bloomsbury Publishing Plc
50 Bedford Square, London, WC1B 3DP, UK
1385 Broadway, New York, NY 10018, USA
29 Earlsfort Terrace, Dublin 2, Ireland

BLOOMSBURY, BLOOMSBURY ACADEMIC and the Diana logo are
trademarks of Bloomsbury Publishing Plc

First published in Great Britain 2019
This paperback edition published in 2021

Cover design: Charlotte Daniels
Cover image © Pine District Pictures / Collection Christophel / ArenaPAL

A catalogue record for this book is available from the British Library.

A catalog record for this book is available from the Library of Congress.

ISBN: HB: 978-1-7883-1318-6
         PB: 978-1-3501-9474-8
         ePDF: 978-1-3501-1563-7
         eBook: 978-1-3501-1562-0

Series: International Library of the Moving Image

Typeset by Integra Software Services Pvt. Ltd.

To find out more about our authors and books visit www.bloomsbury.com
and sign up for our newsletters.

Contents

Contributors

Johan Andersson is Lecturer in Urban Geography at King's College London. He is the co-editor of *Global Cinematic Cities: New Landscapes of Film and Media* (2016) and co-author of *Planning on the Edge: The Context for Planning in the Rural-Urban Fringe* (2006). His work has appeared in numerous journals, including *Antipode, Environment and Planning A, International Journal of Urban and Regional Research, Society and Space, Transactions of the Institute of British Geographers*, and *Urban Studies*.

Amy Corbin is Associate Professor of Film Studies and Media & Communication at Muhlenberg College. Her research focuses on racial and cultural geography in film and on the intersection of film spectatorship and senses of place. Her book, *Cinematic Geographies and Multicultural Spectatorship in America* (2015), explores the ideologies of cinematic landscapes in the post–Civil Rights era and theorizes the sense of virtual travel inherent in films about place. She has also published essays on narrative map-making, the films of Charles Burnett, and whiteness in Southern films.

Stanley Corkin is the Charles Phelps Taft Professor of English and History, and Niehoff Professor of Film and Media Studies at the University of Cincinnati. He is the author of *Connecting the Wire: Space, Race, and Post-Industrial Baltimore* (2017), *Starring New York: Filming the Grime and the Glamour of the Long 1970s* (2011), *Cowboys as Cold Warriors: The Western and U.S. History* (2004), and *Realism and the Birth of the Modern United States: Cinema, Literature, and Culture* (1996). He also co-edited, with Phyllis Frus, The New Riverside Edition of *Stephen Crane: The Red Badge of Courage, Maggie, A Girl of the Streets, and Other Selected Writings* (2000). Professor Corkin's peer-reviewed articles, essays, and reviews have appeared in a number of journals, including *Jump Cut*, the *Journal of Urban History, MFS: Modern Fiction Studies, Prospects: An American Studies Annual, Journal of American History, Cinema Journal, College English, College Literature*, and *Cineaste*.

Camilla Fojas is Professor of American Studies and Media Studies at the University of Virginia. Her most recent books are *Zombies, Migrants, and Queers: Race and Crisis Capitalism in Pop Culture* (2017) and *Migrant Labor and Border Securities in Pop Culture* (2017).

Nick Jones is Lecturer in Film, Television and Digital Culture at the University of York. He is the author of *Hollywood Action Films and Spatial Theory* (2015), and his work on digital effects, spatial theory, and contemporary cinema has also appeared in numerous journals, including *Cinema Journal, New Review of Film and Television Studies, Journal of Popular Film and Television* and *Continuum*. He is currently completing a monograph on digital 3D cinema.

Nathan Koob is Special Lecturer at Oakland University. He received his PhD from the University of Michigan in 2015. His work examines texts through their spatial and industrial contexts, such as in his dissertation *Outsiders: Auteurs in Place*, where he studied auteurs who forged consistent production relationships with cities. Further work has explored industrial and exhibition contexts associated with the concepts of place and space such as the history of the development of Midnight Movie exhibition and the re-coding of theatrical spaces for live streaming and comedy events.

Brendan Kredell is Assistant Professor of Cinema Studies at Oakland University. His teaching and research focus on the intersection of media and urban studies. With Marijke de Valck and Skadi Loist, he co-edited the collection *Film Festivals: History, Theory, Method, Practice* (2016). He also serves as co-editor of *Mediapolis: A Journal of Cities and Culture*, and is currently working on a book on American cinema and urban development in the postindustrial era.

Carlo Rotella's books include *October Cities* (1998), *Good with Their Hands* (2002), *Cut Time* (2003), *Playing in Time* (2012), and, most recently, *The World Is Always Coming to An End: Pulling Together and Apart in a Chicago Neighborhood* (2019). He contributes regularly to the *New York Times Magazine* and his work has also appeared in *The New Yorker, Harper's, Slate, The Believer*, and *The Best American Essays*, and on WGBH FM. A recipient of Guggenheim, DuBois, and Howard fellowships, the Whiting Writers Award, and the L. L. Winship/PEN New England Award, he is Professor of American Studies, Journalism, and English at Boston College.

Martha Shearer is Teaching Fellow in Film Studies at King's College London. She is the author of *New York City and the Hollywood Musical: Dancing in the Streets* (2016) and a member of the editorial board of *Mediapolis: A Journal of Cities and Culture*.

Mark Shiel is Reader in Film Studies and Urbanism at King's College London. He is the author of *Hollywood Cinema and the Real Los Angeles* (2012) and *Italian Neorealism: Rebuilding the Cinematic City* (2005). He is the editor of *Architectures of Revolt: The Cinematic City circa 1968* (2018) and co-editor of *Screening the City* (2003), and *Cinema and the City: Film and Urban Societies in a Global Context* (2001).

Erica Stein is Assistant Professor in the Department of Film at Vassar College. Her research concerns the relationship between media and the built environment, focusing on the political function of space in independent cinema. Her work has appeared in *Journal of Film and Video*, *Camera Obscura*, and *Studies in the Humanities*. She is the co-founder and managing editor of *Mediapolis: A Journal of Cities and Culture* and recently completed a manuscript on mid-century independent film and city planning called *Seeing Symphonically: Avant-Garde Film, Urban Renewal, and New York as Utopian Image*.

Lawrence Webb is Lecturer in Film Studies at the University of Sussex. He is the author of *The Cinema of Urban Crisis: Seventies Film and the Reinvention of the City* (2014), and co-editor of *Global Cinematic Cities: New Landscapes of Film and Media* (2016), and *Hollywood on Location: An Industry History* (2019).

Acknowledgments

The editors would like to thank: Maddy Hamey-Thomas, Alexandru Ciobanu, Rebecca Barden, Rebecca Richards, Amy Jordan, Kumeraysen Vaidhyanadhaswamy, and the two anonymous peer reviewers for their generous and constructive comments on the manuscript. We are extremely grateful to *Backstage* magazine and to Joe Conzo for allowing us to reproduce images in Chapter 2.

American Cinema and Urban Change: Industry, Genre, and Politics from Nixon to Trump

Johan Andersson and Lawrence Webb

At the close of an eventful night at the 89th Academy Awards, the producers of *Moonlight* (Barry Jenkins, 2016) famously won the statuette for Best Picture only after it had first been wrongly awarded to the hotly tipped frontrunner *La La Land* (Damien Chazelle, 2016). The slip-up had the immediate effect of placing the two films very publicly in opposition to each other. Regardless of whether such an opposition was fair, both movies had already been widely discussed as cultural touchstones of the previous year, and each one offered audiences a distinctive portrait of a starkly divided American society as the Obama era gave way to the nascent Trump administration. Pitting the spectacular neoclassical Hollywood musical *La La Land* against the small-scale, lyrical realism of *Moonlight* revealed, it seemed, obvious fault lines: the two films split not only by budget, box office, and mode of production, but also according to genre, aesthetics, and cultural politics.[1] At the heart of this division lay the films' strikingly different images of cities and urban life. Both *La La Land* and *Moonlight* are inseparable from their primary setting—Los Angeles, California, and Miami, Florida, respectively—and each film renders its highly specific sense of place by drawing on, and revising, rich yet divergent legacies of urban representation.

Though *La La Land* is not, in fact, a high-budget, major studio production, it is nevertheless steeped in Hollywood history and revels in the expressionistic artifice of studio filmmaking. Its portrayal of Los Angeles is suffused with nostalgia for the glamour and romance of "Old Hollywood" and displays a playful awareness of the city's history as an image factory, drawing influences and references from mid-twentieth-century movies such as *Singin' in the Rain* (Stanley Donen, 1952) and *Rebel Without a Cause* (Nicholas Ray, 1955). Celebrating the tradition of the urban musical, it integrates the utopian dynamism of playful song-and-dance set pieces with a cautiously optimistic, if melancholic, narrative of individual achievement centered on two young, white, heterosexual protagonists. In contrast to the gentrified, affluent setting of *La La Land*, *Moonlight* takes place in Liberty City, an African American neighborhood of Miami, and depicts what is at first glance a familiar cityscape of poverty, drug addiction, violence, and social exclusion. Indeed, for some commentators, the dominating whiteness of *La La Land* contrasted in a stark and unflattering manner with *Moonlight* at a moment when the politics of screen diversity had become a pressing topic at the Oscars and beyond. In its three-part story of a young gay, black man's coming of age, *Moonlight* draws on the legacy of African American social realism while significantly expanding its possibilities. Filmed with a mix of professional and non-professional actors on locations where its director Barry Jenkins had grown up, *Moonlight* offers an image of Miami radically discordant with its conventional screen presence.

As these examples show, contemporary American cinema is unavoidably *located*. This can be explored from a variety of perspectives. From a textual, audience-centered point of view, a film's narrative setting, social milieu, and choice of locations are rich with cultural and political meaning. For viewers, the parameters and possibilities of a film's storyworld are often formed in its opening moments, even its credit sequence, by an establishing shot, a montage sequence, or a place-specific intertitle, or even shaped before the viewing process, by reviews, posters, trailers, and other promotional paratexts that indicate key markers of setting. The spaces and places of films—from everyday, domestic interiors to spectacular, panoramic cityscapes—establish fictional environments and social worlds that are traversed and inhabited by characters and viewers alike. And as *La La Land* and *Moonlight* demonstrate, the way we apprehend cinematic space is deeply intertwined with our understanding of genre patterns and aesthetic conventions. As we have suggested, these two films draw, implicitly or explicitly, on modes of urban representation that can be traced back through the history of cinema, television, literature, and the visual arts. Such legacies of urban representation carry with them viewing strategies, markers of cultural value, and frameworks for reception.

Looking behind the scenes, we can also consider how *La La Land* and *Moonlight* were made using distinctive spatial practices of production, from location shooting and studio sets to sound design and visual effects techniques. Whether shot on location, in a studio, or visualized digitally, a film's narrative space is manufactured by key creative personnel, including the director of photography, editor, art director, sound designer, and visual effects supervisor. From an industrial perspective, the choice to film in a particular city—Los Angeles or Miami, say—is not merely a creative decision, but one bound up with crucial questions of economics, institutions, and labor. And at the level of distribution and exhibition, the release pattern of each film plots a complex social map, telling the story of where these films were seen, by what kinds of audiences, and in what type of space.

The City in American Cinema explores these complex, multilayered relations between cinema, space and place in one specific geographical and historical context: the United States since the 1960s. As the contributions to the volume demonstrate, American cities have transformed during this period. From inner city decay, the loss of industry, and the rapid growth of the suburbs in the postwar decades, to regeneration, gentrification, and downtown redevelopment in the 1980s and beyond, the dynamics of decline and renewal have created complex patterns of urban social change. The causes and effects of such change have long been a pressing subject of debate for academics and journalists, architects and planners, politicians and activists. At the same time, this remarkable story of "decline" and "rebirth" has afforded rich subject matter for filmmakers, just as it has profoundly shaped the cultural and economic conditions in which the movies have been produced, circulated, and consumed. Whether we view American cinema as a set of film texts, a global media industry, or as (trans)national popular culture, its recent history cannot be fully understood outside of this spatial context of economic transformation and social upheaval.

This collection traces the shifting contours of this relationship between the city and the moving image since the 1960s, which we conceptualize as a historic turning point for both Hollywood cinema and North American urbanism. Over this period, the rapidly changing cityscape has offered a constantly evolving diegetic world and social environment for cinema. Consider, for example, the determining, expressive function of urban settings in such disparate films as *Midnight Cowboy* (John Schlesinger, 1969), *Killer of Sheep* (Charles Burnett, 1978), *Chan Is Missing* (Wayne Wang, 1982), *Manhunter* (Michael Mann, 1986), *Strange Days* (Kathryn Bigelow, 1995), *You've Got Mail* (Nora Ephron, 1998), *Somewhere* (Sofia Coppola, 2010), *Magic Mike* (Steven Soderbergh, 2012), *Zootopia* (Byron Howard and Rich Moore, 2016), or *The Florida Project* (Sean Baker, 2017). As these examples suggest, the varied spaces and places of cities—both real and imagined—have played a constitutive role in the development of American filmmaking. The contributions to this book show how American cities and their stories of social change are deeply embedded in the mise-en-scene, stylistic patterns, narrative habits, and genre logics of films in the "postclassical" era. And as many of the chapters in this volume also explore, this relationship goes deeper than subject matter and setting. Looking beyond the film text, the cultural and economic remaking of cities has shaped the development of the motion picture business and the structure of its audiences, just as media industries have become increasingly important to the success of urban economies.

Postindustrial cities and cinema

Marking a definitive break point in film history or urban history is never straightforward. Nevertheless, many scholars in both fields see the 1960s and 1970s as transitional decades. For film historians, this period is widely seen as a watershed for the history of American cinema, when the classical Hollywood studio system—which had already experienced deep changes during the postwar decades—finally gave way to New Hollywood and what has often been characterized as a "postclassical" cinema.[2] Likewise, for geographers, the crises of the 1960s and 1970s set off a series of restructuring processes that would profoundly reshape the urban environment. The racialized media discourse of the urban crisis and the ghetto uprisings in Watts (1965), Detroit (1967), and Newark (1967) brought the material decline and deep social inequality of the inner city into sharp focus, heralding a breakdown of the established urban order. Fractures appeared in the political frameworks and regulating ideologies of the postwar era: Fordism, Keynesianism, modernist urban planning, and the gendered division of labor. For American cities and cinema, these were years of intensive and far-reaching change.[3]

From the late 1960s, manufacturing decline and "white flight" accelerated, fueling an interconnected set of crises in American society that impacted on cities and culture alike. These crises—among them the urban crisis, the oil crisis, the crisis of masculinity, and Hollywood's own financial crisis— are commonly understood as ushering in a new era variously characterized, with differing emphases, as "postindustrial," "post-Fordist," "postmodern," or "neoliberal."[4] These interlinked discourses and the explanatory models they offer are used throughout this book, though "postindustrial" is especially frequently deployed. If post-Fordism refers to new ways of organizing production and consumption, and neoliberalism to the laissez-faire economic ideology underpinning them, postmodernism is often viewed as their cultural and architectural expression. But the "postindustrial," which we have chosen to include in the title of the book, provides a useful way for many authors to capture interconnections between space, society, and culture. Beyond the shift in employment structure forecasted by Daniel Bell, "postindustrial" is useful both as a marker of deep changes to the uses and functions of city space, and as an umbrella term for political and social upheaval, corporate restructuring, and an array of new cultural expressions and consumer tastes. As such, it provides an especially productive way to position cinema within broad historic shifts in urban space, business organization, patterns of labor and consumption, as well as emerging social practices and political trends.[5] The 1960s and 1970s can be seen as a foundational moment, then, and as the chapters in this book explore, the years that followed would bring cities and cinema together in new configurations.

As the varied contributions to this book make clear, individual cities experienced these shifts in different ways: what holds true for New York, Boston, or Austin does not necessarily pertain to Baltimore, Kansas City, or Detroit. Nevertheless, we can map several broad trends. In contrast to optimistic predictions of a "postindustrial society," Barry Bluestone and Bennett Harrison's landmark study *The Deindustrialization of America* (1982) offered a critical perspective on the potential dissolution of the industrial order. As their research showed, large numbers of manufacturing jobs had been automated, moved offshore to factories in the developing world, or relocated to "Right to Work" states in the South. Such precipitous industrial decline devastated "Rust Belt" cities across the Northeast and Midwest, especially manufacturing powerhouses such as Detroit, Pittsburgh, and Cleveland, which suffered soaring unemployment, population loss, decaying infrastructure, and rising crime.[6] In contrast to the landscapes of abandonment and ruin found in cities such as Detroit, urban centers in the "Sun Belt" states of the South and West experienced rapid economic growth and the expansion of high-tech sectors, such as aerospace and semi-conductors. Coastal cities, such as New York, Boston, and San Francisco, emerged as flagships for a "new economy" based on finance, insurance, real estate, and the service sector more generally. Industrial zones and declining port areas, such as New York's Battery Park and Baltimore's Inner Harbor, were redeveloped and reinvented as centers of consumption and leisure while specific areas of major cities began to experience localized redevelopment. In Lower Manhattan, for example, the formerly industrial area of SoHo transformed into a bohemian, mixed-use neighborhood, its warehouses repurposed as artists' studios and loft apartments, while an influential set of self-styled "pioneering" middle-class homeowners refurbished brownstones in areas such as Park Slope and Brooklyn Heights.[7]

This transformation of inner city neighborhoods would later be codified as gentrification, a term first coined by sociologist Ruth Glass in 1964, which remained obscure in academic debates until the late 1970s when Neil Smith's work on the "rent-gap" provided an influential neo-Marxist model that viewed capital as the principal driver of inner-city rehabilitation.[8] The long-standing and overly schematic arguments over production-side versus consumption-side explanations took shape at this time, although Smith's early work acknowledged the role of consumer preferences while still arguing that these were largely constrained by the availability of mortgage capital. Those who have instead emphasized shifting consumer tastes have pointed to structural changes in the labor market overlapping largely with the shift from manufacturing to services and the new centrality of science-based industries predicted by Daniel Bell.[9] In this context, the associated expansion of higher education has also been seen to foster new preferences for urban living. As David Ley has argued, "the demographic bulge of the baby boom reaching college age in the 1960s" often lived in the "emergent youth ghettos nestled symbiotically around inner city university campuses."[10] This college-educated demographic who attended university during the political fervor of the late 1960s would in many instances develop an experiential and ideological commitment to diverse urban neighborhoods over homogeneous suburbs. These college-educated baby boomers would become a key target audience for the New Hollywood cinema that developed in the late 1960s and 1970s.

While the role of fine art in gentrification is relatively well understood—and the idea of artists and galleries driving neighborhood regeneration is almost a cliché—cinema is much less often discussed in these terms. From a production point of view, this may be because the transitory nature of location shooting makes organic connections with local communities harder to establish. Equally, filmmakers have not been accorded the same high-culture status as visual artists in the discourses of gentrification, and below-the-line crew for a feature production fit less easily into preexisting notions of what Richard Lloyd calls "neo-bohemia."[11] Accordingly, the history of gentrification, which runs like a thread throughout this book, has only recently become a topic in the cinema and the city literature. Thus, while it is commonplace to understand 1970s urban cinema in the context of deindustrialization and demographic change, films from the 1980s and 1990s onwards, when gentrification spread and accelerated, remain comparatively less explored from an urban geography angle. Yet looking across the 50-year time-span of this book, we argue that it is no coincidence that cities such as New York and San Francisco, which became successful film production centers in the late 1960s and 1970s, are now the most expensive and gentrified in the whole of the United States and that their perceived attractiveness should be understood in relation to their cinematic image and the employment opportunities associated with their media industries.

In the 1980s and 1990s, however, when the first generation of cinema and the city literature emerged, many urban theorists pointed to the dispersed, polycentric development of the Los Angeles metropolitan region as *the* paradigmatic urban form of the late twentieth century. For Los Angeles School geographers such as Michael Dear and Edward Soja, Los Angeles was an urban laboratory and a prototype for urban growth for cities worldwide.[12] The urban and architectural forms of Los Angeles also inspired cultural theorists such as

Fredric Jameson, for whom the postmodern "hyperspace" of the Bonaventure Hotel in downtown Los Angeles famously offered an object lesson in the cultural logic of late capitalism.[13] In turn, discussions of the contemporary "cinematic city" in the pathbreaking work of the 1980s and 1990s—from Giuliana Bruno and David Harvey to Mike Davis and David Clarke—placed Los Angeles at center stage and looked to *Blade Runner* (Ridley Scott, 1982) as a key cinematic text of the postmodern or postindustrial city.[14] Yet the centrality of Los Angeles to urban and cultural theory has since been challenged by the accelerated gentrification of American cities from Pittsburgh to Portland. Many of the contributions to this book explore the effects of this emphatic revival of central cities as commercial and residential spaces for the middle class. As they suggest, the Los Angeles blueprint for rapid, decentralized peripheral expansion therefore coexisted with a counternarrative of downtown revival and the return of affluent city-dwellers to the urban core. The tension between these two tendencies generated protracted debates between proponents of density (such as Richard Florida) and those who champion sprawl (such as Joel Kotkin), but the reassertion of the urban center has nevertheless been striking.[15]

As we have suggested above, the period covered by this book has also seen far-reaching changes in American cinema. From the late 1960s, the Hollywood studios sought to recapture the young, affluent, college-educated consumers that Ley describes. Though relatively deep industrial and aesthetic change had occurred during the previous decade or so, there was nevertheless a palpable cultural shock to the first stream of films that unapologetically addressed this audience. Championed by a new generation of critics such as Pauline Kael and Vincent Canby, iconoclastic, sexually frank, and sometimes violent movies, such as *Bonnie and Clyde* (Arthur Penn, 1967), *Point Blank* (John Boorman, 1967), *The Graduate* (Mike Nichols, 1967), *Easy Rider* (Dennis Hopper, 1969), and *Midnight Cowboy*, appeared to dispense with the stylistic conventions, narrative principles, and regulating moral codes of the classical Hollywood cinema. Taken together, the critical (and sometimes commercial) success of this American "New Wave" or "Hollywood Renaissance" from 1967–8, the end of the Production Code in 1968, and the industry financial crisis of 1969–71 marked the transition between the "old" and the "new" Hollywood. As numerous histories of the period explain, the auteur-driven, socially critical cinema of the 1970s produced a series of now-canonical films that refracted the widespread sense of social turmoil and political disillusionment in the wake of the urban crisis, the Vietnam War, global recession, and Watergate.[16] In the second half of the decade, the box office dominance of blockbusters *Jaws* (Steven Spielberg, 1975) and *Star Wars* (George Lucas, 1977) signaled a different kind of post- (or perhaps neo-)classicism and more substantive set of economic and industrial shifts toward "global" or "conglomerate" Hollywood that would set the stage for the decades to come.

Although many of the landmark films of the sixties and seventies did not have urban settings—especially in key genres such as road movies, war films, and revisionist westerns—location shooting in the streets of American cities such as New York, Philadelphia, Los Angeles, and San Francisco was a defining feature of the period. There is now a relatively developed literature on the urban film cycles of the 1970s, which explores how the shifting terrain of the city provided a key narrative space for socially questioning, genre-revising crime films, paranoid thrillers, "blaxploitation" films, dramas, musicals, and comedies, from *The French Connection* (William Friedkin, 1971), *Dirty Harry* (Don Siegel, 1971), *Klute* (Alan J. Pakula, 1971), *Super Fly* (Gordon Parks Jr., 1972), and *The Long Goodbye* (Robert Altman, 1973) to *Claudine* (John Berry, 1974), *Rocky* (John G. Avildsen, 1976), *New York, New York* (Martin Scorsese, 1977), *Annie Hall* (Woody Allen, 1977), and *Girlfriends* (Claudia Weill, 1978).[17]

Beyond this especially fertile period, scholars have focused on key areas of intersection between the city and cinema, which have included the suburban themes and yuppie tropes of the 1980s; the new black cinema of the early 1990s; the postmodern spatiality of Los Angeles; cyborg urbanization; the relationship between indie cinema and gentrification; the impact of 9/11 on urban representation in genres such as horror, action, and superhero films; posthuman love in the digital city; as well as the relationship between the disaster movie and the environmental crisis.[18] In the context of these debates, specific films have recurred and become central reference points, including such diverse examples as *Ferris Bueller's Day Off* (John Hughes, 1986), *Robocop* (Paul Verhoeven, 1987), *Boyz N the Hood* (John Singleton, 1991), *You've Got Mail* (Nora Ephron, 1998), *The Day After Tomorrow* (Roland Emmerich, 2004), *American Psycho* (Mary

Harron, 2000), *Cloverfield* (Matt Reeves, 2008), the *Dark Knight* trilogy (Christopher Nolan, 2005–2012), and *Her* (Spike Jonze, 2013).

This body of scholarship demonstrates the continuing productivity of the spatial turn in film studies, which has explored the manifold relations between screen media and the urban environment. Drawing on the foundational work of critical spatial theorists such as Henri Lefebvre, Edward Soja, and Doreen Massey, film scholars have increasingly focused on geography as well as history, space as well as time.[19] This has led to rich insights into the spatiality of American cinema, whether we think of studies of screen cities and landscapes, specific genres and cycles, narratives of urban life (especially in relation to race, gender, and sexuality), or the geographies of production and exhibition.[20] This book builds on and extends this existing work, offering a geographically and historically specific exploration of a single national context over a defined historical period. Rather than rely on ahistorical conceptual generalizations about cinema and cities, the scholarship in this book often draws on close-grained historical research on individual cities, bringing insights from urban studies to bear on the study of Hollywood and American independent cinema.

In the remainder of this introductory chapter, we offer an extended overview of some key historical contexts and conceptual approaches, which doubles as an argument for the continued relevance both of spatial approaches to film studies and of cinematic analysis to cultural geography. This material is intended to both to frame and to complement the book chapters, which are summarized separately from pages 26–34. Our first section focuses on the geographical dynamics of production and discusses how aspects of urban political economy have interlocked with developments in the American film industry. The second section focuses on issues of representation and cultural discourse, and discusses issues of politics, identity, and agency in relation to city narratives and genres.

Locating the film industry: the place of production

One of the key interventions of this book is to bring together industrial and textual approaches to the study of cinema and cities, both within individual chapters and across the collection as a whole. In this section, we provide a broad overview of the interlocking industrial and urban trends that have shaped the geography of American filmmaking since the emergence of New Hollywood in the 1960s.

As the contributions to this book show, the media industries have operated as a spearhead of the cultural economy over the last four or five decades. For cities such as New York, Boston, and San Francisco, and more recently, Portland, Austin, and Atlanta, the growth of media production has played a central role in their economic prosperity. According to a think tank report published in 2015, creative economy growth in New York City outperformed sectors such as finance, insurance, real estate, and legal services during the previous decade. Moreover, employment in film and television constituted the largest single contribution to that growth, placing it above performing and visual arts, architecture, advertising, and design.[21] As these trends suggest, film and television production has made a significant economic impact on cities beyond the industry's historic base in Los Angeles.

But what is the historical backdrop to this closely intertwined relationship? We might begin the story in the 1960s, when Hollywood responded to and help to shape the various interlinked crises of the period with a new economic organization that geographers have characterized in terms of "vertical disintegration" and "flexible specialization." Whereas the classical studio system had been vertically integrated and resembled the serial manufacturing processes of other major industries in important respects, the New Hollywood studios frequently subcontracted aspects of production to specialized firms that could more quickly respond to market niches, avoid unionized labor, and capitalize on production incentives offered by city governments outside Los Angeles. As the economic geographers Susan Christopherson and Michael Storper have argued, the Hollywood firms were therefore at the cutting edge of post-Fordist restructuring and might be considered pioneers of the postindustrial economy.[22]

Location shooting was central to this flexible mode of production, which opened up a wider range of filming locales and narrative settings than possible under the relatively restricted practices of the studio era, though the postwar tendency toward "runaway production" overseas was temporarily constrained by the falling value of the dollar and studio belt-tightening at the end of the 1960s. Throughout the 1970s, this decentralization of Hollywood production intensified. As the industry's spatial practices were reconfigured, the two meanings of the term "studio" diverged. While it had made sense to conflate the motion picture corporations and their primary site of production in the classical era, this model was now out of date. From a corporate perspective, the "studios" (as companies) became primarily financier-distributors, while the "studios" (as physical sites of production) underwent significant change. The majors sold off or redeveloped large tracts of their studios and backlots, which had become highly valuable Westside real estate, and though soundstage production continued to play an important role in the filmmaking process, studios functioned as rental operations and their routine functions were largely maintained by the high demand for television production.

Such major shifts in the film industry constituted part of a wider process of urban and industrial restructuring, both in the immediate context of the Los Angeles urban region and across the United States more generally. As cities sought to manage the transition toward a postindustrial economy, their governments looked to Hollywood location shooting as a lucrative part of the expanding cultural sector. New York City and San Francisco were the primary beneficiaries of this dispersal of production, though filming also surged in Southern states, such as Texas and Florida. This turn toward location shooting meshed with a new spirit of entrepreneurialism in local government. Faced with the decline of industrial production, many cities aggressively encouraged the growth of what Sharon Zukin terms the "symbolic economy." "What is new about the symbolic economy since the 1970s," writes Zukin, "is its symbiosis of image and product, the scope and scale of selling images on a national and even a global level, and the role of the symbolic economy in speaking for, or representing the city."[23]

This new emphasis on images and brands evinced a sea change in urban political economy. As David Harvey argued in an influential article, the focus of municipal governance had shifted from "managerial" approaches in the 1950s and 1960s to "entrepreneurialism" in the 1970s and 1980s.[24] For Harvey, the primary role of local government was no longer seen as the provision of services and welfare for its citizens, but rather the creation of economic activity and luring inward investment. City governments now operated as entrepreneurial agents, competing nationally and internationally for flows of capital, labor, and tourism. In this context, practices of branding and place marketing took on new significance. Urban leaders and business elites made global branding a core strategy, creating new kinds of institutions and agencies to promote—and in some cases rehabilitate—the image of their cities in the public imagination. Alongside flagship renewal schemes and iconic buildings by star architects, a successful media sector and thriving art scene became among the most visible markers of a city's perceived prosperity and cultural dynamism.

Since the 1980s the film industry has bifurcated, with the dominance of conglomerate Hollywood offset by the rise of a substantial independent sector. Though "indie" cinema became partially commercialized and co-opted with the rise of mini-majors (such as Miramax and New Line) and studio specialty divisions (such as Focus Features and Fox Searchlight), significant differences in production methods persist. Though there are no clear-cut distinctions, major studio movies and independent productions can often be differentiated by their distinctive spatial logics and operational geographies. Limited by budget, indie filmmakers have often developed close ties with particular cities or locales—for example, Richard Linklater and Austin, Texas—and based their fictional worlds and auteur brands around the specificity of place. In turn, local governments have also seized on such directors as cultural assets and promotional tools for the film industry and the city more generally. Placed against the ersatz cosmopolitanism of the blockbuster, independent and studio specialty division productions are frequently embedded in a bounded and highly localized diegetic world. This attachment to place specificity is notable in the titles of films such as *Fruitvale Station* (Ryan Coogler, 2013), *Manchester by the Sea* (Kenneth Lonergan, 2016), and *Paterson* (Jim Jarmusch, 2016). At one level, this type of spatial difference obviously correlates with a film's budget and is an index of the opportunities and constraints offered by different levels of financing. But it also reflects a different approach to dramaturgy. Smaller scale films often develop more intimate connections between character and place, and in contrast to the high-stakes, globalized conflicts of the blockbuster, they tend to embed narrative development within a carefully rendered and relatively contained social world.

In contrast, major studio productions are characteristically transnational. One of the defining factors behind this globalization of Hollywood has been the rise of government tax breaks and production incentives, which have played an important role in transforming the geography of film production. In 1997, the launch of federal and state tax credit programs in Canada launched Toronto and Vancouver into the top tier of production destinations for Hollywood. State governments in the United States followed suit, as did national governments such as Great Britain, kicking off a period of intensive competition for Hollywood production that continues today. Within this political–economic framework, film commissions have played a key role in selling cities and states to the industry as viable production hubs, and in advertising key assets, such as distinctive locations, studio infrastructure, and a specialized workforce. From an aesthetic standpoint, the frequency with which a city is filmed can also depend on its ability to capitalize on an aura of "authentic" local specificity, or alternately, on qualities of versatility and generic "urbanness." The most successful screen cities, from Boston to Toronto, have generally been able to offer both.

At a city level, these entrepreneurial cultural policies have been driven forward by the work of Richard Florida, who argued in the early 2000s that an army of young city-dwelling professionals—the "creative class"—had become the primary agents of economic growth and prosperity. As Florida saw it, city governments should focus less on attracting economic investment and more on enticing affluent cultural workers to move in.[25] These insights, along with Florida's ranking of cities by intangible (yet apparently calculable) qualities of "creativity" and "buzz," were highly influential among civic leaders and city planners, for whom they provided an off-the-peg narrative for urban regeneration. As a result, jobs in media, advertising, and other types of notionally cultural activity became especially valuable to city governments chasing the ideal of the "creative city." The success of the film industry, and a highly visible and proactive film commission, had become attractive at both city and state levels, despite question marks over the efficacy of film subsidy programs. Indeed, this ubiquitous creative city "script" was widely critiqued by academics such as Jamie Peck for its complicity with neoliberal political agendas, and in due course, Florida himself would acknowledge some of the limitations of his ideas.[26]

Today, the assembly of a film, from principal photography to postproduction, is often globally dispersed. High-budget production is routed through transnational supply chains that enable the studios to source cost-effective labor, "film friendly" regulatory regimes, and substantial tax incentives. A typical live action production for one of the majors will shoot extensive green-screen sequences in a studio, frequently located outside Los Angeles (current hotspots include Atlanta, Vancouver, and London). This is characteristically augmented with location shooting, which may occur in generic spaces close to the studio, specific locales in the United States or Canada, or in a range of global destinations that provide distinctive, authentic, and sometimes marketably exotic settings. Principal photography for *Doctor Strange* (Scott Derrickson, 2016), for example, was carried out primarily at Longcross Studios in Surrey, England, with additional location shooting in Kathmandu, Nepal, and in New York City, while visual effects work was subcontracted to firms in Los Angeles, Vancouver, and London.

These international networks of production service—and to some extent also drive—a transnational, though US-centric, approach to narrative that speaks to Hollywood's self-understanding as a global popular culture and to the interests of its increasingly lucrative overseas audience. The Hollywood blockbuster is therefore characteristically mobile and flexible in its approach to story space. Characters move smoothly across national borders and hop between global destinations with ease. Such transnational mobility is a key component of action franchises, such as the *Fast and Furious, Mission Impossible*, and *Bourne* series, as well as the Marvel Cinematic Universe, which frames narrative conflicts and resolutions at an emphatically global (even galactic) scale. Nevertheless, global franchises frequently stage action globally but underscore the narrative with a specific American setting. Much of the action in *Doctor Strange*, for example, takes place in Nepal and Hong Kong, but the film reserves some of its most iconic visual effects sequences for New York City. As with the Marvel Cinematic Universe in general, *Doctor Strange* draws on precise New York locations—such as the specifically named Bleecker Street setting of the Sanctum Sanctorum—to generate narrative meaning.

As the Marvel films demonstrate, the North American city still anchors many Hollywood productions both industrially and textually, and we argue that though Hollywood may be global in reach, it remains deeply embedded in Southern California and retains close operational links with other urban centers. Despite persistent claims about the globalization of the industry, recent research shows that around 70 percent of production still takes place in the United States and Canada, largely in key urban production hubs.[27]

Los Angeles remains the nerve center for Hollywood financing, distribution, and marketing. It is the primary place where scripts are green-lit, packages put together, and roles are cast, and its infrastructure and talent pool is still unchallenged by any North American city. However, though Los Angeles and New York are still dominant, other production centers have recently emerged. In particular, Georgia and Louisiana have been strikingly successful in using tax breaks to attract major productions. Offering up to 30 percent rebates to Hollywood producers, Georgia's incentive scheme was worth $606m in financial year 2016, making it the largest film tax credit program on record.[28] As a result, Georgia has quickly moved into pole position: in 2016, it narrowly beat California, Louisiana, Canada, and the UK to become the most popular primary filming location for Hollywood features. Studios such as Pinewood Atlanta have hosted high-profile productions, such as *Spider-Man: Homecoming* (John Watts, 2017), while the relatively generic modern spaces of downtown Atlanta have doubled for a range of other cities, including Los Angeles itself—for example, in *The Nice Guys* (Shane Black, 2016).[29] However, though the influx of Hollywood shoots has been celebrated by Atlanta's city government, intensified global competition for production has significant downsides. Feature film production offers relatively short-term and precarious employment, and as Michael Curtin and Kevin Sanson have shown, the global mobility of filmmaking has driven what they describe as a "race to the bottom" in terms of pay and conditions for below-the-line crew.[30] Furthermore, as Vicki Mayer observes, Georgia and Louisiana not only offer the most generous tax program, but are also among the poorest states in the United States, and their use of dwindling public funds to subsidize multinational media corporations has been widely critiqued.[31]

Arguments about the hypermobility and placelessness of the industry have also been fueled by the rapid development of visual effects technology, which has indeed altered the spatial dynamics of production. In the first instance, a high proportion of principal photography for high-budget, effects-driven projects necessarily takes place in studios, to some extent reversing the earlier trend toward location shooting. Computer-generated imagery CGI has made it possible to render highly detailed and plausible visual environments that are able, in some cases, to dispense with the need for physical locations. For example, a short behind-the-scenes documentary about the making of *The Walk* (Robert Zemeckis, 2015) shows how digital effects techniques were used to reproduce the twin towers of the World Trade Center for the film's dramatic tightrope walking sequences. Shooting in Montreal to take advantage of Quebec's competitive tax regime, the filmmakers also used the streets of the city, digitally augmented in postproduction, to double for New York and Paris exteriors. However, such industry paratexts double as promotional films for VFX houses and tend to present an overly celebratory account in which the "magic" of visual effects can overcome any challenge or reproduce any setting. The reality is somewhat more complicated. Although the workflow of a contemporary blockbuster is now fully digitized, resulting in a blurring of boundaries between visual effects and production design, CGI has not supplanted location shooting, which remains an important component of the filmmaking process and a marker of authenticity, even if on-location sequences are frequently redesigned and composited with digitally created environments. And though it is rarely, if ever, acknowledged in behind-the-scenes materials, visual effects work remains highly-labor intensive and costly. The location of postproduction is therefore bounded by the need for material infrastructure, workforce availability, and government tax regimes. Thus, despite the industry's vision of a frictionless digital pipeline, the geography of digital postproduction remains embedded in the concrete political and economic realities of key VFX hubs, such as Vancouver, London, and Wellington, New Zealand.

Indeed, at the local scale, the trend of digital convergence has also helped to create media industry clusters in urban redevelopment zones. Occupying 300 acres of ex-industrial waterfront space, the Brooklyn Navy Yard is a case in point. In addition to the Steiner Studios (opened 2004), a major facility that regularly hosts high-profile film and television productions, the Navy Yard is home to a flourishing ecology of small companies offering postproduction, visual effects, and ancillary services, alongside firms in related sectors such as new media, advertising, design, and consultancy. Hailed by Governor Andrew Cuomo as a "transformative project," the broader redevelopment of the Brooklyn Navy Yard as a high-tech industrial park has provided an influential model for culture-led regeneration and postindustrial aspiration (as the website puts it, "the 300-acre waterfront asset offers a critical pathway to the middle class for many New Yorkers," while Steiner Studios chairman Doug Steiner opines that the Navy Yard has helped make Brooklyn "the home, and now workplace, of the creative class").[32] As the case of the Navy Yard suggests, the film industry in the digital age is far from placeless: rather, film and television production frequently plays a flagship role in specific urban redevelopment programs, even as it has become recontextualized under the umbrella of the digital cultural economy.

Figuring the city: genre, politics, identity

While institutional and economic factors often determine the site of production, the symbolism and cultural image of individual cities also play an important role. As the contributors to this volume explore, the city is refracted through diverse genres, which offer varied ways of capturing and imagining urban experience and which tend to be associated with particular cities. Here we can think of the romantic comedies of New York, crime dramas of Boston, and more recently, horror-themed films set in Detroit, which often take their narrative dynamism and character types from their specific cultural milieus. Different genre forms have also lent themselves to different modes of urban experience and vision: the musical, for example, has conventionally been understood as portraying the city in a utopian or nostalgic light, whereas urban science fiction films are primarily associated with dystopian futures.[33] However, such easy categorizations are often defied by the complex and flexible relationships between genre and setting, and as recent films such as *Magic Mike* (Steven Soderbergh, 2012) and *Her* (Spike Jonze, 2013) suggest, genres are frequently responsive to processes of cultural change. Indeed, though there are a range of industrial and cultural factors that shape the ebb and flow of specific genre formats and cycles over time, such shifts have nevertheless been understood as responses to shifting public values and sociocultural concerns. From this perspective, genres can be read as barometers of changing attitudes about the American city, from fears and anxieties to aspirational dreams and glamorized myths. In historical terms, for example, scholars have often placed cycles such as blaxploitation and the vigilante thriller in the context of deindustrialization, "white flight" and rising crime rates in the 1970s, while the return of the romantic comedy in the following decades has correspondingly been associated with accelerated gentrification. Directly shaped by the city's social and geographical topographies, narrative devices such as the car chase and shoot-out of the crime film and the "meet cute" of the romcom communicate very different ideas about public space and have historically drawn from distinct character repertoires. Perhaps these two broad genre categories—crime films, on the one hand, and romantic comedies, on the other—reveal the most about the trajectory of the postindustrial American city from "crisis" to "regeneration", although the horror film and financial drama have also become popular forms in which to dramatize gentrification and neoliberal restructuring.

In the crime film, wider anxieties about the city and the breakdown of social order have often been projected directly onto racialized understandings of urban space. Scholarship on the original cycle of film noir from the 1940s and 1950s, for example, has linked its anti-urban themes to the processes of suburbanization and "white flight," while following the publication of Richard's Dyer's influential *White* in the 1990s, new attention has been paid to the peculiar whiteness of film noir's depictions of the American city at exactly the time when it was becoming more racially diverse. In this context, the cycle has been characterized by a "racial unconscious" in which even the high contrast lighting, which emphasizes shadows and juxtaposes black and white, can be understood to create metaphors of race.[34] In contrast with this structuring absence of blackness, subsequent postclassical cycles of crime films have often been explicitly concerned with questions of territory and the ethnically bounded affiliations of the neighborhood. As several of the films discussed in this book highlight, ethnicity and territorial identities have been central to the crime genre, whether in the Irish mob themes of *The Friends of Eddie Coyle* (Peter Yates, 1973) or the racialized gang conflicts of *King of New York* (Abel Ferrara, 1990). Indeed, the genre has linked a whole range of ethnic groups to criminality, from the Italian Americans in *Mean Streets* (Martin Scorsese, 1973), the Puerto Ricans in *Fort Apache, the Bronx* (Daniel Petrie, 1981), the Cubans in *Scarface* (Brian de Palma, 1983), the Chinese Americans in *Year of the Dragon* (Michael Cimino, 1985), the Japanese in *Rising Sun* (Philip Kaufman, 1993) and the Russian Americans in *We Own the Night* (James Gray, 2007), although the most persistent link has been made between crime and African Americans from the blaxploitation cycle to the so-called "hood" films of the 1990s.

The frequent deployment of specific neighborhoods as settings in many of these films has been motivated by conventions of realism and facilitated by the increased importance of location shooting, but it also reveals how local territorial solidarities have gained in political (and for Hollywood, commercial) importance in the postindustrial period. As Jefferson Cowie and Joseph Heathcott have argued, the acceleration of manufacturing decline had social and political consequences extending beyond the issue of job losses. As they argue, deindustrialization captures a wider set of processes that include "the de-linking of investment and place, the deinstitutionalization of labor relations machinery, de-urbanization (and new forms of urbanization), and perhaps even the loosening of the connection between identity and work."[35] This partial decoupling of identity from work in tandem with changes to the gendered division of labor has shaped some of the key political developments of the postindustrial era with its rise of new social movements. Not least, the spatial concentration of minority votes within specific electoral districts enabled ethnic and other minority groups to use the neighborhood and its community institutions to promote territorial identities and democratically elect politicians on platforms defending local communities. While this has clearly been empowering, it has also led to divide and rule tactics among local politicians and a fragmented electoral picture overall with many American cities resembling "mosaics" of different communities dotted side by side rather than "melting pots." In Ira Katznelson's stark phrase, deindustrialization opened up "city trenches" between the class-based politics of work and the racial and ethnic solidarities of the neighborhood with the latter now beginning to dominate.[36]

At the same time, historical narratives that view the gradual erosion of the Fordist-Keynesian compromise as the end of a relatively harmonious and prosperous era clearly risk idealizing the postwar decades, when, as the parallel processes of white suburbanization and inner-city ghettoization illustrate, the economic distribution of the period's economic gains was highly uneven. If the classical studio system had constituted a Fordist mode of production (a frequently debated point) and its genre system and censorship regimes were forms of cultural reproduction that valorized the white heterosexual nuclear family, then the film industry's economic reorganization in the late 1960s and 1970s might be seen partly as a response to the era's political fragmentation and the emergence of new market niches. In this context, the blaxploitation cycle from the 1970s is often considered a key example of Hollywood's market diversification in response to demographic change and inner city white flight. Yet if flexible specialization was supposed to have helped Hollywood to respond more quickly to new market niches, it is nevertheless striking how little diversification of narrative perspectives it initially led to. There is no studio-backed gay cinema from the 1970s and black leads tended to be confined to blaxploitation films and occasionally comedies. Overwhelmingly, the theme of postindustrial restructuring features in gritty crime films by white male directors with white male protagonists in which the female experience only appears in relation to the central theme of the crisis of masculinity.

In response to this, debates about the lack of female and minority perspectives as well as about exploitation and negative stereotyping became increasingly politicized and intertwined with overlapping academic research agendas in the 1970s. Now questions of representation were key political battlegrounds, with research focusing on the relationship between oppression and persistent negative stereotyping in popular culture. In the context of Hollywood cinema, works such as Molly Haskell's *From Reverence to Rape: The Treatment of Women in the Movies* (1974), Randall Miller's edited collection *The Kaleidoscope Lens: How Hollywood Views Ethnic Groups* (1980), and Vito Russo's *The Celluloid Closet: Homosexuality in the Movies* (1981) are early examples of such approaches which quickly filtered into the public and activist political consciousness.[37] Throughout the decade, grassroots mobilizations—mirroring arguments in cultural studies and feminist film theory—began to highlight how exploitative representations were not detached from structural and physical violence, but rather directly interwoven. Protests targeting the location shooting of films such as *Cruising* (William Friedkin, 1980) and *Fort Apache, the Bronx* (Daniel Petrie, 1981) in early 1980s New York, for example, illustrate the new emphasis on the identity-based allegiances of the neighborhood. These demonstrations were not about individual texts—the demonstrators had not seen the scripts—as much as about principled objections to recurring genre tropes and narrative structures of oppression which reinforced stereotypical links between violence, deviance, specific communities, and their neighborhoods.

In contrast to crime films, in which genre tropes of urban space as inherently dangerous have tended to be mapped onto particular social groups, the romantic comedy, which returned in the late 1970s and 1980s in tandem with the economic restructuring of its preeminent setting, Manhattan, instead seems symptomatic of gentrification both in terms of its narrative themes and target audience. The whiteness of the genre and the demographic whitening of its key settings have gone hand in hand while the idealized framing of the city around affluent consumption often presents a homogenized articulation of "global cityness." At the same time, Romeo and Juliet-scenarios in which love transgresses social divides—especially in rags-to-riches stories such as *Pretty Woman* (Garry Marshall, 1990)—clearly have the potential to explore socioeconomic and intra-urban differences in polarized cities. Romcoms set in New York, for example, have often been structured as narratives about the geographical and social divisions between Manhattan and the outer boroughs or New Jersey. Yet in spite of these geographies having clear ethnic and racial dynamics, the dominant romcom formula from *Desperately Seeking Susan* (Susan Seidelman, 1985) to *Frances Ha* (Noah Baumbach, 2012) has instead been to center on gendered ideas of bohemian eccentricity within a white milieu. In fact, since *Guess Who's Coming to Dinner* (Stanley Kramer, 1967)—set in San Francisco and released in the same year as the US Supreme Court's *Loving v. Virginia* ruling invalidated prohibitions against interracial marriage—very few romcoms have explored love across racial boundaries. In an overview of the genre from the early 1990s, Steve Neale highlighted the total absence of any deviation from the white heterosexual formula.[38] Since then, some commercially successful films such as *Jungle Fever* (Spike Lee, 1991), *Maid in Manhattan* (Wayne Wang, 2002), and *Hitch* (Andy Tennant, 2005) have used aspects of the romcom formula to explore various constellations of interracial love, although they remain exceptions to the white norm. And as the hype surrounding *Love, Simon* (Greg Berlanti, 2018) as the first major-studio romcom highlights, the genre remains almost exclusively heterosexual. The setting of *Love, Simon* in the new production powerhouse of Atlanta arguably illustrates the geographical diversification of the genre, although strictly speaking its generic upper-middle-class suburban landscape draws more from the traditions of the "coming-of-age" high school drama than the romcom. Generally, however, the romcom has expanded its geographical repertoire to include historically less pedestrian- and "meet cute"-friendly cities such as Houston in *Reality Bites* (Ben Stiller, 1994), Los Angeles in *500 Days of Summer* (Marc Webb, 2009), and the Rust Belt settings of Pittsburgh in *She's Out of My League* (Jim Field Smith, 2010) and Detroit in *The Giant Mechanical Man* (Lee Kirk, 2012).

As the emblematic city of postindustrial urban decay—and more recently of innovative solutions to that decay—Detroit has also emerged as a contemporary setting for horror films such as *It Follows* (David Robert Mitchell, 2014), which is partly set in the abandoned Packard Plant. Because of their historical reliance on creepy and haunted houses, horror films are well suited to narratives about housing and gentrification. "Apartment plots," such as *Rosemary's Baby* (Roman Polanski, 1968), *Single White Female* (Barbet Schroeder, 1992), and *Panic Room* (David Fincher, 2002), explore domestic anxieties about cohabitation with neighbors and "roomies" under different levels of real estate pressure on Manhattan's Upper West Side, whereas the topic of racial displacement has been addressed directly in *The People Under the Stairs* (Wes Craven, 1991) and *Candyman* (Bernard Rose, 1992).[39] The latter, which was filmed in Chicago's now demolished Cabrini-Green housing project, illustrates the genre's fondness for a picturesque ruin aesthetic, also frequently deployed in anti-gentrification narratives such as *Wolfen* (Michael Wadleigh, 1981), which was filmed at the time of housing abandonment and arson in the Bronx of the early 1980s.[40]

Following the financial crisis of 2008 and the ensuing "great recession", landscapes of dispossession and decline not witnessed since the depths of the urban crisis in the 1960s and 1970s reappeared. This crisis, which had its roots in the collapse of the subprime mortgage market, had less dramatic effects on the central areas of most cities, but impacted in particular the surrounding peri-urban areas. Over the coming months and years, images of foreclosures, abandoned houses, and evictions created a familiar media iconography of the crisis, but filmmakers found it hard to capture the complexity of its financial underpinnings in visual or narrative form. How could credit default swaps or collateralized debt obligations be grasped by existing conventions of narrative and genre? In practice, many films evaded questions of systems and structures by telling stories about flawed individuals, personal hubris, and the redemptive power of family and community. As Jeff Kinkle and Alberto Toscano write in their analysis of *The Company Men* (John Wells, 2010), *Up in the Air* (Jason Reitman 2010), and *Wall Street: Money Never Sleeps* (Oliver Stone, 2010): "Filmmakers have struggled to incorporate economic turmoil into their works without reverting to longstanding and ultimately comforting tropes; families reuniting to overcome hardship, the machismo and malevolence of stockbrokers, the corrosive power of greed."[41] Indeed, Hollywood dramas have often dramatized the economic opportunities and losses of postindustrial restructuring as bargains between the traditional values of family, honesty, and community, on the one hand, and greed, individualism, and hedonism, on the other.

Moreover, films about the great recession have arguably prioritized its impact on the upper echelons of society. In a critique of *The Company Men*, Derek Nystrom has highlighted how the film promotes the misleading idea of cross-class precarity or even implies that the executive class is more vulnerable than the traditional working class by concluding that "during an economic crisis catalyzed by the collapse of the housing bubble, one can always fall back on construction work as a reliable Plan B."[42] Dramas about Wall Street and the financial sector have also in many instances reinforced the focus on the "1%" and now constitute a separate sub-genre, which typically draws on the familiar trope of young ambitious men arriving in the city only to be corrupted by it. Many of these narratives can be mapped spatially as divided between small-town America and New York, "Main Street" versus Wall Street, or within intra-urban New York narratives as expressing a tension between the blue-collar outer boroughs and white-collar Manhattan, as in *Wall Street* (Oliver Stone, 1987), *Working Girl* (Mike Nichols, 1988), and *Boiler Room* (Ben Younger, 2000). *Wall Street* has become a textbook example of a film which ended up glamorizing the very culture it intended to critique through its glossy style, production values, and the star quality of Michael Douglas—a critique leveled at other examples of the genre too, including *The Wolf of Wall Street* (Martin Scorsese, 2013). What is at stake here is the frequently delicate balance between depicting a greedy and sexist culture of excess without seemingly endorsing it. Following the 2008 financial crisis, the emotional register of some Wall Street films such as *Margin Call* (J.C. Chandor, 2011) and *The Big Short* (Adam McKay, 2015) have arguably moved away from these glossy glamorizing tendencies in favor of questions of corporate and individual responsibility. The anger directed at the financial industries following the great recession—from which some of these films draw their emotional impact—has also been held up as an explanation for the rise of populism, although Donald Trump, who campaigned on some of these sentiments, is himself a real estate mogul who stacked his cabinet with former Wall Street executives.

As we write, long-standing geographical rifts in American society have resurfaced in which the "liberal elites" of the coastal cosmopolitan cities are pitted against the entrenched conservatism of small towns and rural areas. While crime and Wall Street films have continued to feed some of the historically negative associations of the big cities (while also glamorizing them), Hollywood today is arguably more anti-rural and anti-small-town than anti-urban. The diversification of urban locations that we have discussed above and to which some of the chapters in this book testify has arguably not been matched by any corresponding interest in small-town America beyond recurring caricatures of rednecks and hillbillies. Thus, a film such as *Three Billboards Outside Ebbing, Missouri* (Martin McDonagh, 2017)—often discussed in the context of Trump's America—has been critiqued both for its narrative of redemption for a white racist cop and for its condescending views of Middle America. With regard to the latter critique, the film, which is set in a fictive Missouri town, but shot in North Carolina, has been seen to flatten geographical and cultural specificity in favor of well-trodden tropes of the reactionary Midwest and South.[43] As Christian Long has argued in his mapping of US cinema since the 1960s, the notion of "Middle America" as "less an actual place than ... an ideology" was influential in the critical discourse and the films of the New Hollywood, which frequently catered for "metropolitan tastes."[44] Yet at the same time, this period saw the long history of anti-urbanist thought in American culture stretching back to Thomas Jefferson mobilized in political rhetoric about metropolitan liberals and the "silent majority." Such an anti-urban animus was a decisive force in debates about the "urban crisis" in the 1960s and early 1970s, when urban issues became problematically displaced onto racial ones and vice versa.

In this respect, the political schisms of contemporary America can be traced back at least as far as the Nixon era. Following the inner-city race riots of the 1960s and the Lyndon B. Johnson administration's landmark legislative achievements—the Immigration and Nationality Act of 1965, which ended the discriminatory preference for Northern European migrants, and the Fair Housing Act of 1968—the Republican party under Nixon and his vice-presidential candidate Spiro Agnew began the dog-whistling white electoral strategy it has never since fully abandoned and of which the election of Donald Trump in 2016 is the most recent culmination. In many ways, Trump's personal biography embodies the same historical trajectory, from early 1970s racist landlord in New York's outer boroughs, to glitzy real estate mogul after the city's fiscal crisis and his more recent forays into media and politics. Revealingly perhaps, the most high-profile films perceived as critical of Trump so far—*The Post* (Steven Spielberg, 2017) and *BlacKkKlansman* (Spike Lee, 2018)—have deployed the period drama form to analogize aspects of the Nixon-era with the contemporary political moment. These attempts to understand the present through a return to the early 1970s suggest an explanatory historicization similar to the framing of this book, which views postindustrial restructuring, identity politics, and the geographical divides of the culture wars as deeply interconnected. Whether Trump's presidency ultimately constitutes a rupture or the end of an era remains unclear at this point. On the one hand, his domestic agenda of tax cuts and deregulation merely accelerates the neoliberal dogmas that have shaped US postindustrial restructuring, yet, on the other hand, his nationalistic protectionism—and the nostalgia for an industrial past epitomized by coal and steel—indicate a withdrawal from the globalizing forces that underpinned both the urban crisis and its "renaissance."

Overview of the chapters

The book is divided into three parts, "Film Production and the Postindustrial Turn," "Postindustrial Narratives and Aesthetics," and "Cinema and Gentrification."

The contributions to the first part consider film production in the postindustrial city at different scales, from individual cities (including Los Angeles, New York, Kansas City, and Boston), to specific neighborhoods (such as South Boston, the West Village, and the South Bronx) and redevelopment zones (Century City). Mark Shiel's opening chapter focuses on the center of the

American film industry, Los Angeles. As the business underwent restructuring in the 1960s, large tracts of Hollywood studio real estate were sold off and redeveloped. Shiel examines Century City, an extensive commercial and residential complex built on a section of the former Twentieth Century Fox backlot, as an illuminating case study of the postindustrial built environment and its presence onscreen. For Shiel, Century City offers a privileged site for understanding the often unacknowledged social fractures that lay behind theories of the postindustrial. Tracing the historical development of the term, Shiel demonstrates that the "technocratic utopianism" of Daniel Bell's ideas in the 1960s would later become overshadowed by critiques of the "postindustrial society." An emblem of the postindustrial economy and its implementation through architecture and planning, Century City briefly became a flashpoint for protest in 1967, when anti-war demonstrators and police clashed outside the Century Plaza Hotel. Shiel explores two films partly shot on location at Century City as popular culture counterpoints to contemporary theories of the postindustrial city. Whereas the sex comedy *A Guide for the Married Man* (Gene Kelly, 1967) offered a light-hearted vignette of the white collar worker, the science fiction dystopia of *Conquest of the Planet of the Apes* (J. Lee Thompson, 1972), with its evocation of a futuristic police state, reckoned allegorically with the systemic violence and racial injustice underpinning Los Angeles in the 1970s.

Moving from Hollywood to the East Coast, Lawrence Webb's chapter focuses on New York City as a key production center in the late 1970s and early 1980s. Webb shows how the Mayor's Office of Motion Pictures and Television, established in 1966, developed into a flagship institution of the entrepreneurial city and its neoliberal governmental project during the first Mayoral term of Edward Koch. Analyzing promotional materials and articles from the trade press, Webb shows that the branding activities of the Mayor's Office intensified as part of an increasingly aggressive pro-business agenda at the city level. But the presence of Hollywood location crews on the streets of the city led to local struggles over the right to film in specific areas and the representation of neighborhoods and minority communities. Focusing in detail on the campaigns against *Cruising* (William Friedkin, 1980) and *Fort Apache, the Bronx* (Daniel Petrie, 1981), which were organized by gay and Puerto Rican groups respectively, the chapter examines how activists created media-savvy "urban interruptions" at location shoots, projecting their political agenda onto the national and global stages. Yet, in the long run, city and state governments found new ways to co-opt the more "edgy" qualities of urban culture into their media strategies.

While New York established a blueprint for municipal government engagement with Hollywood, treating it as a paradigmatic case can be misleading. As Nathan Koob's chapter suggests, we also need to pay attention to the variations between different types of city and their relative place within the media industries landscape. Koob brings this discussion of the film office up-to-date with three comparative case studies: Austin, Texas; Baltimore, Maryland; and Kansas City, Missouri. Taking a production studies perspective, Koob draws on interviews with film commissioners and production crew to explore the work of the film office in detail. As Koob demonstrates, these three film offices perform broadly similar functions, yet each city has also developed distinctive strategies to navigate local conditions. Whereas the Austin film office was formed to service an already-flourishing production culture, an index of the city's thriving cultural economy, Baltimore established its commission with the express intention of creating such a demand (in turn, bringing much-needed tax dollars to an ailing industrial city). And as Koob's case study of Robert Altman's *Kansas City* (1996) shows, an individual high-profile project may fuel local hopes for both neighborhood redevelopment and media industry growth, though creating a sustainable production culture over the long term is a more complex proposition.

As Webb and Koob make clear, the entrepreneurial activities of film offices have helped specific cities to become successful production centers. But what other factors contribute to a city's relative popularity as a narrative setting? As Carlo Rotella's chapter shows, institutional arrangements are just one thread in the complex web of economics and culture that influences filmmaking in any specific locality. Rotella takes twenty-first-century Boston and its film boom as a case study. By the mid-twentieth century, Boston was a declining industrial town. Why did it become such a popular and evocative setting for Hollywood movies in the 2000s? As with New York, Boston's postindustrial turn catalyzed local government support via tax incentives and industry liaison. Yet this alone did not distinguish Boston from its competitors. Alongside such crucial institutional backing, Rotella points to the "layered versatility" of the Boston cityscape, which has appealed to filmmakers as both distinctively photogenic and productively generic. But perhaps most importantly, Rotella argues, Boston is popular as a narrative setting because it stands in for authentic locality in the age of globalization, and as the well-spring of Irish American identity, it forms a resonant backdrop for stories about (un)reconstructed white masculinity. While some films, such as *The Company Men*, have meditated overtly on the shifting status of the city, most of the emblematic films of the cycle—such as *The Departed* (Martin Scorsese, 2006) or *The Town* (Ben Affleck, 2010)—are not typically about the financial sector or the knowledge economy of the "New Boston." Rather, they draw on the "authentic" textures of the city's rapidly disappearing industrial past. Boston's success as a narrative setting therefore rests on its ability to capitalize on the stories and signifiers of a lost urban world.

The second part of the book focuses on the narrative and aesthetic forms that have emerged from the postindustrial city, and considers how films engage with and shape urban imaginaries. Stanley Corkin's chapter pushes back further into Boston's cinematic history to consider a moment when the city was poised between historical stasis and far-reaching change. Drawing on the theories of Kevin Lynch and Sharon Zukin, Corkin explores how a physically legible "image of the city" gave way to a more diffuse, digitally mediated sense of urban branding that transcends and reconfigures material space. Corkin's point of entry is the 1970s and early 1980s, and a set of films that sit at the cusp of this historic shift. For Corkin, *The Friends of Eddie Coyle*, *The Brink's Job* (William Friedkin, 1978), and *The Verdict* (Sidney Lumet, 1982) capture a liminal and transitional city, caught between the grip of tradition and its postindustrial reinvention. Tracing cinematic pathways through the city's shifting physical and social environment, Corkin shows how these films evoke a turning point between the "regional past" and the "globalized future." Exploring what he calls a "recessed racial commentary" in the three films, Corkin attends to the divisions of class and race that are embedded in the traditional cinematic image of the city, and which inform the white working-class identity that Rotella also explores in his chapter.

While Boston has been able to present itself as a success story, Detroit has remained a media symbol for urban failure, despite significant efforts toward regeneration and rebuilding. Camilla Fojas focuses on representations of ruined and abandoned Detroit after the financial crisis of 2008, from fiction films *Only Lovers Left Alive* (Jim Jarmuch, 2013), *It Follows* (David Robert Mitchell, 2014), and *Lost River* (Ryan Gosling, 2014), to documentaries *Detropia* (Heidi Ewing and Rachel Grady, 2012) and *Requiem for Detroit* (Julien Temple, 2010). Placing these films within in a wider field of photography and visual culture, Fojas focuses on the persistent motif of postcrisis Detroit as haunted or undead. But rather than reading the trope of the "undead" city in a pessimistic light, she argues that it offers a mode of resistance and a means to project alternative futures to the capitalist city. For Fojas, films such as *Only Lovers Left Alive* and *Detropia* reject the idea that the city is subject to organic cycles of crisis and renewal, decline and regeneration. By imagining Detroit beyond the confines of both "ruin porn" on the one hand, and optimistic narratives of rebirth and progress on the other, these films reject the dominant narrative tropes of crisis capitalism. As she puts it, "Post-crisis stories of ruin, failure and devastation contain imaginaries of new formations, of alternate ways of living in capitalism, of refusing its storylines and rerouting its linear course."

Nick Jones and Amy Corbin both address the impact of digital technology on the urban imaginary through their respective analyses of the Hollywood blockbuster and independent cinema. For Jones, high-tech, high-budget science fiction movies, such as *Inception* (Christopher Nolan, 2010), *The Adjustment Bureau* (George Nolfi, 2011), and *Doctor Strange*, are key texts for understanding what he calls the "dominant spatial imagination" of contemporary urbanism: the city as a flexible, virtualized space that can be digitally manipulated and remixed by architects, planners, and users. Rather than grappling with the complex social reality of actual cities, these films project an idealized space of flexible, post-Fordist capitalism, in which privileged "creative" protagonists can reshape and redesign the city to their will. Drawing on Anna Secor's notion of "topological cities," Jones shows how key action sequences visualize urban spaces as modular and malleable, existing between the material and the virtual, and operating beyond the constraints of the body's lived experience. As Jones shows, Hollywood's digital engineering of screen space is linked to contemporary architectural practice both through applications such as Maya and through shared conceptions of space as fractal and algorithmic, as exemplified in the designs of Gehry, Koolhaas, and Hadid. But as Jones points out, drawing on the critical tradition of Lefebvre and

Harvey, these cinematic projections should be viewed primarily as celebrations of postindustrial capitalism and framed in the context of emerging "smart cities" (such as Songdo, South Korea) that place flexibility and virtuality at their core.

Whereas the films Jones discusses tend to put the protagonist in a position of control over the urban environment, Corbin's chapter discusses ambivalent relationships between film characters and the networked cities they inhabit. Corbin's chapter provides an in-depth analysis of Ryan Coogler's debut feature, *Fruitvale Station* (2013), which dramatizes the real events leading up to the killing of Oscar Grant by a BART police officer in Oakland in 2009. Though Corbin emphasizes the film's neorealist bond between protagonist and environment, she also argues that the film moves beyond the conventional "hood film" tropes of containment and immobility. For Corbin, *Fruitvale Station* is a social realist film that attests to the lived urban experience of African Americans, but as she argues, it also grapples with the complex ways that locality and "networked life" interact. Coogler's film shows how Grant's movements through city space are accompanied by the virtual connections of his cell phone usage, which allow him to partially (though not fully) move beyond the constraints of the physical and social environment. Nevertheless, as Grant's death makes only too clear, digital networks do not necessarily liberate people from their surroundings, and the geographies of racial inequality have not been dissolved by smart phones. Still, as Corbin points out, Grant's case was transformed by the availability of cell phone video footage, and although digital connectivity cannot erase geographical boundaries, it increasingly enables oppression to be witnessed.

The third section of the book examines the intersections of gentrification and screen media via a range of industrial, historical, and textual approaches. Brendan Kredell argues that alongside representational approaches to cinema and gentrification, we should also focus critical attention on audiences and the sites of media consumption. For Kredell, zooming out from the film text allows us to consider connections between movie theaters, the areas they are situated in, and the audiences they primarily serve. As he puts it, we need to know "which films are screened where, by whom, and for which audiences." Such geographical and demographic questions about patterns of distribution and exhibition are inherently political: by asking "where are the movies?," he suggests, we are also asking "for whom are the movies?" As a starting point for this research agenda, Kredell traces some of the key trends in domestic exhibition over recent decades. While consolidation in mainstream exhibition led to fewer, high-budget tentpole films being shown on a greater number of screens, especially in suburban multiplexes, "post-arthouse" chains, such as Landmark Theatres and Alamo Drafthouse, prospered in gentrifying areas of major cities. The opening of a new movie theater in a neighborhood is what Kredell calls "the capstone of gentrification": a sure sign that the character of the area has changed enough to make such an enterprise commercially viable. But as Kredell points out, "the movie theatre is never a culturally neutral site," and exhibition geared toward the shared taste preferences of these affluent, largely white consumers necessarily excludes other audiences and alternative conceptions of what cinema might mean for urban communities. However, as Kredell suggests, streaming services Netflix and Amazon may yet disrupt the existing spatial relations between movie consumption and cultural identity in the years to come.

The traditional neighborhood theater was just one aspect of the social experience of the industrial city that was first destroyed, then later revived in the age of the gentrified "post-arthouse." As Erica Stein argues in her chapter, such loss has been a defining experience of postindustrial New York, whether one thinks of the loss of unionized manufacturing jobs and the dissolution of once tight-knit local communities, or the loss of coherent public space and a legible and readily "imageable" cityscape. Many independent films of the 1980s and 1990s traded in nostalgia for this lost industrial city, expressing a longing for the past which, for Stein, plays into the dominant narrative of the "revanchist city" and the exclusionary processes of hyper-gentrification. Stein focuses on three outer borough films which appear to offer an alternative to this narrative: *The King of New York, Smoke* (Paul Auster and Wayne Wang, 1995), and *Blue in the Face* (Paul Auster and Wayne Wang, 1995). In contrast to the prevailing theme of loss, these films construct their outer borough neighborhoods as monuments to the industrial city. Yet, as Stein's close analysis of the films demonstrates, these films still evoke the revanchist logic of the postindustrial city in their fetishistic image of the neighborhood-as-monument. Emphasizing "monumental structures of transit and communal performance," such as the Brooklyn, Manhattan, Triborough, and Queensboro Bridges, these films recreate the neighborhood as an "authentic" site of (heterosexual) white male identity. Nevertheless, films such as *Smoke* also suggest how cinema might be called on to produce the city as a genuinely collective work, rather than a dead monument to its industrial past.

The final two chapters by Johan Andersson and Martha Shearer focus on the romantic comedy, which both authors see as an especially important genre for understanding cinema and gentrification. Andersson's chapter examines *Desperately Seeking Susan* (Susan Seidelman, 1985) as an example of screwball-influenced comedy from the 1980s in which New York's geography is used to set up gendered tropes around conventional masculinity and eccentric femininity. In contrast with the frequent (but not exclusive) use of escapist luxury settings in the Depression-era screwball cycle, characters across a range of films from the booming mid-1980s instead go slumming in SoHo, which at this point has replaced Greenwich Village as New York's erogenous zone. As Andersson argues, the romantic comedy brings the libidinous elements of gentrification into focus by investing erotic capital into specific locations. In the second half of the chapter, Andersson expands this discussion via an intertextual queer reading of the film by highlighting the understated homoerotic potential of the protagonists mobilized by a series of cinematic references, including *Marnie* (Alfred Hitchcock, 1964), *Midnight Cowboy*, and *Ms. 45* (Abel Ferrara, 1981). These "allusions," Andersson argues, constitute a form of dual address which bypasses the obligatory heterosexuality of the romcom while also communicating a form of subcultural distinction associated with the film's downtown bohemian settings.

Martha Shearer unpacks the relationship between the contemporary romantic comedy and the gendered discourses of the "creative city." In her focus on genre developments following the 2008 financial crisis, Shearer analyzes indie romcoms—including what she calls "post-romcom" elements openly critical of dominant notions of romance—in which the genre's traditional framing of the city around affluence and consumerism has been replaced with a new focus on housing and employment precarity. Both her main examples— *Frances Ha* (Noah Baumbach, 2012) and *The Giant Mechanical Man*—center on young white women who while in precarious employment have their lives thrown into personal crisis in cities with distinct experiences of urban crisis:

New York and Detroit. These narratives with "recessionary resonances" deal with the themes of "time crisis" and arrested development for protagonists prevented from "progressing." Ultimately, however, Shearer argues that these films evade structural and systemic forms of precarity in favor of individual solutions and personal networks. And equally damning, her critique highlights how the films' settings in Brooklyn and Detroit whitewashes their historical and contemporary associations with African Americans. As Shearer concludes, these films' "endorsement of the creative city not only sidesteps the concerns it raises about precarity but also depicts such concerns purely as they affect white people."

Notes

1   However, despite the obvious differences between *La La Land* and *Moonlight*, both films (and, perhaps, their audiences) can arguably be placed on the same side of another contemporary political divide—the apparently widening gap between predominantly conservative rural areas and small towns on the one hand, and on the other, the large, diverse coastal cities that have been repeatedly denigrated in right-wing rhetoric. See the final section of this introduction for further discussion of Donald Trump and the political urgency of thinking about the urban geography of cinema in the context of postindustrial America.

2   On the debates around the term postclassical, see Barry Langford, *Post-Classical Hollywood: Film Industry, Style, and Ideology since 1945* (Edinburgh: Edinburgh University Press, 2010).

3   For a more detailed discussion of this period and the relations between film and urban change, see Lawrence Webb, *The Cinema of Urban Crisis: Seventies Film and the Reinvention of the City* (Amsterdam: Amsterdam University Press, 2014).

4   On post-Fordism, see Ash Amin, ed., *Post-Fordism: A Reader* (Oxford: Blackwell, 1994); on postmodernism, see Fredric Jameson, *Postmodernism, or, the Cultural Logic of Late Capitalism* (London: Verso, 1991); on neoliberalism, see David Harvey, *A Brief History of Neoliberalism* (Oxford: Oxford University Press, 2005).

5   However, we should also be aware of the various critiques of the postindustrial and take into account its conceptual limitations and blind spots. See Mark Shiel's chapter in this volume for a discussion of the term's historical development.

6   Barry Bluestone and Bennett Harrison, *The Deindustrialization of America* (New York: Basic Books, 1982).

7   See Sharon Zukin, *Loft Living: Culture and Capital in Urban Change* (Baltimore and London: Johns Hopkins University Press, 1982); Suleiman Osman, *The Invention of Brownstone Brooklyn: Gentrification and the Search for Authenticity in Postwar New York* (New York: Oxford University Press, 2011); Christopher Mele, *Selling the Lower East Side: Culture, Real Estate, and Resistance in New York City* (Minneapolis: University of Minnesota Press, 2000).

8   Ruth Glass, *London: Aspects of Change* (London: MacGibbon & Kee, 1964); Neil Smith, "Toward a Theory of Gentrification: A Back to the City Movement by Capital, Not People," *Journal of the American Planning Association*, 45.4 (1979), 538–548.

9   Daniel Bell, *The Coming of Post-Industrial Society: A Venture in Social Forecasting* (New York: Basic Books, 1999).

10 David Ley, *The New Middle Class and the Remaking of the Central City* (Oxford: Oxford University Press, 1996).

11 Richard Lloyd, *Neo-Bohemia: Art and Commerce in the Postindustrial City* (New York: Routledge, 2006).

12 See Scott, Allen J. and Edward W. Soja. *The City: Los Angeles and Urban Theory at the End of the Twentieth Century* (Berkeley and London: University of California Press, 1996); Michael Dear, *The Postmodern Urban Condition* (Malden, MA: Blackwell, 1999).

13 Jameson.

14 Giuliana Bruno, "Ramble City: Postmodernism and 'Blade Runner,'" *October* 41, Summer (1987), 61–74; David B. Clarke, ed., *The Cinematic City* (London and New York: Routledge, 1997); Mike Davis, *City of Quartz: Excavating the Future in Los Angeles* (London: Pimlico, 1998); David Harvey, *The Condition of Postmodernity: An Enquiry into the Origins of Cultural Change* (Oxford: Basil Blackwell, 1990). See also Mark Shiel and Tony Fitzmaurice, eds., *Cinema and the City: Film and Urban Societies in a Global Context* (Oxford and Malden, MA: Blackwell, 2001).

15 On Florida vs. Kotkin, see Joshua Keating, "Urban Warfare: Joel Kotkin vs. Richard Florida on Cities and the Creative Class," *Foreign Policy*, March 22, 2013, http://foreignpolicy.com/2013/03/22/urban-warfare-joel-kotkin-vs-richard-florida-on-cities-and-the-creative-class/.

16 However, as a number of scholars have stressed, the canonical "Hollywood Renaissance" films were only part of the story. In the early-to-mid 1970s, the box office was also dominated by more conventional fare such as *Airport* (George Seaton, 1970), *Love Story* (Arthur Hiller, 1970), *The Poseidon Adventure* (Ronald Neame, 1972), and *The Sting* (George Roy Hill, 1973). From another

perspective, feminist critics such as Molly Haskell have also critiqued the mythos of the "auteur renaissance" for its valorization of male authorship and its marginalization of important female creative figures such as Carol Eastman, Joan Tewkesbury, and Dede Allen. However, if auteurism—if by that we mean the perpetuation of a male white canon and romanticized ideas about individual creativity—may now seem dated, the centrality of the director as a commercial entity that organizes marketing, consumption, and reception practices remains a lasting legacy of the "Hollywood Renaissance." Indeed, the work associated with many of the directors featuring in this book—for example, Noah Baumbach, Christopher Nolan, Susan Seidelman, and Ryan Coogler—tends to be marketed and received in that context. As the varied approaches here illustrate, however, their films can also be analyzed from a range of spatial perspectives which emphasize settings, production contexts, and genre topographies.

17 See Lawrence Webb, *The Cinema of Urban Crisis: Seventies Film and the Reinvention of the City* (Amsterdam: Amsterdam University Press, 2014); Stanley Corkin, *Starring New York: Filming the Grime and the Glamour of the Long 1970s* (Oxford and New York: Oxford University Press, 2011); Carlo Rotella, *Good with their Hands: Boxers, Bluesmen, and Other Characters from the Rust Belt* (Berkeley: University of California Press, 2002), 105–166; Sabine Haenni, "Geographies of Desire: Postsocial Urban Space and Historical Revision in the Films of Martin Scorsese," *Journal of Film and Video* 62.1 (2010), 67–84; Art Simon, "'One Big Lousy X': The Cinema of Urban Crisis," in *The Wiley-Blackwell History of American Film, vol. 3, 1946 to 1975*, ed. Cynthia Lucia, Roy Grundmann and Art Simon (Hoboken, NJ: Wiley-Blackwell, 2012), 470–489.

18 See, for example, Christian B. Long, *The Imaginary Geography of Hollywood Cinema, 1960–2000* (Bristol: Intellect, 2017); Barry Keith Grant, "Rich and Strange: The Yuppie Horror Film," *Journal of Film and Video* 48.1–2 (1996), 4–16; Paula Massood, *Black City Cinema: African American Experiences in Film* (Philadelphia, PA: Temple University Press, 2003); Brendan Kredell, "Wes Anderson and the City Spaces of Indie Cinema," *New Review of Film and Television Studies*, 10.1 (March 2012), 83–96; Lawrence Webb, "When Harry Met Siri: Digital Romcom and the Global City in Spike Jonze's *Her* (2013)," in *Global Cinematic Cities: New Landscapes of Film and Media*, ed. Johan Andersson and Lawrence Webb (London and New York: Wallflower Press, 2016); Nick Jones, *Hollywood Action Films and Spatial Theory* (Abingdon and New York: Routledge, 2015); Stephen Keane, *Disaster Movies: The Cinema of Catastrophe* (London: Wallflower Press, 2012); Westwell, Guy, "Acts of Redemption and 'The Falling

Man' Photograph in Post-9/11 US Cinema," in *American Cinema in the Shadow of 9/11*, ed. Terence McSweeney (Edinburgh: Edinburgh University Press, 2016), 67–88.

19 See Edward W. Soja, *Postmodern Geographies: The Reassertion of Space in Critical Social Theory* (London and New York: Verso, 1989); Doreen Massey, *For Space* (London: Sage, 2005); Henri Lefebvre, *The Production of Space*, trans. Donald Nicholson-Smith (Oxford: Blackwell, 1991).

20 Key texts include Edward Dimendberg, *Film Noir and the Spaces of Modernity* (Cambridge, MA, and London: Harvard University Press, 2004); Pamela Robertson Wojcik, *The Apartment Plot: Urban Living in American Film and Popular Culture, 1945–1975* (Durham, NC: Duke University Press, 2010); Mark Shiel, *Hollywood Cinema and the Real Los Angeles* (London: Reaktion, 2012); Massood; Merrill Schleier, *Skyscraper Cinema: Architecture and Gender in American Film* (Minneapolis: University of Minnesota Press, 2009); Corkin.

21 Center for an Urban Future, "Creative New York," June 2015, www.nyc.future.org.

22 Michael Storper and Susan Christopherson, "Flexible Specialization and Regional Industrial Agglomerations: The Case of the US Motion Picture Industry," *Annals of the Association of American Geographers* 77.1 (1987), 104–117.

23 Sharon Zukin, *The Cultures of Cities* (Oxford: Blackwell, 1996).

24 David Harvey, "From Managerialism to Entrepreneurialism: The Transformation in Urban Governance in Late Capitalism," *Geografiska Annaler. Series B, Human Geography* 71.1, The Roots of Geographical Change: 1973 to the Present (1989), 3–17.

25 Richard Florida, *Cities and the Creative Class* (New York: Routledge, 2005).

26 Jamie Peck, "Struggling with the Creative Class," *International Journal of Urban and Regional Research* 29.4 (December 2005), 740–770; Richard Florida, *The New Urban Crisis* (London: Oneworld, 2017).

27 Film L.A., "2016 Feature Film Study" (Film L.A. Inc. 2016), https://www.filmla.com/our-services/research/.

28 Ibid., 7.

29 The rise of Atlanta has been reported widely. See, for example, Alison Herman, "How Atlanta Is Taking over the Entertainment Industry," *The Ringer*, August 22, 2017, https://www.theringer.com/pop-culture/2017/8/22/16181284/georgia-filming-credit-south-week.

30 Michael Curtin and Kevin Sanson, eds., *Precarious Creativity: Global Media, Local Labor* (Oakland: University of California Press, 2016), 1–18.

31 Vicki Mayer, *Almost Hollywood, Nearly New Orleans: The Lure of the Local Film Economy* (Oakland: University of California Press, 2017), 16.

32 On the Brooklyn Navy Yard, see https://brooklynnavyyard.org/about/mission; "Brooklyn Navy Yard: An Analysis of Its Economic Impact and Opportunities for Replication," Pratt Center for Community Development, 2013, prattcenter.net/sites/default/files/web_2013_bny_full_report_0.pdf. The Steiner quotation is taken from "De Blasio Administration, Brooklyn Navy Yard and Steiner NYC Break Ground at 399 Sands Street, City Invests $40 Million in Manufacturing Jobs," https://www1.nyc.gov/office-of-the-mayor/news/294-18/de-blasio-administration-brooklyn-navy-yard-steiner-nyc-break-ground-399-sands-street-city.

33 On the musical and utopia, see Scott Bukatman, *Matters of Gravity: Special Effects and Supermen in the 20th Century* (Durham, NC: Duke University Press, 2003), 157–183. For a detailed discussion of the historical relationship between the musical and New York City, see Martha Shearer, *New York City and the Hollywood Musical: Dancing in the Streets* (London: Palgrave, 2016). As Shearer points out, even outwardly "utopian" films such as *On the Town* negotiate anxieties about the nature of urban change.

34 On suburbanization, white flight, and film noir, see Eric Avila, *Popular Culture in the Age of White Flight: Fear and Fantasy in Suburban Los Angeles* (Berkeley: University of California Press, 2004) and for analyses of the whiteness of film noir following Richard Dyer's *White* (Routledge, 1997), see Julian Murphet "Film Noir and the Racial Unconscious," *Screen* 39.1 (1998), 22–35 and Eric Lott "The Whiteness of Film Noir," *American Literary History* 9.3 (1997), 542–566.

35 Jefferson Cowie and Joseph Heathcott, eds., *Beyond the Ruins: The Meanings of Deindustrialization* (Ithaca: Cornell University Press, 2003), 15.

36 Ira Katznelson, *City Trenches: Urban Politics and the Patterning of Class in the United States* (Chicago: University of Chicago Press, 1981). Another key text on the new urban social movements is Manuel Castells, *The City and the Grassroots: A Cross-Cultural Theory of Urban Social Movements* (London: Edward Arnolds, 1983).

37 The questions around minority representation (or the lack thereof) explored in Molly Haskell's *From Reverence to Rape: The Treatment of Women in the Movies* (New York: Holt, Rinehart & Winston, 1974), Randall Miller's *The Kaleidoscope Lens: How Hollywood Views Ethnic Groups* (Englewood: Jerome S. Ozer, 1981) and Vito Russo's *The Celluloid Closet: Homosexuality in the Movies* (New York: Harper & Row, 1981) remain central to many social struggles as exemplified by recent campaigns such as *#OscarsSoWhite*. While recent Best Picture Oscar winners such as *Moonlight* (Barry Jenkins, 2016) and *The Shape of Water* (Guillermo del Toro, 2017), which both tackle questions of discrimination and bigotry through an intersectional lens rather than singular identity politics, suggest that questions

of diversity are being addressed by Hollywood, the success of these individual films perhaps conceal the broader underlying picture. The annual Annenberg Media, Diversity and Social Change studies published by the University of Southern California, which have analyzed the top 100 grossing films between 2007 and 2016, paint a static picture in which white able-bodied men remain the overwhelming norm.

38   Steve Neale "The Big Romance or Something Wild?: Romantic Comedy Today," *Screen* 33.3 (1992), 284–299.

39   The term "Apartment Plot" is defined in Wojcik, *The Apartment Plot: Urban Living in American Film and Popular Culture, 1945–1975.*

40   Johan Andersson "Landscapes of Gentrification: The Picturesque and the Pastoral in 1980s New York Cinema," *Antipode* 49.3 (2017), 539–556.

41   Jeff Kinkle and Alberto Toscano, "Filming the Crisis: A Survey," *Film Quarterly* 65.1 (2011), 39.

42   Derek Nystrom, "Haut-Bourgeois Precarity in Boston: The Company Men," *Post-45* (2013), http://post45.research.yale.edu/2013/01/haut-bourgeois-precarity-in-boston-the-company-men/.

43   Tim Parks, "The Feel-Good Fallacies of 'Three Billboards Outside Ebbing, Missouri'," *The New Yorker*, March 1, 2018.

44   Christian B. Long, *The Imaginary Geography of Hollywood Cinema, 1960–2000* (Bristol: Intellect, 2017), 61.

Part One

Film Production and the Postindustrial Turn

1

Daniel Bell, Post-Industrial Society, and Los Angeles Cinema circa 1967–72

Mark Shiel

Varieties of the "post-industrial"

Since the 1960s, the adjective "post-industrial" has been widely used as a broad category to describe the economy and society of various countries, primarily in North America, Western Europe, and Asia. For a long time its use in film and media studies was sporadic, but it has gained currency in the early twenty-first century and is now widespread: for example, Liam Kennedy has examined "the postindustrial ghetto" as "a highly visible signifier of urban decline" in American independent films about race, such as *Boyz N the Hood* (John Singleton, 1991) and *Falling Down* (Joel Schumacher, 1993); Laura Rascaroli and Ewa Mazierska have explored "postindustrial economy and landscape" in European city films such as *Kika* (Pedro Almodóvar, 1993) and *Teatro di guerra* (Mario Martone, 1998), set in Madrid and Naples, respectively; and Michael Witt has argued for the perceptiveness of Jean-Luc Godard's "radically new post-industrial kaleidoscopic form of vision."[1] These books use the term profitably, but they deploy it briefly, and mostly without considering its critical history or etymology, although a few others have used it at greater length. For example, Hamid Naficy valorizes the "artisanal" qualities of "exilic and diasporic filmmaking" in contemporary Iran and Turkey over and against "American post-industrial cinema"—that is, the New Hollywood, which Naficy associates with "globalization, privatization, diversification, deregulation, digitization, convergence, and consolidation" as well as "centralization of the global economic and media powers in fewer and fewer hands."[2]

Two important books of sociology—by Margaret Rose and Krishan Kumar—have analyzed the "postindustrial" at great length and in relation to the "postmodern", which is often considered the cultural expression of the postindustrial.[3] Both provide valuable investigations of the term and some commentary on media, with reference to Marshall McLuhan and Jean Baudrillard, but almost exclusively in relation to television and with no attempt at textual analysis.[4] Perhaps the most well-known use of the "postindustrial" category in film analysis, therefore, remains Giuliana Bruno's examination of the futuristic and dystopian sci-fi film *Blade Runner* (Ridley Scott, 1982). In that essay, published in 1987, Bruno influentially argued that the film's postmodern style was an expression of the "postindustrial" configuration of the economy and society of Los Angeles as the film imagined it would be in 2019.[5] The city was "postindustrial" in its "polyvalent" and "hybrid" architecture, its rampant consumerism, its "society of the spectacle," and juxtaposition of high technology and garbage: "It is not an orderly layout of skyscrapers and ultra-comfortable, hyper-mechanized interiors. Rather, it creates an aesthetic of decay, exposing the dark side of technology, the process of disintegration."[6]

It is notable, however, that the most important source on the "postindustrial" cited by Bruno is Paolo Portoghesi's *Postmodern: The Architecture of the Postindustrial Society* (1983) in which Portoghesi proposes postmodern architecture as a promising response to the challenges posed by the contemporary "crisis of the city"—that is, economic bankruptcy, organizational breakdown, traffic, waste, the "blind alley" of the Modern Movement and "the myth of infinite development [...] hypothesized in the sixties."[7] Portoghesi proposes optimistically that the "postindustrial city" will be able to *correct for* these ills by incremental change, including careful decentralization, mixed-use and medium density development, allowing for the citizen's "right to the city," respect for urban history, creativity and the arts, and a "culture of complexity" in architectural design.[8] So Bruno is indebted to Portoghesi, but there is a difference between his relatively hopeful use of the term "postindustrial" to point to a better future and her use of it to describe an urban dystopia in which the idea of a better future has come to nothing.

This leads us to the important observation that there have been optimistic and pessimistic uses of the term and that it is important not only to have a precise sense of the economic and social characteristics typically enumerated under the "postindustrial" heading but also to understand the temporal and geographical context, as well as the tone in which the term is being used. For example, perceptive recent analyses by Stanley Corkin and Lawrence Webb have used the term extensively to highlight representation of the seemingly perpetual and deeply stubborn inequality and injustice of the "postindustrial" city in crime films, melodramas, and comedies. In his book *Starring New York* (2010), Corkin highlights films of the 1970s, such as *Annie Hall* (Woody Allen, 1977) and *Kramer vs. Kramer* (Robert Benton, 1979), which were centered on a "new class" of well-to-do people working in "information industries," such as entertainment, media, and finance, who express themselves through cosmopolitan lifestyles and consumer choice but struggle emotionally in their intimate relationships with family and lovers.[9] The latter are associated with the romance and sentimentality of late nineteenth- and early twentieth-century architecture (the 59th St Bridge, Upper East Side lofts, the Museum of Modern Art), which provides a nostalgic counterpoint to the traumatic "postindustrial" restructuring of New York from its legendary bankruptcy in 1975 to its reconfiguration as a leading center in global capitalism in the Reagan era.

Lawrence Webb, in *The Cinema of Urban Crisis* (2014), extends this theme in relation to an international variety of cities, including San Francisco in *The Conversation* (Francis Ford Coppola, 1974) and Paris in *Peur sur la ville* (Henri Verneuil, 1975), which he interprets as "deeply divided cities, with images of poverty and urban blight thrown into relief by a more characteristically postindustrial, commodified cityscape, ... the corporate architecture of the central business district and the omnipresence of advertising, television and the media."[10] Like Corkin, Webb is careful to see the postindustrial city as a function of "emerging neoliberal approaches to urban governance" and to insist that, although widespread, its emergence is highly uneven.[11] Corkin makes this especially clear in his most recent book, a close study of the acclaimed television crime series *The Wire* (HBO, 2002–8), which he characterizes as "a highly articulate vision of life among the underclass—poor African Americans, struggling working-class whites, the homeless—in a city, Baltimore, that is pictured as having seen better days."[12] He then traces into the twenty-first century the expansion of the

American "rust belt" as a function of deindustrialization and globalization and the aggressive shrinking of government expenditures, especially on public housing, in favor of private sector speculation and greed.

Notably, both Corkin and Webb take inspiration from the Marxist geographer David Harvey, who uses the term frequently but cautiously—for example, in *The Condition of Postmodernity*, when reviewing what he sees as the "new round of 'time-space compression' in the organization of capitalism" which began in the 1970s, but which he sees more as "shifts in [the] surface appearance" of capitalism rather than "some entirely new ... postindustrial society."[13] Indeed, it is important to note that several geographers and urban planners have consciously refrained from using the term "postindustrial." For example, many of those who work on Los Angeles argue that while the city experienced a profound and highly influential restructuring of its economy and culture in the 1970s–'90s, it remained essentially *industrial*.[14] Michael Storper has overtly declared his dislike of the term "post-industrial," arguing that in the "flexible specialization" of its economy since the 1960s, Los Angeles has not been driven by "a post-industrial economy, but a different kind of industrialism from that which had propelled the development of such cities as Detroit or Chicago."[15] Allen J. Scott has questioned the value of the "post-industrial" as "a meaningful category of analysis" too, preferring the term "post-Fordist" because it entails much of what is usually meant by "post-industrial" but implies that the economy continues to be industrial despite mutations in industry's forms and distribution.[16] Edward Soja detected influential new trends in the society and built environment of Orange County, which he described as an "exopolis" in which the city is turned "inside-out and outside-in at the same time," but he also resisted calling it "post-industrial," just as he resisted calling it "suburban," because he saw it as industrial and urban in new ways—that is, characterized by rapid economic and physical growth, deep social and economic segmentation, resurgent political conservatism, technocracy, and high-tech, defense, and media industries manifest in a series of "breathtaking industrial-cum-commercial-cum-cultural landscapes."[17] Indeed, Soja directly referred to the "post-industrial" as a "myth."[18]

Notably, one of the earliest uses of the term "post-industrial" in close film analysis was Fredric Jameson's essay on "Class and Allegory in Contemporary

Mass Culture: *Dog Day Afternoon* as a Political Film" (1977), in which Jameson also dismissed "post-industrialism" as a myth:

> One of the most persistent leitmotivs in liberalism's ideological arsenal, one of the most effective anti-Marxist arguments developed by the rhetoric of liberalism and anticommunism, is the notion of the disappearance of class. The argument is generally conveyed in the form of an empirical observation, but can take a number of different forms, the most important ones for us being either the appeal to the unique development of social life in the United States, or the notion of a qualitative break, a quantum leap, between the older industrial systems and what now gets to be called post-industrial society.[19]

Indeed, in his later famous essay on "Postmodernism, or the Cultural Logic of Late Capitalism" (1984), Jameson was even more direct, arguing that what should really be called "multinational capitalism" is often "wrongly called post-industrial."[20]

A book chapter like this one cannot possibly hope to resolve all of the complexities, nor the tensions, that inevitably accompany such a variety of uses, but it is important to note the variation, and sometimes the crankiness, of the term "postindustrial," rather than to restrict its use, and to balance the need to understand it in general terms with an attentiveness to the discrete contexts in time and place in which the term has come to prominence. In the rest of this essay, learning from Raymond Williams's example in *Keywords*—his compendium of historically important ideas in literary criticism—I want to propose that it is useful to return to first principles by examining the concept and the articulation of "post-industrial society" as it was originally set out in the 1960s.[21] Especially in the work of the sociologist Daniel Bell, who was then based at Columbia University, that era was the point of origin of the term and of its normalization and widespread use. Reflecting on it suggests that there have been two waves of usage of the term "post-industrial"—the first, from the late 1950s through the early 1970s having been primarily optimistic and futuristic in tone, and the second, since the late 1970s, using the term primarily as a sign of dejection, if not apocalypse (as Bruno, Corkin, Webb, and Harvey have done).[22] The first wave was formative but a lot shorter because hyperbole was quickly overtaken by reality.

Daniel Bell's *The Coming of Post-Industrial Society* (1973)

In *The Coming of Post-Industrial Society*, Bell sets out his thesis largely without reference to geographical variation, as a description of the United States as "a singular unit of illustration."[23] Where the Industrial Revolution had entailed a shift from the "primarily extractive" labor of agrarian times to "primarily fabricating" activities, the late twentieth century witnessed a further shift in emphasis in the economy from the manufacture of goods to the provision of services, or from fabrication to "processing," from "machine technology" to "intellectual technology," and from "capital and labor" to "information and knowledge."[24] These shifts entailed a displacement of previous concerns with scarcities of raw materials by new "scarcities of information and of time," and a shift from physical transportation and utilities to "digital information technologies" as the most important means of communication.[25] These economic and technological changes brought with them social change too, especially "a change in the character of work," which was no longer "a game against nature" or a game against machines but was now primarily a series of transactions between persons in a relatively flexible meritocracy. In this meritocracy, age-old class antagonisms were replaced by four "statuses" (the professional class, technicians, clerical and sales workers, craftsmen, and semi-skilled workers) and four more or less equal "estates" (scientific, technological, administrative, and cultural), among which the most important feature was the "spread of a knowledge class."[26] These developments entailed some limited risk of greater bureaucracy and militarization, of "communications overload" by "the greatest bombardment of aural and visual materials that man has ever experienced," and of a "hedonistic way of life" based superficially on the "promotion of pleasure."[27] But, for Bell, post-industrial society promised a mostly positive redefinition of social relations, the economy, and technology (including rapidly expanding fields such as computing, electronics, systems analysis, optics, and plastics), and it also seemed to promise greater participation—for example, in expanded opportunities for women in the workforce because of the new priority of mental over physical labor, of services over manufacturing.[28] Laurence Veysey correctly ascribed to Bell a "technocratic utopianism" in which long passages of optimistic prognosis are punctuated by occasional notes of caution "sprinkled here and there throughout."[29]

Many of Bell's ideas have been naturalized in the forty-six years since the publication of *The Coming of Post-Industrial Society*. One of the most prominent of the many former leftists who were turned into liberal anti-communists not only by Stalinism but by the ideological pressures of life in the Cold War United States, his prognoses have often been incorporated into government and corporate policies worldwide, though they have also been questioned, not least because many of them came to play central roles in the neoliberalism which subsequently emerged and which is in crisis at the time of writing.[30] There is much that is prescient and interesting to read in Bell's work, but also much wishful thinking—Timothy Tilton put it well in his review of Bell's book in *Social Research* in 1973 when he pointed to a somewhat frustrating "fuzziness" in the book between "forecasting" the future and describing actually existing conditions.[31] And yet from the vantage point of the present day, the genesis of the idea of the postindustrial seems closely identifiable with the growth-oriented Keynesian economics that dominated the United States in the twenty-five years following World War Two. Bell identified 1956 as the "symbolic turning point" in the emergence of the "post-industrial," because it was the first year white-collar workers outnumbered blue-collar workers in the US economy.[32] He explained that he first started using the term in teaching and conversation in 1959 and first put the concept forward in a conference paper on technology and social change delivered in Boston in 1962. The concept was then elaborated by Bell and others throughout the 1960s, especially in the journal *The Public Interest*, and it became quite well-known even in popular discourse—for example, it was frequently reported on in the *New York Times* and the *Los Angeles Times* from 1966 and 1969, respectively.[33] In such discourse, the post-industrial thesis often had a utopian or fanciful ring to it: while many reports predicted a new role for personal computers in everyday life, one report in the *Los Angeles Times* argued that the obsolescence of the nation state in the post-industrial world meant that war would be far less likely and, in another, Bell proposed that in the 1970s "three-day weekends will be common."[34]

Almost as soon as it had gained currency, however, and contrary to its initial optimism, the notion of a "post-industrial society" became deeply implicated in the violent polarization of US politics, culture, and society, especially with the massive intensification of the Vietnam War in 1968 and the resulting rapid expansion of critiques of "the Establishment," many of which latched onto the idea of a "post-industrial" future as an empty or false promise. Hence, the idea of the "post-industrial" became a key lens through which the New Left and counterculture were examined in several contemporary analyses. For example, Massimo Teodori depicted the New Left as "the first, embryonic expression of a new force which confronts the problems of post-industrial society"[35]; Alain Touraine presented a Marxist analysis of the post-industrial centered on the opposition of technocracy, the student movement, and workers in France around May 1968[36]; and Theodore Roszak argued, contrary to Bell, that there *should* be a post-industrial future, but that it should be "a graceful symbiosis of people and nature, an organic community" founded on New Left, Black Power, and hippie principles.[37] The idea also began to be linked to cinematic representation when Richard Schickel, in the *New York Times*, praised the critique of "postindustrial societies" in then-recent art films such as Michelangelo Antonioni's *Blow Up* (1967) and John Cassavetes's *Faces* (1968).[38]

Daniel Bell's *The Cultural Contradictions of Capitalism* (1976)

Daniel Bell became implicated in these conflicts not only because his ideas were frequently cited but because he chose to take sides, publishing in *The Public Interest* a condescending and irate critique of the April 1968 student occupation of Columbia University, which complained of the students' "underlying vague, inchoate, diffuse dissatisfaction with our society and its liberal culture" and the "self-inflated posture of revolution" of the leading student organization, Students for a Democratic Society.[39] In retrospect, this can be seen as one of the first of a long line of attacks by Bell on what he later called "the sensibility of the Sixties."[40] The phrase was prominent in Bell's book *The Cultural Contradictions of Capitalism* (1976), which is less often attended to by commentators on the post-industrial but which,

I would argue, is vital for an understanding of it because in a real sense it and *The Coming of Post-Industrial Society* were really two volumes of one larger work. As Veysey has explained, not only were the two books published very close together in time but they were both products of one long period of research and writing throughout the previous decade and both show signs of the progression from optimism to apocalyptic fears which marked the 1960s as a whole.[41] Bell liked to insist on the separation of economics and culture, but the post-industrial thesis is cited throughout *The Cultural Contradictions of Capitalism* as a precondition of the cultural trends Bell claims to detect.

The later book starts positively enough with a lengthy recapitulation of the achievements of various twentieth-century avant-gardes, including appreciative commentary on the Soviet montage school of cinema, Dada and Surrealism, the Bauhaus, and Antonin Artaud.[42] But the majority of the book is a dismissive appraisal of "the sensibility of the Sixties," which Bell sees as a counterfeit recycling of the avant-garde by a younger generation in over-reaction to the "normative consensus" of the 1950s, which Bell himself had famously theorized in his earlier study *The End of Ideology* (1960).[43] Echoing concerns he expressed in *The Coming of Post-Industrial Society* about possible "communications overload" and the prevalence of a "hedonistic way of life," in *The Cultural Contradictions of Capitalism*, Bell argues against what he sees in 1960s counterculture as "violence and cruelty; a preoccupation with the sexually perverse; a desire to make noise; an anti-cognitive and anti-intellectual mood; an effort once and for all to erase the boundary between 'art' and 'life', and a fusion of art and politics."[44] By "fusion," however, he really means an unwelcome destruction of "bourgeois culture" by psychedelic experience, rock music, happenings, and the like, all driven by what he calls a new "scale and intensity of feeling that [is] not only anti-government, but almost entirely anti-institution and ultimately antinomian as well."[45]

Worryingly for Bell, "the sensibility of the Sixties" is characterized by the new prominence of a "cultural class" of writers, artists, and filmmakers who are "no longer … outcasts, or a bohemian enclave, in the society. They function institutionally as a group, bound by a consciousness of kind."[46] But the culture they create is an excessively rebellious and unedifying "adversary culture" in cinema, art, and literature, which dominates now because "bourgeois culture has been shattered."[47] As a prominent element of this thesis, and contrary to Schickel's praise of late 1960s cinema for its perceptive critiques of post-industrial society, in *The Cultural Contradictions of Capitalism* Bell complained that recent cinema seemed fascinated by "expressions of shock and ... the exploration of extreme situations."[48] He accused films such as *Bonnie and Clyde* (Arthur Penn, 1967) and *M*A*S*H** (Robert Altman, 1970) of an excessive violence and gore, and objected to an "obsessive preoccupation" with the "sexually perverse" in *Chelsea Girls* (Andy Warhol and Paul Morrissey, 1966) and *I Am Curious (Yellow)* (Vilgot Sjöman, 1967)—all films which are regularly cited by film scholars, to this day, as among the most artistically and politically important works of the post–World War Two era.[49] In Bell's argument, one clearly sees the "neo-conservative" attitudes with which he was increasingly associated in the 1970s and '80s, although Bell disliked that label.[50] It is also notable that Bell deeply distrusts the creative workers whom later characterizations of the postindustrial economy would foreground in a positive way.[51]

Materializing the "post-industrial" in Los Angeles

Bell's references to movies are not numerous, but they allow me to now bring my summary of his thinking about post-industrial society to bear on the actual history and cinematic representation of one post-industrial site. In doing this, in addition to historicizing the term, I want to suggest that it is also important to *place* it in so far as its history can be better understood the more precise we are about where and how the "postindustrial" has been most visible.[52] Notwithstanding the reasonable objections to the term of Storper, Scott, and Soja, at the time the term was first developed, few places seemed to match the characteristics of what was called "postindustrial" society more than Los Angeles—or at least certain well-to-do parts of it, especially in the northwestern quadrant of Los Angeles often referred to as "Westside," which was primarily white and middle class. This was partly because it was home to the Hollywood film industry and its "studio system," which was then undergoing dramatic restructuring in response to the coming of television, suburbanization, and changing audience demographics; and it was also because Los Angeles boosters in big business and local government liked to present the place in exceptionally upbeat and futuristic terms. Indeed, I want to suggest that both Los Angeles and Hollywood in the 1960s deserve special consideration in light of the post-industrial thesis, although Bell lived and worked most of his life in New York and, after 1969, in Cambridge, Massachusetts, where he taught at Harvard.

Primarily concerned with structures and processes, thinking sociologically more than geographically, Bell did not write at length about Los Angeles or other cities but he did single out Los Angeles as a place of rising crime in comparative data on several US cities in the 1950s.[53] Among the key features of post-industrial society, he pointed to the rise of "the megalopolis," of which he pinpointed the Los Angeles-San Diego urban corridor as one of three, along with the Boston-Washington corridor and the Chicago region.[54] One of Bell's most important public airings of his post-industrial thesis, prior to his book, was in the major symposium on "Scientific Progress and Human Values," which took place at the California Institute of Technology in October 1967 to mark the 75th anniversary of its founding and its rise from local technical college to "national scientific and technological pre-eminence."[55] Soon after, Alain Touraine developed much of *his* post-industrial thesis while teaching at UCLA in 1969. And an innovative seminar at UCLA in the summer of 1973, funded by the National Endowment for the Humanities to examine "growing concern ... with technology's alleged effects on American society and values," was predicated on a view of Los Angeles as "the capital of America's postindustrial society ... Nowhere are the problems and promises of a technological society more vivid than in this Southern California megalopolis."[56]

Moreover, as I have argued elsewhere, even in the first half of the twentieth century, Los Angeles was already notable for qualities that would later be called "postindustrial" in so far as its film industry demonstrated an intense interaction of culture and commerce, a relative priority of creative- and knowledge-based work over manufacturing and physical labor, and a hyperactive image-based consumer culture.[57] On the one hand, the relatively early displacement of downtown Los Angeles by a multi-centered regional network of suburbs would also correspond to the expansive "change of scale" of urban societies pointed to by Bell as "post-industrial."[58] On the other hand, because Los Angeles was a relatively disciplinary society, outwardly democratic but harboring widespread inequality and injustice, and underwritten by the soft power of capitalism and the hard power of the police, it is also one of the places where Bell's idea of a "normative consensus" in the postwar United States was most dramatically called into question, especially in the calamitous events of the Watts riots of 1965.[59]

Century City, Los Angeles

One of the most telling sites in which this argument can be tested is Century City—a luxury complex of offices, apartments, shopping mall, and hotel, which was built between 1961 and 1972 on three quarters of the former 20th Century Fox film studios in the well-to-do Los Angeles district of Westwood, about half way between Hollywood and the Pacific Ocean.[60] In its architecture, organization, and ideological underpinnings, Century City is a manifestation of many of the tendencies spelled out by Bell and because of its proximity to the Fox studios it featured in several notable feature films, of which I will briefly examine two as revealing pop culture counterpoints to Bell's sociological theses: *A Guide for the Married Man* (Gene Kelly, 1967), a romantic comedy in which Century City typifies the white-collar workplace of the "organization man"; and *Conquest of the Planet of the Apes* (J. Lee Thompson, 1972), a post-apocalyptic science fiction film in which it plays the nerve center of a police state.[61] Hence, the remainder of this chapter will be a case study of the ways in which Century City's history and representation do and do not confirm Bell's ideas of the post-industrial society. I will argue for the usefulness of the term "postindustrial" to historical analysis of Los Angeles and Hollywood cinema in the 1960s, or to other specific contexts of place and time, as long as its limitations are clearly recognized.

In legend, Century City is often said to have been "built on the wreckage caused by booze, drugs, adultery, and workplace absenteeism" on the parts of Elizabeth Taylor and Richard Burton, who caused repeated delays in the filming of the historical epic *Cleopatra* (Joseph L. Mankiewicz, 1963) on the Fox studio lot in the early 1960s and, hence, that film's famously inflated budget and the subsequent insolvency of 20th Century Fox, as a result of which Fox sold off most of its 176-acre back lot for real estate development.[62] In fact, however, the sell-off occurred a number of years earlier, first announced in 1958, and it happened largely for two reasons: first, the already precarious financial position of Fox given the accelerating decline of the studio system; and, secondly, an increase in the value of land in the area as a result of the 1956 Federal Highways Act, which encouraged the growth of Los Angeles's freeway system in the form of a so-called Beverly Hills Freeway, which was planned to run right past Century City but ultimately was never built.[63]

Century City was adjacent to Beverly Hills but, according to developer William Zeckendorf, it was intended to be "almost twice the size" of it in population and "to overshadow Rockefeller Center in New York" in architectural design.[64] The new complex exemplified the work of Welton Becket and Associates (WBA), one of the leading US architectural firms of the post–World War Two era, headquartered in Los Angeles, but with offices nationwide employing about 500 people. In the early 1960s, WBA generated a sizeable revenue through commissions valued at about $100 million per year, growing to about $200 million per year by 1970, with a client list including many of the most important corporations in the Los Angeles region and the United States as a whole. Specializing in large-scale commercial buildings and public facilities, designed along the rationalist lines of Mies van der Rohe, it designed office buildings for General Petroleum, Prudential Insurance, and California Federal Savings and Loan, several key buildings at Los Angeles International Airport, department stores for Bullocks and other major retailers, much of the Westwood campus of UCLA, the Beverly Hilton Hotel, the Capitol Records Building in Hollywood, and the Music Center for the Performing Arts in downtown Los Angeles. In *Total Design: The Architecture of Welton Becket and Associates* (1971), WBA proudly called itself a firm of "Corporate Architects."[65] It emphasized "organization" and "accounting" as much as "design," and it insisted on "total design"—master planning, architecture, industrial design, and interior design "down to the last detail of furniture, sculpture, and other art, landscaping, and furnishings, even to ashtrays, menus, and matchboxes."[66] In other words, WBA created not just buildings but also a whole new way of life (indeed, it moved its own headquarters to Century City as well).

In its architecture and planning, therefore, Century City instantiated a number of the features of "post-industrial society" as enumerated by Bell and it definitively displayed the "orderly layout of skyscrapers and ultra-comfortable, hyper-mechanized interiors," which Bruno saw decaying in her later analysis of *Blade Runner*. The design of Century City by WBA was carefully presented as a function of processes and systems of engineering carried out and managed by specialists, very much epitomizing Bell's idea of a new "knowledge class." The development pointed to the new size and power of corporations, not only in WBA's own organization and ethos but also in its clients, Fox Realty Corporation and the aluminum manufacturer Alcoa, whose building materials were widely used throughout the site.[67] It gained widespread media attention, locally and nationally, not only as a real estate development but also as a sign of a cultural and economic shift, especially in seeming to confirm the new importance of shopping malls as agents of poly-nuclear urban growth and consumer culture, in a city which had become the sixth largest metropolitan area in the world by 1965.[68] The chronology of the site's development closely matched that of Bell's post-industrial thesis, from initiation in the late 1950s to completion in the early 1970s. And, in retrospect, it might even be seen to anticipate Robert Fishman's idea of the "technoburb," a move beyond ordinary suburbanization, which Fishman identifies as a function of the "postindustrial" and which he describes in terms of "the breakaway of the urban periphery from a central city it no longer needs, and the creation of a decentralized environment that nevertheless possesses all the economic and technological dynamism we associate with the city. ... not suburbanization but a *new city*."[69]

At the same time, however, it is important to note that, like other late modernist building programs, Century City had a controversial environmental impact, significantly altering the skyline of west Los Angeles at a time when Bunker Hill in downtown Los Angeles was also being overhauled by skyscrapers. Hundreds of local residents objected to what they saw as Century City's excessive size and massive intrusion in the landscape, the loss of sunlight which would be caused by its multiple skyscrapers, and the rushing of its planning and official approval to please its large corporate backers (although local government lobbying and public relations activities by Fox Realty Corporation and Alcoa won out in making the case for the local and regional benefits of a project valued at up to $500 million).[70] Sylvia Lavin convincingly argues that "the cool and neutral spaces of modernism" and its "perfected abstraction of space" were increasingly threatened during the 1960s by pressures of over-population, urban sprawl, and environmental destruction, and were increasingly viewed as repressive and repressed.[71] Such a view is also described by Meredith Clausen in *The Pan Am Building and the Shattering of the Modernist Dream*, which documents the bitter public controversy which surrounded the construction of Walter Gropius's building in New York, completed in 1963.[72] Such concerns with urban environment and habitability were compounded by even more urgent crises of socioeconomic and racial inequality in cities as a result of the riots in Watts in 1965, which claimed thirty-four lives, as well as other riots in Newark, Detroit, Baltimore, and other cities in 1967–68. These seemed to make clear that the decentralization which was a prominent feature of the "postindustrial" city was not neutral but morally unjust.[73] As Fishman puts it: "The late twentieth century American environment thus shows all the signs of the two nations syndrome: one caught in an environment of poverty, cut off from the majority culture, speaking its own languages and dialects; the other an increasingly homogenized culture of affluence, more and more remote from an urban environment it finds dangerous."[74]

In this respect, I find Reinhold Martin's otherwise invaluable documentation of postwar modern architecture for American corporate clients insufficiently critical of the "merger between architectural experimentation and the military-industrial complex."[75] Not citing WBA itself, but writing of the work of comparable architectural firms, such as Eero Saarinen and Associates and Skidmore, Owings & Merrill, Martin explicitly connects them to "the emergence of what might be called a 'postindustrial' or even a 'posthuman' subject, a subject immersed in and constructed by data flows."[76] However, he downplays "ideological struggles" and "the constructions of gender, class, or race within the enforced normalcy associated with the corporations."[77] Instead, he declares a preference for detecting "the complex intertwinings of discourse ... the intertwinings of words, images, and things" in postwar corporate architecture, arguing that the repetitive and geometric patterns and shapes which it favored were powerful expressions of the visual and managerial organization of the corporation and a manifestation of a new postwar consumer economy in which mass production guaranteed individualized choice.[78]

But here is one way in which it is quite complicated to map Century City onto Bell's theses, because, although he did not write much about architecture, he seems to have been ambivalent about International Style design of the kind of which Century City and other 1960s buildings represent a high water mark before the advent of postmodernism in architecture in the 1970s. In *The End of Ideology*, Bell complained briefly that, beginning with the Bauhaus, through the later work of Mies and Gropius, the priority given in "modern style" architecture to the dictum that "form follows function" had led to a "loss of the human scale" and to "asceptic and sterile" buildings.[79] However, in *The Cultural Contradictions of Capitalism*, he wrote quite respectfully of the modern city:

> The use of steel, replacing masonry, allowed architects to erect a simple frame on which to "drape" a building, and to push that frame high into the sky. The use of reinforced concrete allowed the architect to create "sculptured" shapes that have a free-flowing life of their own. In these forms one finds a powerful new comprehension and organization of space.[80]

Then, in an afterword to the latter book published in the twentieth anniversary edition in 1996, Bell returned to his previous criticism, associating architectural modernism in the 1960s, like literary and artistic modernism, with an "exhaustion," evident in its "spare geometric forms."[81] He contrasted these with architectural postmodernism, which he cautiously approved as "a somewhat serious effort to define a new style" in the work of Michael Graves, Charles Moore, Aldo Rossi, Renzo Piano, Richard Rogers, and Frank Gehry.[82]

On the face of it, this might seem to place Bell on the same page, in his views of modern architecture, as so many of the most insightful filmmakers of the late 1960s for whom modern architecture of the corporate kind became a metaphor for the existential crisis of society in general. But Bell's concerns seem to be primarily aesthetic where most architecturally aware films of the era went beyond aesthetic judgment of building styles to ethical and moral evaluation and political critique: for example, the underground political documentary *Columbia Revolt* (Newsreel, 1968) identified modern architecture with the increasing corruption of higher education by corporations and the military-industrial complex, and feature films such as *Hi, Mom!* (Brian De Palma, 1970) and *Zabriskie Point* (Michelangelo Antonioni, 1970) linked it to the stultifying effects of mass media and the destructive capitalism of the real estate industry, respectively.[83] In other words, Bell's criticism of modern architecture would seem to have come from a conservative rather than progressive position (and I have previously noted Bell's negative judgment of much 1960s art cinema).

In any case, notwithstanding Bell's apparent impatience with the Miesian cube, the latter had been strongly supported by the increasingly corporatized, technological, and services-oriented economy, which Bell described as post-industrial, and which, as Martin astutely observes, was drawn to architectural modernism for its pure expression of efficiency.[84]

A Guide for the Married Man (Gene Kelly, 1967)

Without wanting to draw too straight a line between them, this observation of increasing dissatisfaction with modern architecture in the 1960s leads me to consider the sex comedy *A Guide for the Married Man*, in which Walter Matthau plays Paul Manning, an investment adviser who works in an office building at Century City and who chafes at the mundane and repressive routines of corporate life which the architecture seems to embody. Revolving around Paul's boredom with married life, and his desire to have an affair like most of his married friends seem to be doing, *Film Daily* called the film a "Comedy Spoof for Mature Audiences [with the] Makings of Big Box Office Hit," although Charles Champlin in the *Los Angeles Times* argued that the film was a curious mix of old and new, with some moments of humor and good acting, but generally frivolous and overdone.[85] Champlin called it an "outspoken adult comedy which says and shows nearly everything there is to say and show about sex and cheating and marriage and the way pretty ladies look in tight dresses, or none."[86] Full of slapstick, innuendo, and Johnny Williams lounge music, the film's mise-en-scène is sumptuous, filmed in Panavision with Color by Deluxe and mixing affluent bungalow, apartment, cocktail bar, and insurance office studio sets, with some rear projection and prominent Century City locations. The trade paper *Variety* praised the film's upbeat suggestion that "Southern California is peopled by attractive married couples, living attractive lives, having lots of fun, and getting considerably more out of adultery than children get out of childhood."[87]

The film depicts Century City as a relatively self-contained place, where Matthau works in Welton Becket's Gateway West building and spends long lunch breaks around the Broadway department store and surrounding mall (Figures 1.1 and 1.2). It also situates Century City by counterpointing cutaways to secondary narrative lines featuring middle-aged TV stars, such as Jack Benny, Phil Silvers, Sid Caesar, Lucille Ball, and Art Carney, which, though not unentertaining, seem to confirm the film's intention to appeal to a middle-aged audience. Of special interest to the analysis of the

Figure 1.1 Lower level frontage of Welton Becket's Gateway West building at Century City in *A Guide for the Married Man* (1967).

Figure 1.2 Paul (Walter Matthau) and Ed (Robert Morse) at the Century City shopping mall in *A Guide for the Married Man* (1967).

postindustrial, in one of these secondary narratives, Carney plays a foreman at a construction site and is filmed in hard hat, blue jeans, and rolled up shirt sleeves in the foundations of one of the Century City buildings under construction at the time of the film's principal photography. This provides an interesting, and knowing, contrast with the financial milieu of Matthau's lead character, although the two men get on well in the film, interacting cordially in a way which seems to mirror the relatively stable worker–manager labor relations which, according to Bell, characterized much of the US economy in the late 1950s and '60s and which was one of the preconditions of his theses of both the "end of ideology" and the "post-industrial society."[88] The contrast of the two men also reinforces the viewer's awareness that the protagonist makes his living not in a "game against Nature" but in the processing of information by a "knowledge class." In another remarkable sequence, montage situates Century City globally by cutting to an anecdote about two lovers who go to great lengths to disguise the fact they are having an affair, arranging to meet in a chalet in the Italian Alps but flying in opposite directions around the world from Los Angeles—he via New York, London, and Paris, she via Honolulu, Hong Kong, and Cairo—only to find his wife and press photographers waiting for them at their secret rendezvous. Here, another aspect of the services economy—tourism—is foregrounded in a rapid succession of shots and scenes, together with a map which charts the global navigation and the multiple forms of transportation the lovers avail of (among which United Airlines has a prominent place).

Hence, Century City becomes the linchpin in a carefully structured geography, which is global on one level and entirely suburban on another—downtown Los Angeles, notably, does not appear in the film at all, nor does any other industrial setting besides the construction site. Racial diversity is absent too, as the entire cast and nearly all of the extras are white, and none of the film's action takes place outside of the largely white and middle-class neighborhoods between Century City, the San Fernando Valley, and Malibu. Indeed, like many studio-produced feature films emanating from Hollywood in the 1960s, *A Guide for the Married Man* acts now as a kind of index of the studio system's decline because its overblown studio-bound production values, all-star cast, and light-hearted escapism can be seen so clearly to have been at odds with the increasing social discord and violence of Los Angeles and the United States at the time. On the other hand, the film seems to be in harmony with large parts of Bell's thesis of a new post-industrial economic and social order, enjoying it, albeit with a little more humor and self-mocking.

For example, the fact that all women in the film are either housewives, swingers, or clerical or retail workers, with little apparent social agency that does not derive from motherhood or sex appeal, attests to the film's underlying conservatism while echoing Bell's somewhat condescending insistence that in the post-industrial society "the proportion of women in the labor force is bound to rise—the efforts of women's lib apart—simply because of the expansion of the service industries."[89] Similarly, the absence of any racial tension in the film tallies with Bell's tendency to keep it at arm's length in his post-industrial thesis: he makes no reference to Watts or any other specific large metropolitan race riots of the era; he mentions civil rights marches in Selma, Alabama only to argue that they would not have gained national significance before television; he admits that black Americans tended to have less social mobility and social capital than white Americans, but emphasizes "striking" gains in the proportion of blacks employed in several economic sectors and recent new appointments of black men to the boards of some major US corporations; and he expresses skepticism of affirmative action because, in his view, it is contrary to the principles of meritocracy.[90]

The film also skirts around profound social fractures. For although the narrative places the protagonist in various unlikely predicaments, he is never in real danger and ultimately finds that he enjoys his life, routinized though it is. This is made clear in the film's dénouement when Paul invites a woman to a motel but recoils from her at the last minute, returning to his wife and kids to the accompaniment of sentimental strings and a tongue-in-cheek rendition of "There's no place like home." Hence, Century City and the mid-century modern bungalow form the two poles of a balanced and satisfactory way of life—indeed, in so far as the protagonist chooses domesticity and corporate life and rejects hedonism, the film may be read as an endorsement of Bell's view that "the cultural estate" was "hostile to the functional rationality [of] the technological and administrative estates."[91]

However, the libidinous urges that fuel the film's comedy—and the gentle irony of its closing sequence—ensure its endorsement of postindustrial society is not too straitlaced or functional. Rather, the film seems on the cusp of something, having its premiere in New York in May 1967, at the beginning of the Summer of Love and just before the collapse of the US film industry's long-standing censorship regime known as the Production Code Administration. Not a radical film by any means, it *flirts with* promiscuity, nudity, the rejection of middle-class mores, and the replacement of professionalism by decadence, as if aware of hippie counterculture but unable to *represent* it directly. This makes the film seem a little anxious about what Bell called the "adversary culture" of the Sixties, although a lot less anxious than he was, and in any case what counterculture there is in the film is very mild indeed, epitomized by the opening theme song by The Turtles, a light-hearted pop version of the sound of folk–rock groups like The Byrds. Then again, *A Guide for the Married Man* was also released just before the wave of riots which would engulf so many US cities in July and August of 1967 and into the following year, and which significantly ratcheted up the sense of gravity which surrounded the nation's social problems. This is a timing which also makes it comparable to the two essays by Bell which would form the core of his post-industrial thesis, and of his later book—they were published in *The Public Interest* in Winter and Spring 1967, also just before that turbulent summer.

"Day of Protest, Night of Violence"

The dramatic effects of actual urban conditions on the idea of the "postindustrial" can be further gauged by considering subsequent events at Century City. When President Lyndon Johnson visited Los Angeles on June 23, 1967, he was met by one of the largest political demonstrations in the city's history—an antiwar march by about 10,000–15,000 people, which led to one of the worst outbreaks of street violence the city has ever seen.[92] This took place on Avenue of the Stars, right outside the flagship Century Plaza hotel, a luxurious 20-storey, 800-bedroom facility designed by Minoru Yamasaki in keeping with Century City's modernist aesthetic. Johnson hosted a $500-a-plate fundraising dinner inside the hotel, protected by 1,300 police, about three times the number the Los Angeles Police Department (LAPD) had deployed during the much deadlier riots in Watts, about twelve miles southeast of Century City. Outside the hotel, the peace marchers were a diverse group, led by the Student

Mobilization Committee, Young Democrats, Progressive Labor, Students for a Democratic Society, and the Black Power-dominated Student Non-violent Coordinating Committee. After several hours of speeches, marching, and a stand-off, LAPD officers charged the protestors lines en masse, fragmenting and scattering the crowd.

A photo-journalistic account of the events published by the American Civil Liberties Union recorded the shocking effect of the police action not only on the marchers but also on well-to-do and conservative passers-by who became caught in the melée: "A substantial portion of the community which before June 23rd had regarded the city's police department as competent and dedicated learned that these men were capable of indiscriminate violence, of relentless intolerance, of a careless indifference to the civil liberties which they were sworn to uphold. 'The brutality was so unnerving', a 40 year old real estate agent wrote, 'that my attitude toward the police has taken a complete turn from admiration to fear.'"[93] The New Left-ist *Los Angeles Free Press* reported that what began as a peaceful act of dissent was met by

> wave after wave of remorseless sadism motivated by the uneasiness and fear the officers felt before the agitated crowd. … With every blow the nightsticks struck a few more layers of the rationalization and self-deception that insulates the lives of those in WASP society from the violence of American wars and racist programs was stripped away. … the Asian War that had been so far off was coming home.[94]

Public reaction to the violence outside the Century Plaza Hotel split dramatically along political lines, with conservative opinion backing police assertions the protest had to be suppressed to make sure that what happened to John F. Kennedy in Dallas would not happen to Lyndon Johnson in Los Angeles. Among liberals and the left, however, there was outrage and the police response to the protest had a very significant chilling effect on political protest in Los Angeles, during the remaining six years of the Vietnam War. Like Watts and periods of labor unrest in Los Angeles history such as the Hollywood studio strikes of 1945–7, the Century Plaza protest demonstrated the unusual difficulty of popular protest in an extremely decentralized and automobile-oriented environment like Los Angeles.[95] As contemporary reports made clear, the violence stemmed from the enforcement by police of a very rigid separation between pedestrians and automobilists, on the one hand, and, on the other, between protestors and office workers, hotel patrons, and shoppers in Century City—or, to put it another way, between the notionally public space of the street and the privatized, corporate space of the postindustrial new town.[96]

We do not have a record of any opinion Daniel Bell may have held about the Century Plaza protest, but we can imagine what his view might have been from his negative judgment of the New Left-inspired student occupation of Columbia University the following spring. Noted above, his Fall 1968 article in *The Public Interest*, entitled "Columbia and the New Left," was an attack on the individuals and organizations that led that protest (Mark Rudd, Students for a Democratic Society), but it was also an indignant defense of the university as "*the* paramount institution" in "the post-industrial societies of tomorrow."[97] Bell mildly criticized Columbia's administration and the New York Police Department (NYPD) for heavy-handed management and crowd control but effectively argued that the striking students brought violent repression on themselves through their intemperate views and actions. This suggests that he would have been equally impatient toward protestors at Century City, albeit mildly critical of the LAPD's use of physical force. For this reason, although I find much to agree with in Howard Brick's analysis of "the decline of intellectual radicalism" in Bell's work, I have difficulty with his argument that "Bell's intellectual development, particularly his involvement with the 'new radicalism' of the mid-forties, suggested more of an affinity with the New Left than either he or his young antagonists would easily admit. ... [S]ignificant remnants of radical ideas remained to enrich his thought."[98] Bell wrote a letter to the *New York Times* in 1969, in which he objected to what he saw as Noam Chomsky's mis-characterization of Bell's "end of ideology" thesis and declared that he had opposed the Vietnam War since 1965.[99] And yet, in the five hundred pages of *The Coming of Post-Industrial Society*, for all of its comprehensive discussion of economics, politics, technology, and social change, there are only two brief references to Vietnam—one when Bell points non-judgmentally to the calculation of bombers' flight paths as an example of the new "intellectual technology" of planners and the other when he calmly identifies inflation in the US economy after 1968, caused by Vietnam War expenditures, as a potential constraint on change.[100] The failures and wrongs of the Vietnam War are more candidly acknowledged by Bell in *The Cultural*

Contradictions of Capitalism, in which he comes across as a disenchanted liberal, admiring President Kennedy and his idea of a "New Frontier" but annoyed by what he sees as the incompetence and deceit of Kennedy's successor, Johnson, and his military strategists.[101] Perhaps Alain Touraine—to Bell's left, in political terms—put it best when he acknowledged Bell's "well-informed scrutiny" of society and culture, but implied Bell's version of the post-industrial thesis was a kind of "technological optimism," which was "full of nostalgia for this Great Society which was destroyed with human beings and trees in the hills of Vietnam."[102]

Conquest of the Planet of the Apes
(J. Lee Thompson, 1972)

Where Bell was increasingly concerned about "the sensibility of the Sixties," and *A Guide for the Married Man* was relatively relaxed and jovial, another significant film was made on location in Century City five years later which depicted a dystopian science fiction future in opposite terms by zooming in on and amplifying the negatives which Bell admitted secondarily in his post-industrial thesis. *Conquest of the Planet of Apes* was a film horrified by the future and antithetical to the form and ideology of Century City.[103] Indeed, filmed in the spring of 1972 and released that summer, near the end of the mass protest movements of that era, it was just one of a large cluster of distinctly pessimistic and critical Los Angeles-based films which ran from *The Graduate* (Mike Nichols, 1967) and *Point Blank* (John Boorman, 1967) to *Sweet Sweetback's Baadasssss Song* (Melvin Van Peebles, 1971), *Cisco Pike* (Bill L. Norton, 1971), and beyond.[104] *Conquest* was the fourth film in the famous first *Planet of the Apes* series (the series having started in 1968), and while the film blended in some sequences filmed at the University of California Irvine most of its location shooting was done at Century City, called "Civic Center" in the film. An apocalyptic film about a future United States in which apes are kept as pets and slaves by humans, but rebel against their oppression, the *Los Angeles Times* reviewer Kevin Thomas called *Conquest* the best and probably the most bleakly totalitarian film of the *Apes* series, noting its technically impressive setting in "an undesignated city-state (not unlike Fritz Lang's *Metropolis*)."[105]

Welton Becket's architecture is very prominent in the film, especially in a long sequence early in the action in which a human, Armando (Ricardo Montalban), leads a chimpanzee, Caesar (Roddy McDowell), around the Century City shopping mall to advertise the arrival of a circus (Figures 1.3 and 1.4). The setting is notable for the ostensibly open comfort

Figure 1.3 Armando (Ricard Montalban) and Caesar (Roddy McDowell) at the "Civic Center" shopping mall, actually Century City, in *Conquest of the Planet of the Apes* (1972).

Figure 1.4 A low-angled long shot of Century City shopping mall and office buildings, from behind the jackboots of the police in *Conquest of the Planet of the Apes* (1972).

of the mall, which is low-rise and horizontal, but it is overshadowed by tall towers whose height is exaggerated because almost the whole sequence is filmed with the camera set low down, as if at the eye level of an ape, and pointed upward in a suggestion of imbalanced power relations. Hence, even though most of the action occurs by day, and often in bright sunlight, the mise-en-scène expresses a sense of foreboding or latent violence, and this intensifies as the film builds to a final violent confrontation between apes and men overlooking the Avenue of the Stars at night—the cinematographer Bruce Surtees had recently been commended for his work on Don Siegel's police thriller *Dirty Harry* and Clint Eastwood's neo-noir *Play Misty for Me* (both 1971).

In *Conquest of the Planet of the Apes*, Century City is again populated by well-to-do and *mainly* white men and women shopping and sitting in cafés, but this time they have a prominent SS-style police presence to protect them from an equally large underclass of primates engaged in all sorts of menial roles—personal servants, street cleaners, bus boys, and hairdressers' assistants. This underclass is managed by occasional arbitrary police violence in the mall itself and by a ruthless technocracy behind the scenes which runs torture centers and an early form of computer-controlled security and environmental management system. These kick into high gear when groups of apes begin to protest their conditions, only to be met by a stern warning on the automated public announcement system: "Attention, attention. The labor demonstration on the south plaza will be terminated in ten minutes. Repeat ... Failure to comply with this order can result in a one-year suspension of your right to bargain collectively." Arrests and beatings swiftly follow.

The film has been analyzed well by Eric Greene in his book *Planet of the Apes as American Myth* (1996) as a progressive allegory of racial oppression and early 1970s Black Power, which it surely is—but it also lends itself very effectively to analysis as a critique of the soft power of the corporation, the hard power of the police, and their mutual support of a particular kind of "postindustrial" urban space.[106] This becomes especially clear in the closing scenes of riot, which are rightly said by Green to echo Watts in 1965—although they also uncannily recall the Century Plaza protest of 1967. The Century City we see in this film is a relentlessly built environment, a kind of "systems analysis" in pure form, with technocratic management of large structures and intellectual and physical control of behaviors so rigorous and minute that they suggest a critique not only of corporate power but also of education (in keeping with the New Left critique of higher education).[107] This, together with the entirely service-based economy of the "Civic Center," dedicated to shopping, personal hygiene and beauty, cleaning and landscape gardening would seem to confirm elements of Bell's post-industrial thesis but present them in a far more critical light. The film insists that the postindustrial demarcation of private and public space, and of acceptable and unacceptable behavior, is not accidentally violent, but fundamentally unjust and built on indentured labor. Moreover, the film's insistence on giving Century City buildings a prominent place in so many scenes associates brutal coercion with grid-based rationalist architecture, its hard and straight lines, blank and flat surfaces, muted spectrum of colors, and supposedly open-plan arrangement.[108]

Of course, neither *A Guide for the Married Man* nor *Conquest of the Planet of the Apes* corresponds to Bell's "post-industrial" vision in every respect, but counterpointing them makes plain that that vision was very much on the public's mind and evolved dramatically in a turbulent era. Counterpointing them with the realities of the Century Plaza protest (and related conflagrations such as Watts) reminds us that the official preoccupation with the supposed promise of a postindustrial future tended to mask social discord, conflict and violence, downplaying them and their human costs (Hollywood cinema had also tended to mask such things but did so less successfully in the era in question because of its own "postindustrial" crisis). Grandiose claims were made for the postindustrial in the primarily optimistic way the term was used at this time, and its adherents—whether government, futurologists, capitalists, or academics—gave capital, technology, and science too much benefit of the doubt while underestimating the challenges and the potential for unexpected catastrophe which could derail postindustrial plans. In what was then often called the Establishment, faith in Bell's prognosis did not end, and it was resurgent in the 1980s and '90s; but it was thrown into crisis and redefined—with its social costs in sharp relief—by the intervening economic collapse of the 1970s, which took the shine off the term and left it ripe for appropriation by progressive critics, whether in scholarship, public policy, or on the screen.

Notes

1   Liam Kennedy, *Race and Space in Contemporary American Culture* (London and New York: Routledge, 2000), 12; Laura Rascaroli and Ewa Mazierska, *From Moscow to Madrid: European Cities, Postmodern Cinema* (London and New York: IB Tauris, 2003), 11; Michael Witt, *Jean-Luc Godard: Cinema Historian* (Bloomington: Indiana University Press, 2013), 112. The majority of references to the term "post-industrial" in this essay are not hyphenated, although I have hyphenated the term when quoting from, or referring to, a secondary source in which the term is hyphenated.

2   Hamid Naficy, *An Accented Cinema: Exilic and Diasporic Filmmaking* (Princeton, NJ: Princeton University Press, 2001), 42.

3   Margaret Rose, *The Postmodern and the Postindustrial: A Critical Analysis* (Cambridge: Cambridge University Press, 1991); Krishan Kumar, *From Post-Industrial to Post-Modern Society: New Theories of the Contemporary World* (Oxford and New Malden, MA: Blackwell, 2005).

4   Another short but useful discussion of the "postindustrial" is provided by Douglas Kellner, who argues that it has some limited analytical value but often tends toward hyperbole and underestimates the economic and ideological power of spectacle and entertainment. See Kellner, *Media Spectacle* (London and New York: Routledge, 2003), 11–13.

5   Giuliana Bruno, "Ramble City: Postmodernism and 'Blade Runner'" *October* 41 (Summer 1987), 61–74, 62.

6   Ibid., 63. Science fiction film has proven especially fertile ground for analysis of the "postindustrial." See also, for example, Ian Conrich, "Metal-Morphosis: Post-Industrial Crisis and the Tormented Body in the *Tetsuo* Films," in *Japanese Horror Cinema*, ed. Jay McRoy (Edinburgh: Edinburgh University Press, 2005), 95–106; Claudia Springer, *Bodies and Desire in the Postindustrial Age* (London: Athlone Press, 1996).

7   Paolo Portoghesi, *Postmodern: The Architecture of the Postindustrial Society* (New York: Rizzoli, 1983; first published in Italian in 1982), 48, 68. When referring to the postindustrial, Bruno cites three books: Portoghesi; Charles Jencks, *The Language of Post-Modern Architecture* (New York: Rizzoli, 1977); and Robert Venturi, Denise Scott Brown, and Steven Izenour, *Learning from Las Vegas* (Cambridge, MA: MIT Press, 1972). For further consideration of the similarities and differences in their uses of the terms "postindustrial" and "postmodern," see Rose, 101–149 and 152–158. Broadly speaking, Jencks and Venturi assent to the

description of the "postindustrial" by Daniel Bell, which I set out in this essay. Jencks approvingly cites Bell in *Critical Modernism: Where Is Post-Modernism Going?* (Chichester and Hoboken, NJ: Wiley-Academy, 2007), 98.

8 Portoghesi, 72–77. Portoghesi uses the phrase "right to the city" when alluding to urban protests of the 1960s, but without citing Henri Lefebvre's earlier use of the term, i.e., Lefebvre, *Le Droit à la ville* (Paris: Éditions Anthropos, 1968). Portoghesi's main source on the "postindustrial" is Alain Touraine rather than Daniel Bell. See Touraine, *The Post-Industrial Society: Tomorrow's Social History: Classes, Conflicts, and Culture in the Programmed Society* (New York: Random House, 1971).

9 Stanley Corkin, *Starring New York: Filming the Grime and the Glamour of the Long 1970s* (New York: Oxford University Press, 2010), 163–164.

10 Lawrence Webb, *The Cinema of Urban Crisis: Seventies Film and the Reinvention of the City* (Amsterdam: Amsterdam University Press, 2014), 9.

11 Webb, 30.

12 Stanley Corkin, *Connecting The Wire: Race, Space, and Postindustrial Baltimore* (Austin: University of Texas Press, 2017), 1, 87.

13 David Harvey, *The Condition of Postmodernity* (Oxford and Malden, MA: Blackwell Publishing, 1990), vii. Harvey sometimes uses the term pragmatically—for example, when recognizing the undeniable growth in the relative importance of the services and cultural sectors of the economy under Keynesian economic policies in Western Europe and North America since the Second World War. But he also argues against the term—for example, in *The Urban Experience*, he suggests that "the ideology of the post-industrial city" is beginning "to wear thin" and that the increasing importance of sweatshop labor from London to New York and Singapore means that "behind the illusions of the post-industrial city lie the realities of a newly industrializing city." See Harvey, *The Urban Experience* (Baltimore, MD: Johns Hopkins University Press, 1989), 53. He also sometimes argues that "post-industrial" discourse is pro-capitalist and right-wing in tendency—see, for example, Harvey, *Justice, Nature, and the Geography of Difference* (Oxford: Blackwell, 1997), 12–14.

14 Writing primarily about New York, Sharon Zukin has used the term "post-industrial" occasionally—for example, to describe a certain kind of suburban landscape of "shopping malls, ranch houses, and office parks" in specific places such as Silicon Valley or Westchester County, New York—but she too generally seems to find other terms more useful. Zukin, *Landscapes of Power: From Detroit to Disney World* (Berkeley: University of California Press, 1991), 17, 177. See also

Zukin, *Loft Living: Culture and Capital in Urban Change* (New Brunswick, NJ: Rutgers University Press, 1989), 18.

15 Michael Storper, "The Poverty of Paleo-Leftism: A Response to Curry and Kenney," *Antipode* 31.1 (1999), 37–44, 39; Storper is referring to Michael Storper and Susan Christopherson, "Flexible Specialization and Regional Industrial Agglomerations: The Case of the U.S. Motion Picture Industry," *Annals of the Association of American Geographers* 77.1 (March 1987), 104–117.

16 Allen J. Scott, "Los Angeles and the LA School: A Response to Kenney and Curry," *Antipode* 31.1 (1999), 29–36, 33–34; and Scott, ed., *Global City-Regions: Trends, Theory, Policy* (New York: Oxford University Press, 2001), 6.

17 Edward Soja, *Postmetropolis: Critical Studies of Cities and Regions* (Oxford and Malden, MA: Blackwell Publishing, 2000 [1996]), 239, 266. See also *My Los Angeles: From Urban Restructuring to Regional Urbanization* (Berkeley: University of California Press, 2014), 99, 202. The latter book contains a later reiteration of Soja's famous essay on Orange County, California, "Inside Exopolis."

18 Soja, *My Los Angeles*, 32, 56 fn. 4, 123. Soja also faults the idea of the "postindustrial" several times in *Postmodern Geographies: The Reassertion of Space in Critical Social Theory* (London and New York: Verso, 1989), 62, 160, 204, 212.

19 Fredric Jameson, "Class and Allegory in Contemporary Mass Culture: Dog Day Afternoon as a Political Film," *College English* 38.8, Mass Culture, Political Consciousness and English Studies (April 1977), 843–859, 843.

20 Jameson, Fredric, "Postmodernism, or the Cultural Logic of Late Capitalism," *New Left Review* I 146 (July–August 1984), 53–92, 78. When referring to the "postindustrial," Jameson singles out Bell for criticism on 55 of the same article and also in *Postmodernism, or, the Cultural Logic of Late Capitalism* (London: Verso, 1991), 3 and 159.

21 Raymond Williams, *Keywords: A Vocabulary of Culture and Society* (Oxford and New York: Oxford University Press, 2014 [1976]).

22 Kumar asserts that "following the 1973 oil shock, one had the distinct impression that 'post-industrialism' had had its day" and that postindustrial theories of the 1970s and 1980s "lack the confident optimism of the 1960s varieties." Kumar, 30.

23 Bell suggests his thesis also applies to some of the latest tendencies in Western Europe, the USSR, and Japan, but these are not the focus of his book. Bell, *The Coming of Post-Industrial Society: A Venture in Social Forecasting* (New York: Basic Books, 1976 [1973]), x.

24 Bell presents a lot of statistical evidence to demonstrate these shifts, especially in the 1960s. For example, he cites data to show that in 1969, services generated

60 percent of US GNP and 61 percent of US employment (higher than any other country), by comparison with industry (36 percent and 34 percent, respectively) and agriculture (3 percent and 5 percent, respectively). See "Table 2, Labor Force and GNP in Western Europe and United States by Sectors, 1969," in Bell, *The Coming of Post-Industrial Society*, 17.

25 Ibid., xviii, 456–475.

26 Ibid., xvi–xvii, 374–375.

27 Ibid., 316, 477.

28 Ibid., 146.

29 Laurence Veysey, "A Postmortem on Daniel Bell's Postindustrialism," *American Quarterly* 34.1 (Spring 1982), 49–69, 52.

30 Zbigniew Brzezinski, "Crises Blur Reality Of Slow Basic Change: Ideology Losing Impact," *The Washington Post*, July 9, 1967, B2; Daniel Patrick Moynihan, "Toward a Post-Industrial Social Policy," *The Public Interest* (Summer 1989), 16–27. This chapter was written between summer 2017 and summer 2018, not long after the US presidential election victory of Donald Trump and the British referendum vote for "Brexit," as well as during a rise in far-right populist movements in many parts of Europe, including general election victories in 2018 for the Fidesz party in Hungary, the Freedom Party in Austria, and the Northern League in Italy. To varying degrees, all of these political events were driven by strongly nationalistic and masculinist reactions to developments commonly associated with the postindustrial, such as the automation and globalization of manufacturing industry.

31 Timothy A. Tilton, "The Next Stage of History?," a review of Bell's *The Coming of Post-Industrial Society*, with a rejoinder by Bell, *Social Research* (Winter 1973), 728–760, 729.

32 Bell, "Notes on the Postindustrial Society," *The Public Interest* (Winter 1967), 24–36, 28. Howard Brick further examines the chronology of the term "post-industrial" in its first expressions by Bell and David Riesman, identifying 1958–1967 as the key phase of its formation. See Brick, "Optimism of the Mind: Imagining Postindustrial Society in the 1960s and 1970s," *American Quarterly*, September 1992, 348–380, 351.

33 The first reference to "postindustrial" society in a *New York Times* article occurred in a report on the annual meeting of the American Institute of Planners, which sought to address the "pressing urban problems of postindustrial America" in light of recent street violence in Harlem and Watts; "City Planners Told They Forget People And Stress Things," *New York Times*, August 17,

1966, 40. Bell's work as chair of the American Academy of Arts and Sciences' so-called "Commission on the Year 2000" also drew high-profile attention to his work. See Daniel Bell and Stephen R. Graubard, eds., *Toward the Year 2000: Work in Progress*, American Academy of Arts and Sciences, Commission on the Year 2000 (Cambridge, MA: MIT Press, 1997 [1968]).

34　Robert M. Hutchins, "Aims of Industrial Society No Longer Satisfying: Industrial Society's Aims No Longer Satisfy Aspirations," *Los Angeles Times*, August 10, 1969, F1; Arelo Sederberg, "The Sensate '70s: $17,000 Incomes, Computers in Homes, 4-Day Week Seen," *Los Angeles Times*, June 20, 1969, 1. It should be acknowledged that Bell was generally said (by himself and others) to be less inclined to futuristic hyperbole than some of his peers, such as Herman Kahn of the RAND Corporation and Hudson Institute, or some of his popularizers, such as Alvin Toffler, author of the best-selling *Future Shock* (1970) and *The Third Wave* (1980). See also William H. Honan, "'The Futurists' Take Over the Jules Verne Business: They Live In The Year 2000," *New York Times*, April 9, 1967, 243; Langdon Winner, 'Postindustrial Man', *New York Times*, March 30, 1980, BR1.

35　Massimo Teodori, ed., *The New Left: A Documentary History* (New York: Bobbs Merrill, 1969), 90.

36　Touraine's postindustrial thesis, less widely popularized than Bell's in the English-speaking world but otherwise influential, retains a larger place for political and class antagonisms, and for manufacturing industry, and is more critical of technocracy. For a usefully sceptical account of all uses of the term postindustrial, see Peter Kivisto, "Touraine's Post-Industrial Society," *Humboldt Journal of Social Relations* 8.1 (Fall/Winter 1980), 25–43.

37　Theodore Roszak, *Where the Wasteland Ends: Politics and Transcendence in Postindustrial Society* (New York: Doubleday, 1972). Roszak does not cite Bell in that book but does cite futurologists such as Alvin Toffler who helped to popularize postindustrial thinking. Roszak's version of the "postindustrial" also differs from Bell's in leaning toward West Coast experience and reference points—a feature evident in the distinctive blend of ecology, New Age spiritualism, and computing as subjects in his work, as well as in the fact Roszak was based in Berkeley, California. See Roszak, *From Satori to Silicon Valley* (San Francisco: Don't Call It Frisco Press, 1986), and Dave McBride, "Counterculture," in *A Companion to Los Angeles*, ed. William Deverell and Greg Hise (Oxford and New Malden, MA: Blackwell Publishing, 2014), 327–345.

38　Richard Schickel, "The Movies Are Now High Art," *New York Times*, January 5, 1969, SM32.

39 Daniel Bell, "Columbia and the New Left," *The Public Interest* (Fall 1968), 61–101, 90.

40 Daniel Bell, *The Cultural Contradictions of Capitalism*, 20th anniversary edition (New York: Basic Books, 1996 [1976]), 120–145.

41 Veysey, 56–57. The main argument of Bell's book was first published in long essay form as "The Cultural Contradictions of Capitalism," *The Public Interest* (Fall 1970), 16–43. For a contemporary critique of Bell, see Christopher Lasch, "Take Me to Your Leader," *New York Review of Books*, October 18, 1973, http://www.nybooks.com/articles/1973/10/18/take-me-to-your-leader/; and replies by Bell and Lasch, in "An Exchange on Post-Industrial Society," *New York Review of Books*, January 24, 1974, http://www.nybooks.com/articles/1974/01/24/an-exchange-on-post-industrial-society/.

42 Notably, for film scholars, in this discussion, Bell advances an early version of the thesis linking cinema and urban modernity by arguing that cinema epitomized "new conceptions of space" in the early twentieth century and was accompanied by "a new emphasis on travel and the pleasure of seeing" together with a reduction in the "psychic and aesthetic distance between the viewer and the visual experience"; the cinema, Bell opined, "in its use of montage, goes further than any other contemporary art in the direction of 'regulating' emotion, by selecting the images, the angles of vision, the length of a single scene, and the 'synapse' of composition." Bell, *The Cultural Contradictions of Capitalism*, 106–107.

43 Daniel Bell, *The End of Ideology: On the Exhaustion of Political Ideas in the Fifties* (Cambridge, MA: Harvard University Press, 1988; originally Glencoe, IL: Free Press, 1960), 419.

44 Bell, *The Coming of Post-Industrial Society*, 316, 477, and *The Cultural Contradictions of Capitalism*, 121.

45 Bell, *The Cultural Contradictions of Capitalism*, 123.

46 Ibid., 41.

47 Ibid.

48 Ibid., 108.

49 Ibid., 122. For histories of cinema at this time, See Paul Monaco, *The Sixties, 1960–1969*, History of the American Cinema, vol. 8 (Berkeley: University of California Press, 2003); Geoffrey Nowell-Smith, *Making Waves, Revised and Expanded: New Cinemas of the 1960s* (London: Bloomsbury Publishing, 2013).

50 In his later life, Bell worked hard to maintain distance between himself and the neo-conservative counter-reaction which came to dominate American

society in the aftermath of the Sixties. In 1978, he described himself as "a socialist in economics, a liberal in politics, and a conservative in culture" (Bell, "Modernism and Capitalism," *Partisan Review* 45 (1978), 206–222, 206); however, the following year, Ron Chernow reported that, whatever Bell's self-image, he was widely associated with neoconservatism in the public eye (Chernow, "The Cultural Contradictions of Daniel Bell," *Change: The Magazine of Higher Learning* 11.2 (1979), 12–17, 13). In Veysey's interpretation, Bell took positions "somewhere between [Ted] Kennedy and [Jimmy] Carter" in the Democratic Party of 1980 (Veysey, 58); and in the Afterword to the 1988 edition of *The End of Ideology*, he retrospectively aligned himself with the Democratic Party's Great Society reform program and what he continued to insist was the well-intentioned anti-communism of the U.S. war effort in Vietnam (Bell, *The End of Ideology*, 419). Malcolm Waters discounts Bell's claimed liberalism and socialism, asserting that "Despite all interest in the future possibilities of technology and post-industrialism, Bell is an old-fashioned, traditionalistic, elitist conservative." See Malcolm Waters, *Daniel Bell* (London and New York: Routledge, 2002), 169.

51 For example, Richard Florida, in his influential book *The Rise of the Creative Class*, both acknowledges his debt to Bell as a "far-seeing thinker" and criticizes him for castigating 1960s bohemianism. Florida, *The Rise of the Creative Class* (New York: Basic Books, 2012 [2002]), 163, 166.

52 As I have tried to suggest, my view is that theories of the postindustrial have too often relied on generalization, often while making grand futuristic claims, at the expense of spatial understanding, a sense of uneven development, dialectics, and regional variation. This seems to me an important limitation of postindustrial thinking in the form it took in the 1960s and 1970s.

53 Bell, *The End of Ideology*, 154–155.

54 Bell, *The Coming of Post-Industrial Society*, 320–321.

55 Lee Alvin DuBridge (physicist, president of CalTech, 1946–1969), "Preface," in *Scientific Progress and Human Values, Proceedings of the Conference Celebrating the 75th Anniversary of the California Institute of Technology in Pasadena, California, October 25–27, 1966*, ed. Edward Hutchings and Elizabeth Hutchings (New York: Elsevier, 1967), viii; Bell's paper in the same volume, 154–170, is very similar to his aforementioned Winter 1967 article on postindustrial society in *The Public Interest*. Bell did not refer to Los Angeles in his CalTech paper, though he did refer to California as a place of "excitement" in *The Cultural Contradictions of Capitalism*, 70–71.

56 H.J. Eisenman, "Technology, Society, and Values in 20th-Century America: The
    UCLA 1973 Summer Seminar," *Technology and Culture* 16.2 (April 1, 1975),
    182–188, 182, 187. Eisenman was chair of the seminar and wrote the official
    report. It might also be noted here that one of Daniel Bell's collaborators in
    the early to mid-1960s, Harvey S. Perloff, then of the Washington, DC-based
    environmental and natural resources think tank Resources for the Future, was
    Dean of the Faculty of Architecture and Urban Planning at U.C.L.A. from 1968
    until 1983. See Harvey S. Perloff, *The Art of Planning: Selected Essays of Harvey
    S. Perloff*, ed. Leland S. Burns and John Friedmann (New York: Plenum Press,
    1985).

57 Mark Shiel, *Hollywood Cinema and the Real Los Angeles* (London: Reaktion,
    2012), 14, 16, 171.

58 Bell, *The Coming of the Postindustrial Society*, 171.

59 I address the spatial and political specificity of Los Angeles at length in relation
    to the Hollywood strikes of 1945–1947, in *Hollywood Cinema and the Real Los
    Angeles*, 211–72, and have examined it also in two recent essays: "Los Angeles
    and Hollywood in Film and French Theory: Agnès Varda's *Lions Love* (1969) and
    Edgar Morin's *California Journal* (1970)," in *Cinematic Urban Geographies*, ed.
    François Penz and Richard Koeck, Screening Spaces series (London: Palgrave
    Macmillan, 2017), 245–268, and "'It's a Big Garage': Cinematic Images of Los
    Angeles circa 1968," in *Architectures of Revolt: The Cinematic City circa 1968*, ed.
    Shiel (Philadelphia, PA: Temple University Press, 2018), 164–188.

60 The evolution of the site was fairly rapid and dramatic—a ground-breaking
    ceremony was held in late May 1959, construction began in 1961, and the
    first phase of construction ended in 1972. See "Century City Now to House
    50,000, Zeckendorf Says," *Westwood Hills Citizen*, October 8, 1959, unpaginated
    photocopy, Los Angeles City Planning Commission, City Plan Case CPC9838,
    Los Angeles City Archive file CPC9838-22-144-2-loc24121.

61 Most of the feature films shot on location at Century City in the 1960s were 20th
    Century Fox films and most were romantic comedies or sex comedies: *What
    a Way to Go!* (J. Lee Thompson, 1964, with Shirley MacLaine), *The Swinger*
    (George Sidney, 1966, with Ann-Margret), *A Guide for the Married Man* (Gene
    Kelly, 1967), *Caprice* (Frank Tashlin, 1967), and *Live a Little, Love a Little*
    (Norman Taurog, 1968, with Elvis Presley). Bell cites the idea of the "organization
    man" as an icon of 1950s conformism, originally made famous by William H.
    Whyte in his study of management, *The Organization Man* (1956); but Bell
    suggests that conformism in mass society has been overstated, that society is

more diverse and freer than the idea suggests. See *The End of Ideology*, 34 and *The Coming of Post-Industrial Society*, 288.

62 Frank Sanello, "L.A.'s Century City—An Unrecognized Monument to Substance Abuse," writers' blog, http://redroom.com/member/frank-sanello/writing/century-city-%E2%80%93-an-unrecognized-monument-to-substance-abuse, posted July 6 2010; also Sam Kashner and Nancy Schoenberger, *Furious Love: Elizabeth Taylor, Richard Burton, and the Marriage of the Century* (New York: Harper, 2010); and "Mapping L.A.>Westside, Century City," *Los Angeles Times*, June 2010, http://maps.latimes.com/neighborhoods/neighborhood/century-city/. For a contemporary account explaining how Century City would displace the former movie studios, see Tom Cameron, "Century City: 'Frontier' Movie Towns Supplanted by Huge $500 Million Development," *Los Angeles Times*, June 10, 1962, M1; and Ray Hebert, "Century City Makes Magic Where Film Studio Used to Spin Fantasy: Century City," *Los Angeles Times*, April 17, 1966, G1.

63 "Century City Now to House 50,000, Zeckendorf Says," *Westwood Hills Citizen*, October 8, 1959, unpaginated photocopy, Los Angeles City Planning Commission, City Plan Case CPC9838, Los Angeles City Archive file CPC9838-22-144-2-loc24121.

64 Ibid.

65 William Dudley Hunt, *Total Design: Architecture of Welton Becket and Associates* (New York: McGraw-Hill, 1972).

66 Ibid., 4.

67 Although it's not an example he cites, Century City would seem to fit a trend which Reinhold Martin calls especially important in postwar corporate architecture—that is, "the use of materials representative of the industry to which the corporation belonged"—by which the office building became a consumer-oriented advertisement of the corporation's particular expertise, in an intermingling of architecture and media representation. Martin cites the corporate headquarters of Alcoa in Pittsburgh, in which aluminum was especially important, and the way in which the clean lines and materials of Lever House in Manhattan expressed the hygienic values of its owner, the soap company Lever. Reinhold Martin, *The Organizational Complex: Architecture, Media, and Corporate Space* (Cambridge, MA: MIT Press, 2003), 102.

68 See, for example, reporting on Century City's development by Gladwin Hill for the *New York Times*: "Huge Metropolis Rising on Coast," *New York Times*, October 6, 1963, 315, and "Century City: New Stop on the Tourist Map," *New York Times*, June 26, 1966, XX1.

69 Robert Fishman, "Beyond Suburbia: The Rise of the Technoburb," in *Bourgeois Utopias: The Rise and Fall of Suburbia* (New York: Basic Books, 1987), 184. Emphasis in original. Although Fishman does not use the term "postindustrial" frequently, he refers to it twice in a way that connects the "technoburb" and the "postindustrial." See Fishman, 199 and 206.

70 "Rezoning for Fox Approved," *Westwood Hills Citizen*, August 20, 1959, unpaginated photocopy, Los Angeles City Planning Commission, City Plan Case CPC9838, Los Angeles City Archive file CPC9838-22-144-2-loc24121.

71 Sylvia Lavin, *Form Follows Libido: Architecture and Richard Neutra in a Psychoanalytic Culture* (Cambridge, MA: MIT Press, 2004). Lavin is writing about modernist domestic architecture in Los Angeles–that is, the work of Neutra–but her characterization of the crisis of modernism applies to corporate modernism too. Indeed, Lavin briefly notes that Neutra reframed the architecture/nature relationship for a "postindustrial" environment. Lavin, 96.

72 Meredith Clausen, *The Pan Am Building and the Shattering of the Modernist Dream* (Cambridge, MA: MIT Press, 2005).

73 By "spatially unjust" here I mean to evoke the argument for "spatial justice" in Los Angeles effectively put forward by Edward Soja in *Seeking Spatial Justice* (Minneapolis: University of Minnesota Press, 2010).

74 Fishman, 200.

75 Martin, *The Organizational Complex*, 11.

76 Ibid, 12.

77 Ibid.

78 Ibid.

79 Bell, *The End of Ideology*, 244.

80 Bell, *The Cultural Contradictions of Capitalism*, 106. There is no discussion of architecture in *The Coming of Post-Industrial Society*.

81 Bell, *The Cultural Contradictions of Capitalism*, 283–284.

82 Ibid., 297. Bell's discussion of architecture is hardly long enough to allow for authoritative assessment of his position, but my reading of it is that he is somewhat drawn to postmodernism in architecture, sharing some of the opinions of Charles Jencks and Robert Venturi, whom he cites, and both of whom appear to have largely accepted Bell's postindustrial thesis. See Jencks, *Critical Modernism*, 98, and Venturi, *Learning from Las Vegas*, 151.

83 See Stanley Corkin, "New York, 1968," in *Architectures of Revolt*, ed. Shiel, 141–163.

84 There is also the complication that when referring to steel and concrete in architecture in *The Cultural Contradictions of Capitalism*, Bell calls them "[t] he key materials of an *industrial* civilization" (my emphasis), which, of course,

they were to a great extent. But Bell does not elaborate and, naturally, steel and concrete remained key materials for the postmodernists, even if their organization of space evolved. Bell, *the Cultural Contradictions of Capitalism*, 106.

85 *Film Daily*, April 24, 1967, 3, and Charles Champlin, "'Guide for Married Man' Outspoken and Tattling," *Los Angeles Times*, June 14, 1967, C1–C2.

86 Champlin.

87 "A Guide for the Married Man," *Variety*, April 19, 1967, press clippings file, Academy of Motion Picture Arts and Sciences, Margaret Herrick Library, Beverly Hills.

88 For an account of American labor history very different to Bell's, which characterizes the 1950s and '60s as a period of renewed and often bitter subordination of workers to corporate management, see Mike Davis, *Prisoners of the American Dream: Politics and Economy in the History of the U.S. Working Class* (London: Verso, 2007 [1986]), 102–156.

89 Bell, *The Coming of Post-Industrial Society*, 146.

90 Ibid., 145, 315, 416.

91 Ibid., 376.

92 See, for example, Paul Houston, "10,000 in Melee: War Protest Mars LBJ Visit—Police Clash With Crowd," *Los Angeles Times*, June 24, 1967, 1, 15; "10,000 Battle Police During LBJ Visit," *Chicago Tribune*, June 24, 1967, 2; and James Shafikh, "Police Riot Mars Peace March," *Los Angeles Free Press*, L.B.J. in L.A. on Bloody Friday special edition, June 26, 1967, 1, 7.

93 American Civil Liberties Union of Southern California, *Day of Protest: Night of Violence: The Century City Peace March, A Report of the American Civil Liberties Union of Southern California* (Los Angeles: Sawyer Press, 1967), 33.

94 H. Lawrence Lack, "The Asian War Is Coming Home," *Los Angeles Free Press*, June 26, 1967, 5.

95 See Shiel, *Hollywood Cinema and the Real Los Angeles*, 211–272.

96 The ACLU report was not written as an architectural critique, but reads like one in places as it reports that protestors, when trying to disperse, were hemmed in by the automobile-dominated layout of roadways, overpasses, street furniture, and limited pedestrian walkways that characterize the site.

97 Bell, "Columbia and the New Left," 101.

98 Howard Brick, *Daniel Bell and the Decline of Intellectual Radicalism: Social Theory and Political Reconciliation in the 1940s* (Madison: University of Wisconsin Press, 1986), xi. Brick does not cite Bell's essay on Columbia in his 1986 book, though he does briefly footnote it in his 1992 essay, "Optimism of the Mind," *American Quarterly*, September 1992, 376, fn. 33. See also Nathan Liebowitz, *Daniel Bell and the Agony of Modern Liberalism* (Westport, CT: Greenwood Press, 1985).

99 Daniel Bell, "Ends and Means," *New York Times*, May 11, 1969, BR38.

100 Bell, *The Coming of Post-Industrial Society*, 32, 156.

101 Bell, *The Cultural Contradictions of Capitalism*, 178–179, 187, 190–191.

102 Touraine, "What Is Daniel Bell Afraid of?," *American Journal of Sociology*, September 1977, 471. For a contemporary identification of Bell with the crisis of American liberalism in the 1960s, see Norman Birnbaum, "The Coming of Post-Industrial Society," book review, *New York Times*, July 1, 1973, 219 and Norman Birnbaum, reply to Daniel Bell, *Letters to the Editor, New York Times*, August 12, 1973, 329. I see an analogy between what I would call a blind spot in Bell's thinking with regard to the Vietnam War and his remarkable lack of attention to the reliance of the so-called "post-industrial" society upon the outsourcing of manufacturing industry to "Third World" or "developing" countries—realities which other commentators, such as Harvey, have been better at accounting for and evaluating.

103 *Conquest of the Planet of the Apes*, like *A Guide for the Married Man*, uses Century City as a filming location but the place is not identified by that name in either film. However, the reviewer Kevin Thomas, in the *Los Angeles Times*, did note that the former filmed on location at Century City and the University of California Irvine. Kevin Thomas, "'Conquest' No. 4 of 'Apes'," *Los Angeles Times*, June 14, 1972, H19.

104 Principal photography took place from January to March 1972 and the film was released in June. "4th 'Apes' Roll Jan 31," *Variety*, January 14, 1972; and "AMPAS Date for Bulletin of Screen Achievement Records," dated October 6, 1972; *Conquest of the Planet of the Apes* press clippings file, Academy of Motion Picture Arts and Sciences, Margaret Herrick Library, Beverly Hills.

105 Kevin Thomas, "Third 'Ape' Film Opens Engagement," *Los Angeles Times*, May 12, 1971, G12.

106 Eric Greene, *'Planet of the Apes' as American Myth* (Jefferson, NC and London: McFarland, 1996). Bell is well known for his opposition to totalitarianism—whether Nazism or Stalinism—and his own family had been displaced from eastern Poland in the early twentieth century. However, it seems possible that his belief in American exceptionalism would have led him to object to the characterization of totalitarianism in *Conquest of the Planet of the Apes* given the fact that, like the whole *Planet of the Apes* series, the film's mise-en-scène, characterization, and plot details emphasize that what is being depicted is totalitarianism in a future United States of America.

107 Bell proposed that "systems analysis," so much in vogue in the 1960s, was one of the most promising manifestations of the new "intellectual technology" of the

postindustrial society. He called systems analysis "a social alchemist's dream: the dream of 'ordering' the mass society." Bell, *The Coming of Post-Industrial Society*, 1999, 33.

108 Some scenes in *A Guide for the Married Man* provide a light-hearted version of the Miesian bureaucratic office environment analyzed in the conspiracy thriller by Fredric Jameson, *The Geopolitical Aesthetic: Cinema and Space in the World System* (Bloomington and London: Indiana University Press and British Film Institute, 1992), 75–76.

2

Made in New York:
Film Production, the City Government,
and Public Protest in the Koch Era

Lawrence Webb

During Edward Koch's first mayoral term (1978–81), feature film production in New York City appeared to hit an all-time high. As the city began to recover from the fiscal crisis of the mid-1970s, the local film industry boomed. Boosted by the promotional activities of the municipal film office, the Mayor's Office of Motion Pictures and Television, and by the success of the recently re-opened Astoria Studios in Queens, the city attracted record numbers of shoots from Hollywood studios and independent producers alike. High profile productions lensed in the city, in whole or in part, in the late 1970s and early 1980s included *An Unmarried Woman* (Paul Mazursky, 1978), *The Wiz* (Sidney Lumet, 1978), *Kramer vs. Kramer* (Robert Benton, 1979), *Manhattan* (Woody Allen, 1979), *Hair* (Milos Forman, 1979), *The Warriors* (Walter Hill, 1979), *All That Jazz* (Bob Fosse, 1979), *Cruising* (William Friedkin, 1980), *Dressed to Kill* (Brian De Palma, 1980), *Fame* (Alan Parker, 1980), and *Raging Bull* (Martin Scorsese, 1980). Alongside these flagship movies, a profitable stream of lower budget films, television programs, and commercials helped to maintain a sustainable local production culture.

For the city government, the success of the media industries was both good business and good public relations. In early 1980, a statistical study published by the Office of Economic Policy and Development reported that film and

Note: Research for this chapter was supported by grants from the British Academy/Leverhulme Trust, and the Birgit and Gad Rausing Foundation.

television production generated direct expenditure of $650 million, with a potential multiplier effect of up to $4 billion a year.[1] Such demonstrable financial benefits were matched by the less quantifiable but perhaps equally important branding effects created by Academy Award-winning movies shooting in the streets and refurbished studio spaces of the Big Apple. "Mayor Koch should give Woody Allen the key to the city," gushed Joy Gould Boyum in her review of *Manhattan* in the *Wall Street Journal*. "After all, no one has been a greater contributor to the 'I Love New York' campaign than the city's literate, witty and immensely gifted native son."[2] From this point of view, the box office success and cultural impact of distinctively East Coast films, such as *Manhattan* and *Kramer vs. Kramer*, not only supported the image of a resurgent local film industry, but also bolstered the city's official narrative of economic recovery, urban regeneration, and cultural renaissance.[3]

Yet this narrative was repeatedly disrupted by a series of highly visible public protests against the production and exhibition of specific films between 1979 and 1981. The two most sustained and widely reported of these—and the focus of the second half of this chapter—were the protests around *Cruising* (William Friedkin, Orion Pictures, 1980) and *Fort Apache, The Bronx* (Daniel Petrie, Time-Life Films, 1981). In both instances, activists and local citizens mounted widespread, well-organized campaigns against the negative representation of minority groups and local subcultures. In the case of Friedkin's serial killer thriller *Cruising*, largely set in the leather clubs of the West Village, an increasingly self-confident, post-Stonewall gay community mobilized against the film, which was widely perceived as violently homophobic in its voyeuristic and exploitative image of life in the neighborhood. Around a year later, drawing inspiration from the *Cruising* protests, black and Puerto Rican activists coordinated an equally prominent campaign against Daniel Petrie's cop drama *Fort Apache, the Bronx*, claiming the film's depiction of policing in the notorious 41st Precinct was racist in its treatment of local citizens. Each campaign sought to disrupt the film's progress at every phase, from location shooting to exhibition, and both were arguably designed and staged as media events, with the express intention of engaging the studios, the city government, and the public through local and national media coverage.

Reporting for the *Los Angeles Times* in April 1980, Clarke Taylor captured the discord for the New York City government and the film office in particular.

As Taylor reported, while more than one hundred film commissioners, including New York's Nancy Littlefield, convened at the Association of Film Commissioners International (AFCI) Cineposium in San Antonio, Texas, to discuss the booming locations business across the country, trouble had surfaced again in New York in the aftermath of the *Cruising* protests. On Roosevelt Island, Sylvester Stallone was booed out of a town meeting about the filming of *Nighthawks* (Bruce Malmuth, 1981), while "angry youths" disrupted the shoot of *Fort Apache, the Bronx* in Hunts Point. Meanwhile, lawyer William Kunstler sought a New York State Supreme Court injunction against *Fort Apache* on behalf of black and Hispanic residents of the Bronx. As the headline put it, the Big Apple was "turning sour." "Screams, picket lines, lawsuits; these are not what Nancy Littlefield and Theodora Sklover, energetic representatives of the New York mayor's and governor's film offices, respectively, have in mind when they boost New York as a free and easy location site," noted Taylor.[4]

The struggles over *Cruising* and *Fort Apache, The Bronx* in the streets of New York bring into focus some of the tensions and contradictions of the postindustrial city and its cultural economy. By many measures, New York's financial position had improved since its near-bankruptcy in 1975, but the city was still beset by soaring crime rates and profound social inequality. Local media coverage seemed to oscillate between celebratory and dystopian perspectives. In a cover feature for the upscale lifestyle magazine *New York*, Nicholas Pileggi articulated both sides of the story. "Despite an extraordinary midtown building boom, unprecedented tourist growth, 120,000 new private sector service jobs, and a balanced municipal budget," wrote Pileggi, "there is a pervasive feeling among New Yorkers that their city is falling apart."[5] "Besides street crime, robberies, and burglaries—in which New York leads the nation and to which New Yorkers are almost inured," Pileggi continued, "there has been a deterioration in the kind of behavior that traditionally made urban life bearable."[6] As the city struggled to recover from the traumatic crises of the 1970s, it became a testing ground for neoliberal economic policy at an urban level. The sociologist John Mollenkopf explains: "Between the economic nadir of the mid-1970s and the explosive prosperity of the 1980s, New York City experienced the culmination of a postindustrial revolution."[7] However, as Koch's city "came to epitomize the debt-driven, deal-oriented economic frenzy of the Reagan era," it also created what Mollenkopf calls "new, distinctly postindustrial planes of conflict."[8] Such planes of conflict materialized in the protests against *Cruising* and *Fort Apache, The Bronx*, which articulated both a sense of disjuncture between local citizens and the city government, and a new sense of organization and media awareness in the political strategies of minority groups—a marker of a broad shift from class-based organizing toward the identity politics of the 1980s and beyond.

The campaigns against *Cruising* and *Fort Apache, The Bronx* are now primarily remembered as interventions into debates about minority representation onscreen, but placed within the specific context of film production in the postindustrial city circa 1980–1, they take on added significance.[9] As I will detail below, we might now conceptualize these protests as "interruptions" of the functioning of the neoliberal city—as events that dramatized how the emergence (and rise to dominance) of the neoliberal paradigm was far from smooth and uncontested. These activists used protests at location shoots and outside film theaters to effectively "jump scale" from the local to the global. If the location shoot already plugged the neighborhood into the global media network, this was a chance to seize control of that connection and commandeer it for different political outcomes. Though the protests were, of course, largely unsuccessful in their efforts to derail the production and release of the two films, they nevertheless helped to shape their assembly and frame their critical reception. In this sense, paying close attention to these turbulent production and exhibition contexts can also help us understand the films' complex and ambivalent textuality, as previously noted by scholars such as Amy Corbin, Derek Nystrom, Robin Wood, and Guy Davidson.[10]

By placing the Mayor's Office of Motion Pictures and Television and citizen protests alongside each other, this chapter considers the role of government institutions, as well as the agency of local citizens, in the relations between local place and global media production. A key aim here is therefore to suggest that as a complement to textual studies of screen space, we should also focus critical attention on the role played by municipal governments and other urban institutions in shaping the complex relations between culture and cities. Such questions of institutions, agency, and governmentality have become increasingly important to film studies in recent years.[11] For Lee Grieveson, focusing on institutions and cultural policy as well as representation can provide alternative models for questions of ideology.[12] In particular, Grieveson explains how Michel Foucault's concept of "governmentality" offers a less hierarchical, top-down account of the technologies of power, suggesting how (neo)liberal rationalities establish the "cultural shaping of self-regulating citizens and populations."[13] In this chapter, I emphasize the urban scale as a productive area of focus for governmentality, especially in the era of neoliberalism. As numerous scholars have emphasized, the city has been at the cutting edge of neoliberal practices since the 1970s, providing a testing ground for policy that would later be rolled out at a national level.[14] As such, this chapter emphasizes the institutional role of the city government in shaping the city's production culture, the process of filming, and the reception of films in the urban environment. Furthermore, as James Hay has argued, media has played a constitutive role in the birth of the neoliberal city and its governmental structures.[15] As my analysis of the film office and location protests suggests, viewing the neoliberal city as a "media city" is fundamental to our understanding of cultural industries, government institutions, and urban publics.

The first section of this chapter conceptualizes the Mayor's Office of Motion Pictures and Television as a prototypical agency of the neoliberal city and discusses how its activities were bound up in wider strategies to reposition and rebrand New York. In this section, I argue that the work of the film office was caught between opposing conceptions of cinema as an economic activity and as a cultural practice. While film revenues soared, the late 1970s and early 1980s saw an unprecedented level of public disquiet over individual film projects. As the above examples show, minority groups took to the streets to disrupt location shooting, picketed theaters, and waged a public relations war against both Hollywood and the city government. In the second section, I discuss these local citizen responses to *Cruising* and *Fort Apache, The Bronx* in detail. Aside from their scale and intensity, what made the protest against these films distinctive was their focus on the point of production as well as exhibition, and the extent to which they were able to mobilize local and national media to generate publicity, shape public discourse, and create a framework for reception. Taken together, these case studies show how the widespread use of New York for Hollywood location shooting catalyzed tensions and conflicts on the streets of the city. At the same time, they also suggest that the intensified media environment of the postindustrial city had created a public sphere in which minority groups could intervene and participate.

The film office, neoliberalism, and urban governance

As I have argued elsewhere, the resurgence of New York as an important production center in the 1960s and 1970s was emblematic of two wider trends.[16] In the first instance, the viability of the city as a filmmaking hub was a product of the industrial and cultural shifts associated with the breakdown of the studio system and the rise of New Hollywood. The revived popularity of the city as a destination for Hollywood film crews was premised on the fact that location filming had become relatively standardized, logistically feasible, and cost effective by the mid-1960s, thus lowering economic barriers to extensive shooting—even making entire features—outside Los Angeles. And in the cultural turmoil of America in the late 1960s and early 1970s, New York's "edgy" or "gritty" qualities were eminently marketable as the backdrop for Hollywood Renaissance films, which often capitalized on East Coast talent both behind and in front of the camera. At the same time, emerging policy agendas for the postindustrial city favored media and culture as major revenue streams for the reconfigured urban economy.

The film office worked as a key switching point between Hollywood and the city government. First established in 1966 by Mayor John V. Lindsay (1966–73), the Mayor's Office of Motion Pictures and Television (later renamed the Mayor's Office of Film, Theatre and Broadcasting) was initially located in the Economic Development Administration. Its primary purpose was to fulfill a long-standing ambition of city leaders to "bring back" film production from the West Coast (and to stem the ongoing flow of television production away from the city). It revolutionized the logistical and bureaucratic process of filming overnight with newly streamlined permitting processes, proactive industry liaison, cooperative links between filmmakers and city departments, and a liberalized approach to municipal censorship. Though the Mayor's Office was only one factor behind the subsequent success of New York as a film center, it certainly played a key role in creating the institutional infrastructure for competitive on-location filming.[17] Equally importantly, it was widely viewed within the industry and by city leaders elsewhere as a template for effective municipal interaction with Hollywood, catalyzing the "film bureau phenomenon" that would proliferate in the United States and internationally in the 1970s and 1980s.[18]

As well as recognizing its impact on the film industry, recent scholarship has established the Mayor's Office as a landmark development for urban policy. Both James Sanders and McLain Clutter have convincingly shown how the Mayor's Office and its new conjunction of economics, media, and culture played a significant role in the social and architectural transformations of New York in the late sixties and early seventies.[19] For Sanders, the creation of the Mayor's Office is best viewed as part of a wider change that occurred during Lindsay's two terms, a paradigm shift that recast the city as a place of pleasure rather than a place of function. As Sanders argues, the urban vision promoted by Lindsay reimagined the city as somewhere to be enjoyed, a visual landscape or "giant playground" for its citizens. While filmmakers transformed the city's streets and public spaces into an open-air stage set, this theatricalization of the urban environment also animated the Lindsay administration's creative and playful approach to parks, public events, community art, and questions of urban design more generally.[20] From this perspective, the Mayor's Office wasn't just deeply intertwined with the city's postindustrial turn and its reorientation from production to consumption, but equally helped transform New York from the rational, functionalist city of the past toward a postmodern sensibility that placed the "cinematic" at the core of the urban experience.

Clutter pushes these insights a stage further, drawing parallels between Mayor Lindsay's innovative film policy and city planners' concurrent use of multimedia techniques to engage New Yorkers. As he shows, the city planning commission and media organizations such as CBS not only shared key personnel, but also deployed similar aesthetic strategies—a convergence readily visible in the "Plan for New York" and its documentary counterpart *What Is the City but the People?* (1969). Drawing on ideas from Michel Foucault and Christian Metz, Clutter conceptualizes the city government as an "apparatus" that produces urban subjectivity, shaping and modulating the experience of the city for its users. For Clutter, this analysis of the city-as-apparatus provides a useful way to connect the Mayor's Office of Motion Pictures and Television laterally with the activities of other organizations and institutions in the urban realm. While Sanders points to the agency of the citizen who is invited to enjoy the "adventure playground," Clutter shows how that citizen is hailed by a governmental apparatus operating through urban planning and media policy.[21]

Building on this work, I want to reorient the discussion here by placing emphasis not on the creation of the film office under Lindsay, but rather on its development under the more characteristically neoliberal framework of the Koch administration. This helps us to consider some methodological and political questions that are not fully addressed by Sanders and Clutter. While Sanders usefully contextualizes filmmaking within wider shifts in municipal governance and urban design, he shies away from the political ramifications of his argument. If filmmaking helped transform the city into an "adventure playground," we might question who benefited most from this repurposing of urban space. The gentrification of large swathes of Manhattan and Brooklyn has created an urban environment tailored to middle-class leisure and upscale consumption, but it has done so at the cost of severe economic and racial inequalities. If the Mayor's Office and the filmmaking it supported has contributed, perhaps unintentionally, to this transformation of sections of the city into a playground for the affluent, then questions remain about the consequences of the new "sensibility" that Sanders sketches and the political–economic realities with which it intersected. Furthermore, presenting the postindustrial city as predominantly a place of pleasure and spectacle also risks eliding the material processes that necessarily undergird it. While movies might be construed as "intangible" goods, their manufacture still requires labor power and physical infrastructure. In short, Sanders is right to argue that the Mayor's Office helped revise the use and meaning of public space in the city, but we need to frame these shifts within a more grounded, material account of the film industry and urban political economy.

Clutter's analysis is more politicized, but there are some limitations to his image of the city government as cinematic apparatus. First, the implication of top-down control—the city "positioning" urban subjects—doesn't quite grasp the messy, lived experience of the city for its inhabitants, or the complexity of relationships between local government, Hollywood studios, and filmmakers that characterizes the production of feature films. Secondly, apparatus theory has long been critiqued within film studies for its deterministic view of spectatorship, with many scholars preferring to view audiences as actively engaged in a complex process of interpretation and negotiation. Rather than theorize an idealized, universal subject positioned by the apparatus or the operations of the text, film scholars have long paid close attention to specific historical audiences, to the processes of film exhibition and reception, and to the inherent complexity of the viewer–film relationship. In this respect, though slightly later than Clutter's period of focus, the examples of *Cruising* and *Fort Apache, The Bronx* reveal a more nuanced, multidirectional relationship between citizens and the media networks of the city than his account suggests.

As Miriam Greenberg has demonstrated, the Mayor's Office of Motion Pictures and Television was one of a number of public and private institutions involved in rebranding the city after its fiscal crisis of the mid-1970s. Greenberg shows how city leaders and business elites worked together to repair New York's public image and promote the city as a safe place for businesses, tourists, and consumers. Public–private partnerships such as the Association for a Better New York led the way with coordinated advertising and PR campaigns. At the same time, the counter-hegemonic practices of graffiti artists and hip-hop pioneers challenged this official branding.[22] But locating the Mayor's Office (and the films it helped to produce) within these categories is not so easy, however. As an agency of the municipal government, the film office might have been expected to promote officially sanctioned texts that worked with rather than against the grain of the city's brand management. Yet the laissez-faire approach of the city prioritized economic growth over issues of representation, which in the final instance, they were unable to control. Some films undeniably offered celebratory views of the city, while other films were uncomplicatedly negative, even anti-urban, at least on the surface. But individual films have a tendency to frustrate categories of this kind, and the complexity of cinematic texts tends to elude binary oppositions between branding and counter-branding. Did rich and multivalent films such as *Midnight Cowboy* (John Schlesinger, 1969), *The French Connection* (William Friedkin, 1971), or *Dog Day Afternoon* (Sidney Lumet, 1975) operate either as branding or its opposite? One way to sidestep this opposition is to refocus attention away from reading film texts as inherently "positive" or "negative" in relation to the city's image. Rather, we might instead view the branding potential of the film office as encapsulated in its media strategy, rather than in the films that it helped to sponsor, and to view the location shooting it enabled as a spatial practice with its own dynamics, as well as the precursor to the cinematic text it created.[23]

Because the Mayor's Office did not directly finance or distribute films, or even seek to regulate their content, its function is best described as that of a mediator. From an industry perspective, the film office operated as a switching point between a range of actors and stakeholders, including municipal government, Hollywood studios, independent firms, unions, and local communities. From the standpoint of urban political economy, the Mayor's Office can be seen as a prototypical agency of the neoliberal city and a spearhead of the cultural or "creative" economy more generally. At the heart of the film office's activities was the creation of a business environment and a regulatory regime that supported a neoliberal governmental project. These objectives can clearly be framed within the broader contours of the "entrepreneurial city."[24] Consider the basic activities of the Mayor's Office: it supported cultural activity as a means to attract inward investment and generate economic growth; it promoted the city as a competitive, business-friendly environment for a specific sector and directed public subsidy to further that objective; it operated an organizational structure that could nevertheless simultaneously claim itself to be streamlined and offer reduced regulation; and it generated public relations and marketing campaigns that exploited synergies with the city's wider efforts in strategic branding and image management. As these interlocking objectives suggest, the film office created a nexus between public and private actors and worked to establish a viable production "ecology," though its activities have always been broadly skewed toward attracting Hollywood shoots rather than prioritizing a genuinely independent sector.

For Ed Koch, a noted cinephile who would later become a movie critic, attracting filmmakers to the city was equal parts personal ambition and political strategy. In the late 1970s and early 1980s, the activities of the Mayor's Office of Motion Pictures and Television supported Koch's distinctively pro-business policy agenda. For Jonathan Soffer, Koch's rebuilding of the city after the fiscal crisis provides "a history of the postwar shift in New York City's political economy, away from a manufacturing center with a welfare-state orientation to one dominated by neoliberalism." As Soffer explains, Koch's policies "pioneered the Democratic Party version of neoliberalism, which allowed for government intervention to shape and subsidize private enterprise."[25] Writing in a special advertisement feature for *Forbes*, Koch argued that the city's "remarkable recovery" stemmed from what he termed an "aggressive pro-business policy." In the same piece, Karen Gerard, Deputy Mayor for Economic Policy and Development, described public–private partnerships as "the driving force behind the economic renaissance of New York City," creating a model of "interplay between government and the private sector that is both subtle and complex." "Government's role," she explained, "is to identify natural forces at work and nurture their growth." Gerard pointed to the collaboration between the film office and the Public Development Corporation on the Astoria Studios Project as one of the most "visible examples of how government attitudes and government programs have complemented and stimulated natural forces to increase private sector jobs."[26]

From 1978 to 1983, the linchpin of this public–private collaboration in the Mayor's Office of Motion Pictures and Television was Nancy Littlefield, a former television producer and assistant director who had worked for Columbia Screen Gems on the groundbreaking New York series *Naked City* (CBS, 1958–9, 1960–3). When she arrived at the Mayor's Office in the late 1970s, Littlefield brought extensive industry contacts on both coasts, local production knowledge, and a distinctly private sector style.[27] Littlefield and Koch had a close working relationship that the Mayor liked to celebrate in the press. As Koch repeatedly expressed, Littlefield and the Mayor's Office were central components of his economic and cultural program. "You want to know why I love Nancy Littlefield?," asked Koch. "Night and day I dream of bringing more bucks here—revitalizing the city's economy—and Nancy's making some of that dream come true."[28] Littlefield also mused on the direct relationship between filmmaking and the city's reputation. "I compare bringing film production into the city with tourism," Littlefield said. "When the image of the city is up, tourism is rising. When every day you hear that the city is going bankrupt, people don't want to come."[29] As Deputy Mayor Peter Solomon underlined, Littlefield was more executive than bureaucrat, and her interests were also those of the city, "since filmmaking here meant steak (jobs) and sizzle (image)."[30] "She applies a private-sector mentality to the bureaucracy," said another admirer, pinpointing her especially smooth fit within the new entrepreneurial culture of the city government.[31]

Under Littlefield, the Mayor's Office functioned at one level as a switching point between institutions, corporations, filmmakers, and urban publics, but it also slotted neatly into a broader media strategy for the postindustrial city. One of the key operational activities of the Mayor's Office in this period was to create a public profile for New York as a production center by managing media relations. In the first instance, its primary objective was to persuade Hollywood decision-makers to consider the city for principal photography, but an important by-product of this activity was to project the city as a business-friendly and entrepreneurial environment with a world-class cultural sector. From this perspective, then, the primary output of the Mayor's Office was not feature films, but rather a diversified media image of the city as a streamlined, competitive, and creative filmmaking environment—an image we can view across press releases, newspaper reports, trade press articles, and marketing campaigns.

The traces of this strategy are visible both in the limited materials present in municipal archives and in the pages of the local, national, and trade press. However, one of the complications of studying an institution such as the Mayor's Office is that one of the primary sources of study—articles in newspapers and trade publications—were, of course, prompted by the agency's own press releases, which exerted a strong influence on their reporting. In this respect, the relatively regular reports of a "boom" in New York filmmaking should not necessarily be taken at face value, or viewed in isolation. Tracked over time, they reveal a consistent attempt to produce a narrative about the "revival" of New York City as a production center, to celebrate its success at attracting Hollywood shoots, and to bolster the image of the city as a center of creative activity. Each report tends to identify a spike in filmmaking which is then supported with a quantitative assessment of the financial contribution to the city economy. Alongside the headline figures, the reports frequently provide boosterish commentary on the city and its positive qualities: its entrepreneurial spirit, competitiveness, iconic global status, distinctive culture, and creative talent. For example, a typical piece published in *Back Stage*—itself a New York publication with a vested interest in ballyhooing the local industry—argued that the city offered "a freewheeling creative atmosphere, a deep pool of talent, equipment and services, and an unlimited variety of rich and gritty settings, all set in the financial hub of the western hemisphere."[32] As they put it, New York provided Hollywood producers with unique "economic and social environments" that combined "tangibles as well as intangibles."[33]

In 1980, the year that *Cruising* was released and *Fort Apache, The Bronx* was filmed, the Mayor's Office embarked on an extensive publicity campaign that pushed their promotional efforts into the public and commercial spaces of the city. The centerpiece of the campaign was "Motion Picture and Television Production Week," organized in May that year. A retrospective of New York-made films included unsurprising choices such as *Breakfast at Tiffany's* (Blake Edwards, 1961) alongside grittier fare such as *Midnight Cowboy* (John Schlesinger, 1969), while a radio series about city location shooting aired on WNYC. Corporate tie-ins were established with the airline TWA, who produced subway posters, while Eastman-Kodak furnished tote bags with the Mayor's Office logo and department store windows displayed promotional materials. Parties were held at the Mayor's official residence, Gracie Mansion, and at the nightclub Studio 54.[34]

In the trade press, Mayor's Office advertising had previously emphasized services, industry liaison, and infrastructure, but now it began to move firmly into the territory of urban branding. The first gambit was to capitalize on the city's creative assets and existing reputation as an unparalleled center of culture. Drawing on the New Hollywood valorization of the auteur as a marker of distinction, a series of print commercials used the directorial prestige of famous New Yorkers Woody Allen, Sidney Lumet, Martin Scorsese, and Paul Mazursky to brand the city. For example, under the headline, "Why Sidney Lumet Makes Films in New York City," the director describes Astoria Studios as a "magnificent facility" and dubs the city "the creative capital of the world." Below, the copy appeals to New York's exceptional status—"the place you can't compare to anywhere"—and underlines its historic connection with the early years of film and television. At the same time, this image of the city as "creative capital of the world" supports the Mayor's Office narrative of revival and "rebirth" for the industry and, implicitly, the city itself. In a similar ad based around Scorsese, the copy is forced to somewhat awkwardly sidestep the edgy and frequently violent image of the city found in his films, referring to New York as "where a 'Taxi Driver' takes you through 'New York, New York' and four other boroughs vibrant with energy, ideas and limitless locations" (Figure 2.1). "I work at a very high energy level and so does this city," offers Scorsese, identifying New York with his own intense authorial persona.

Figure 2.1 Advertising for the Mayor's Office of Motion Pictures and Television, *Back Stage*, 1980.

Following this appeal to cultural prestige and cinephilia, a second wave of print adverts focused squarely on the relationship between location shoots and specific city landmarks, tourist sights, and other distinctively marketable aspects of New York. Focusing both on iconic visitor destinations such as Central Park and the Brooklyn Bridge, as well as the layered, historic streetscapes of downtown Manhattan, the ads presented New York's varied visual environment with a touristic sensibility. Such use of landmarks and monuments operated in a similar register to parallel city marketing campaigns, which likewise projected a spectacular and commodified urban landscape to reassure tourists and executives that the city was once more a safe place to visit or do business in.

Placed alongside the citywide events of "Motion Picture and Television Production Week," these advertising campaigns demonstrate the confluence between attracting location shooting and intersecting interests of the city government. While the film office primarily sought to reach film producers, it also participated in the rebranding of the city as spectacular landscape of scenic attractions and landmarks. At the same time, as the auteurist ads make clear, the Mayor's Office helped to shape a broader discourse of New York "creativity" and "independence"—branding the city as simultaneously attractive to the major studios and yet distinctively "off"-Hollywood in its artistic merits. Such imagery drew on preexisting ideas about New York as a distinctive cultural environment, but also meshed with emerging narratives about the city as the locus of enterprise culture. In the second half of this chapter, I consider how local activists captured this intensified media interest in city film production to further their own agendas and to assert their right to the (media) city and the self-representation of their neighborhood.

Film protests: urban interruptions, media activism, and the right to the city

The presence of Hollywood location crews on the streets increasingly brought up thorny questions of the "right to the city."[35] The Mayor's Office held the regulatory power to grant filming permits, but beyond that, who could claim a cultural or moral right to film in a particular street or neighborhood? And who had the ability to control the media image of a specific area and its citizens? In the post–civil rights era, minority groups had become closely attuned to the potentially exploitative relationship between media corporations and the areas they used as filming locations.[36] In New York, the promotional activities of the Mayor's Office had established a heightened public awareness of film production, while the city's position as publishing and media hub meant that debates that might have remained locally contained in alternative outlets such as *The Village Voice* soon became circulated and amplified by the national press. Consequently, activists began to understand how the global and the local intersected at the site of a Hollywood location shoot, and to discern how apparently micropolitical actions such as interrupting filming or picketing a movie theater could become media events with national or even international reach.

With the benefit of hindsight, we might now conceptualize the protests against *Cruising* and *Fort Apache, The Bronx* as "interruptions" in the terms developed by Shirley Jordan and Christoph Lindner.[37] As they argue, the concept of "interruption" captures a diverse array of interventions that have sought to challenge and resist the speed, mobility, and flow of the global city. For Jordan and Lindner, interruptions are "unruly practices that deflect, divert, decelerate or put on hold, and thus create the conditions for considering not only the object of interruption (what has been interrupted) but also the agent of interruption (who or what is causing the interruption)."[38] For local citizen-activists, film sets and movie screenings offered highly visible opportunities to interrupt the functioning of media corporations and the city agencies that supported them. Though they did not manage to stop the production or distribution of the films in question, the protestors nevertheless generated national debate about minority representation and censorship.[39] However, as Jordan and Lindner note, interruptions can easily be co-opted by the forces they seek to resist. As I will return to below, we might question whether the protests ultimately had counterintuitive effects—for example, by generating extra publicity for the films and potentially bolstering the image of the "edgy" city that would be so thoroughly commodified in the years to follow.

Why, then, did these particular protests "kick off"? Though there are some notable differences between the two films, there are nevertheless strong similarities. Both *Cruising* and *Fort Apache* were filmed in neighborhoods immediately identifiable with specific minority groups. In the 1960s and 1970s, these areas had also incubated political radicalism: while the South Bronx had catalyzed black and Puerto Rican movements, the West Village had been the crucible for the gay liberation struggle after Stonewall. The bohemian but increasingly affluent enclave of Greenwich Village was a far cry from the devastated cityscape of the South Bronx, but the clubs and bars of the West Village S&M scene (largely located in what would later become rebranded as the Meatpacking District) were also habitually constructed as dangerous and "other" in relation to normative views of the city. Each film drew, in different ways, on established representational tropes that had become familiar during the urban crisis: the city as ruin, the city as frontier, and the city as urban underworld. Both productions capitalized on edgy subject matter and used their cop protagonists to provide an entry point for a mainstream audience. Such an institutional, outsider point of view of a particular area or subculture could easily take on touristic or even voyeuristic qualities, which amplified an existing distrust of law enforcement. In each case, politically engaged citizens were primed to respond vigorously to what they perceived as the continued misrepresentation of both minority groups and the local neighborhood.

Yet initial protests took place well before either film had finished shooting, and although activists later picketed theaters, their primary target was the process of production. As this suggests, the two campaigns were not mobilized in response to the finished movies, or even the scripts in the first instance, but rather a relatively nebulous sense of each project that had circulated in the media. In both cases, the source material was an initial warning sign. *Cruising* was based on Gerald Walker's eponymous 1971 novel, which had become something of a bête noire for the gay community for its salacious portrayal of a homosexual serial killer, and drew further inspiration from a series of real-life murders that had been linked to gay clubs in the local press. Heywood Gould's screenplay for *Fort Apache, The Bronx* was not, as a court case would later rule, adapted from Tom Walker's infamous police memoir, *Fort Apache: New York's Most Violent Precinct*, but it drew from the experiences of NYPD cops Thomas Mulhearn and Pete Tessitore, and as I will explain below, its title alone was an incitement to protest.[40] Moreover, activists also based their understanding of each production based on press reports and marketing materials in the local and national media. In this respect, it's important to stress that the protests were not a product of the films' ambiguous textuality. In fact, the reverse may well be the case: to some extent, the complexity and even incoherence of these two films was influenced by the protests, which pushed their producers to make ad hoc changes during filming and editing.[41]

Questions of representation aside, we should also view these protests as responses to the practice of location shooting itself, and more broadly, to the neoliberal governmentality embodied by the Mayor's Office of Motion Pictures and Television. As I have suggested, the Mayor's Office prioritized filmmaking as an economic activity, and their primary aim was to smooth the way for Hollywood producers to shoot on the city streets. But location shooting is always implicitly a matter of territory and politics, in the sense that governments regulate where and when camera crews are allowed to film, and because filming necessarily occurs in places that are embedded with social meaning. At this historical moment, shooting a major film in a leather club or in the streets of the South Bronx was inevitably a political gesture, and although the city government did not fund films directly, activists were well aware that municipal support for mainstream movies constituted a form of indirect subsidy. For radical groups, then, the location shoot symbolized both the city government's laissez-faire film policy and the incursion of corporate America—here, Time-Life Inc. and TransAmerica Corporation—into the neighborhood. Nevertheless, this incursion also offered opportunities for publicity and a means to jump scale from the local to the global, connecting the micropolitics of the street to transnational media networks.

Cruising and gay activism in the West Village

Such media awareness had become a hallmark of gay activism in the post-Stonewall era. During the 1970s, the Gay Activists' Alliance (GAA), the National Gay Task Force (NGTF), and the Gay Media Task Force (GMTF) had coordinated demonstrations and boycotts of film releases, including an earlier William Friedkin film, *The Boys in the Band* (1970), alongside titles such as *Some of My Best Friends Are ...* (Mervyn Nelson, 1971), *The Laughing Policeman* (Stuart Rosenberg, 1973), and *Busting* (Peter Hyams, 1974).[42]

Initially sparked by Arthur Bell's call-to-arms in the *Village Voice*, the action against *Cruising* was spearheaded by the GAA, of which Bell was a founding member.[43] Although the protests built on tactics that had been developed over the previous decade, they added a new dimension. Whereas earlier campaigns had primarily focused on picketing theaters and creating media awareness at the time of the film's release, the movement against *Cruising* targeted the location shoot and the interaction between the filmmakers, local citizens and businesses, and New York's gay community.

The campaign began with a local publicity drive about the forthcoming production, with volunteers distributing leaflets in public spaces across the city from street corners to gay bars and local beaches. Activists appealed to local citizens and to gay businesses, especially clubs and bars, asking them not to cooperate with the film production.[44] As they explained in the press, their intention was not censorship: Friedkin was free to make any film he wanted, but he would not make it unimpeded in the West Village (as one activist put it, "he will be prevented from shooting the rest of the film *here*"). This sense of territorial ownership over the neighborhood and its public spaces was a central part of the campaign, but also a source of tension. As one gay leader explained, "Not only have film makers come to New York to shoot a film which a large portion of the population might find offensive, they have come to Greenwich Village (traditionally, gay turf) for most of the filming, to our streets, our bars, into our lives!"[45] Nevertheless, the production depended on a degree of cooperation both from the general gay population and individuals in the leather scene more specifically. Reports suggest that more than 500 gay men worked as extras on the film for $50 a day. This was enabled by the actions of the Screen Actors Guild (SAG), who gave Lorimar a waiver allowing them to recruit non-union extras. As SAG representatives explained, this was necessary given the difficulty of sourcing guild actors with a "leather look" or who would agree to "explicit sexual acts."[46] Despite the campaign, local businesses also played a key part, with the film shooting in leather clubs such as the Anvil, the Ramrod, and the Eagle. Though the campaign had gained significant momentum, there remained splits and tensions in the gay community about participation in the production that prefigured the subsequent ambivalence about the finished film.[47]

The next stage saw a series of carefully coordinated demonstrations and actions designed to disrupt the location shoot. The strategy was to delay the film as a means of escalating its budget, to the point where location shooting in New York would become untenable. Then, if the picture were to be completed, boycotts would ensue against United Artists and its parent company, Transamerica Corporation. Pre-existing communication networks were used to manage the action: *Variety* reported that information about the daily location schedule had been given out on the Gay Switchboard, a recorded hotline number.[48] Protestors were instructed to "mill within camera range, cause a barrage of noise via loud radios, block streets, remove no parking signs, etc." Over fourteen days of production, activists chanted, made noise with bullhorns and whistles, flashed lights, and threw eggs and bottles. On July 25, several hundred demonstrators marched from 9th Avenue to 14th Street, where a scene was being filmed in a bar, moving through the West Village to assemble in front of the Sixth Precinct station house. Having created a public platform, representatives called on Koch and Littlefield to withdraw the film's shooting permit, arguing the film would cause "a potentially inflammatory and explosive reaction to the homosexual community."[49] Speaking on behalf of the activists, Ethan Geto clarified they were not asking for the movie to be banned, but rather requesting the city "stop allocating taxpayer resources to this particular project through the Mayor's Office of Motion Pictures and Television and to deny the movie permits to use the city's streets for filming." Littlefield and the Mayor's Office held firm, however, and Koch's official response underlined the city's business-oriented approach to the film industry. "It is the business of this city's administration to encourage the return of film making to New York City by cooperating to whatever extent feasible with film makers," Koch said, adding that the city does not "accord its approval or disapproval of film content by offering that cooperation."[50] Littlefield's appraisal was even more to the point: "Anything that brings in $7m is good for New York."[51]

Though the protestors repeatedly disrupted exterior filming in the West Village, the overall impact to the film's production schedule was not especially significant. Daily reports filed by the Production Manager record trouble on-set on only fourteen out of forty-five days of shooting in the city (around 31 percent), and show an overall delay to the schedule of three-and-a-half days in total (partly due to more run-of-the-mill challenges such as bad weather).[52] Disruption to sound recording presented perhaps the most pressing problem, with many scenes requiring dialogue to be rerecorded with ADR (though this in itself was not an unusual occurrence). A studio lawyer advised Lorimar that an insurance claim for $100,000 could be filed, largely to due to the costs of extensive dubbing, but this is likely to be an inflated figure.[53] Yet the public image created by the protests had already become a defining aspect of the film's media profile.

As the release date approached, United Artists attempted to assert control over the media circus that had developed around the film. On February 4, 1980, the distributor took out a full-page advert in the *New York Times* (at a reported expense of $15,000) that reproduced a telegram to Jerry Weintraub from A. Alan Friedberg, President of the National Association of Theatre Owners.[54] Friedberg's letter implicitly addressed both exhibitors and the general filmgoing audience. "As an American citizen, a husband, a father, and a theatre owner," wrote Friedberg, "I strongly support the right, if not the obligation, of the American creative film making community to address itself to any subject worthy and susceptible of filming." Exhibitors had an obligation to offer a diverse slate of film fare; anything less would be a "voluntarily imposed form of censorship which is anathema to a free society." The telegram was not only a call for exhibitors to exercise first amendment rights in showing the film, but also doubled as a subtle piece of consumer marketing. "In my opinion, it is admittedly a very violent and explicit film," wrote Friedberg, conveniently pinpointing two of the movie's key selling points. Moving into full reviewer mode, he added that "it is also powerful, compelling, serious, well directed by William Friedkin, and well acted by Al Pacino and the supporting cast." Ultimately, the letter concluded, "those who are interested in seeing a film which breaks new ground in dealing powerfully with a slice of life subject should have the unfettered right to choose for themselves to do so."[55] The same day as the advert appeared in the newspaper, UA held a screening and press conference. *Variety*'s Stephen Klain, who had been explicitly barred from the event, nevertheless noted that UA's maneuvers offered an object lesson in "how to manipulate media controversy ... into marketability on a film about which a broad sampling of early viewers has reacted to with revulsion and anger in a highly negative manner." Noting that "UA execs admit privately that the dispute is gaining the film 'more publicity than money could buy'," Klain reasoned that "UA's bid letters ... 'alert' exhibs to the inevitable public and media controversy not as a warning, but as 'selling points' they (theatres) can count on for the film."[56] The campaign had certainly created media awareness, then, but it also raised questions about who was able to shape or control the outcome of the publicity.

Defending the South Bronx

The strategies pioneered by the *Cruising* protestors provided the template for the following year's action against *Fort Apache, The Bronx*, which was orchestrated by various intersecting groups of Puerto Rican and black activists via the ad-hoc pressure group Committee Against Fort Apache (CAFA).[57] A flyer produced by CAFA set out the case against the film: "*Fort Apache, The Bronx* comes at a time when our communities are under attack from every side. It blames us for worsening conditions and will set public opinion against our struggles for survival and advancement. This is not a question of just a movie. *Fort Apache, The Bronx* is an anti-Puerto Rican and anti-Black movie." Such a rapid response attested to the rising confidence and organization of local political groups in the South Bronx. However, whereas gay activists targeted media representation throughout the 1970s, black and Puerto Rican groups in the borough had tended to focus on local issues, especially urban renewal projects. During the Lindsay administration, community boards and antipoverty organizations were given participatory roles in planning decisions in an explicit attempt to move beyond the top-down "bulldozer approach" of the Robert Moses era. As a *New York Times* piece explained, "Black pride and self-assurance have worked in combination with the Federal anti-poverty program to produce a sophistication and a battery of neighborhood organizations that have enabled some slum dwellers to find the pressure points of city government."[58] Such community organizations were complemented by radical leftist groups such as the Young Lords, who were frequently discussed in the press as the Puerto Rican answer to the Black Panthers.[59]

In this respect, the movement against the film was the product of an increasingly well-organized local political apparatus that had been fueled by neighborhood-level struggles over the fate of the South Bronx.

The campaign was initially catalyzed both by the film's title and pre-publicity circulating in the media. But what was so inflammatory about the title *Fort Apache, The Bronx* in the first place? Far from being created by the film's scriptwriters, "Fort Apache" had been used as a nickname for the 41st Precinct and the Hunts Point district since at least the late 1960s, and at the time of the film's release, it had long been associated with negative media imagery about the area.[60] By the late 1960s, the decaying landscape of the South Bronx had become a national symbol for the urban crisis. The plight of the area was captured in two high-profile special series for the *New York Times* in 1969 and 1973, which cemented a set of representational tropes that would define its public image throughout the following decade. The press repeatedly presented the South Bronx as disconnected from the rest of the city—a dangerous, virtually lawless zone standing outside and apart from New York, or even the United States. "In basic ways," wrote Richard Severo and Barbara Campbell, "portions of the Hunts Point section of the southeast Bronx have ceased to be a part of New York City."[61] Noting the near-collapse of city services and the ever-present threat of crime and social disorder, Martin Tolchin amplified this theme. "Even for a native New Yorker," he wrote, "the voyage across the Willis Avenue Bridge is a journey to a foreign country where fear is the overriding emotion in a landscape of despair."[62] The racial coding of this sense of otherness was forcefully mobilized by the repetition of the term "jungle" and via the metaphor of the frontier, which was extrapolated from the existing "Fort Apache" nickname to describe a generalized breakdown in civil society. "Repeated visits to Hunts Point," wrote Severo and Campbell, "uncover so much that is not supposed to be America in 1969 that the visitor wonders if he has suddenly entered a time machine and been transported to frontier days. Nearly everything seems touched by lawlessness."[63]

Such accounts implicitly drew on a long tradition of slum writing and street photography. Offering the reader a vicarious journey into the urban underworld, these *New York Times* articles combined socially conscious reportage with an uneasy tone of voyeuristic fascination. In most cases, each report began on the front page of the newspaper, accompanied by images of abandoned lots, ruined buildings, and gangs of non-white urban youth. This quasi-ethnographic approach was also deployed by contemporary television documentaries such as "New York Illustrated: Saturday Night at Fort Apache" (WNBC, 1973) and "The Police Tapes" (PBS, 1977), both of which presented outsider views of the South Bronx that were filtered through the first-hand experience of the police. Through such repeated exposure in both local and national media, the reputation of the South Bronx as blighted and crime-ridden area of the city long preceded its use as a movie location for *Fort Apache, The Bronx*. By 1977, the area's status as a resonant political symbol was crystallized by Jimmy Carter's notorious photoshoot in the burnt out ruins of Charlotte Street—a stunt later to be repeated by both Ed Koch and Ronald Reagan. When a feature film about the "Fort Apache" precinct was first mooted in the mid-1970s, then, its commercial viability was therefore partly premised on the public familiarity with the South Bronx that this flow of media imagery had created.

Fort Apache, The Bronx would remain stuck in development for several years at the end of the decade, but had come close enough to starting principal photography that, in February 1976, the production company, Bryanston, jumped the gun and bought a full-page advertisement in *Variety* to announce the imminent location shoot. In the minimally designed ad, the film title is presented in bold, block capitals alongside one simple, striking image: an NYPD badge with a Native American arrow cutting through it diagonally. The tagline announces "Principal photography begins in the Bronx, May 1976." The simplicity of the design and the lack of contextual information suggests that the basic premise and the motif of the "urban frontier" was clear enough to both audiences and industry insiders. As well as pushing the basic marketable elements of the film—a police thriller or urban western set in a notoriously dangerous neighborhood—the advert implies that the idea of principal photography in the Bronx also held promotional value. A film shot in such an infamous location might be a risky venture, it suggested, but it could be daringly authentic. Cameras did not roll in the South Bronx in 1976, however, and production was delayed until early 1980, after the project had been picked up by Time-Life Films. Under the creative directorship of David Susskind, well-known to television audiences for his syndicated chat show,

Time-Life Films extended the media organization's portfolio into mainstream feature films.

Production finally started on March 10, 1980, on location in the South Bronx and at the recently reopened Astoria Studio in Queens. The unusually slow gestation period for the film may have given local activists a head start. But with the *Cruising* controversy still playing out in the city, black and Puerto Rican activists in the South Bronx were galvanized and ready for action. Aside from the title, the initial community reaction to the production was shaped by another advert in *Variety*, this time a double-page spread. Though the ad's visual focus was on Paul Newman and the frontier imagery of the 1976 marketing was notably absent, the advert offered a gritty vignette of the South Bronx to set the scene for the film. Promising viewers "A chilling and tough movie about the South Bronx," it described the neighborhood in dystopian language as "a 40 block area with the highest crime rate in New York. Youth gangs, winos, junkies, pimps, hookers, maniacs, cop killers and the embattled 41st Precinct, just hanging in there." This attempt to market *Fort Apache* with the area's negative reputation—described as an "inflammatory ad" in the press—was directly blamed with inciting the controversy in court, when CAFA's attorney William Kunstler produced it in his attempt to block production of the film.[64]

Drawing inspiration from the ongoing brouhaha over *Cruising*, activists demanded a temporary halt to filming while copies of the script were distributed to locals for approval and feedback. As the press were quick to note, the protracted disturbance of the shoot during spring 1980 clashed with the attempts of the Mayor's Office to rebrand the city. While reports of marches and demonstrations (Figure 2.2) took the shine off Koch and Littlefield's "Motion Picture and Television Production Week," the film's publicist Bobby Zarem was "chased out of the courthouse by a group of angry young blacks who claimed the movie company had reneged on a promise to give them parts in the picture." Zarem, as the activists were keen to point out, was perhaps better known as the PR mastermind behind the city's "I Love New York" branding campaign. Given the circumstances, it was not easy for the activists to extricate the movie, Time-Life, and the city government. For his part, Koch attempted to head off the widespread sense

Figure 2.2 Protests against *Fort Apache, The Bronx*, 1980. Photograph: Joe Conzo.

of a burgeoning rift between his administration and its citizens. The film could be construed as racist, Koch averred, because of its largely negative depiction of Puerto Ricans and blacks, but it would not damage the city's image because people would be able to see the film wasn't "kosher."[65] As it had with *Cruising*, the Mayor's Office of Motion Pictures and Television asserted its laissez-faire policy. "It's a $500 million annual business for us," a spokesman said. "We're not about to revoke people's permits."[66] Meanwhile, star Paul Newman and director Daniel Petrie—both outspoken political liberals—expressed dismay at the action against the film. While Petrie declared himself "appalled at the accusations of racism," Newman offered that the film might be taken as "the positive catalyst needed to rebuild the inner cities and better the lives of their inhabitants."[67] Nevertheless, on the film's opening in February 1981, the campaign retained national momentum. As pickets formed outside theaters in New York and Philadelphia, the *Washington Post* quoted Bronx congressman Rep. Robert Garcia: "I'm not saying the world is perfect in the South Bronx, but this movie so distorts and will leave you with such a negative impression that any effort to rebuild the area will be thwarted."[68]

Reception and recuperation

In both cases, the protests against location shoots were matched by extensive picketing of theaters on the release of the film, which spilled out from New York to other major cities. Over an extended period, the two actions received significant media coverage and drew public attention to issues of minority representation and social justice. But to what extent were the activists successful in their efforts to challenge the nexus between Hollywood, the city government, and the Mayor's Office of Motion Pictures and Television? And had these controversies helped or hindered the critical and commercial success of the films?

Measured by box office receipts, the campaigns had mixed results. Despite the protests and distinctively lukewarm reviews, *Fort Apache, The Bronx* was a resounding commercial success. Even in New York, the epicenter of the protest movement, *Fort Apache* opened in 37 theaters and grossed what *Variety* called a "formidable" $1m on its opening weekend—as they facetiously suggested, the film "evidently had even its pickets buying tickets."[69] Taking a characteristically industry-friendly position, the Hollywood trade paper further noted that "very likely, the general public doesn't see the picket lines outside the theatres when it wants to see the film showing inside."[70] Likewise, *Screen International* reported that "the controversy seems to have hyped, rather than hurt, attendance."[71] The film was an international hit too, topping weekly charts in cities from Paris and Stockholm to Buenos Aires and Tel Aviv.[72]

Cruising, on the other hand, was a more complex case. United Artists had promoted the film with substantial television and newspaper advertising and had managed somewhat unexpectedly to receive an R rating for the film (following some minor cuts) rather than the widely predicted X. The New York opening was impressive, pulling in $800,000 from 30 cinemas, and the film continued to do brisk business throughout the first two weeks of release. Again, many commentators explicitly argued that the controversy had helped rather than damaged *Cruising*. "If these protests hadn't happened, this picture would have died in 10 days or less," confided one senior United Artists executive to the *Los Angeles Times*.[73] But after initial success in New York and Los Angeles, the box office tailed off, and the film failed to connect with audiences in small towns and cities in the mid-West. As several papers noted, this was more likely because of poor word of mouth and a mismatch between the film's lurid content and the taste of mainstream audiences in Middle America. Several theater chains cancelled screenings, and one Kansas City theater publicly apologized to patrons for showing the film, but this was more likely motivated by concerns over obscenity (and perhaps homophobia on the part of the exhibitors) than issues of gay representation. Indeed, *Variety* noted in its rather reactionary review that "from a trade standpoint, 'Cruising' may be remembered in the future as a picture that caused exhibitors more concern over the rating system than it agitated the gay community. If this is an R, the only X left is actual hardcore."[74] In the trade paper *Boxoffice*, one article gamely proposed that exhibitors might even play up the controversial aspects of the film to revive its prospects: "Theatre owners could explore with local radio and TV stations the idea of organizing talk shows or listener call-in forums where guests could discuss gay rights, artistic freedom, Hollywood's depiction of homosexuals, whatever."[75] As this suggests, many in the industry were perfectly willing to capitalize on controversial content, but the film was just as likely to enrage conservatives as it was gay rights activists.

But industry insiders and the trade press could be expected to play down the impact of the protests. As it turned out, Lorimar executives would rather claim that *Cruising* had tailed off at the box office because "it just wasn't a very good movie" than admit that the activists had been successful.[76] Though the campaigns had failed to halt shooting or force meaningful concessions from the filmmakers in terms of content, they had nevertheless garnered substantial media coverage. Measured in terms of column inches, the protests were highly effective. In addition to news coverage of the demonstrations, numerous articles and editorials on minority representation and gay rights appeared in the national press. Though many of these articles posed the question as one of censorship and first amendment rights, they nonetheless brought significant exposure to causes such as gay liberation, Latinx representation, and social justice in the South Bronx. In the case of *Fort Apache*, the court case was also instrumental in raising the campaign's media profile. As CAFA's legal representative William Kunstler explained:

The point is that you have to use the courts any way you can. Maybe we didn't get the script changes, and we haven't stopped the movie, but look at what we did get—eight stories in the *New York Post*, seven stories in the *New York Times*, four stories in the *Village Voice* and a lot of TV and radio time.[77]

Similarly, though the *Cruising* activists admitted they had not stopped the movie, the NGTF nevertheless discovered that the protests had galvanized their network across the United States. "Because of the *Cruising* thing," said spokesman Tom Burrows, "we now have organizations in Vermont, Maine, California, Indiana, New Jersey, Ohio, Ottawa, Houston, DC … The list goes on."[78] New York was the crucible in which the protests were forged, but their effects were felt far beyond the city.

The critical reception of the films also reveals the extent to which the campaigns were able to set the agenda for debate. Reviews of both films in major publications made reference to the protests and the issues that they had brought to the fore. In the *Los Angeles Times*, Charles Champlin opened his review of *Cruising* with a discussion of the protests, noting that "it will probably be difficult for anyone, gay or straight, to view it coolly on its own terms as a movie."[79] Similarly, reviews in *Variety*, the *New York Times*, and the *Washington Post* all placed the controversy center stage.[80] In the *New York Times*, Vincent Canby agreed with the protestors' charge that *Cruising* presented a distorted view of homosexual life.[81] However, Champlin, Canby, and the *Washington Post*'s Gary Arnold all predominantly critiqued the film for its ambiguity and lack of coherence, rather than issues of minority representation. While Arnold dubbed it "dramatically evasive and incomprehensible," Champlin described the film as "baffling, vague and deliberately misleading about its own contents."[82] For Canby, this lack of clarity was itself likely a product of the protests. As he put it, "Perhaps because of the complaints he received during production, Mr. Friedkin has ended up with a movie that is still in a closet."[83]

In her *Washington Post* review of *Fort Apache*, Judith Martin humorously flagged up the controversy around the film as an attraction for a lackluster cop picture: "The movie that managed to libel the South Bronx! See famous bleeding-heart liberals Paul Newman and David Susskind set themselves up for the dreaded charge of racism!"[84] As she put it, "This excitement has been added to […] an otherwise unremarkable cops-and-addicts story."[85] In reviews, the protests helped to frame what was already a key component of the film: what Joy Gould Boyum called "that emphatically New York neighborhood which, in the extremes of its deterioration and as an expedient campaign stop for politicians, has become a national symbol of urban blight."[86] The protests also enabled reviewers to make connections between the two films. Arnold dubbed *Fort Apache* "an uptown variation on *Cruising*" and noted that "each begins as a would-be topical, urgent police melodrama about the search for a homicidal maniac and then wanders luridly, absent mindedly astray."[87] Adding that the film "exploits the troubled, blighted urban landscape of the South Bronx for picturesque squalor and gratuitous, grandstanding sensationalism," Arnold observed that "both movies inspired protests by offended interest groups while they were on location."[88] As with *Cruising*, reviewers criticized the film's lack of narrative coherence. Though *Fort Apache* does not deploy the strategic, art cinema ambiguity of Friedkin's film, Arnold was still able to describe it as "a hopeless tangle of loose threads and discarded hooks."[89] In a characteristically even-handed review, Canby argued that despite the film's outwardly authentic, semi-documentary register, it had failed to live up to the standards it set for itself. While the protestors had arguably read the film almost naively as a documentary, Canby suggested, they were correct that it trades on its patina of authenticity without shouldering the social responsibility that comes with it.[90]

However, as Jordan and Lindner suggest, the urban interruption is liable to be co-opted. As *Jaws* (Steven Spielberg, 1975) had shown in the mid-1970s, a challenging production history could easily be repackaged as an asset. Though neither *Cruising* nor *Fort Apache* could be expected to achieve quite the "event" status of Spielberg's blockbuster, the disruption and controversy that attended the production, exhibition, and reception of the two films certainly helped them maintain media presence. As *Cruising* producer Jerry Weintraub put it at the time, "Everything I do has an event aura."[91] In the years since, the disruption of shooting has become part of the film's mythology, even its claim to authenticity, and is discussed in some detail in the film's DVD extras. In this sense, the media attention generated by activist campaigns were double-edged: at the same time as they raised awareness and helped frame the film's reception, they unwittingly fueled publicity and fed the Hollywood marketing machine. And in the case of *Fort Apache*, news reports about dangerous production conditions only helped to reproduce the very imagery of the dangerous South Bronx that the protestors wished to combat.

The incoherence of *Cruising* was seen as a liability by contemporary critics, but it is perhaps this very quality, along with its mix of art and exploitation cinema, that has allowed the film to be recuperated more recently. Its complexity and strategic ambiguity have allowed it to be read as an open, flexible text. And despite its visibly touristic and inauthentic nature, *Cruising* has nevertheless been celebrated for capturing and making visible an underground scene, and an era of New York history, that is now the object of much fascination and nostalgia.[92] Viewed from the gentrified city of the twenty-first century, the thriving community depicted in *Cruising* might offer a lost utopia rather than an urban nightmare, and the shifting critical reputation of *Cruising* has arguably made the campaign against the film seem misguided, even naïve, in its rigid approach to the text. *Fort Apache, The Bronx* has not yet been reevaluated in the same way, but viewed at several decades' remove, the film's politics equally seem much less clear cut. However, the protests against both films need to be understood in the specific historical and geographical context of early eighties New York. As the campaigns began *before* the release of the film, activists were unable to respond sensitively to their textual complexities. Rather, they are best understood not only as important moments in the struggle for positive media representation, but also as disruptive interventions into the emergent neoliberal city. From this perspective, the protests contested Hollywood's incursion into the streets, resisted the city government's entrepreneurial policies, and made visible some of the social fractures of Koch-era New York.

However, while *Cruising* and *Fort Apache, The Bronx* were widely received at the time as dystopian views of the city, it is also important to note that the protests could be construed not as markers of social alienation but as symbols of success. Rather than unfocused disturbances, these were well-coordinated, multilevel campaigns that evinced the rising capability of activist groups to engage with the media at urban and national scales. Beyond these two cases, protestors mounted numerous actions against films including *Dressed to Kill* (Brian De Palma, 1980), *Windows* (Gordon Willis, 1980), *American Gigolo* (Paul Schrader, 1980), and *Charlie Chan and the Curse of the Dragon Queen* (Clive Donner, 1981). This burst of protest was not sustained throughout the 1980s, though it was to return in the early 1990s when movies such as *Silence of the Lambs* (Jonathan Demme, 1991) and *Basic Instinct* (Paul Verhoeven, 1992) became battlegrounds for the "culture wars," but the connection between identity, place, and the location shoot was less firmly articulated than it had been in Koch-era New York.

Conclusion

This chapter has sought to demonstrate how questions of institutions and agency can develop our understanding of cinema at an urban scale, and to focus attention on the central role of media in the development of neoliberal governmentality. As these case studies suggest, focusing on institutional frameworks alongside local conditions of production and reception allows us to reconceptualize relations between cinema and the city within wider historical shifts in urban centers, their models of governance, and their media networks.

By intertwining cultural production, economic development, and city branding, the Mayor's Office of Motion Pictures and Television operated as a flagship institution of the emerging neoliberal city. This was broadly the case from its inception in 1966, but its entrepreneurial activities intensified under the Koch administration and its aggressively pro-business managerial culture. As I have shown, the competitive activities of the Mayor's Office under Nancy Littlefield worked not only to establish a dominant narrative of the city's rebirth and continuing success as a production center, but also meshed with wider efforts to rehabilitate the city's public image. Rather than look for traces of this strategy in films—which inevitably rendered images of the city that were complex and ambivalent—we can more readily grasp it in the promotional materials produced by the Mayor's Office, and through its work as a mediator between various public and private agencies. The Mayor's Office therefore makes visible how urban institutions embraced culture as part of a neoliberal project, and underlines the role of Hollywood and the media industries within that unfolding story. However, the protests against *Cruising* and *Fort Apache, The Bronx* make clear that such a vision of the city streets as an "adventure playground" for filmmakers was contested. Koch had risen to power by exploiting the social and racial fault lines of postindustrial New York, but those fractures created cultures of resistance. As the protests discussed in this chapter show, citizens are not passive users of the city or its media networks, and while the urban "interruptions" they produced did not, in the long run, seriously damage the films or challenge the policies of the Mayor's Office, they nevertheless revealed how minority groups might use the location shoot to project the local space of the neighborhood onto the global media stage.

Postscript: one of the gang?

Institutions can quickly adapt to cultural change, however. In 1984, the New York State film office published a full-page advertisement in the trade paper *Back Stage*[93] (Figure 2.3). A multi-ethnic, mixed gender group decked out in an eclectic range of street fashion stands against the backdrop of a graffiti-covered wall, staring nonchalantly at the camera. "Shooting On Location Can Be Tough When You're Not Familiar With The Turf," the tagline announces, adding: "New York State Makes You Feel Like One of the Gang." In this image and its accompanying text we can read the State film office's attempts to negotiate the tensions and cultural shifts that took place in the wake of the film protests. It is clearly addressed to an outsider—someone "not familiar with the turf," let's assume a producer from out of town—and readily acknowledges the well-known problems with location shooting in New York. What the film commission has to offer, it suggests, is a guide to the city, an insider point of view. It is both honest and reassuring: shoot your film in New York City, it says, and we will help you avoid any problems you might face. But we can also read in the image a sea change in the way that city and state institutions interacted with the city's subcultures. It's clear from the image that the "gang" in question is supposed to look more hip than threatening. The staged visual presentation suggests a fashion shoot, or a band photograph, rather than street ethnography. The image feels diverse and inclusive—white and black, male and female—and is carefully pitched to avoid some obvious pitfalls (such as associating "gang" too closely with young black men). While the text suggests that location shooting can be "tough," the image plays up New York's ethnic diversity and subcultural cool. In this respect, it shows how city agencies learned to incorporate New York's "edgy" sensibility into its vision of the city.

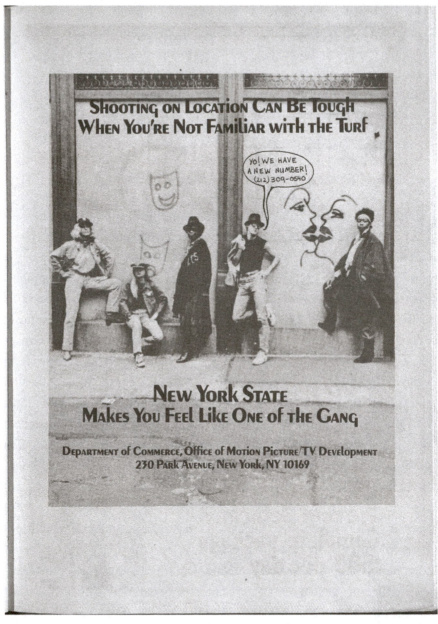

Figure 2.3 Advertising for the New York State Office of Motion Picture/TV Development in *Back Stage*, 1984.

In contrast to the city landmarks of the earlier Mayor's Office materials, it emphasizes a street-level view, and markets the city to filmmakers not so much as a set of static, historical landmarks, but as a living, breathing space filled with vibrant urban culture. Whether one reads this as a story of institutions adapting positively to social change, or less charitably as a narrative of co-optation, even gentrification, remains open for debate. Either way, such marketable, edgy cool would soon be mined cinematically by hip-hop crossover vehicles such as *Beat Street* (Stan Lathan, 1984) and hit downtown Manhattan films such as *Desperately Seeking Susan* (Susan Seidelman, 1985).

Notes

Research for this chapter was supported by grants from the British Academy/ Leverhulme Trust, and the Birgit and Gad Rausing Foundation.

1 Sherry Eaker, "NY Film Production Sets Record Levels," *Back Stage*, January 16, 1980, 57.

2 Joy Gould Boyum, "Woody Allen's Heartbreak Town," *Wall Street Journal*, April 27, 1979, 17.

3 On the city's recovery after the fiscal crisis, see Miriam Greenberg, *Branding New York: How a City in Crisis Was Sold to the World* (New York: Routledge, 2008). On *Manhattan* and *Kramer vs. Kramer*, see Stanley Corkin, *Starring New York: Filming the Grime and the Glamour of the Long 1970s* (Oxford and New York: Oxford University Press, 2011), 162–193, and Lawrence Webb, *The Cinema of Urban Crisis: Seventies Film and the Reinvention of the City* (Amsterdam: Amsterdam University Press, 2014), 104–108.

4 Clarke Taylor, "The Big Apple Turns Sour for Makers of 'Ft. Apache, The Bronx,'" *Los Angeles Times*, April 7, 1980, G2–3.

5 Nicholas Pileggi, "Wounded City: What's Happened to Our Life Here?," *New York* 14.3 (November 2, 1981), 27.

6 Ibid.

7 John Hull Mollenkopf, *A Phoenix in the Ashes: The Rise and Fall of the Koch Coalition in New York City Politics* (Princeton, NJ: Princeton University Press, 1994), 3.

8 Ibid., 3–4.

9 On *Cruising* and the representation of sexuality, see Harry M. Benshoff and Sean Griffin, *Queer Images: A History of Gay and Lesbian Film in America* (Lanham, MD: Rowman & Littlefield, 2006), 181–184. On the protests against both films in the context of censorship, see Charles Lyons, "The Paradox of Protest: American Film, 1980–1992," in *Movie Censorship and American Culture*, Second Edition, ed. Francis G. Couvares (Amherst: University of Massachusetts Press, 2006).

10 See Amy Corbin, *Cinematic Geographies and Multicultural Spectatorship in America* (New York: Palgrave Macmillan, 2015), 113–166; Derek Nystrom, *Hard Hats, Rednecks, and Macho Men: Class in 1970s American Cinema* (Oxford and New York: Oxford University Press, 2009), 138–155; Robin Wood, *Hollywood From Vietnam to Reagan… And Beyond* (New York: Columbia University Press, 2003), 52–62.; Guy Davidson, "Contagious Relations: Simulation, Paranoia, and the Postmodern Condition in William Friedkin's *Cruising* and Felice Picano's *The Lure*," *GLQ: A Journal of Lesbian and Gay Studies*, 11.1 (2007), 23–64.

11 See, for example, two special issues on "Institutions and Agency" in the journal *Film Studies*, no. 13 (Autumn 2015) and no. 14 (Spring 2016).

12 Lee Grieveson, "On Governmentality and Screens," *Screen* 50.1 (Spring 2009), 180–187.

13 Grieveson, 181.

14 See, for example, Neil Brenner and Nik Theodore, eds., *Spaces of Neoliberalism: Urban Restructuring in North America and Western Europe* (Walden, MA and Oxford: Wiley, 2002). On Ed Koch, New York, and neoliberalism, see Jonathan Soffer, *Ed Koch and the Rebuilding of New York City* (New York: Columbia University Press, 2010).

15 James Hay, "The Birth of the 'Neoliberal' City and Its Media," in *Communication Matters: Materialist Approaches to Media, Mobility and Networks*, ed. Jeremy Packer and Stephen B. Crofts Wiley (London and New York: Routledge, 2012), 121–140.

16 For an account of New York filmmaking and the Mayor's Office of Motion Pictures and Television in the 1960s and 1970s, see Webb, 75–81.

17 Ibid.

18 On "the film bureau phenomenon," see Gary Edgerton, "The Film Bureau Phenomenon in America: State and Municipal Advocacy of Contemporary Motion Picture and Television Production" [*Audiences, Economics, and Law*, vol. 2, ed. Bruce Austin (Norwood, NJ: Ablex, 1986), 204–224.]. See also Noelle Griffis, "The New Hollywood," in *Hollywood on Location: An Industry History*, ed. Joshua Gleich and Lawrence Webb (New Brunswick, NJ: Rutgers University Press, 2019).

19 James Sanders, "Adventure Playground: John V. Lindsay and the Transformation of Modern New York," *Places*, May 2010, https://placesjournal.org/article/john-lindsay-adventure-playground-new-york/ (accessed April, 2014); McLain Clutter, *Imaginary Apparatus: New York City and Its Mediated Representation* (Zurich: Park Books, 2015).

20 Ibid.

21 Clutter.

22 Greenberg.

23 For a useful discussion of film and television production as spatial practice, see Helen Morgan Parmett, "Media as Spatial Practice: *Treme* and the Production of the Media Neighborhood," *Continuum* 28.3 (2014), 286–299.

24 The foundational article on urban entrepreneurialism is David Harvey, "From Managerialism to Entrepreneurialism: The Transformation in Urban Governance in Late Capitalism," *Geografiska Annaler. Series B, Human Geography* 71.1, The Roots of Geographical Change: 1973 to the Present (1989), 3–17. See also Tim Hall and Phil Hubbard, *The Entrepreneurial City: Geographies of Politics, Regime and Representation* (Chichester: Wiley, 1998).

25 Soffer, 4.

26 "New York City: A Forbes Special Advertising Supplement," *Forbes*, July 5, 1982.

27 Clarke Taylor, "Bringing Film to the Big Apple," *Los Angeles Times*, July 18, 1979, G7. Much of the reporting of Littlefield in the press was also disconcertingly gendered. For example, Koch repeatedly described her "feminine" qualities as an important part of her success at "luring" in production. As he put it, "She's tough and soft… Soft and womanly enough to entice filmmakers here, tough enough to stand up for the movie industry against the city bureaucracy."

28 Ibid., G7.

29 Arnold Schmidt, "Littlefield, NYC Film-TV Director, Discusses Gotham Prod'n Outlook," *Back Stage*, February 16, 1979, 37.

30 Ibid., G8.

31 Ibid., G8. Littlefield talks about her contribution in an interview for the DGA: "There was no marketing when I first took that job. There was no marketing. It had no brochures. They had nothing that was telling people what we had. The first thing that I did was, I went out to Los Angeles because I had been there, so I knew where I was going." https://www.dga.org/Craft/VisualHistory/Interviews/Nancy-Littlefield.aspx (accessed May 5, 2014).

32 Tom Tolnay, "NYC Is 'Action' Again—City Passes Own Screen Test," *Back Stage*, May 2, 1980, 1.

33 Ibid. By 1975, *Back Stage* had offices in other cities, but its headquarters remained in New York.

34 Jim Robbins, "City Office Helps Filmmakers Love New York," *Box Office*, May 5, 1980, 2.

35 The term was coined by Henri Lefebvre in his 1968 essay *La Droit à la ville*, later
    published in English as "The Right to the City," in *Writings on Cities*, selected,
    translated and introduced by Eleonore Kofman and Elizabeth Lebas (Oxford:
    Blackwell, 1995). On the history and development of the slogan within urban
    debates, see Margit Mayer, "The 'Right to the City' in the context of shifting
    mottos of urban social movements," *City* 13.2–3 (June–September 2009),
    362–374. Though it is unlikely that the activists described in this chapter used
    the precise term "right to the city," it nevertheless usefully captures some of the
    motives and strategies of post-1968 social movements and their approach to
    urban politics, as well as the essentially territorial nature of the film protests.

36 Organized protest against minority representation in cinema dates back at least
    as far as *The Birth of a Nation* (D.W. Griffith, 1915). Conflicts between African
    American groups and filmmakers had flared up in the late 1960s, as Hollywood
    studios started to take an interest in the marketability of crime films set in
    Harlem. For example, there were disturbances on the sets of *Cotton Comes to
    Harlem* (Ossie Davis, 1970) and *Come Back, Charleston Blue* (Mark Warren,
    1972). Italian American groups had also mounted a campaign against *The
    Godfather Part II* (Frances Ford Coppola, 1974). See Noelle Griffis, "Filmmaking
    to Save the City in Crisis: New York on Location, 1966–1975," PhD dissertation,
    Indiana University, 2018.

37 Shirley Jordan and Christoph Lindner, "Visual Culture and Interruption in
    Global Cities," in *Cities Interrupted: Visual Culture and Urban Space*, ed. Shirley
    Jordan and Christoph Lindner (London: Bloomsbury Academic, 2016), 1–13.

38 Ibid., 9.

39 See, for example, articles such as Allen Woll, "How Hollywood Has Portrayed
    Hispanics," *New York Times*, March 1, 1981, D17, D22; Christian Williams,
    "Minorities Are Rising up against Their Stereotypes on the Silver Screen,"
    Washington Post, May 4, 1980, H1, H5; Carrie Rickey, "Why They Fight: Subjects'
    Rights and the First Amendment," *American Film*, October 1, 1981, 57–60.

40 The court case was widely reported in the press. See, for example, Anon.,
    "Gotham Cop Sues 'Ft. Apache' Filmers; Charges Story Lift," *Variety*, June 4,
    1980, 4, 28. Mulhearn and Tessitore worked in the 41st Precinct in the 1960s, so
    by the time the film was released, its image of the South Bronx was somewhat
    dated.

41 Critics such as Guy Davidson, Robin Wood, Derek Nystrom, and Amy Corbin
    have written very perceptively about these films as complex and ambiguous texts.
    I won't attempt to provide an alternative reading of the films or unravel their

ambiguity here, nor will I intervene in the debates they generated about minority representation, artistic expression, and free speech. Rather, I want to suggest that to grapple with the ambiguous textuality of these films we need to attend to their turbulent production and reception contexts. In the case of *Cruising*, the multiple versions of the script held in the William Friedkin papers show that a number of significant changes were made during the production process, including the ending of the film, partly in response to the protests. William Friedkin Papers, Margaret Herrick Library, Academy of Motion Picture Arts and Sciences, Los Angeles.

42 Matt Connolly, "Liberating the Screen: Gay and Lesbian Protests of LGBT Cinematic Representation, 1969–1974," *Cinema Journal* 57.2 (Winter 2018), 66–88.

43 Arthur Bell, "Bell Tells," *Village Voice*, July 18, 1979. Bell implored the reader "to give Friedkin and his production crew a terrible time if you spot them in your neighbourhood" and suggested that "owners of gay establishments would do well to tell Friedkin to fuck off." The protests were widely covered in the *Village Voice* and discussed from multiple angles. See Richard Goldstein, "Why the Village Went Wild," *Village Voice*, August 6, 1979, 1, 16, 18; John Rechy, "A Case for *Cruising*," *Village Voice*, August 6, 1979, 1, 18, 20.

44 Clarke Taylor, "N.Y. Gays Rally against 'Cruising,'" *Los Angeles Times*, July 20, 1979, F19.

45 Clarke Taylor, "Gay Drama Offscreen on 'Cruising,'" *Los Angeles Times*, August 19, 1979, N32.

46 Ibid., N33.

47 The split attitudes of the community were discussed at the time in the gay magazine *Mandate*, which published a cover feature titled "The Men of Cruising." See John Devere, "On the Set," *Mandate*, February 1980, 20–23, 48–51.

48 Anon., "Manhattan Homosexual Circles Fight Lorimar's 'Cruising' Pic," *Variety*, July 25, 1979, 34.

49 Anon., "Protestors Call the Film 'Cruising' Antihomosexual," *New York Times*, July 26, 1979, B7.

50 Les Ledbetter, "1,000 in 'Village' Renew Protest against Movie on Homosexuals," *New York Times*, July 27, 1979, B2.

51 Edward Guthmann, "The *Cruising* Controversy: William Friedkin vs. the Gay Community", *Cineaste* 10. 3 (Summer 1980), 4.

52 William Friedkin Papers, Margaret Herrick Library, Academy of Motion Picture Arts and Sciences, Los Angeles. Folder f. 165, Production Reports.

53 Interoffice memo from Bob Finkelstein to Bruce Liliston. William Friedkin Papers, Margaret Herrick Library, Academy of Motion Picture Arts and Sciences, Los Angeles. Folder f. 135 (Legal: Casting and Locations). Friedkin also investigated taking legal action against the *Village Voice* for inciting the protests, but this was not pursued.

54 Advertisement, *New York Times*, February 4, 1980, B10.

55 Ibid.

56 Stephen Klain, "Weintraub to Media: 'Fan Dispute, But Hold Your Critics,'" *Variety*, February 6, 1980, 4.

57 The *Village Voice* usefully listed some of the groups involved: "United Bronx Parents, Black United Front, Association of Hispanic Arts, United Tremont Trades, New Rican Village, Museo del Barrio, Puerto Rican Educator's Association, Community Association of Progressive Dominicans, MECHO (Chicano student movement), Reverend Neil A. Connolly, vicar of the Bronx for the New York Archdiocese, City Councilman Gilberto Gerena-Valentin, and Bronx Community Boards 1, 2, 4, and 6." See Richard Goldstein, "Footnote to the Above," *Village Voice*, May 5, 1980, 2.

58 David K. Shipler, "Urban Renewal Giving the Poor Opportunity to Increase Power," *New York Times*, November 9, 1969, 1, 80. See also Murray Schumach, "Puerto Ricans Strengthen Political Power," *New York Times*, March 27, 1971, 31, 43.

59 For a detailed insider discussion of the Young Lords and the background to CAFA, see Richie Perez, "Committee Against Fort Apache: The Bronx Mobilizes against Multinational Media," in *Cultures in Contention*, ed. Douglas Kahn and Diane Neurnoier (Seattle: Real Comet Press, 1985).

60 The first reference in the *New York Times* to "Fort Apache" in conjunction with the South Bronx appears in September 1969. The report suggests that the term already had widespread local usage. See "Addict Control: No Solution in Sight," *New York Times*, September 5, 1969, 1, 50.

61 Richard Severo with Barbara Campbell, "Hunts Point: Ruled by Addicts," *New York Times*, September 24, 1969, 1.

62 Martin Tolchin, "South Bronx: A Jungle Stalked by Fear, Seized by Rage," *New York Times*, January 15, 1973, 1.

63 Severo and Campbell, 1.

64 Taylor, "The Big Apple Turns Sour for Makers of 'Ft. Apache, The Bronx'", G3.

65 Selwyn Raab, "Film Image Provokes Outcry in South Bronx," *New York Times*, February 6, 1981, C6.

66 Williams, H5.

67 Ibid.

68 Betsy Kennedy, "'Fort Apache' Under Fire," *Washington Post*, February 6, 1981, C6.

69 Anon., "B'Way Teepees Come to Life; 'Apache' Encircles $1,000,000; 'Fear' 800G; 'Maniac' 750G," *Variety*, February 11, 1981, 8; Anon., "French Fried Broadway as 'Cage II' Gay $125,000; 'Metro' Big 80G; 'Apache' 900G, 2d," *Variety*, February 18, 1981, 8.

70 Anon., "B'Way Teepees Come to Life; 'Apache' Encircles $1,000,000; 'Fear' 800G; 'Maniac' 750G," *Variety*, February 11, 1981, 8.

71 Anon., "'Apache' Opens Well despite Controversy," *Screen International*, February 14, 1981, 1.

72 Advertisement in *Screen International*, August 22, 1981.

73 Dale Pollock, "'Cruising': Protests on the Picket Lines," *Los Angeles Times*, February 18, 1980, E1.

74 Har., "Cruising," *Variety*, February 13, 1980, 16.

75 Jim Robbins, "Cruising," *Boxoffice*, March 24, 1980, 14.

76 Dale Pollock, "'Cruising' Tails Off," *Los Angeles Times*, March 16, 1980, N36.

77 Williams, H5.

78 Ibid.

79 Charles Champlin, "'Cruising'—Looking Past the Images'", *Los Angeles Times*, February 10, 1980, M1.

80 Har., 16; Vincent Canby, "Screen: Pacino Stars in Friedkin's 'Cruising'", *New York Times*, February 15, 1980, C6; Gary Arnold, "'Cruising' Off Course," *Washington Post*, February 18, 1980, B1, B13.

81 Canby, February 15, 1980, C6.

82 Champlin, February 10, 1980; Arnold, "'Cruising' Off Course," B1.

83 Canby, February 15, 1980, C6.

84 Judith Martin, "'Fort Apache'", *Washington Post*, February 13, 1981, 17.

85 Ibid.

86 Joy Gould Boyum, "Urban Blight; Suburban Fright," *Wall Street Journal*, February 6, 1981, 21.

87 Gary Arnold, "Bronx Cheer: Trouble at 'Fort Apache,'" *Washington Post*, February 7, 1981, C1.

88 Ibid.

89 Ibid.

90 Vincent Canby, "Screen: 'Fort Apache, the Bronx', with Paul Newman: In Hostile Territory," *New York Times*, February 6, 1981, C6.

91   Clarke Taylor, "Weintraub Defends 'Cruising,'" *Los Angeles Times*, August 8, 1979, E10.

92   See, for example, Melissa Anderson, "Rawhide: *Cruising* Comes Out of the Closet and into the Dungeon," *Film Comment* 43.5 (Sept/Oct 2007), 36–37.

93   This chapter has focused primarily on the Mayor's Office of Motion Pictures and Television, a city institution, but from 1979, filmmaking in New York has also been promoted at a state level by the New York Governor's Office for Motion Picture and Television Development. See Anon., "Governor Promoting Filmmaking in N.Y. Thru State Office," *Independent Film Journal* 82.8 (July 1, 1979), 5, 18.

3

You Don't Have to Call Us Home, but Please Stay Here: The City Film Commission

Nathan Koob

Many have argued that the development of film commissions in the United States followed the economic development strategies of municipal powers within postindustrial cities to move to a more service-based economy.[1] The later rise of state subsidies and tax incentives has made the film commission all the more central to contemporary film production and as a result we must gain a better understanding of how these offices function. While performing field research for a past project on production relationships between filmmakers and cities, I first thought that the best use I had for the local film commission would be as a good place to get general information. However, my unintentional reduction of their role quickly became clear when I found they were central to understanding how filmmakers worked with places and, in turn, how those places influenced productions and texts. Due to the wide range of my research, which examined a variety of cities with different levels of scale and production infrastructure, I somewhat stumbled on a tangential examination of the postindustrial city film commission. I found that while film offices all purport to serve similar basic functions, their success and survival often require much more specific strategies that correlate the local production environment and available resources with the much broader industrial landscape. Through my interviews and conversations with film commissioners and production crew, I discovered how these cities and offices work to construct each other.

Film commissions have grown into almost a local standard. In an early piece studying film offices and their relationship to independent filmmaking, Gary

Edgerton notes that by 1986 there were already ninety-three city and state film offices—seventy of which developed after 1976.[2] Today, the Association of Film Commissioners International (AFCI) website lists 135 city and state film offices in 42 states.[3] It is worth noting, however, that many cities, regions, and states also have unofficial film offices not registered with the AFCI. If we were able to reliably count these offices, it would undoubtedly show a much more dramatic increase. To understand the functions of the local film office, we must begin by realizing that they often act as the first official voice of the city that production personnel hear. City film commissions sell their locale, manage location difficulties, work in conjunction with the state film commission, react to/influence the local production infrastructure, and in turn sell the production's presence to local residents. The majority of film commissions begin within departments of economic/urban development or tourism, though the strategies they must use to produce benefits to the locality differ significantly depending on the needs, resources, and hindrances of any given city. In other words, having a film office and a film production in the city does not guarantee successful economic stimulus. Most film offices manage some variation of four primary functions: Organization, Enticement, Tax Incentives, and Economic Stimulus.[4] This chapter shows film commissions as a larger part of production cultures by drawing from personal interviews with film commissioners from a variety of cities as well as production personnel who have long worked with film offices on location shoots. The examples studied here come in part through my past research, but also show a selection of cities and film offices with distinctly different histories: Austin, Texas; Baltimore, Maryland; and Kansas City, Missouri. Interactions between productions and cities rely on unique production strategies entwining with local place dynamics and resources—much of which is organized, managed, set up, and negotiated by a local film commission at some level.

'Tis impossible to be sure of anything but film commissions and tax incentives

To look at how film offices present themselves, one might think that their functions have not changed much since their inception—comprised of primarily organization, enticement, and economic stimulus.[5] When looking at how film offices began developing historically in the United States, the context of the postindustrial city and related issues such as white flight, the downsizing of manufacturing jobs, gentrification, and uneven development are important.[6] In "Performing the New Economy," Stanley Corkin notes:

> New York City had declined as a manufacturing center in the 1950s and 1960s and also experienced a related flight of the middle class. As a consequence, the prospect of meeting the city's considerable financial obligations appeared particularly daunting for successive New York City mayors. When the liberal John Lindsay was elected in 1966, then, one of his early acts was to create the Mayor's Office of Film, Theater, and Broadcasting.[7]

Mayor Lindsay reached to film production as a possible savior of the local economy and in doing so created an office with functions that would become standard for other film commissions that followed. McLain Clutter, in an essay also focused on Mayor Lindsay's film office and urban development, further outlines how Lindsay established what soon became the primary functions of film commissions across the country:

> [The] Mayor's Office of Film, Theatre, and Broadcasting streamlined film-production permitting to one standard document that would apply to all filming locations. While mounting a national letter-writing campaign to attract film productions, the mayor and his staff made every effort to alleviate the obstacles to filming in the city. Lindsay removed film censorship powers from municipal agencies, negotiated with the local industry labor unions to offer competitive rates, and even created a division in the police department composed of officers specially trained in the "cinema arts."[8]

Lindsay used the office to simplify local bureaucratic obstacles in order to aid organization. The office also created a letter-writing campaign to entice productions into the city, all for the hope of creating economic stimulus with the money spent by film productions. There was no guarantee this would work, but the strategy revealed how city governments had begun to view film production as one potential panacea for urban decline.

Today, film office websites appear to offer roughly the same things: links to local filmmaking resources, including information on permits; information about diverse locations along with promotional advertisements about the city; links for local media industry workers; and information about how the film commission's efforts have aided local economic stimulus. For instance, the Kansas City Film Office website outlines, "The Kansas City Film Office attracts film, television and media (including new media) production to the Kansas City area [...] In addition to production assistance, the Office actively builds relationships with producers and filmmakers marketing Kansas City as a production location"[9] and the Baltimore Film Office website similarly states, "It's our mission here at the Baltimore Film Office to provide exceptional service to all productions scouting and filming in Baltimore [...] We strive to facilitate the growth of the film industry in Baltimore and to create an awareness of the economic and cultural benefits of filmmaking and film-related events."[10] These statements highlight many of the aforementioned general functions of film offices. Wilmington Regional Film Commissioner Johnny Griffin perhaps most aptly characterizes the general sense of what film commissions do in the current industry environment by referring to them as "a combination of travel bureau and concierge."[11] Yet in reality film commissions are as distinct as the places they represent, and their roles change distinctly over time. Some have started out of necessity, such as Austin, Texas, because productions began swooping in to film in that area and someone needed to liaise with the producers and manage the potential impact of multiple film projects in the city. However, much more frequently cities develop a local film office with the specific hope of aiding economic development and rejuvenation.

The success of some early film commissions made the consistent enticement of new productions even more central to their functioning. Writing about the Mayor's Office of Film and Television in New York, Clutter argues, "Although the long-term economic effects of these policies are difficult to calculate, when one considers that the motion picture and television economy in New York had reached a level of $500 million a year by 1980, the contribution of Lindsay's policies seems significant."[12] Similarly, a study performed by a Texas Tech University professor found that in 1980, after establishing state and local film commissions, visual media production contributed over $500 million to the Texas economy.[13] Cities offer attractive enticements like tax credits because the reported economic benefits of having a film shoot within an area can be quite large, even if it is a bit difficult to pin down exactly how much money is spent and where it will be spent. As reported by the Nassau Film Office, "The indirect economic impact in 2008 came to $67.75 million, according to a formula from the New York State Governor's Office of Motion Picture and Television Development. It's people eating, paying location fees, staying at hotels, going to Home Depot because they have to build something, services to clean up."[14] Although these numbers are impressive, the impact of an individual production depends on a large number of factors, such as its scale, the length of stay in the area, and the amount of local resources used. Of course, the overall impact on a specific city or state varies depending on the number of productions within (in this case) the year that come to the area. None of these aspects are really guaranteed, however, as producers enticed by a tax incentive are likely to be looking to cut costs wherever possible and will be most interested in getting their film made rather than necessarily contributing to the local economy. Further, such strong numbers require a consistent wave of films. Thus, given that many more states, cities, and regions have created film commissions since the 1990s, making the market increasingly competitive, it stands to reason that the organization function has become less of a priority than enticement.

Production designer Stephen Altman, who began his career working for his father Robert Altman, testifies to such as distinct change in the strategies of film commissions over the years. Robert Altman is well known for filming on location outside of California. Early examples include *That Cold Day in the Park* (1969), filmed in Vancouver, British Columbia, and *Brewster McCloud* (1970), filmed in Houston, Texas. Stephen Altman's first film as production designer was *Secret Honor* (1984), filmed in Ann Arbor, Michigan, and he continued to build his career working on location shoots outside of Hollywood well before it was fashionable to do so. He explains how the role of the film commissioner has changed from a part-time government job, which focused primarily on organizational functions, to a full-time endeavor active primarily in enticing films to the area:

> Some film commissions and film commissioners back in the day were really ex-location managers. I remember, maybe it was New Mexico on *Fool for Love* (1985) where we ended up hiring the guy who was on the film commission, it was a part-time job for him, and then we had him on as a location manager [...] now it's like a full-time job for those guys. Every time I go on a film and move in to another town usually we're driving around

with all the film commissions and they're actively participating and picking up our lunch, getting us acclimated. Then as soon as we start production they sort of bow out, go away [...] A lot of them these days are just like, "Ok, great, thanks, make sure that locations get all the permits."[15]

According to their websites, film commissions are generally run either by local industry professionals, whose careers can range from experience in Hollywood to commercial production work, or by local government administrators. Yet, Altman notes that whereas once a film office was dedicated to working with productions throughout shooting, the job has changed to simply getting the film there and then shifting focus to getting the next film there. It is a distinct change from a focus on organization (production personnel being shepherded and helped during production) to enticement (being wined and dined during pre-production and left virtually alone once in the city).

Such a shift in emphasis from organization to enticement has further resulted in increased attention on subsidies, especially tax incentives, as a consistent means to draw in production. In a 2013 interview on the increasing importance of production tax incentives, Regional Commissioner Johnny Griffin recalls: "About twelve years ago, we didn't have incentives and, in that point in time, people looked all over the place to scout movies, but now certain areas are not even considered because they have no incentive."[16] It is no secret that Hollywood filmmaking has quickly become reliant on incentives. Anyone doing localized research on productions, especially in the 2010s, has likely run into stories about large production decisions being made, or hindered, due to availability of state and local tax incentives. In their study of state-level strategies used to lure in film productions, Susan Christopherson and Ned Rightor note that "by 2009, over forty U.S. states were offering tax-based incentives or rebates to film or television producers."[17] The AFCI recognizes the importance of the rise of tax credits in their mission statement: "We provide invaluable tools for producers searching for the right location, or looking to capitalize on the latest tax incentives."[18] Griffin's comments highlight that the film commission now works primarily in service to its tax incentive instead of directly in service to its community—as if the incentive will lead to automatic stimulation and renewal. Altman's above example further underlines this trend, as many film commissions have removed the personal organizational attention they used to provide and shifted to a working structure built on promoting tax incentives.

Tax incentives have become so important because they have proven extremely effective in enticing production, but often what is most needed is not just *a* tax incentive, but instead *the best* tax incentive. States offer films significant return in exchange for having their film produced locally, so it is no wonder that producers are primed to take advantage of them. For instance, in 2011, Ohio's tax incentives provided "a 25% rebate on expenditures in the state with an additional 10% for the wages of Ohio native cast and crew."[19] Since 2008, Georgia has had one of the most robust tax credits—sitting at 30 percent if the production is over $500K and if the Georgia logo appears in the end credits.[20] The Atlanta Journal-Constitution reports that due to this incentive, "Atlanta has played backdrop to more than 140 films and TV shows, according to the Georgia Department of Economic Development."[21] Arguably, if productions simply seek out the best tax credit then they will flock to whichever state provides the best incentive. Thus, tax incentives are not really a viable mass strategy for enticement as long as a handful of incentives are conceivably better than the rest. It is also not a particularly viable local strategy without a commitment to retaining one of the best incentives packages even as the market and industrial landscape changes. From this perspective, then, it is worth questioning how much a competitive incentives package gives and takes away from a local economy.

We now live in an industrial moment where all states and most big cities feel they *need* a film commission to be able to compete for film and television production. The demand created by incentive schemes in turn creates the need for a film office to manage it, however, and as we have already started to see, the benefits of attracting productions are not so cut and dried. In his focused work on the Philadelphia Film Office, Paul Swann argues:

> The claims regarding the benefits of transforming major cities into sound stages and backlots warrant close scrutiny. Such an audit would reveal whether the tax rebates and free or heavily discounted municipal services that are now standard packages for film shoots are justified. In the short term, they offer temporary employment for taxpaying citizens as well as some longer-term benefits, including the prospect of many more jobs being created over a longer time frame, and more nebulous gains such as promoting and advertising the city itself.[22]

Swann points out that it is hard to know what film productions actually bring to cities beyond the more obvious short-term gains. Films both build and restore, but do both cosmetically, not functionally, so it is not clear what these productions actually *do* long term for these cities that justifies all the effort and money given to entice them.

Such valid political concerns regarding the effectiveness and long-term viability of tax incentives have largely been reinforced by subsequent research. Christopherson and Rightor found discrepancies among different research studies on the effects of tax incentives, but the overall picture their collection of these studies paints is a rather bleak one:

> The overwhelming majority of fiscal impact analyses of film and TV subsidy programs conclude that the subsidies have a negative impact on state revenues, particularly if they take the form of saleable tax credits. The tax implications of the 2008 legislation passed by the State of Michigan, for example, have been assessed by the State Senate Fiscal Agency [...] The incentive program is anticipated to cost $127 million in the 2008 fiscal year, only $10 million of which will be offset by income and sales tax receipts [...] The State of Rhode Island Department of Revenue calculated that for every dollar invested in motion picture production tax credits, the state earns back $.28 from direct economic investment [...] A Connecticut study of their 2007 incentive program showed a loss of $14.5 million in state revenues.[23]

Looking at the benefits of tax incentives makes it difficult to calculate how much money is actually spent in the local economy: real gains are almost impossible to quantify reliably. In response to the trend of government reports showing significant losses due to tax incentive programs, some states with historically robust tax credits have begun to cut back or cap the amount that productions can claim. Louisiana offers up to 30 percent tax credits to big productions and another 10 percent payroll credit if they use local crew. However, they recently capped the amount of credits which can be claimed to $180 million.[24] The only way, it would seem, to track reliable economic stimulus from tax incentives is with the consistent presence of film productions, yet this scenario is unlikely to develop in most places without establishing a highly competitive tax credit. The huge rise of productions in Georgia in recent years, allowing the local industry to establish a formidable production infrastructure, does showcase how effectively one of the most generous tax incentives can be used for real gain. However, only a handful of locations will ever be able to boast that they have one of *the best* tax credits for a given period and, as Christopherson and Rightor show, the tipping point where productions ultimately take much more than they provide may already be upon us in many locations.

Actual long-term benefits, which can exist, need to be more carefully considered. Janet Wasko mirrors Altman's earlier sense of changing roles though ascribes the rising *expectation* of economic stimulus as key to this change:

> As more production companies began to look for realistic and varied locations, more cities and states began to see the need for production coordination. But most importantly, they were also keenly aware of the economic benefits brought by film and video production companies to their areas. Indeed, a multiplier effect is often experienced as the local economy can take in as much as three times the amount that a production company actually spends on location.[25]

Wasko suggests here that the possible benefits of having a production in town can be theoretically limitless. Media productions bring in money to lease location sites, but also serve to hire and train local media industry workers, often through union deals negotiated through the producers and municipal tax incentives, hire and train production support services, and of course patronize local hotels and restaurants. As Swann argues above, though, many of these gains are quite obviously short term and longer-term gains require a constant presence of productions so it raises the question of whether tax incentives lead to the formation of self-sustaining industry services that can contribute to the local economy in the long term. As suggested above, the answer to this question likely has more to do with the old adage: location, location, location.

"Nothing succeeds like success": Austin, Texas

As a model for what consistent outside production can do for cities we can look to Austin, Texas.[26] While Texas established a state film commission in 1971, Austin did not form its local film office until more than a decade later at a time when film productions were viewed more as a local nuisance than an economic savior. It is easy to say that today Austin is booming; the 2015 census places Austin's population at 900,000, in large part due to the development of the city as a center for the creative industries.[27] Austin epitomizes the organizational function of film offices in that its film office originally formed out of necessity due to productions just cropping up there. In the mid-1980s, Austin's basic film commission functions were performed part-time by the City Inter-Governmental Affairs Officer, who was appointed by the local government to be in charge of wrangling permits and checking for production insurance. In 1985, when the city's population was at around 400,000, Gary Bond took over the position of Austin Film Commissioner from his original post in the Communications Department.[28] Bond describes the job in the mid-1980s as organizational: "I don't think it had really occurred to anyone at the time to encourage films to come. We had one every five years or so, a made for TV movie or something. The main interest of the city was making sure they followed the rules: that they had liability insurance, got their permits, all of that kind of thing."[29] At first, and unlike the earlier New York examples, it seemed that the city was not quite aware of what economic potential they had with the success of early films like *The Texas Chainsaw Massacre* (Tobe Hooper, 1974). As Bond suggests, filmmaking in general was seen by locals as a lower-class industry and was not directly encouraged by the city.

Bond paints the city of Austin at that time very much as a postindustrial city, in the sense that its economic expansion was occurring primarily in high-tech, white-collar work and cultural industries, but one that had not yet realized the possibility of filmmaking as a source of economic growth. The relevance of film productions in the area took on increasing importance, however, as Austin began to notice how integral films were becoming to the local economy. Bond explains:

> I've said too many times that nothing succeeds like success. Once you start doing something, it began to kind of get on a roll and coincidentally Austin had overbuilt the hotels, there was a real estate bust, and oil bust [...] Austin kind of took a downturn and the city was very receptive to anything that would generate a little more economic development. Their hotels were running at 25% occupancy so it was a perfect storm for me signing up with the Association of Film Commissions [...] and beginning to actually market the city as a film location.[30]

Bond describes, for Austin, the shift from city film commissioner as a government job focused primarily on regulation and organization to a job more focused on enticement. In his description he uses the term "marketing" instead of "tax incentive", which helps show that, at least in Austin, the tax incentive strategy came out of a desire to market locations beyond simply appealing to available local resources.

The shift to enticement as a strategy, however, was more specifically to help a growing local media industry infrastructure than it was to vaguely create economic stimulus. As Bond describes, the influx of productions caused the development of support services and local crew, ultimately organizing Austin into a film production center. "I think it was a happy accident," Bond explains. "Again, it's the success. It's also a very imitative industry. People came here, did a movie, it went well for them, they went back to talk to their 35 friends in Los Angeles and then they wanted to hire the same people, stay in the same hotel, go right in the footpath that came before them."[31] The consistent influx of much-needed money into the local economy led to a wider acceptance of filmmaking which, in turn, led to more productions and more locals becoming involved—especially in the way of support services. The early word-of-mouth, happening at a time before many productions were leaving Hollywood to film elsewhere, led to Austin gaining a reputation as a viable production center, which helped direct productions there even without the film office. In 2014 Bond estimated Austin had around 600–700 fully trained crew who work full-time. Therefore, after creating a solid infrastructure, Austin does not primarily attract media productions in order to aid its economic development, but has instead shifted its focus to attract productions in order to support an already existing local workforce.

Austin's history and thriving film culture put its film office in a different league than a more typical contemporary example such as Baltimore or Kansas City, which are discussed below. Drawing on its status as a film production center, Austin is portrayed by the Film Commission website as something akin to film location royalty: "Austin is a leading destination for independent and large budget films as well as television & commercial productions."[32] Austin relies on its history, but Austin's film commission also has a distinct tinge of not trying so hard. They rely on very confident and quickly communicated facts for their sales pitch, including "Austin's talented crew base will give you more production value per-dollar spent; Austin has hill country, lakes & farmland all within 30 minutes of downtown; Austin is surrounded by small towns time has forgotten, perfect for a period piece; Austin's mild climate provides over 300 days of sunshine a year."[33] The Austin Film Commission does remain active in recruiting films to the area, though its success came out of a growing film culture that needed a film commission, not the more contemporary case of a city wanting to forge a film culture. As Bond suggests, Austin has become economically successful in further encouraging a film culture (seen today most prominently in the SXSW Film Festival, The Austin Film Festival, The University of Texas at Austin Department of Radio-Television-Film, and the start of the Alamo Drafthouse theater chain) around the rise of incoming productions, which has in turn helped to sustain its production culture long term. In the case of Austin, its history of productions in many ways sells itself.

The long game: Baltimore, Maryland

Austin could conceivably act as a model of what a film commission can do to help economic stimulation in a city or locality, yet its history raises the question of whether or not it's viable for other cities to productively forge the demand for productions, which Austin was receiving much more naturally at first. Whereas Texas has developed tax incentives to remain competitive, their incentives are not the highest in the nation. In fact, Texas incentives become more competitive *outside* larger cities such as Austin or Dallas which are felt to receive, at least for now, enough production attention to sustain the local infrastructure. This more comfortable situation is not the case for most film commissions across the country, however, which have developed out of desire or even desperation to use outside production to stimulate the local economy and reap long-term benefits. In short, the battle to attract productions is real and is happening everywhere.

In comparison to Austin, Baltimore has taken a longer road to find some measure of success with economic redevelopment and media production. As a big city, Baltimore has suffered from urban decline due to the loss of manufacturing. Cultural geographer David Harvey, who has worked extensively in Baltimore, explains that after 1960 Baltimore lost two-thirds of its manufacturing jobs; the major industry employers which severely cut back or left Baltimore included shipbuilding, Bethlehem Steel, and General Motors, the loss of which put much of Baltimore into crushing poverty.[34] Over the past three to four decades Baltimore has undergone extensive urban development and gentrification. This development has not, however, resulted in overall prosperity in the city. In 2001 Harvey pointed out, "The redevelopment has certainly brought money into the city through a rapid growth of the convention and tourist trades. But there is no guarantee that money stays in Baltimore. Much of it flows out again, either as profits to firms or payments for goods."[35] Furthermore, he adds that "there are some 40,000 vacant and for the most part abandoned houses in a housing stock of some 300,000 units within the city limits (there were 7,000 in 1970). The concentrations of homelessness [...], of unemployment, and, even more significant, of the employed poor [...] are everywhere in evidence."[36]

Since the 1960s, Baltimore has been host to film productions and television series, but not as consistently as cities such as New York or Austin. Just for the sake of comparison, the 2015 census puts Baltimore's population around 620,000.[37] However, unlike Austin, which has continued to grow significantly since the mid-1980s, Baltimore's population has decreased.[38] This is not to say that population always directly correlates with the success of film productions, but instead to suggest that the arrival of the (or a) film industry does not on its own guarantee successful economic redevelopment for the city as a whole, especially when production work is inconsistent.

The Baltimore Film Office is a division of the Baltimore Office of Promotion & The Arts, thus connecting the drive to bring productions in to promote local Baltimore culture. On its website, the film office uses its history of hosting location shooting as a key motivator for productions to film there: "Baltimore has been the setting for hundreds of movies, television series, documentaries and commercials over the years. We are proud of our cinematic heritage and look forward to continuing our history of being one of the finest moviemaking cities in the country."[39] Focusing on history is a way to suggest that Baltimore is well "trained" as a host for productions, meaning on the side of both local crew *and* its citizens. The Baltimore Film Office professing a history of productions does two things for the purposes of enticing productions. First, people are more used to the level of disruption a production causes and are better able to deal with it. Secondly, with a history of both steady and non-steady production work within the city over the years, the overall local economic benefits of having productions in town become all the more clear. With Baltimore hosting major television series such as *House of Cards* (Netflix, 2013–18) and *Veep* (HBO, 2012—19) along with other productions coming through the area, their current production climate can be viewed as successful, but this was not always the case when looking at the forty years prior. Part of reaching this point involved developing well-trained crew and industry support services in the middle of much more tenuous production environments.

In order to try to reap long-term benefits, many cities want to develop their own local crew base as well as industry support services. Focusing on local labor will not only have the film spending more money in the location, but also creates local jobs and helps to develop infrastructure. However, if a city has no real productions coming through consistently it is difficult to develop and retain trained crew. Stephen Altman relayed the struggles of being a department head and negotiating with film commissions or local union representatives about using local crew:

> There's nothing wrong with locals. It is comfortable to hire the same old people that you always know, but there's always different and better people […] We were just in Cleveland and they had just opened up their tax rebate […] They want me to hire the locals and as many people as possible from there. But they had a really weak crew base, they've not done a lot of films up there […] It gets difficult on that level when you just don't have quality people.[40]

For many cities, a paradox is created where local crew needs to be trained by working on productions, but incoming productions do not want to work with inexperienced crew. Tax incentives sometimes address this inconsistency by offering further benefits to productions that use local crew, as seen above in the example from Louisiana, but as Altman suggests this is not always enough and base training needs to come from somewhere, especially in cities without an active film school. In Austin, Bond made local training seem more like an output which occurred due to the increased presence of production cultures in the area, not to mention the University of Texas at Austin's Department of Radio-Television-Film. However, without the consistent presence of productions in need of workers, such training is not going to happen naturally without some other form of incentive built in.

In the case of Baltimore, the local industry environment has benefited greatly from hometown filmmaking heroes John Waters and Barry Levinson as well as the television writer and showrunner David Simon. Waters, who rose to fame with off-beat hits such as *Pink Flamingos* (1972), *Female Trouble* (1974) and *Hairspray* (1988), made a career out of filming independent productions in Baltimore with city locals as cast and crew—providing a strong basis in industry training. However, in part due to his consistent demand that he shoot only in Baltimore, even at his most prolific Waters was only producing a film once every two to three years, which means he could not provide consistent local work on his own at a time when few films were shooting anywhere outside of Los Angeles or New York. In the 1990s and 2000s, Levinson and Simon are most noteworthy for producing long-running television series which filmed in Baltimore, such as *Homicide: Life on the Street* (NBC, 1993–9) and *The Wire* (HBO, 2002–8), which brought further training as well as consistent work for the local industry. Jed Deitz, Director of the Maryland Film Festival and President of The Producer's Club, which is a nonprofit working in tandem with the Baltimore Film Office, outlines how each hometown figure helped Baltimore escape the more typical pitfall of training locals:

> Barry started with *Diner* (1982), though it was a studio movie. John's first bunch of movies were not at all studio movies. So the combination was pretty powerful because you had Barry's resources and Waters' no resources and that built two different types of groups. And David in a very different way with *Homicide* (1993–1999), *The Corner* (2000), and *The Wire* (2002–2008) did the same thing. The neighborhoods he would shoot in, they would hire people in those neighborhoods. There are people who are union members who were just kids off the street.[41]

Baltimore developed a professional crew base from a variety of different sources, making its crew not only knowledgeable, but also highly traversable regardless of what kind of production came through. However, during the in-between times when these productions have not been active they left a void where local industry workers had to leave the state in order to find work. And whereas hometown creators have shown real interest in Baltimore—in certain cases moving their production locations to areas of the city most in need of development—outside productions typically have no incentive to do anything but film in local places most convenient to them, which are unlikely to be those in need of economic stimulus.

There's no struggle like home: Kansas City, Missouri

It is important to note that for many cities, such as Kansas City, commercial and industrial media production is far more stable and consistently viable than Hollywood or television productions. In San Antonio, for instance, the film commission started as a division of the San Antonio Convention & Visitors Bureau.[42] The goals of the San Antonio Film Commission show its role involves not a lot of discernment regarding *what* comes to shoot in San Antonio, just that *something* comes to shoot in San Antonio—a method shared by most city film offices seeking to feed the economic beast created by the promise of having a local production infrastructure. As Michele Krier puts it, "Dovetailing with the SACVB's efforts to market the city, Chapman says his role is to market San Antonio as a destination for film makers, TV commercials, TV shows, print catalogues, documentaries, music videos as well as news and national talk shows."[43] As a result of such tactics, film commissioners in today's media environment need a broad knowledge of production cultures in order to sustain a viable local industry. In other words, it does not always have to be all about Hollywood when it comes to making ends meet.

As the above examples suggest, while film and television shoots can create substantial economic benefits and help to build a production infrastructure, actual urban renewal in larger cities requires a consistent flow of productions to sustain local support services. In order to achieve this standard, many film offices fetishize the incoming production at the expense of the local community. Writing about film commissions in Hawaii, Julian Stringer notes, "Some local film commissioners are willing to bend over backwards to satisfy the whims of filmmakers, offering to change river flows, grow crops on barren fields, or remove telephone poles so they don't distract camera moves and angles."[44] Stringer describes location alterations which likely do not aid local communities and, in fact, would serve as an incredible nuisance as well as significant cost to the city. Their need to bend over backwards lies in the reality that, as Michael Curtin has argued, locations-seeking film productions have found an increased need to compete over productions in ways that benefit producers, but not creative media workers.[45] In attracting producers (and thus the film productions), then, film commissions are not necessarily all focused on local representation—once felt to be key to aiding local tourism efforts and visualizing urban renewal.[46] The result has been a surge in local film offices along with increased pressure to attract productions. From the perspective of incoming crew, these qualities tend to make contemporary film commissions seem very mechanical and detached. Stephen Altman explains:

> We were in Virginia, North Carolina and South Carolina looking at the three states to decide where we're going to be [...] All three of them take us around, trying to set their best case for why we should do the film here. They couldn't care about the movie we're making they just want us to come here, and once they do that job they're pretty well done.[47]

Such broad-minded city film commissions work to "sell" the places or spaces of the city *in general* to any outside production, ultimately not caring what areas of the city the production locates in, despite their most common position in an economic development council (EDC). If a production decides to situate in more affluent communities it raises the question what, if any, larger economic benefit the production provides to the greater city and its areas in need.

Simply having a production roll through town or through an impoverished area does not guarantee successful economic stimulus, though it is clear the most common narrative among film commissioners involves the "if you build it they will come" mantra. Or, to be more specific, they work under the guise of "if you bring in a production, it will spend as much money as we need." Christopher Crane, Director of the Arkansas Film Commission, provides an example of this argument:

> What impact did the movie *Mud* (2012) have on Arkansas? I can tell you that you should have conversations with many of the vendors used during the filming of "Mud": they will sing its economic praises. These production companies purchase local goods and services and increase short-term employment and spending throughout the area [...] When speaking about just the cast and crew, these people rent houses. apartments, hotel rooms, eat, drink, buy gas, use the dry cleaners, buy local art, go to local entertainment venues, etc.[48]

Crane treats the question very pragmatically, suggesting that if a production comes in and brings many people with it then those people will spend money in this place. Of course this is true, though, it is also true that once all of those people leave they will no longer be spending money there. The need for another production/group of people then gets created to keep that level of income and so on ad infinitum if the city/area wants to gain any kind of long-term benefit. Film producers will not necessarily be concerned about supporting the city; they are typically most interested in just getting their film made. Both producer Matthew Seig and production designer Stephen Altman, who worked together on *Kansas City* (Robert Altman, 1996), suggested that any benefit to the city from their work was great, but their focus was first and foremost getting their film done while trying to stay within budget.[49]

At the time of making *Kansas City* in the mid-1990s, many areas throughout Kansas City, Missouri were in need of redevelopment. The film production ended up focusing on a lot of these areas that acted as markers of an almost postindustrial wasteland. Most strikingly, the giant Kansas City Union Station had fallen into almost total disrepair—complete with a caving-in roof—and in particular, the Historic Jazz District at 18th & Vine, a formerly segregated neighborhood across the city, was now full of mainly condemned buildings long forgotten. Just before the Altman film arrived, Robert T. Trussell gave his own account of the historic neighborhood: "Today the district is a shadow of what it once was. Many of the buildings that existed in 1935 are gone, and you're likely to see street crowds only during the annual 18th and Vine Heritage Festival."[50] Despite gaining an increasing historic significance as an area of much cultural importance, the famed intersection, once home to dozens of jazz clubs and jazz legends, was also unable to sustain itself economically. As Trussell goes on to argue, in part the decline results from the area's history as a highly segregated neighborhood which fell in part due to the white flight of the 1960s: "In 1964 voters in Kansas City approved, by a narrow vote, a public accommodations law lowering racial barriers for which so many people in the 18th-and-Vine area had worked for so many years. One result, ironically, was that the historic intersection became a neglected area of the inner city."[51] What had been a thriving community dispersed once an emptying city was opened up to the residents. Further, the historic neighborhood had received little support or interest from the city up to that point in restoring or maintaining any of its history.

The case of Kansas City sheds some light on what many burgeoning film offices need to survive in the more mobile production environment. Shortly after Mayor Emanuel Cleaver created the Kansas City Film Commission in the late 1990s, Robert Altman decided to scout locations and ultimately shoot in the city for his film *Kansas City* (previously titled *Blondie*). Since it was only just establishing itself, the first film commissioner, Patti Broyles Harper, distinguished her film office by offering both the resources of a larger city with steady commercial production services and the hands-on attention of a smaller locality. Matthew Seig, producer of *Kansas City*, remembered Broyles Harper's attentiveness as a distinct part of the larger Kansas City social environment: "I found them very friendly [...] The film commission was all 'what can we do for you?'—introducing us to people, bringing people around who were helpful, finding connections, opening doors."[52] Such attentiveness during the production process was a part of the Commission's establishment in the municipal EDC and stood to differentiate Kansas City from other areas seeking sustained production revenues by returning to a more personal, organizational approach.

The film commission, placed in the role of economic development stimulus, sits in a strange binary position. At one and the same time the commission must attract films to the area, typically by offering them what they want, and yet they must also strive to bring the incoming economic stimulus to areas of the city in most need of it. Broyles Harper explains their early strategies:

> [The EDC] were very forward thinkers and their minds were totally open to the business of film and the economic impact it would have on the community [...] [we] erred on the side of the movie makers because there's so much value to having them in your area. Employment, very little infrastructure required on their behalf, they come in, spend money and they leave the area for the most part better than they found it.[53]

Broyles Harper suggests that by connecting their overall focus more on the side of filmmakers, the EDC felt as though simply having a film in the city would lead to successful economic development of some kind, though aligning the commission more with the filmmakers also suggests that any development was being placed in the hands of people who had no specific mind to affect economic rejuvenation in the city in any direct way. Through the film commission and local press, Kansas City did attempt to take a more hands-on approach and tried to use Altman's interest in the historic Jazz

District to drum up typically lacking public attention to the area and aid redevelopment efforts.[54] The argument became that the film's interest and use of the neighborhood would lead directly to economic redevelopment through the film's creation of cosmetic period facades—supposedly preserving the almost lost history there.[55] This local media machine allowed the production to work quite smoothly, though little follow-up development to the area resulted after it left, with the exception of some already-planned renovations such as the opening of the American Jazz Museum.

The lack of attention to further development at 18th & Vine is particularly noticeable, especially when compared to the large-scale renovations successfully completed in more affluent areas of the city. Kansas City's Union Station, for instance, used the momentum from the film's presence there to form a bi-state tax that garnered upwards of $180 million dollars for its complete restoration.[56] The historic Jazz neighborhood, however, sits in a similar position to the one it was in before the film came. The film commission, despite being positioned in the EDC, shepherded the film, but despite best efforts was unable to steer lasting economic redevelopment to the historic district. In part, of course, it is arguably not the business of the film commission to continue redevelopment efforts once a film leaves, but given that they were described as leaning more to the side of the filmmakers, the example does highly suggest the value that a film has for long-term economic redevelopment on its own—which is understandably little, unless bolstered by many films consistently occupying the same areas of the city.

Furthermore, the Kansas City Film Commission and the municipal government doubled-down on *Kansas City* by trying to make the film a poster child for their move to become a consistent host of media productions. Mayor Cleaver and Broyles Harper accompanied the film to Cannes, wanting to use its success to breed, borrowing Bond's term, future success in Kansas City productions.[57] Yet now they were applying money and attention toward a film in *post*-production when the film had no more money left to spend in the city. The ultimate commercial failure of *Kansas City* played against the city's constructed narrative. Once the film faltered it left the city with little else to build from it beyond the positive word of mouth garnered through the heightened organizational function Broyles Harper used during production.

Kansas City also, however, serves as an example of the need for some kind of organizational body in the current media industry environment. In other words, if there are local media industry support services, a film office is vital to maintaining them. In the mid-2000s, the city dropped the film commission and stopped funding it, leaving a void for production support services in the area who took it upon themselves to create a privately run, nonprofit film commission. Local industry professionals banded together in order to keep some decorative appearances of film commission services running in order to help keep their own support services more active. Former President of the nonprofit film commission Heather Laird explained: "They just simply stripped the funding, so at that point there was one staffer and then like an intern or part-time staffer and then they pulled the plug. When that happened this not for profit film commission was started."[58] Laird went on to explain that the nonprofit film commission at first functioned as an arm of the State film commission, however, sometime around 2010 the state film office also closed, leaving the nonprofit Kansas City Film Commission to attempt to function on its own. Kansas City's more grassroots film commission was started by Teri Rogers, who ran the largest production house in Kansas City. Her initiative got together a knowledgeable board of local industry practitioners and created an informative website which caters to locals, by displaying available jobs, and attempts to attract outside production to the area. Heather Laird, who was president at the time of my visit in 2013, is a local casting director who openly admitted she does not have the qualifications necessary to run a film commission, but she and her colleagues did so to help their own businesses. Given that these are professionals with full-time jobs, their ability to run a film commission are thus very limited: maintaining the website, managing queries from the State film office, and directing prospective producers to each other's services are all they can conceivably manage. In other words, Kansas City, desperately in need of a contemporary film commission that actively fights to sustain its production and commercial infrastructure, for years had a film commission that served the functions endemic to a city with no need to attract productions and thus was consistently faltering. Over the few previous years, not having a full-time film commissioner, Laird theorized, cost them the chance to host *America's Got Talent* as well as a great number of film productions with stories set in Kansas City, yet they all ended up filming somewhere else when the city could not provide the necessary attention required to entice them.[59]

Paradoxically, in some cases the focus of the film commission has moved almost obsessively to fetishizing imagined benefits of incoming productions at the actual expense of the communities and local industries they are meant to economically stimulate. Among significant changes to the industry film production environment, in Hollywood's move from a California home-base to increasing reliance on tax incentives and localized shooting outside of Los Angeles, film commissions have changed in terms of their basic functions. To some extent, the potential future of these practices is hazy. The move to regarding industry filmmaking as a local economic panacea has made consistently enticing films in for economic stimulus through abandoning potential revenue in tax incentives the most visible contemporary strategy. However, perhaps this is not the most fruitful central function of the film office; it is clear from looking at perspectives of cities, producers, and crew that the film commission can serve different purposes for each. Not every city can be a new Hollywood, and local film commissions have a duty to their cities to find their locational and industrial strengths along with their economic needs, which will allow filmmaking to best serve the community. Despite its storied delivery of dreams on screen, the Hollywood film industry is not magic, and their occasional presence in a city does not, on its own, equate to lasting economic redevelopment. True city-changing economic stimulus comes from the consistent presence of productions *and* the ability to build a sustainable local industry— either through the presence of productions or otherwise. While incoming productions can provide a nice, local, temporary economic boost in primarily the service sector, the revenue lost due to tax incentives likely does not cover it. Without the ability to win the intensely competitive tax incentives, game cities increasingly attempt to build industries that they have no real support for. Kansas City's local industry and support services have survived thus far largely through a long history of commercial and industrial filmmaking—thus Hollywood is not the only fruitful or most reliable support system. Film commissions can have many functions in order to be effective and enticement via tax incentive may not be the most advantageous focus for every city. In a world where cities are increasingly in need of a film commission in order to play the media capital game, they are also in need of the right film commission.

Notes

1   For example, Lawrence Webb argues, "As cities adapted to a predominantly
    service-sector economy, they began to position themselves as global financial
    centres and tourist destinations, hubs of leisure and consumerism... Film
    commissions were therefore one of a number of quasi-public bodies at
    municipal level, such as redevelopment agencies and convention and visitors
    bureaus, that sought to promote the city and its revitalized downtown as a
    safe place for tourists and as an attractive location for company headquarters."
    Lawrence Webb, *The Cinema of Urban Crisis: Seventies Film and the Reinvention
    of the City* (Amsterdam: University of Amsterdam Press, 2014), 37. See also
    McLain Clutter, "Imaginary Apparatus: Film Production and Urban Planning
    in New York City,1966–1975," *Grey Room* 35 (Spring 2009), 58–89; Stanley
    Corkin, "Performing the New Economy: New York, Neoliberalism, and Mass
    Communication in Late 1970s Cinema," *Jump Cut* 54 (Fall 2012); Carlo Rotella,
    October Cities: The Redevelopment of Urban Literature (Berkeley: University of
    California Press, 1998).

2   Gary Edgerton, "The Film Bureau Phenomenon in America and Its
    Relationship to Independent Filmmaking," *Journal of Film and Video* 38.1
    (Winter 1986), 41.

3   "Jurisdiction Directory," *Association of Film Commissions International*, http://
    www.afci.org/jurisdiction/us/all (accessed May 18, 2017).

4   Tax incentives are certainly a form of enticement, though as we will see they
    are a form of enticement that has come to dominate all functions of most film
    commissions—many of which now get created in order to "manage" the tax
    incentive.

5   Adapted from the line: "'tis impossible to be sure of any thing but Death and
    Taxes" from Christopher Bullock. *The Cobler of Preston. A farce. As it is acted at
    the New Theatre in Lincolns-Inn-Fields. By Mr. Christopher Bullock London 1716*,
    in *Eighteenth Century Collections Online*, Oakland University, Gale, http://find.
    galegroup.com.huaryu.kl.oakland.edu/ecco/infomark.do?&source=gale&prodId
    =ECCO&userGroupName=lom_oaklandu&tabID=T001&docId=CW112605340
    &type=multipage&contentSet=ECCOArticles&version=1.0&docLevel=FASCIMI
    LE (accessed May 18, 2017), 14.

6   Carlo Rotella more specifically explains: "At the same time, industrial jobs and
    capital of all kinds moved to the suburbs and the Sunbelt (and, in some cases, to
    other countries), departing the old Northeastern and Midwestern manufacturing

cities that were still the leading models of American urbanism. Both public and private investment in the inner city began to shift toward service industries rather than manufacturing, and wealth and resources re-concentrated in the redeveloped downtown cores, where developers produced masses of steel and glass skyscrapers in the matrix of ramifying highway systems built by the state." Rotella, 5.

7   Corkin, 25. See Lawrence Webb's chapter in this volume for further discussion of the Mayor's Office of Motion Pictures and Television in New York City.

8   Clutter, 61–62.

9   *KC Film*, MMGY Global, 2017, https://www.visitkc.com/kansas-city-film-office (accessed January 3, 2017).

10   *Baltimore Film Office*, Mission Media, http://www.baltimorefilm.com/index.cfm (accessed January 3, 2017).

11   Ivy Burridge. "*Local Liaison:* Interview with Wilmington Regional Film Commission Director, Johnny Griffin," *Film Matters* (Fall 2013), 66–68.

12   Clutter, 63.

13   Edgerton, 43–44.

14   Claude Solnik, "Q&A with Debra Markowitz, Director of Nassau's Film Office," *Long Island Business News* 25 (June 2009).

15   Stephen Altman, (production designer), phone interview with the author, August 13, 2013.

16   Burridge.

17   Susan Christopherson and Ned Rightor, "The Creative Economy as 'Big Business': Evaluating State Strategies to Lure Filmmakers," *Journal of Planning Education and Research* 29.3 (2010), 340.

18   "History," Association of Film Commissions International, http://www.afci.org/about-afci/history (accessed May 18, 2017).

19   Michael Sullivan, "Film Office Exits en Masse," *Daily Variety*, January 7, 2011, 5.

20   Tiffany Stevens, "Lights, Camera, Atlanta, Action," *The Atlanta Journal-Constitution*, http://stories.accessatlanta.com/movies-tv-filming-atlanta/?ecmp=AJC_filmfreesite1 (accessed January 3, 2017).

21   Ibid.

22   Paul Swann, "From Workshop to Backlot: The Greater Philadelphia Film Office," in *Cinema and the City: Film and Urban Societies in a Global Context*, ed. Mark Shiel and Tony Fitzmaurice (London: Blackwell, 2001), 92.

23   Christopherson and Rightor, 341.

24 *Louisiana Economic Development*, https://www.opportunitylouisiana.com/ business-incentives (accessed January 3, 2017).

25 Janet Wasko. "Financing and Production: Creating the Hollywood Film Commodity," in *The Contemporary Hollywood Film Industry*, ed. Paul McDonald and Janet Wasko (Malden, MA and Oxford: Blackwell, 2008), 55–56.

26 Gary Bond, (Austin Film Commission Director), personal interview with the author, Austin, TX, April 15, 2014.

27 *United States Census Bureau*, https://www.census.gov/quickfacts/table/ PST045215/4805000 (accessed January 3, 2017).

28 Bond. Population figures are from: "City of Austin Population History 1840 to 2016," US Census Bureau and the City Demographer, Department of Planning, City of Austin (Austin, TX, 2017).

29 Bond.

30 Ibid.

31 Ibid.

32 *Made in Austin Texas*, http://www.austintexas.org/film-commission/ (accessed January 3, 2017).

33 Ibid.

34 David Harvey, *Spaces of Hope* (Berkeley and Los Angeles: University of California Press, 2000), 151.

35 Harvey is specifically referencing the Inner Harbor development. David Harvey, *Spaces of Capital: Towards a Critical Geography* (New York: Routledge, 2001), 142–143.

36 Harvey, *Spaces of Hope*, 133.

37 *United States Census Bureau*, http://www.census.gov/quickfacts/table/ PST045215/2404000 (accessed January 3, 2017).

38 The 1990 census lists the city population at 730K. *Maryland at a Glance Population Growth Rates*, US Census Bureau, http://msa.maryland.gov/msa/ mdmanual/01glance/html/pop.html#rates (accessed January 3, 2017).

39 *Baltimore Film Office*.

40 Altman.

41 Jed Deitz, (Director, Maryland Film Festival), personal interview with the author, Baltimore, MD, August 19, 2013.

42 Michele Krier, "Film Commission," *San Antonio Business Journal*, September 14, 2001, 12.

43 Ibid.

44 Julian Stringer. "The Gathering Place: *Lost* in Oahu," in *Reading Lost*, ed. Roberta Pearson (London and New York: I.B. Tauris, 2009), 77.

45 Michael Curtin, "Regulating the Global Infrastructure of Film Labor Exploitation," in Nobuko Kawashima and John Hill (eds), *International Journal of Cultural Policy*, special issue "Film Policy in a Globalized Cultural Economy," 22.5 (2016), 673–685.

46 See in particular Corkin, Clutter, and Webb.

47 Altman.

48 Christopher Crane, "This Week: Christopher Crane: Director of the Arkansas Film Commission," *Arkansas Business*, November 4, 2013, 38.

49 Matthew Seig, (producer), phone interview with the author, New York City, August 1, 2013.

50 Robert T. Trussell "Dreaming of 18th and Vine," *The Kansas City Star*, 1992, E1.

51 Ibid. E9. See also Frank Driggs and Chuck Haddix, *Kansas City Jazz: From Ragtime to Bebop—A History* (New York: Oxford University Press, 2005).

52 Seig.

53 Patti Broyles Harper, (former Kansas City Film Commissioner), personal interview with the author, Lawrence, KS, October 13, 2013.

54 As stated by Broyles Harper: "We did some things with music with the jazz community and opened that to the public [....] [The Altmans worked] with Bob Butler at the time, who was the writer at *The Star*, who was a huge Altman fan [....] and casting totally involved the community [....] all the extras just weren't extras and that kind of thing involved so much of the community and everybody was excited about it. It was a fun time."

55 "It took Hollywood to discover the 4600 block of St. John Avenue [....] The [*Kansas City*] crew tore down an overhang from the brick storefronts on the south side of the street. Lo and behold, long-forgotten stained glass windows emerged [....] Truth is, if you like cities and neighborhoods and nostalgia, the 4600 block of St. John has always been a gem. And there are dozens of blocks like it. But sometimes it takes an outsider to find the stained glass beneath the faded boards." Barbara Shelly, "Commentary," *Kansas City Star*, July 27, 1995.

56 Through interviews with those involved in the redevelopment process throughout its history I heard figures ranging from $160 million to over $200 million. The most common figure given by those involved in the redevelopment of Union Station is approximately $180 million. A Union Station History pamphlet created by Union Station Kansas City, Inc. in March 2012 estimates $118 million from the bi-state tax, $100 million from private donors and $40 million from private funds which would bring the cost of restoration up to $258 million.

57 Robert W. Butler, "At Long Last, 'KC' Is in the Cannes," *The Kansas City Star*, May 12, 1996, 1.

58 Heather Laird, (casting director), personal interview with the author, Kansas City, MO, October 15, 2013.

59 Kansas City now, once again, has its own film office, reestablished in late 2014 as a part of Visit KC, Kansas City's convention and visitors association. *KC Film*.

4

The Boston Movie Boom

Carlo Rotella

There's a priceless moment in *Gone Baby Gone* (Affleck, 2007) when a little boy on a bike cuts in front of a car on a street in Dorchester and, when the driver tells him to move, yells back, "Go fuck ya mothah." It's pure Boston-style unpleasantness—bad traffic skills, bad manners, nastiness to strangers, refusing to pronounce the r in "mother"—and it's like a shot of a yak herder or a snake charmer in a movie set in Mongolia or India: a moment that's there primarily for the citational pleasure of tasting an exotic locality that moviegoers can be counted on to recognize.

In recent years such Boston-area movie moments have become frequent to the point of becoming conventional. *Gone Baby Gone* is full of them, including some memorable variations on the great Boston theme of resentment between class fractions so close to each other that they may well appear identical to an outsider: "I remember you from high school; I see you're still a little conceited," for instance, or "Make me a fuckin' mahtini, you fat fuckin' retahd." Then there's Ben Affleck's dress-up fantasy as a series of twonic(not soda or pop)-drinkin' regular-guy icons—EMT (emergency medical technician), cop, MBTA bus driver, neighborhood hockey god—in *The Town* (Affleck, 2010); Fenway Park's cameo in *Moneyball* (Miller, 2011), in which it figures as a figurative combination of Harvard and the Death Star; and the victim-finding sequence in *Spotlight* (McCarthy, 2015) in which Standard American English-speaking reporters from the *Boston Globe* go among the no-r-pronouncing Walshes and Kennedys of the city's church-haunted immigrant-ethnic neighborhoods to catalogue the devastation wrought on traditional rank-and-file Catholics by sexually predatory priests.

Over the past decade such moments have become familiar enough to serve as the butt of celebrated parodies and needling on *Saturday Night Live* and *Late Night with Seth Meyers*, in the Golden Globe Awards ceremony, and in other such general-interest forums. It requires an intellectual effort to step back and appreciate how startling it is that Boston, of all places, has become such a prominent feature in the cinematic map of the world imagined by the movie industry and the viewing public. Boston was for much of the twentieth century strictly the sticks, a parochial dump in perennial decline that had peaked not long after the Civil War as both cultural and industrial capital. If the city was known for anything film related, it was the banning of interesting movies, as well as books and plays, by its killjoy guardians of civic virtue. But in the twenty-first century not only do homegrown notables like Ben and Casey Affleck, Matt Damon, and Mark Wahlberg make Boston movies and build their local identity into their star personas, but celebrated mythmakers from elsewhere—Clint Eastwood, Martin Scorsese, Mel Gibson—have felt drawn to get in on the action.

That action is concentrated in the subset of the movies made in and about Boston that make a conscious effort to establish a conventional local feel. This subset would not include, say, *Paul Blart, Mall Cop* (Carr, 2009), which was shot on location in malls in the Boston area but could take place just about anywhere in the nation. It would include *The Friends of Eddie Coyle* (Yates, 1973), *The Brink's Job* (Friedkin, 1978), *Good Will Hunting* (Van Sant, 1997), *Monument Ave.* (Demme, 1998), *Next Stop Wonderland* (Anderson, 1998), *The Boondock Saints* (Duffy, 1999) and its inevitable sequels, *Mystic River* (Eastwood, 2003), *Fever Pitch* (Farrelly and Farrelly, 2005), *The Departed* (Scorsese, 2006), *Gone Baby Gone, Black Irish* (Gann, 2007), *What Doesn't Kill You* (Goodman, 2008), *Shutter Island* (Scorsese, 2010), *Edge of Darkness* (Campbell, 2010), *The Town, The Company Men* (Wells, 2010), *The Fighter* (Russell, 2010), *Ted* (MacFarlane, 2012), *The Heat* (Feig, 2013), *Ted 2* (MacFarlane, 2015), *Black Mass* (Cooper, 2015), *Spotlight, Patriots Day* (Berg, 2016), *Manchester by the Sea* (Lonergan, 2016), TV shows like *Wahlburgers* and the short-lived *Breaking Boston*, and other films and shows currently in production that will have been released by the time this chapter sees publication.[1]

What does it mean that this batty old Norma Desmond of a city finds itself ready for one close-up after another? How did such a traditionally uncool, stodgy, in-turned place come to be regarded as possessing a potent cultural–historical mojo on which outsiders as well as natives place special value?

Properly answering these questions begins with following the money, which leads to considering the effect of policy decisions that cut the cost and increase the convenience of filmmaking in Massachusetts. And the visual distinctiveness as well as the versatility of the Boston area also contributes to its appeal. But these and any other explanations should be framed in a larger postindustrial picture. The Boston movie boom of the late twentieth century and early twenty-first century can be understood as in large part a product of postindustrial transformation, and as a series of commentaries on what has been gained and lost in the course of that ongoing seismic shift. The movies of the Boston boom exploit the artistic and economic possibilities—for cheap production, resonant storytelling, and meaning-making—that opened up as the closing of factories and the rising importance of services, education, biotech, and finance reconfigured the economic, social, and cultural orders of Boston and its region. Exploiting those possibilities constitutes these movies' meta-theme and signifying context. That's what the boy on the bike is implicitly and even explicitly *about*.

*

The short answer to "Why Boston?" is "follow the money." Since 2007, movies and TV productions shot in Massachusetts have received tax credits equal to 25 cents on every dollar of new spending they bring to the state.[2] That has attracted movie studios, which will go wherever they can turn out an acceptable product as cheaply as possible. The tax credit extends and enormously multiplies the investment in film production begun with the founding of the state film office in 1979, which helped attract some productions to Massachusetts by making it somewhat easier and therefore more cost-effective to make movies.[3]

It wasn't easy to shoot in Boston back then, as a famous story about the making of *The Brink's Job* illustrates. When word got around that the production had paid a family in the North End to remove an air conditioner from its window to improve the mid-century verisimilitude of a scene, other families up and down the block borrowed window units or painted up fake ones overnight, demanding their own payoff. That wasn't the only hardship encountered by the production, which was beset by armed robbers who stole footage and tried to ransom it back to the producers, and by Teamsters who were later investigated by federal authorities for trying to extort money from *The Brink's Job* and other productions.[4] Boston's reputation for prickliness, both internecine and directed toward outsiders, has not abated since then. Tina Fey joked at the Golden Globes ceremony in 2013 that Ben Affleck's "first two movies took place in Boston but he moved this one"—*Argo* (Affleck, 2012)— "to Iran because he wanted to film somewhere that was friendlier to outsiders." Her comic partner, Amy Poehler, followed up by putting on a cartoonish Boston accent to tell Affleck, "I'm from Boston too, so you're looking great, good for you," before dropping the false cheer to close on a regionally pitch-perfect note of class resentment: "You're not better than me."

Without the tax credit, the sustained boom in production would never have happened. Movies were indeed made in Boston before the tax-credit program reached mature strength in 2007, but moviemakers have not kept coming to Boston just because the city's so damn fascinating, photogenic, or welcoming. It may come as news to some state legislators whose belief in the region's superiority and attractiveness attains the level of delusion, but the boom will end as soon as it's more efficient to go somewhere else. If it becomes cheaper to simulate Southie in Romania, Hollywood will do that, assuming it remains at least a little interested in telling Boston stories. A public discussion in early 2010 about possibly limiting the tax credit, initiated by critics who plausibly argued that there were more cost-effective ways to attract more reliable jobs, was enough to drive away productions for the rest of that year. Business picked up again only when the studios felt sure that the policy wouldn't change anytime soon.[5] The tax credit has been the essential material fact sustaining the Boston movie boom.

But the short answer won't suffice, not all by itself. Not only did at least some of Hollywood's interest in making Boston movies precede the tax credit, but Louisiana, Connecticut, New Mexico, and other states have also offered film tax credits, some with more generous rates—like Michigan's 42 percent credit.[6] That Massachusetts has been consistently successful in the competition to draw and retain Hollywood's interest means that we need a longer answer. A more complete answer must include the city's reputation for unreconstructed white, especially Irish, ethnicity—a reputation that, outmoded though it may be in some ways, attracts white stars (news flash: they're still mostly white) eager to play tough guys and gals from the Old Neighborhood. Boston is in fact a majority–minority city, but it's still famous for the production of what a character in *The Town* calls Serious White People. We will return to that shortly, after attending to other salient factors.

One principal factor is that Boston and its region offers a balance between a visual distinctiveness that enables the metro area to stand out from other places and a layered versatility that allows it to stand in for other places and times. Contemporary Boston certainly has its own iconic features—Fenway, the State House, Harvard Yard, the triple-decker block, the bridges over the Charles and Mystic rivers—but its age and multilayered architecture also allow it to easily stand in for a wide range of other places and periods: Rust Belt, Sun Belt, and Old World cities; colonial or Civil War-era America; visions of the near future or alternate realities; Paris, Tokyo, New York, Mars. Furthermore, the compactness of New England geography means that no more than an hour's driving can take you from mountains to ocean, from all kinds of cityscapes to all kinds of suburbia, farmland, or woodlands. And then there's the quirkiness of the city's cow-path-based street net, which actually does make the city uniquely photogenic.

"It feels like Universal Studios' backlot here," said James Lin, who was supervising location manager for the action movie *R.I.P.D*, in 2011. "There are so many obtuse angles and perpendicular dead ends and curves, you don't get that endless chasm of the avenue extending away behind the scene that you get in L.A., New York, or Chicago, which are all on a grid." Instead, Boston's dense, nodal layout offers picturesque backdrops. "If you're, like, on Charles Street with the Red Line T structure on the side and three or four lanes of traffic coming together, or Post Office Square, with everything converging on the intersection, you get a kind of forced perspective," Lin told me. "It looks great."

The film tax credit has made it possible for Hollywood to get and stay excited about Boston's Bostonness—a combination of weathered elegance, dinge, compactness, and perspective-rich geography that adds up to an ineffable quality movie people like to call "authentic." What they really mean is that Boston looks like a place where people have lived for a few centuries and that's not exactly like everywhere else and actually has four seasons, but they can still get it to look like whatever they want it to look like. Charlie Harrington, a veteran location scout, told me, "When I was a location manager in L.A., we had to work incredibly hard to find places that looked like the East Coast. But here, the director will get off the plane at Logan and ride into town through one of the old tunnels and he'll say, 'This tunnel is fantastic! I want to shoot in here!'"

Harrington has worked all over the world but he is from Cohasset, 25 miles southeast of Boston, and he moved back to the area once the film tax-credit renaissance got under way in earnest. He represents one more crucial supporting factor in understanding the staying power of Hollywood on the Charles: the local talent pool. The filmmaking boom has encouraged the growth of a corps of experienced, locally based crew and other craft professionals, enough to mount two or three midsize productions at the same time. This matters a great deal to studios, which save money when they don't have to fly in crew from Los Angeles. Producers can now draw on the expertise of location scouts like Harrington, who intimately know the lay of their native land; makeup artists like Trish Seeney, who gave Amy Ryan her Dorchester party-girl up-all-night look for *Gone Baby Gone*; construction coordinators like Kurt Smith, who told me, "They want the local flavor, but it's not reality," which means that he spends a lot of time removing storm windows from New England houses because directors don't like the way they look; casting consultants like Angela Peri, who told me, "They wanted a Cambodian crack whore, so I went to Lowell and found some girls who could play a Cambodian crack whore"; and, of course, dialect coaches, whose work with actors playing neighborhood types attends to nuances of class and ethnic difference that would otherwise matter to only a handful of locals but now circulate around the world.

At this point, there are probably attentive moviegoers in Jakarta or Kiev, with a dozen Boston movies under their belts, who sit there in the dark, thinking, "This guy's supposed to be from Southie? Come on, that's more of an Eastie inflection!" The authenticity police devote much of their attention to the accents, and Boston is a city overendowed with volunteer authenticity police, but they're often really talking about something else when they slag Kevin Costner's unconvincingly dropped r's (What do you expect? He's from California) or applaud the Falmouth-born, Cambridge-bred Casey Affleck's pitch-perfect use of "guy." Rebekah Maggor, a dialect coach who has worked on Boston-area productions, told me, "Dialect is often a stand-in for a general judgment of authenticity in a movie, which has as much to do with the script or the setting or something else."

Exhibit A in support of Maggor's point is *The Friends of Eddie Coyle*, generally regarded as the grandaddy of all Boston movies. Its leads, Robert Mitchum and Peter Boyle, and many of the other actors don't even bother to try imitating a serious Boston accent, but the movie gets everything else so ecstatically right—the gluey cream pie and watery coffee served in diners, the Dutch Masters-toned interiors of bars and apartments, the left-out-in-the-rain look of early-1970s Boston—that some of the most overweening zealots of localism remember the accents as impeccably rendered.

*

Now for the long answer. As time and space are measured by Hollywood, Boston and the other Massachusetts cities are strange, ancient places with distinctive physical forms, curious folkways, and alien languages, like Jerusalem or the cities of the Silk Road. Their quality of familiar exoticism only intensifies as New England's industrial era recedes into history, joining the transcendentalists and Paul Revere's ride. The industrial city's gradual decay into romantic ruin, forming another layer atop the remains of the eighteenth-century commercial city and the seventeenth-century religious colony, is the bigger story about the changing form and function of Rust Belt cities that moves behind the formula plots of the crime stories, comedies, and family dramas shot in Boston and environs. The state's efforts to woo film and TV production by establishing a film office (now part of the travel and tourism office) and a tax credit are classic postindustrial economic development strategies. The decline of manufacturing opens up a gap that can be filled, in part, by other sorts of enterprise as the New England mill city becomes a backwater in the industrial economy and acquires a new role in the postindustrial economy, especially the production of culture. Becoming a backwater enabled and demanded the policy moves that put Massachusetts back in the center of the cultural action as a hotbed of film production, and it added a crucial layer to the local aura of history and character.

Old manufacturing capitals that don't make things anymore have turned to providing services, information, images, history, experiences. You can see the process in action in the repurposing of factory buildings to house museums, arts spaces, loft housing, convention centers, and places to eat, drink, and shop—and make movies. And you can see the process onscreen in scenes like the long shot in *The Fighter* of Charlene knocking on the door of Micky's apartment with dark mill buildings looming in the background. Whatever's going on in the plot, scenes like this one are also about the possibilities that opened up when the factories closed.

So, drawing on the rich body of work supplied by Boston movies, let's sample some scenes from the postindustrial transformation of eastern Massachusetts.

The story begins with *The Friends of Eddie Coyle*, and it begins in New York City, which set the template for urban movie style in the 1970s and provided the era's model of a city reinventing itself as a center of film production. Until the late 1960s, New York was known for documentaries and art films, but not for feature or TV production. That's when John Lindsay, a mayor looking for high-profile ways to attract new business to a city that was losing industrial jobs and restore glamour to a civic reputation damaged by the urban crisis, declared that he would "throw open the city to producers from Hollywood." He made a well-publicized recruiting visit to Los Angeles, founded a City Hall office to help with permits and police assistance, and otherwise made it attractive to shoot in New York. A lot of feature films and TV shows took advantage of the new policies, among them a stylistically distinct subset that did all they could to give themselves a timely New York street feel. *Midnight Cowboy* (Schlesinger, 1969), *The French Connection* (Friedkin, 1971), *Shaft* (Parks, 1971), *Super Fly* (Parks, 1972), and other New York movies that appeared at the end of the 1960s and the beginning of the 1970s pioneered an influential new stylistic synthesis, enlivening traditional Hollywood storytelling with extensive location shooting, documentary-style mobile cameras, traffic wipes, informal lighting and sound, informal and improvised line readings, and other elements borrowed from the French New Wave, Italian neorealism, and the documentaries and art films that had previously dominated the city's filmmaking scene. Especially when applied to the formula conventions of crime stories, this became the canonical style for telling stories of the postindustrial inner city, the emergence of which had helped to bring on the national urban crisis of the 1960s.[7]

Hollywood had avoided the inner city for much of that decade, but it returned to the subject with a vengeance once it had restocked its stylistic armament and its repertoire of landscape features, character types, and storytelling habits. The industry now had the equipment it needed to explore the ghetto, barrio, white-ethnic enclave, embattled business district, and other features of the postindustrial metropolis of inner city and suburbs that was emerging through and around the receding industrial city of downtown and neighborhoods. If the resulting stories felt new, with wah-wah-pedaled guitar wailing in the background as characters said things like "Everything's everything, baby," it's also true that D. W. Griffith would have had no trouble recognizing the chases and racial melodrama of *The French Connection* or *Super Fly*.

The insurgent New York-flavored style heavily influenced the director Peter Yates when he set out to adapt George V. Higgins's Boston novel *The Friends of Eddie Coyle* for the big screen. The film tracks a crew of bank robbers and their associates, exemplary denizens of the dumpy old Boston who, like dinosaurs after a comet strikes the earth, can feel the world changing around them. Some respond by changing their ways, principally by giving up on old-school gangster omerta and learning to snitch to the feds; others, like the small-time knockaround guy Eddie "Fingers" Coyle, fail to adjust or come to it too late. Marrying style to theme, the movie stages a series of cold, distanced encounters between desperate characters who demonstrate and at times manage to articulate a distress and alienation that resonates with the processes of change visible in the city in which they move.[8]

Yates relies on the relationship between his camera and the landscape of Boston to do much of the work of communicating his characters' anomie, disorientation, and sense of impending doom. J.D. Connor has observed that Yates sets their interactions as often as he can against notable examples of recent modernist architecture, especially the New Brutalism just beginning to emerge as the house style of monumental redevelopment in Boston at the time.[9] The hit man Dillon meets with Foley, the federal agent who pays him to snitch, on City Hall Plaza against the backdrop of City Hall, the pièce de resistance of Government Center, a massive redevelopment project erected on the semi-blank slate created by the eradication of the Scollay Square neighborhood. Other characters meet at the parking garage at Government Center, with Walter Gropius's JFK Federal Building in the background, and on Day Boulevard with the Prudential building rising up in the distance behind them. A gun dealer does business with hippie revolutionaries on a riverside park bench in Cambridge with views of the Hancock building across the Charles and Alvar Aalto's Baker House dormitory at MIT across Memorial Drive. Dillon meets with a mobster at the new North Quincy Station on the T's Red Line, a strange angular landscape that appears to leave Dillon bemused.

The characters are like astronauts floating in an alien and potentially lethal void, but the architectural cues identify it as not a void so much as an emergent order. Postindustrial Boston was in that moment beginning to visibly succeed industrial Boston, which had been aging out for half a century or more. That older Boston's signature features—clusters of dense low-rise workers' housing, redbrick factory buildings, rail lines, waterside industrial facilities, neighborhood dives and hangouts—had been redefined as blight in the age of urban renewal, and some of that older landscape had been cleared to make way for poured-concrete and steel-and-glass structures suited to information-handling service work. We can see remnants of the older city in the glimpses we catch of Eddie Coyle's natural habitat: the cramped kitchen where he and his wife, who still has a strong Irish accent, use appliances that haven't been updated in decades; and the dark, woody bars and diners where Eddie hangs out with his cronies, places that reek of history—which, framed by the advance of the New Brutalist landscape, feels like obsolescence.

Jump ahead a generation or so to *Good Will Hunting*, skipping over *The Brink's Job*, *The Verdict* (Lumet, 1982), and a handful of other Boston movies made in the interim. By the late 1990s the state's film office had been up and running for decades, but the tax credit was still in the future. *Good Will Hunting* serves as the next major landmark because in it the phase of Boston just emerging in *The Friends of Eddie Coyle* has matured to the point that it's competing for primacy with the old Boston, which has proportionally receded. Will Hunting, a hard-handed blue-collar genius from Southie, is a fantasy figure designed to bridge the two Bostons: he's good with his hands, a streetfighter who does demolition work that looks like the brick-by-brick disassembly of the old Boston; and he's also brilliant enough to succeed across the river in Cambridge, where he wows the mathematicians of MIT and, in the movie's most famous scene, humiliates an impossibly snooty and aggressive Harvard graduate student in a bar with a recitatif on the subject of the colonial American history that builds to a soaring cadenza of regular-guy rank-pulling:

"You dropped a hundred and fifty grand on a fuckin' education you could have got for a dallah fifty in late chahges at the public library."

By the late 1990s, Boston's reputation had largely turned around, with the city increasingly regarded as a center of research, education, high tech, and high-end services that made it a poster child for postindustrial comeback rather than a sad exemplar of deindustrialization. The tag line "The New Boston" had been adopted by the city's progrowth coalition of government and business interests and had become semi-canonical. In the movie the New Boston has progressed to the point of incipient dominance and the old neighborhoods of the city's receding industrial order have begun to acquire an idealized gloss of esoteric potency, a figurative Old Country situated in the heart of the American city. Unlike the unevolved Eddie Coyle, Will Hunting, who's so wicked smaht that he can crush you with his wits but can also kick your ass, has adapted to travel back and forth between the Old Neighborhood and the New Boston. As such, he serves as a one-man template for the glut of Boston movies to come, which will be populated by two main kinds of (largely male) characters: a majority of Irish and other white-ethnic tough guys from remnants of the immigrant-ethnic industrial neighborhood order in Southie, Dorchester, Charlestown, and outlying cognates like Lowell; and a minority of fast-talking overeducated types from elsewhere, often associated with Harvard or MIT.

By the time we get to *The Departed*, just on the cusp of the implementation of the full 25 percent tax credit, habits for representing Old Neighborhood guys (Will Hunting's regular-guy side, as opposed to his genius side) have been worked out in greater detail in *Monument Ave., The Boondock Saints,* and *Mystic River,* among others. In these and other movies the Old Neighborhood, a physical and cultural holdover of the urban orders fashioned by white-ethnic immigrants to the industrial city, has become a mythic space on a par with the frontier in the Western: a territory understood to produce character types whose violent potency fancifully expresses their connection to history. As the prominent Boston writer Dennis Lehane (several of whose novels have been adapted into movies) and others have pointed out, this idealization of Boston's avatars of the Old Neighborhood has happened as the places in the city that once exemplified the industrial neighborhood order have lost much of the immigrant-ethnic and blue-collar character that the movies fetishize.[10] Young professionals have descended on Southie and Charlestown, in particular, and you have to look harder and harder in such places to find old-school tribal street culture rooted in manual labor and a set of high-industrial-era institutions that included the parish church, saloon, union hall, immigrant social club, and neighborhood-level organizational strata of the ethnic political machine. This arrangement, rooted in the nineteenth century, once tended to foster the sort of clannish criminality traditionally practiced by do-or-die newcomers to America from Ireland and Italy, but that was long ago.

Two early scenes exemplify how *The Departed* wallows in the notion that this kind of tribalism persists in Boston. The movie's opening sequence, set to the Rolling Stones' "Gimme Shelter," offers images of Boston's school desegregation crisis of the 1970s as a nonfiction frame around the movie's fictional crime-story plot. In a voice-over, Frank Costello, a character played by Jack Nicholson and based on the Boston archcriminal James "Whitey" Bulger, recasts the story of Boston's notorious struggles over school busing as a tale of white-ethnic potency. The busing crisis, which in the past helped give Boston a reputation as America's most racist city (though there have been many claimants to that distinction), is now ripe for rereading. First, though, Costello offers a thumbnail history lesson. Italian "headbreakers, true guineas," showed their strength when they "took over their piece of the city," and the Irish rose up from abjection to seize not just their own neighborhoods but the presidency as well. In his view, "the niggers" haven't learned the fundamental Old Neighborhood truth that you take what you want because nobody's going to give you your fair share, no matter how eloquently or insistently you ask for it. Costello's use of the n-word, like the vivid memories evoked by the movie of white Bostonians chanting and throwing rocks at school buses full of black children, has been recast here as a sign not of atavistic racism but of atavistic potency derived from the Old Neighborhood's ethnic and class cohesion. Costello's not afraid to use the word because he's strong enough not to worry whether anyone might take violent offense, and of course he doesn't care if black people or overeducated types in Cambridge think he's a racist. What matters most in the world of the movie is the intensity of one's belonging to the Old Neighborhood, and using the word marks him as a supremely unreconstructed old-school exemplar of that place.

The other scene is a similarly introductory montage, set to the Dropkick Murphys' anthem "Shipping Up to Boston," in which we see a policeman named Billy Costigan (Leonardo DiCaprio) serve time in jail to establish his cover as a criminal so that he can infiltrate Costello's gang. The director, Martin Scorsese, apparently went out of his way to recruit the runtiest white guys he could find to play the inmates in the scene, both to help the lissome DiCaprio fit in and also to emphasize the notion that they're terrifying simply because they're white guys from Boston, not because they're intimidatingly enormous. The black inmates appear to be tiptoeing around them, a dynamic exemplified by the image of Costigan doing dips in his cell as a black inmate prays fervently in the next one. Later, on his way out of lockup, Costigan runs into a guy who asks if he's related to Sean Costigan from L Street, in Southie—Billy's cousin, of course. "Connected, not too bright," says the other guy; "I mean, no offense." Hey, none taken. You can feel the delight of Scorsese, whose body of work displays a tendency toward hero-worship of white-ethnic gangsters (lightly covered by the occasional headfake toward recognizing their monstrousness), at having discovered a fresh motherlode of Serious White People. Ripe for imbuing with traits associated with the increasingly myth-encrusted industrial neighborhood order, his Boston Irish tough guys have arrived in his oeuvre just in time to augment the nearly tapped-out supply of Italian American hardcases from New York.

The Departed is a remake of a Hong Kong movie, *Infernal Affairs* (Lau and Mak, 2002). *Fever Pitch*, a romantic comedy about diehard Red Sox fans, is an adaptation of Nick Hornby's novel about diehard Arsenal Football Club fans. In both cases, Hollywood's desire to retell a foreign story in a resonant American location led to Boston, a city that was coming more and more to stand for the general principle of authentic locality.

When the film tax credit went into full effect in 2007, the ground had already been prepared for the glut of movies and TV shows that followed to work out the permutations of the meaning of locality, Boston-style. Not all of those shades of meaning can be labeled as conscious meditations on postindustrial transformation, of course, but that historical process and its consequences suffuses a growing body of work.

Sometimes the relationship is explicit, visible on the surface of the work. Take, for example, *The Company Men*, a male weepie about the sorrows wrought upon corporate executives by deindustrialization. In one crucial scene, two former colleagues take a walk in a silent, rusting, broken-windowed shipyard after the funeral of a third former colleague, Phil, who worked his way up into the executive suite from the shopfloor and committed suicide when he was fired in a round of corporate downsizing. Gene (Tommy Lee Jones) segues from talking about Phil's glory days as a welder to rhapsodizing about the kind of masculinity enabled by industrial work. "We used to make something here, before we got lost in the paperwork," Gene says, while the younger Bobby (the ubiquitous Ben Affleck) listens respectfully.

> Two thousand men, three shifts a day, six thousand men. An honest wage, in that room. Fed their kids, bought homes, made enough to send their kids to college, buy a second car. Building something they could see—not just figures on a balance sheet but a *ship* they can see, smell, touch. Those men knew their worth, knew who they were.

The movie's male characters have lost touch with their worth, with who they are, and it becomes clearer as the story proceeds that the real crisis wasn't getting fired, it was the disorientation of moving from blue-collar to white-collar work. Bobby is tellingly saved from despair by Jack, his brother-in-law (Kevin Costner, whose working-class Boston accent wobbles to the point that he sometimes sounds like Jim Garrison in *JFK* [Stone, 1991]), a contractor who hires him to help rebuild a house. The honest manual labor reconnects Bobby to his working-class roots, and by the end of the movie, with the shipping company that stands for the American manufacturing sector miraculously revived, Bobby has regained his confidence and even begun to recover his own long-suppressed Boston accent.

It requires no interpretive stretch to see *The Company Men* as a meditation on what has been gained and lost in the transformation of work and everything connected to it—which is just about everything—in the former manufacturing capitals of the Rust Belt. The script, the camera, and the characters all oblige us to perform such a reading. In many other cases, though, that meditation proceeds in the background, or sub rosa, and we are invited rather than ordered to read the film in a postindustrial frame. The earlier-mentioned scene from *The Fighter* in which Charlene confronts Micky at his apartment with the brooding textile mill buildings of Lowell in the background would be a good example. The opportunities for storytelling opened up by the closing of those factories form part of that scene's implicit subject matter, even if the usual romantic complications occupy the foreground, and the Oscars handed out to actors in the movie—Christian Bale and Melissa de Leo—can be seen as rewards for the acrobatic feat of inhabiting the consciousness of regular guys and gals from places like Lowell that have been violently reshaped by deindustrialization. Dialect coaches in the Boston area who have long made their living by helping working-class people shed their accents so that they can compete for service jobs can now also profit from reversing the process, securing lucrative assignments from film productions to teach millionaires from elsewhere to sound like local types who will never belong anywhere other than on the shopfloors of defunct factories and in the neighborhoods gutted and cast adrift by the closing of those factories.

As the thematics of the Boston movie become more familiar and redundant, greater and greater compression becomes possible. Asked in *The Town* by Doug (yes, Ben Affleck, again) about the rumor that she recently got into a fight on the street, Krista (Blake Lively) says: "Fuckin' Somalian started talking shit while I was with my daughter. All these here yuppies out here, they think there's no more serious white people in Charlestown. So they can fuckin' talk shit? No." That brief speech renders the Old Neighborhood in schematic perspective: squeezed from above by educated professionals employed in Boston's booming service sector and from below by the waves of post-1965 immigrants who have helped make Boston a majority–minority city. With no more honest skilled labor to support the industrial white working class's former way of life, no more reinforcements coming over from the Old Country, and the institutional and cultural orders of the Old Neighborhood fraying rapidly, what's left, in the logic of the Boston crime movie, besides oxycontin and bank robbery?

The Town imagines a figurative solution to the Old Neighborhood's ongoing crisis of obsolescence by proposing an alliance with "the yuppies," as Doug moves on from Krista, his best friend's sister, to Claire, a clerk who works in one of the banks he has robbed (in a heist scene that pays homage to *The Friends of Eddie Coyle*). Doug's romance with Claire worries his Old Neighborhood associates not only because she's a witness to one of his crimes, but also because she represents the class of educated outsiders moving into Charlestown and encroaching on unreconstructable Old Neighborhood types like Krista and her brother James (Jeremy Renner), Doug's best friend and fellow bank robber. The semi-reconstructed Doug's romance with Claire, and especially the savage beating for bothering Claire that he and James give to an ethnically ambiguous guy who lives in the projects, extends the fantasy project of *Good Will Hunting*: reconciling the old and new Bostons in such a way that the old Boston retains the essence of its potent vitality.

But the principal attraction of the Old Neighborhood remains its insularity and exoticism, its promise of access to a throwback tribalism that is simultaneously disappearing and gloriously persistent. *The Town* offers its own version of *Gone Baby Gone*'s little boy on a bike in a scene in which the FBI agent Adam Frawley, played by Jon Hamm, returns to his car after an unsuccessful stakeout in Charlestown to find that somebody has left a note on the back windshield of his car telling him to go fuck himself. It's from Doug the bank robber, who has used his working-class local knowledge to slip through a massive dragnet, first leaping between rooftops and then borrowing his father's old bus-driver's uniform to escape at the wheel of a city bus (which Doug, being a regular guy, of course knows how to drive). But the note could just as easily be from anyone in the neighborhood: after all, Adam's not from around here. "We are a *national* organization," Adam reminds Claire, and that—plus his scrupulous pronunciation of the r's in "are" and "organization"—is exactly what makes him the logical recipient of such a note.

*

Postindustrial Boston has been on a largely sustained economic upswing since emerging in the 1980s from of its century-long industrial decline, and in that sense is unlike New York in the 1970s, which was descending into a major economic crisis that would lead to the brink of bankruptcy, but the two cities' situations are analogous in that both match a reputation for high-cultural sophistication and wealth with a gallery of stock street and neighborhood characters infused with local color. The Boston boom has been narrower in its exploitation of its resources, however, not only less stylistically innovative but also less inclusive. The New York movies of the late 1960s and 1970s offered a range of representative characters. Think of Jill Clayburgh in *An Unmarried Woman* (Mazursky, 1978) or Diane Keaton in *Annie Hall* (Allen, 1977), for instance, and, even if we just consider standard male action heroes of the kind who overpopulate Boston movies, the New York movies of the period feature white-ethnic regular guys like the Corleones and *The French Connection*'s Popeye Doyle, black Caesars like Shaft and *Super Fly*'s Priest, and migrants from the western played by Eastwood and Charles Bronson. *Good Will Hunting* remains the template for Boston movies because its hero manages to embody both the Irish working-class hero from the Old Neighborhood and the fast-talking savant affiliated with Harvard or MIT, almost exclusively the only two types who matter (the former a great deal more than the latter) in Boston movies so far.

The Massachusetts movie boom may not be as significant as New York's, but it's happening in an era when the continuing expansion of Hollywood's international reach ensures greater circulation. One side effect has been to create an odd wrinkle in the globalization of popular culture. The subset of Boston-area movies that try to achieve an authentic-feeling local quality forms an exception to the general rule that Hollywood has tended to remove specialized regional American content from its movies as it has sold more and more to a world audience. As Boston has come to stand for the principle of authentic locality in American movies, as filmmakers fall into the habit of turning to Boston to exercise an interest in the local as a theme, the fetish for Bostonness has returned regional content to American movies with a vengeance. That's how mythmakers from elsewhere like Scorsese and Mel Gibson have found themselves flocking to Boston to join homegrown stars like the Afflecks and Wahlbergs, and that's how those moviegoers in Jakarta or Kiev come to find themselves exclaiming, "You can't say that in a bar on Dot Ave! Somebody's gonna get tuned up!" It may be that artists and audiences in a self-consciously globalizing age are hungry for any kind of local feel at all— even, weirdly, Boston's.

That local feel has become canonical to the point that it's easily gestured at and made fun of. *Saturday Night Live*'s fake Dunkin Donuts ad starring Casey Affleck and Seth Meyers's trailer for an invented blockbuster entitled *Boston Accent* are the best-known parodies. Meyers's spoof was so spot-on that the trailer for the deadly serious *Patriots Day*, released many months later, appeared to quote one of his joke trailer's intentionally hackneyed images, a close-up shot of Boston police patch. *The Heat*, a comic take on the cop buddy picture, exploits audience assumptions learned from other

Boston movies for many of its yuks. For instance, there's a throwaway scene in which a woman drives by, cranking the band Boston's "More Than a Feeling," and gives the finger to Mullins (Melissa McCarthy), the crude but effective Boston cop. "Who was that?" asks Ashburn (Sandra Bullock), the proper but deceptively tough FBI agent. "My mom," says Mullins. It's a little-boy-on-a-bike scene, this time played for laughs. Then there's the conversation in which McCarthy's relatives try to grill Bullock about whether she's a narc but she can't understand them through their accents. And the very fact of a female buddy picture pokes implicit fun at the unremitting maleness of the Boston movies as a whole.

The formation that produces canonical Boston movies—a set of stylistic and thematic habits undergirded by a material foundation of state economic policy, local governmental cooperation, studio money, and allied local enterprises that feed like oxpeckers off the studios' spending—has become dominant enough to feel oppressive. *Patriots Day*, in particular, inspired even parochially jingoistic Bostonian observers to wonder whether turning the civic trauma of the marathon bombings into the occasion for just another regular-guy wish-fulfillment vehicle for Mark Wahlberg was a good idea after all.[11] One small-time local filmmaker, Garth Donovan, whose productions cost so little that they don't even qualify for the tax credit, has set out expressly to make Boston-area movies that don't conform to the canonical profile. His best-known film, *Phillip the Fossil* (Donovan, 2011), about a thirtyish landscaper in suburban Needham who hangs out with high school kids, features working-class characters who aren't from the myth-encrusted Old Neighborhood. "I'm from Needham, and I wanted to make a movie about people like the ones I grew up with, but I didn't want to make a 'Boston film,'" Donovan told me in 2011.

> Look, I thought *The Fighter*, for instance, was very well done, but that depiction of Boston, I'm tired of it. It's played out. I'm against having to have that accent and tell that same story as 'This is what Boston is.' Some of the Boston films, it's so contrived and forced. There are a lot of other kinds of experiences around here.

One way he tried to give his Boston-area movie an authentic working-class feel, in other words, was to avoid the Boston accent generally regarded as the most reliable marker of the authenticity of a Boston film because it indicates direct connection to the immigrant-ethnic past and the industrial neighborhood order.

Even within the canonical heart of the formation, there are signs of curdling. In very different ways, both *Black Mass*, a by-the-numbers gangster movie, and *Spotlight*, an Oscar-winning prestige production on the model of *All the President's Men*, both released in 2015, locate a systemic and long-festering rottenness at the core of the same Old Neighborhood that has been so passionately idealized by Boston movies. In *Black Mass*, a movie made inevitable by the capture of Whitey Bulger after his many years on the FBI's most wanted list, the neighborhood gangster is more horror-movie villain than hero. Physically repellent (in the Hollywood universe of artificially perfect dentition, Johnny Depp's scrupulously recreated bad teeth serve as shorthand for horribleness) and morally indefensible (he kills helpless, begging victims with the remorseless blandness of Jason in the *Friday the 13th* franchise), Whitey's also a fink and a rat, protected by a childhood buddy from Southie who has become an FBI agent. There's almost nothing left in this movie of the Old Neighborhood aura of old-school masculinity and loyalty; the old ways are just grotesque and cruel. In *Spotlight*, the *Globe's* investigation of sexually predatory priests protected by the archdiocese reveals another racket that has been preying on the good people of the Old Neighborhood for generations, so deeply woven into the fabric of neighborhood institutions that rooting it out means pulling up the whole structure and exposing its hateful true nature to the light. This thematic strain positing some kind of original sin tainting the Old Neighborhood can be detected in earlier Boston movies—in *Mystic River*, when one of the child abductors flashes a Jesuit ring, and in *The Friends of Eddie Coyle*, in which the neighborhood gangsters start informing for the feds to stay afloat in a city that has begun to change around them—but in the two recent films it has moved to center stage and become the principal theme.

The curdling is by no means universal. *Patriots Day*, for example, released in 2016, demonstrates that the Boston movie is still capable of unironic indulgence in its traditional regular-guy pieties. But the inability to sustain the idealized fantasy of the Old Neighborhood seems to be advancing. One way to read its progression, especially if you include *The Heat* and other parodies of

Boston movies, is to recognize that, while the tax credit and Boston's cultural function of standing for locality in American movies may continue to attract production to the city, it's getting harder and harder to tell Old Neighborhood stories with a straight face as industrial Boston and its signature ways of life slip ever farther into postindustrial Boston's past. A self-consciously hard-bitten realism has been the main house style of the Boston movie, but it's getting more difficult to suspend disbelief in that particular fashion, and it's therefore getting easier to see the local as contrived rather than authentic. At this point, as Boston stories about Irish tough guys exemplifying the industrial neighborhood order rapidly approach the status of pure fantasy, such stories increasingly belong to the realm of historical romance. Like smoothbore cannons and crinoline skirts, "Go fuck ya mothah" marks a lost world.

Notes

1   This chapter draws upon, updates, and expands an argument made in partial, preliminary form in three previously published articles: "The Cult of Micky Ward in Massachusetts," in *Rooting for the Home Team: Sport, Community, and Identity*, ed. Daniel Nathan (Urbana: University of Illinois Press, Sport and Society series, 2013), 205–217; "Hollywood on the Charles," *Boston* (January 2012), 39–43; "A Boston Film without the Stereotypes," *Boston Globe*, April 27, 2011, http://archive.boston.com/bostonglobe/editorial_opinion/oped/articles/2011/04/27/a_boston_film_without_the_stereotypes/. Quotations not otherwise cited in this chapter were collected by the author in personal interviews conducted in the course of reporting those three articles.

2   See Massachusetts Film Office, "Production Tax Incentives," http://www.mafilm.org/production-tax-incentives/ and Commonwealth of Massachusetts Department of Revenue, "Report on the Impact of Massachusetts Film Tax Incentives through Calendar Year 2014," http://www.mass.gov/dor/docs/dor/news/reportcalendaryear2014.pdf.

3   Candace Jones and Pacey Foster, "Film Offices as Brokers: Cultivating and Connecting Local Talent to Hollywood," in *Brokerage and Production in the American and French Entertainment Industries: Invisible Hands in Cultural Markets*, ed. Violaine Roussel and Denise Bielby (Lanham, MD: Lexington Books, 2015), 171–188.

4   Paul Sherman, *Big Screen Boston: From Mystery Street to The Departed and Beyond* (Malden, MA: Black Bars Publishing, 2008), i–ii.

5   To track the 2010 dip and 2011 recovery in film production in Massachusetts, compare the key findings of the Commonwealth of Massachusetts Department of Revenue's 2010 "Report on the Impact of Massachusetts Film Tax Incentives," http://www.mass.gov/dor/docs/dor/news/reportcalendaryear2010.pdf to the key findings of its 2011 "Report on the Impact of Massachusetts Film Tax Incentives," http://www.mass.gov/dor/docs/dor/news/reportcalendaryear2011.pdf. The terms of the public debate in 2010 about capping the film tax credit were outlined in a *Boston Globe* editorial: "Film Tax Credit Boosts State, Shouldn't Be Subject to Cap," February 14, 2010, http://archive.boston.com/bostonglobe/editorial_opinion/editorials/articles/2010/02/14/film_tax_credit_boosts_state_shouldnt_be_subject_to_cap/.

6   On various states' film tax incentives, see Peter Caranicas and Rachel Abrams, "Runaway Production: The United States of Tax Incentives," *Variety*, August 27, 2013, http://variety.com/2013/biz/news/runaway-production-the-united-states-of-tax-incentives-1200589317/ and Bryn Elise Sandberg, "Film and TV Tax Incentives: A State-by-State Guide," *Hollywood Reporter*, May 6, 2016, http://www.hollywoodreporter.com/news/film-tv-tax-incentives-a-885699.

7   I have told the story of New York's role in the revision of Hollywood's depiction of the inner city in *Good with Their Hands: Boxers, Bluesmen, and Other Characters from the Rust Belt* (Berkeley: University of California Press, 2002), 105–166; also, See Lawrence Webb's chapter in this volume for further discussion of the Mayor's Office of Motion Pictures and Television in New York City. See Nathan Koob's chapter in this volume for further discussion of city film offices.

8   See Stanley Corkin's chapter in this volume for further discussion of *The Friends of Eddie Coyle*.

9   J.D. Connor, "The Modern Sounds of Modern Massachusetts: *The Friends of Eddie Coyle* and the Voice of Southie," a paper that was part of a session cleverly entitled "The Global Southie: Boston and the Cinema of Class," presented at the Society for Cinema and Media Studies meeting, March 24, 2012. I served as chair and commentator for the session. For more on the New Brutalism and the New Boston, see *Heroic: Concrete Architecture and the New Boston*, ed. Mark Pasnik, Michael Kubo, and Chris Grimsley (New York: Monacelli Press, 2015).

10   Dennis Lehane, "Introduction: Tribalism and Knuckleheads," in *Boston Noir*, ed. Dennis Lehane (New York: Akashic Books, 2009), 12–13.

11 Kevin Cullen, a metro columnist in the Globe who cultivates a regular-guy
    Bostonian persona, devoted multiple columns to thinking about the debate
    over the appropriateness and timing of *Patriots Day*. See, especially, "'Patriots
    Day' Is Not Just a Movie. It's Personal," *Boston Globe*, December 23, 2016,
    https://www.bostonglobe.com/metro/2016/12/23/not-just-movie-personal/
    BqVgBLmPBYbX06IB1KBSmM/story.html and "Marathon Bombings Hero Will
    Look away This Time," *Boston Globe*, March 14, 2016, https://www.bostonglobe.
    com/metro/massachusetts/2016/03/14/the-real-world-and-hollywood/
    e7X2sO6QTkyGYGdfDC5vcM/story.html.

Part Two

Postindustrial Narratives and Aesthetics

5

The New Boston and the Grip of Tradition:
The Friends of Eddie Coyle (1973), *The Brink's Job* (1978), and *The Verdict* (1982)

Stanley Corkin

In 1960 the architectural historian Kevin Lynch, in his landmark study *The Image of the City*, asked about the legibility of a city to its citizens. Lynch, using the city of Boston as an example, felt that a city's "success" depended upon its being apprehended by its populace as a kind of navigable and approachable entity, arguing "structuring and identifying the environment is a vital ability among all mobile animals."[1] Lynch's idea of the "image" of the city was user-based and assumed that an urban entity was largely self-contained and substantially for the use and benefit of its residents. More than half a century after the writing of this important volume, things have changed decidedly. To some degree, in the early twenty-first century, what constitutes success for a city has significantly shifted and what defines its ability to be apprehended has also been altered notably in a world where a digital footprint may bridge the divide between the two-dimensional city and three; but increasingly, the digital city comes to stand for the material one as a matter of its wide dissemination and consumption.

As Sharon Zukin noted in her 2010 study *Naked City*, cities are no longer place-bound in their presentation and audience. They are both entities with a particular material presence *and* digital projections with distinct but varied resonances. In effect, cities are to greater and lesser degrees compendia of meanings that attach to a particular name. "To say that the city is no longer authentic," Zukin explains, "reflects our inability to grasp the shifting meanings of space and time. If this is not the end of history, at least it is the end of place-bound cultures and local identities."[2] Her vision of the discursive aspect of cities, and the powers of definition and articulation that adhere to those representations and association, takes us fully into the postmodern world. Zukin's formulation sets up an interesting dialectic. Cities are far less place-bound by their physical geography than they were in the early 1960s and culture in the twenty-first century is increasingly fluid. As a result, the degree to which a sense of place and culture forms anchors for individuals and their sense of self, or even articulates a relative sense of life's possibilities, may be far more a matter of particularity—class, race, ethnicity, gender—than simply of broadly locational origins. And so much of a sense of a city for a mass population is a matter of what consumers of that urban locale glean from our media-saturated environment. The ways in which representations of a place are involved in conceptions and experiences of a particular locale are significant if not determining.

But what about the moment of transition between these two visions, between local articulation and comprehension and the moment of digital definition and saturation: in effect a pre-saturation moment, but a moment where more embedded ideas of place and space are eroding? What then comes to the fore as culturally and spatially definitional? How is our imagining of discrete and named urban space connected to its preexisting materiality? How do these idealist projections create a subsequent materiality? Is the represented city in a group of mass-cultural texts intelligible as a matter of the relationships between its actuality and virtual mapping? Do we need to see a circuit of locations and relatively familiar locales for it to produce the realist effect and evoke the place that is suggested by a given narrative and which will imbue that narrative with a constellation of meanings and associations? What is the city that conceptually emerges from this arrangement of limited details? It is a place that is broadly construed but which reduces a locale to its perceived and recognizable cultural essence. And those cultural markers become "the city," and remain as touchstones, even as the culture and hardscapes of a place morph into something that is distinctly different.

In this chapter I look at the representations of the city of Boston in a group of films shot somewhat on location—certainly they *claim* an authenticity of place—between the moment that begins to define the postindustrial terms of that city, the early 1970s, and the time when the contours of the emergent social and economic entity of a far more cosmopolitan and prosperous place become clearly visible in the early to mid-1980s. That entity would ultimately be decidedly multi-cultural, international in its flows of capital and commerce, and dynamic in its dramatic reshaping of its physical contours, due to pressures put on its stock of available housing and commercial spaces.[3] These films—*The Friends of Eddie Coyle* (Peter Yates, 1973), *The Brink's Job* (William Friedkin, 1978), and *The Verdict* (Sidney Lumet, 1982)—intrigue me for their representation of a city on the cusp between relative dissolution—in the 1950s and 1960s—and substantial demographic change and economic success in the 1990s and 2000s. In effect, we are viewing an urban entity poised between the terms of its more contemporary visibility and its prior obscurity, in the sense that cities which succeed in the digital age are more importantly about their image and brand, which are synergistically combined with more palpable factors. This judgment suggests we've come to a vision of the urban that is all but in direct contradiction of Lynch's definition of "success." Indeed, we are watching the process of "branding" replace that of "mapping."

All three of these films emphasize elements that become iconic in the far more visible city of the 2000s, even though those elements are in eclipse by that time. These earlier films show us a city dominated by white-ethnic groups, a fact that would materially shift in the next three decades—*Eddie Coyle* and *The Verdict* emphasize the prominence of Irish Americans and *The Brink's Job* more resolutely emphasizes Italian—and all show a class-riven city. Further, these earlier films employ place significantly, but not as aggressively or affirmatively as later Boston-based productions, and, in keeping with that relative use of specific geography, all three offer locations that are more about working-class urban texture than iconic landmarks. In effect, they brand the city by socioeconomic type rather than affirm place through iconic landmarks.

Such a loose employment of locale makes sense in an era of the city's emergence. Boston was neither a usual mass culture touchstone nor a mass of iconic views in the 1970s and 1980s. This is distinct from the later 1990s and 2000s, when the city emerged as a capital-rich postindustrial locale. This burgeoning was a matter of a number of material factors, including its strategic and site-specific arrangement of capital and cutting-edge technology, a result of the infrastructure that arranged around a considerable body of elite educational institutions—Harvard, MIT, Boston University, Boston College, Tufts, and even more specialized entities like the University of Massachusetts campuses (particularly the Lowell campus). This embedded market advantage is mirrored by that of a city like San Francisco, which has its own knowledge and infrastructural capital in the form of educational institutions. But as an enhancer of this success and as an adjunct to this preferred market position in the "knowledge economy," those mass-cultural objects that employ Boston as a brand are also—implicitly or explicitly—able to attach to that tech-heavy success a residual sense of the historical city, which includes its legacy of prosperity from the late eighteenth to the mid-nineteenth centuries, when merchants based in Boston participated in and further developed trade with China and thus created a place-specific wealth. This capital became the basis for elite Protestant families, such as the Forbes, Cushing, and Perkins families, as well as the Bryants, Cabots, Higginsons, Paines, and Peabodys, whose investments and philanthropy would significantly define the city for generations. These fortunes also became involved in the creation of a banking infrastructure that was definitional for the economic life of the region and which was instrumental in funding the next regional boom, in the late twentieth century. These banks with anchors in the China trade include the Bank of Boston, the State Street Bank, and the Shawmut Bank, all of which, albeit in new organizational forms, are still traceable to present financial structures.[4] The Perkins family founded the Bank of Boston and many of these families were involved in the creation of the region's valuable educational infrastructure through their gifts to Harvard and then later MIT.

Almost counterintuitively, Boston in its media form in the 1970s and 1980s emerged as both a place of working-class lives and values and a repository of the connected concept of tradition. But this invoking of the past also invokes a legacy of inherited wealth, even if that legacy is inflected, and largely invisible in textual form. In effect, Boston projects the future as it portrays the past. In its signature redevelopment projects of the late twentieth century, such as the reconstruction of Faneuil Hall and Quincy Market, which were completed in 1976, just in the middle of this cycle of films, the city has served as one of the exemplary places for the development and marketing of what Sharon Zukin has referred to as "festival marketplaces," privatized urban spaces that replaced formerly functioning aspects of the city's commercial core with malls, restaurants, and other urban entertainments for the moneyed classes.[5] Zukin's discussion draws from that of David Harvey, particularly his assertion that the postmodern city is a façade, a compendium of images designed to entrance its participating viewers.[6] These facades are as much about brand differentiation as they are about amenities, offering the uniqueness of these particular edifices and their associated historical meanings, which are distinctly connected to an embedded concept of place. That the inner harbor of Baltimore and Quincy Market were developed by the same company, the Rouse Company, which also was responsible for South Street Seaport and any number of repurposings of moribund urban sites with historical significance, matters only to the degree that consumers are eased into their surroundings by the relative ubiquity of their features. But in all cases the selling of the thin historical residue available in such places connects to the relative distinction of each urban entity's brand.

It is a similarly broad kind of branding that takes place in these three films that emerge in this transitional period, in the relatively early days of neoliberalism and the globalized economy, and define a Boston that is not the bifurcated city we see in more contemporary productions: rather, in an appeal to a thin concept of tradition, the city is caught in the maw of its history and the entrenched definitions of its residual ethnicities, as well as the class resentments of the past. The *Friends of Eddie Coyle*, for example, does not dwell on the divide between the economically struggling Coyle and the more prosperous Bostonians who are the targets of crime. Indeed, the film treats those denizens of the upper class and upper-middle class as a matter of happenstance. They are not robbed in order that they will become less rich; rather, it is so the criminals may become more rich. The more tony suburbs that we fleetingly glance are neither dwelled upon nor envied. And those who are more successful criminals also live modest lives. Similarly, *The Brink's Job* shows us the desire for a transcendent crime taking precedence over the fact of the gains provided by such a crime. It is more the scale and challenge than the cash that motivates these robbers. Indeed, none of the robbers is shown upgrading his station. And though *The Verdict* emphasizes class distinction more, it defines those differences more as a matter of social capital than of class resentment. But, to be sure, then entrenched power structures traceable to both Catholic and Protestant elites, much like in the later film *Spotlight* (2015), are constantly moving the levers of power. These films do not dwell on the massive social gap between the residual working-class population of the city and its entrenched and emergent social elites. Those distinction became central for the Boston films of the later 1990s and 2000s, which all but inevitably show that such stark contrasts are too much a matter of the postindustrial contours of the city, a city of gentrification and finance. In these earlier films, rather than a city of the rich and poor, it is a city that is stuck within the bounds of history and in which a glimmer of an evolving world can be spied, but it is not a world that has clearly changed or even clearly changing.

These earlier films define their communities as not only socially articulate; they are also geographically separated from the core of Boston by a significant expanse, both physical and aspirational. *The Friends of Eddie Coyle* maintains its geographic center in the working-class Irish suburbs to the south, *The Brink's Job* in the Italian suburbs to the north, and *The Verdict* in the decaying inner-city. In these first two films, the modesty of these locales marks them as both distinct and insular. These are neighborhoods that seem self sufficient, places where criminals may conspire uninterrupted by the prying eyes of institutional forces. Their relative claustrophobia is largely read as comfortable. In *The Verdict*, the stately decay of Beacon Hill shows us an infrastructure poised for gentrification. Even Galvin's office is a lovely wreck of a space, in a historic building with a bulls-eye window over his cluttered desk. All three films engage in a kind of temporal vision that is either nostalgic or static. We see a place without dynamism and a social world that is largely static—no character in these films ascends to greater social or economic success.

Of the three films, *The Verdict* is far more centripetal, and therefore the most contemporary in its organization, and almost claustrophobically so, as it is centered around Beacon Hill and the statehouse—though the place-specific articulation of that centripetal organization is very broad. In contrast, these two earlier films look out at a decentered and largely featureless city, still dominated by ethnic tensions between the warring Catholic tribes: the Irish and the Italians, and these groups are subjugated by a still regnant Protestant aristocracy. The city we see in all three films is one anchored in the past with little in the way of momentum to push it out of its doldrums. This vision then imagines the relative non-place of Boston in the moment just before it becomes a national and international presence in its virtual representation—in effect, a place.

Such a vision, of course, has become an entrenched trope, one that has been re-appropriated by those who access the cinematic Boston of the 2000s. These films shot after the 1997 release of *Good Will Hunting* (Gus Van Sant) operate in a shifting cultural terrain. While they seem to articulate a distinct sense of space and time, upon closer scrutiny those anchors to materiality and a clear temporality become less definite. All invoke the "new" Boston but the terms of that place are affixed to a body of landmarks and narrative conventions, all of which summon a mix of history and nostalgia. What is clear is that the brand, this later image of the city, is a narrative feature, a virtual "given." These definitions are connected to earlier representations but far more fully articulated. In these films of the 1970s and 1980s, "Boston" becomes a kind of placeholder for the postindustrial, pre-global city of the Northeastern United States. All reference historically received tropes that evoke "Boston" in a way that defines the nexus between the burgeoning digital city of the 2000s and the crumbling compendium of brick and concrete that marked the city of the 1950s and 1960s.

The Friends of Eddie Coyle was based on the Boston noir novel by George V. Higgins. It depicts a moment when the US economy was shifting toward its current postindustrial state and as such shows us a city and its populace with a foot in the regional past and a foot in its globalized future. The film's central character, Eddie Coyle, is an ex-con, a low-ranking member of an Irish American crime network. He is spatially and socially isolated in the urban sprawl, and, in the end, subject to the violence and duplicity of his ethnic counterparts, people to whom he is connected in unquestioned ways. It is intriguing to think of this character as part of the ongoing Boston–Dublin traffic, a movement that had been going on for over a century at the point of production, but a transfer of humans that, while diasporic, is largely conceived as outside of the conventional definitions of cosmopolitanism. It is a textured narrative and the film version operates within the crime genre with many of the noir trappings that were often employed within the era.

Spatially, *The Friends of Eddie Coyle* is also very much a film of the prior decades. It offers no images of distinctive urban streetscapes nor does it envision urban charm. Indeed, it looks to the sprawl that was so much a feature of the decentered city that was a matter of the 1950s, a city that was conceived as a business center but which was unfit for middle-class residency.

Coyle lives outside of the city, in the Wollaston section of Quincy, the city that was then a predominantly working-class Irish American enclave. Indeed, Coyle's wife is an Irish immigrant. The film more generally takes place in the southern suburbs of the city, showing scenes shot in Dedham, Canton, and the edge of the Boston neighborhood of Dorchester. It also features pivotal scenes in the old Boston Garden, at a Bruins game, and at the then newly constructed Boston City Hall in the newly formed Government Center district of the city—an urban renewal project that razed the historic—and seedy—entertainment district of Scollay Square and replaced it with the sterile and uninviting new development.

The Brink's Job is a quasi-historical drama based on one of the largest robberies in history, the hold-up of the Brink's cash depot in Boston's North End in 1950 (Figure 5.1). In the film, the director William Friedkin attempts to reconstruct a facsimile of Boston in the 1940s and early 1950s, and in doing so develops a film that is spatially constrained and gives a sense of the claustrophobic pre-sprawl city, even as it suggests the existence of contiguous regions that are easily accessed by cars. *The Verdict* is a courtroom drama in which Paul Newman plays a struggling attorney who is pitted against the Protestant legal establishment and the Catholic Church over a wrongful death case that took place at one of the archdiocese's hospitals. All three films trade on Boston textures and embedded sociocultural narratives of place, but each

Figure 5.1 Eddie Coyle tells of his hard luck in *The Friends of Eddie Coyle* (1973)

approaches the city slightly differently, with *The Verdict's* sense of the city and its space being the most distinct—even as that urban depiction is more a matter of texture than specific sites.

The new Old Boston and the old New Boston

The paucity of films shot on location in Boston in this interim period suggests the city was not then prominent in the mass consciousness of the nation. Unlike, say, New York City, which became a signature site during the New Hollywood era, no film producers were taking recurring trips to Boston to scout for locations.[7] While such New Hollywood productions as *The Paper Chase* (James Bridges, 1973) and *The Last Detail* (Hal Ashby, 1973) provide fleeting moments of and references to the city, as do *Altered States* (Ken Russell, 1979) and *Starting Over* (Alan J. Pakula, 1979), Boston did not become a notable place for film shoots until the late 1990s. *Good Will Hunting* was released in 1997 and the Boston-specific *Monument Ave.* (Ted Demme, 1998) and *A Civil Action* (Steven Zaillian, 1998) soon followed. It is also notable that on the way to a more significant Boston brand in feature films in the late 1990s, two successful television series, *St. Elsewhere* (NBC, 1982–8) and *Cheers* (NBC, 1982–93), employed Boston as an ostensible location, employing its embedded cultural meanings and providing some exteriors in their credit sequences and opening establishing shots. Indeed this use of the city has much in common with the deployment of place in these three films.

Each of these shows prominently used iconic regional institutions as points of reference. In *St. Elsewhere*, it was Massachusetts General Hospital that defined the place which the featured medical facility, named St. Eligius, would never be; in *Cheers*, bar-owner Sam Malone was a former relief pitcher for the Red Sox. *Cheers*, the more successful and iconic of the two shows, employed the exterior of the Bull and Finch Inn, a basement bar that occupied the iconic location on the edge of Beacon Hill, on the corner of Beacon and Charles Street. In following the place of this bar's role in the city's imagined lore, its name was officially changed to *Cheers* in 2002 and a second *Cheers* replica bar was opened at Quincy Market in the same year. Thus, place and meaning are transformed by mass-cultural projections of "place" and subsequently such representations have the commercial power to remake place. The simulacra become the real. The timing of this change of name and opening of a second *"Cheers"* is also intriguing, since it came some ten years after the end of the show, but far closer chronologically to the emergence of Boston as a media presence in the late 1990s.

This appearance of an ersatz Boston that primarily existed on Hollywood sound stages is an interesting complement to these three films of roughly the same period, which are both place specific and not so specific. They offer few lingering shots of what were to become iconic locales in these later films: Fenway Park, the Prudential Tower, the Customs House, and even the regions of Harvard Square. Rather, these films bask without comment in the indistinct corners of Quincy, Dedham, East Boston, the relatively unimproved waterfront district of the 1970s, and locations that are in another place all together (as in *The Verdict*); or, in locales that function essentially as sets, since they are built specifically for the film even if mounted on the streets of Boston (as in *The Brink's Job.*). *The Verdict* does *seem* to stake out downtown Boston but provides almost no visuals of external landmarks—no state house, no Boston Common, and no Beacon Hill. Perhaps this is because much of the film was shot in New York with Boston-looking locations. Yet, in this envisioning of the centripetal city, we can see the textual emphases that would become materialized in the later century and then in the 2000s.

By the later 1990s production would pick up—to some degree thanks to the career successes of Matt Damon and Ben Affleck, and the impact of their first film, *Good Will Hunting*, which features not only a fairly articulate view of South Boston, but also significant scenes in Harvard Square and the broader environs of Cambridge, including MIT. It also includes shots of the Boston Public Gardens. This increase in visibility continued and in *Mystic River* (Clint Eastwood, 2003), a success by any measure, views of the fictional East Buckingham section of Boston included a compendium of the decidedly working-class districts of Chelsea, South Boston, Charlestown, Roxbury, and other locales. We also see the iconic Mystic River Bridge (now known as the Maurice Tobin Bridge) looming over the action, and are provided an identifiable view of Franklin Park, the city's largest park, which is bordered by Roxbury and Mattapan. In a later scene Celeste Boyle, the wife of one of the film's principals, considers revealing her husband as a murderer as she looks across the harbor to the shadow of the Prudential Tower. In films such as *The Departed* (Martin Scorsese, 2006), *Gone Baby Gone* (Ben Affleck, 2007), and *The Town* (Ben Affleck, 2010), among many others, we see an identifiable Boston, one that viewers may associate with its presence in other films, television series, news stories (The Big Dig, The Whitey Bulger-saga, the Boston Marathon bombing, the sexual abuse scandal in the Catholic Church), and shots from various blimps and cranes accompanying the many nationally televised Red Sox, Patriots, or Celtics games—but particularly those of the Red Sox, the most resonant and place-specific brand of those three. But all of these images and the narratives they support retain elements of the "Boston" we find in these three earlier films; in effect, the "New" Boston retains residual elements of the older one.

In these later films we see a more iconic city, one that has been refined as a locale for mass-cultural texts, and therefore one more clearly suffused with meanings that are immediately recognizable, a place that is far more prominent in the national consciousness due to its relative prosperity and status as a second-tier participant in the network of world cities that define the moment of globalized trade and neoliberal economics. Arguably, that success creates visibility, and visibility creates success. Yet, that city is connected to these earlier films, and to some degree infused with residual definitions and suffused with notions, broadly construed, of history and "tradition."

Notably, this city is physically and demographically a markedly different city than it was in the 1970s and early 1980s. To take one important indicator, Boston, as of today, is among the most gentrified cities in the United States with some of the most expensive real estate. As Barry Bluestone and Mary Huff Stevenson, both urban economists, tell us in their edited study focused on Boston and its social changes over the last half century, "The price of housing rose faster in Boston between 1980 and 1990 than in any other city in the nation … By the second quarter of 1999 the median sale price of a single family home … was 76 percent higher than the national median."[8]

But this state of prosperity and relative paucity of affordable property is a recent one. To look back at the immediate historical antecedents to the era of these films, the 1950s and 1960s, the city had lost significant population and was decidedly run down. The most prolific historian of Boston, Thomas H. O'Connor, chronicles in his *Building a New Boston: Politics and Urban Renewal,*

1950 to 1970 that, as the 1950s unfolded, Boston was a city in notable decline, featuring a decayed infrastructure, including roads, public transportation, and public buildings. It was also a city with an eroding economic base, due to both middle-class, and substantially white, flight, and a declining industrial and shipping sector. Further its structural and political relationship with the state government severely limited funding for its renewal through the auspices of the state of Massachusetts.[9] Boston in the 1950s was already poised to enter the postindustrial moment. Industries that had thrived in the region (shoes, textiles, clothing, foundries, and ship building) were moving to lower-wage regions—at that point to the non-unionized US South, a phenomenon that also afflicted the economies of most major cities of the Northeast: New York, Baltimore, and Philadelphia.

O'Connor tells the revealing anecdote of a city leader, the Reverend Joyce, Dean of Boston College's College of Business, flying over the city in 1956 and being amazed at what he saw—or did not see. Writes O'Connor, "As he gazed down on the low-lying protuberance of land beneath him, which was completely undistinguished, had no distinctive skyline, not a single identifiable structure, except the old Custom House tower, he exclaimed in a startled voice: 'Where's Boston?'"[10] Three years later, the signature project undertaken by the Prudential Insurance company would result in the construction of a fifty-two-story office tower. Interestingly, that question—"Where's Boston?"— would become the title for a multi-media show that was housed in the very same Prudential Tower as part of the city's bicentennial celebration of 1975 and 1976, which, as noted, was also the moment of the reopening of Faneuil Hall, Quincy Market, and the rededication of the waterfront.[11] The need for a brand was a clear element in the conceiving of the Prudential project, and the success of that project as a means to redefine the city's fortunes and skyline has occurred both symbolically and materially—but it took almost two decades.

But while the "new" Boston was slow to emerge, the "old" Boston is ever present. This view of the city as possessing residual historical significance, one that easily becomes nostalgia and intransigence in its popular rendering, finds its way into these films. Boston in these films is white, ethnic, and built in earlier eras. *Eddie Coyle* is very much a film of the older, working-class suburbs of the inner ring, a film that basks in the long-established criminality of Irish- and Italian American gangs. The same mix is available in *The Brink's Job*, and to some degree in *The Verdict*. In this 1970s and 1980s rendering, Boston is white, graying around the edges, and beset with historical resentments and rivalries. These definitions are so much a "given" that these films offer nothing physically new and provide a Boston that, while not quite a place in itself, does prominently trade in residual definitions that project place. *The Brink's Job* in effect creates its own city, with sets that are built on city streets but which are only specific to the film, functioning as a kind of essence of the city. In the most filmed street scenes, we have a market set up in the region near the Boston Common, but the fronts are far more Hollywood than Boston. The Egleston Diner where Tony, the film's protagonist (played by Peter Falk), works, and which seems to be contiguous to that street, is in East Boston, some distance from that location and renamed. Egleston Square is in Roxbury, a place that is miles away and which has nothing to do with East Boston. The most coherent geographic strategy employed is that which locates the Brink's depot in the North End and which actually films in the contiguous streets, the very same streets Ben Affleck used in *The Town* (2010). But again, the viewer is provided with little sense of distinctive place or space. In 1950, the North End of Boston was a teeming, substantially Italian American neighborhood, where one was as likely to encounter a Napolitano accent as one from Boston. Yet, the film does little with such specific historical details.

The Verdict is even less exacting regarding place. While it does offer some appropriate Boston locations, such as street scenes in South Boston and the Massachusetts statehouse, which stands-in as both a hospital and a courtroom, many of its scenes are, as noted earlier, shot in New York. Its most recurring location is a bar where the failing lawyer Frank Galvin, played by Paul Newman, parks himself for most of his waking hours. His preferred perch is at a pinball machine by a window that overlooks a corner of a park. But the park is neither the Boston Commons nor the Public Gardens. Indeed, the latter location seems to be the one evoked, a place also employed in *Good Will Hunting* to mark and define the context of the narrative. But in this very claustrophobic rendering of a sort-of-particular place, we are given a view of a bar on Avenue B in the Lower East Side of New York, and the park is a corner of Tompkins Square. Similarly, we see street shots of Brooklyn Heights, the Otto Kahn mansion at East 91st Street, and the Tweed Courthouse in Lower Manhattan.

This lack of specificity and context suggests the need for a reiteration of Father Joyce's question: Where's Boston? And perhaps it should be amended to include: What is Boston? As we encounter these three films the answer seems to be an amalgam of fairly particular vocal inflections—though this is less true in The *Brink's Job*, where New York-reared actors like Paul Sorvino and Peter Falk make minimal efforts to capture the local sound. But certainly in the other two films, the Boston accent is an important marker of locale. The other defining characteristic as of the 1970s and early 1980s seems to be a residual racism, one that defines both the parochialism and the class resentments of place; though historically, that world was starting to ebb, at least it was by 1980.

These films are of the moment of the beginning of the re-elaboration of the central city of Boston, a time that can take as its germ the opening of the Prudential Tower in 1965. Yet, they seem to take little specific note of that looming transformation—though *Eddie Coyle* does provide a view of the building. In the decade prior to that construction, the use of federal highway funds had gradually routed both businesses and population out of the city, and it is that reduced urban entity that the three films access. In that era, it was the construction of the inner-belt highway of Route 128, largely completed as a limited access road by 1951, that dispersed population to inner-line suburbs and which created the tech campuses that lined that highway's central section in towns such as Waltham, Newton, Lexington, and Burlington. By 1957 there were 140 companies located on that road; by 1973 the number was over 1,200. And the existence of Route 128 inevitably led to the further construction of major contiguous highways—the I-90 extension, I-495—that ultimately had a related impact on work and residential locales, so that by the early 1970s the city of Boston was languishing in both population and employment capacity. As of 1950, the city's population peaked at 801,000. By 1980 only 562,000 people resided there, which was a low point. Its current population is 685,000.[12] This demographic shift suggests that at the point when these films were released the city was at near its lowest in population and centrality, a fact we can spy in these representations that lack bustling, teeming crowds, central gathering places, and, in the case of *Eddie Coyle*, much of the city itself.

In his excellent study of Boston's rise from the ashes, Elihu Rubin traces both the specific matters that led to the building of the city's Prudential Tower and the symbolic significance of that construction. The Prudential Tower opened in 1965, and immediately became a symbol of the New Boston. This building soon became emblematic of the city's role in the emergent world economy, symbolizing not only investment and significance, but also the role of a major player in the capital-intensive environment that emerged in the post Bretton Woods-world. As blue-collar work and population declined, the city's financial, insurance, and real estate sectors (FIRE), the hallmarks of the urban neoliberal economy of the 1980s to the 2010s, were relatively slow to emerge. Prudential's investment in the city was not only symbolically significant, but it also introduced the insurance sector as a pillar of the new Boston. That John Hancock Insurance built a new, and bigger tower not far away—that was completed in 1976—was a further statement.

In mass-cultural terms, then, the representational irony of these films and virtually all subsequent ones is that the Boston we see as a residual bastion of working-class life is a city in which the working class increasingly ceases to exist as we move from the 1970s to the 2010s. And though these films portray Boston as a locale that is defined by its working-class population, they seem to present little evidence of the locales of work. To be of the working class, then, is more a matter of limited wealth and pedestrian taste than it is of the work one does. The films show us modest living conditions, limited aspirations, and above all a kind of tribalism.

The chronology of these films encompasses both the immediate pre- and the immediate post-bicentennial moment—1976—and chronicles the flux in the city's perceived fortunes and identity that coalesce around the moment. The city received extraordinary attention for its role in the celebration, with a visit by the tall ships, as well as for the fourth of July gala that included a national television audience for Arthur Fiedler and the Boston Pops performing the 1812 Overture from the banks of the Charles River basin; but that notice was of a moment and highlighted the historical deep structure of the city at the expense of the contemporary, emphasizing the city's prominence in the eighteenth century, while largely ignoring its more contemporary decline. The national coverage largely dwelt on the scenic spaces that were geographically definitional to the city's success in the preindustrial age, those that defined its status as a major port city of the emergent economy of the North American continent.

But even as the city's past was being celebrated, its present was visibly fraught. More nationally resonant than the Boston Pops and the tall ships was the negative publicity attached to the city of Boston for the ongoing racial antipathies displayed in response to a court-ordered desegregation order of the city's schools in 1974, an order that resulted from an ongoing refusal of the city's school committee to implement a desegregation order issued some nine years before. The resistance of working-class whites, particularly in Charlestown and South Boston, to school integration provided a vision of a place stuck in time and in antipathies that dated back to the mid-nineteenth century, and in a view of race relations that might have seemed more appropriate to Boston, Georgia. But historically they were consonant with a view of that city that revealed its stark ethnic and class divides: the city where abolitionism had coalesced, and where liberal politicians had long supported civil rights, also included a significant constituency that resisted such causes. While abolitionism had important roots in the city during the period immediately prior to the Civil War, Boston also included a recalcitrant population that resisted the draft for that war and denounced the intention of emancipation. It is a place where a number of white families attended rallies for George Wallace—a candidate over 16 percent of Bostonians voted for in the 1976 Democratic primary—and whose population included the founder of the "Wake Up America" campaign of 1969, Arthur Stivaletta, a self-described super patriot whose cause was a northeastern version of the John Birch Society. Stivaletta's rallies often included pro-war and conservative stalwarts such as Al Capp, the creator of the L'il Abner cartoon strip and a former liberal, and Bob Hope, the pro-Nixon and pro-war comedian. Based in the nearly all-white, southern suburbs envisioned by *Eddie Coyle*, Stivaletta brought out crowds of right-wing populists in the late 1960s and 1970s, and aligned with the anti-busing insurgency. Such historical facts remind us that the working-class dimension of the city, memorialized and romanticized in films, included a significant racist strain.

This racist aspect was buttressed by policies that reinforced it spatially. By the 1960s, red-lining and related and restrictive United States Department of Housing and Urban Development guidelines had created a distinctive concentration of African Americans and other minority populations in the formerly Jewish neighborhoods of Roxbury and Mattapan. These areas abutted the traditional Irish neighborhoods of Dorchester, South Boston, and

Charlestown, areas where suburban migration was less pronounced than in other working-class city sectors due to relatively slow social mobility.[13] This divide along racial and class lines figures in all three of the films, though it's less picturesque and less focal than in the post-*Good Will Hunting* films.

This backdrop of the city where racial, ethnic, and class antipathies abound—a vital dimension of the city's national profile and one which still obtains, but to a lesser degree—forms the broad image of the represented "Boston," and there are certainly many continuities between these earlier films and the later ones. By 1997, the resplendent Fiedler, a child of Jewish, Eastern European immigrants, was mostly forgotten, while the distinct regional accent offered by the likes of Matt Damon, the Affleck brothers, and Sean Penn easily summoned images of angry faces of those stoning the buses bringing African American school children to the white and Irish enclave of South Boston in the 1970s. As historian Louis Masur has written about the crisis and particularly the iconic photograph of an African American lawyer in the new city hall plaza being assaulted with the staff on which an American flag was mounted, "The image ... crystalized Boston's reputation as a racist city," an image that was not so much breaking with broad conceptions but affirming and solidifying them.[14]

The related image that also emerges is of a city constrained by a notion of tradition, which is not an unrelated trope. Within their apparently place-specific narratives of these three films, the meaning of the city includes both a deep parochialism and a residual racism that finds itself into the matter of the texts at certain key moments. The fact and persistence of such sentiments, and related allusions to that narrowness of vision and experience by class, race, and ethnicity became more apparent.

The narrowness and the class distinctions of Boston-world are all over all three films. But mostly we are lodged in the world of those with very modest backgrounds and limited chances for success. In *Eddie Coyle* we are immersed in the world of small-time gangsters and gun-runners. In an establishing scene from early in the film, Eddie meets with a younger man from whom he wants to buy guns in a ghostly and depressing cafeteria of a non-descript region. The type of place and its depiction are emblematic of the world this film inhabits and which becomes a resonant version of the city. The establishing shot finds Eddie opening the door to the cafeteria as we see both the contours of this narrow and decidedly unglamorous place. The scene proceeds to Eddie moving down the chow line, selecting a piece of pie and a cup of coffee with deliberateness. Eddie shows both his world weariness and disappointment as they transact their business. They sit in a booth, narrowly framed and claustrophobic, as Eddie reveals his prior failures. Says Eddie in close-up, showing the face of the world-weary Robert Mitchum (Figure 5.2): "Look, I'm gettin' old, you hear? I spent most of my life hanging around crummy joints with a buncha punks drinkin' the beer, eatin' the hash and the hot dogs and watchin' the other people go off to Florida while I'm sweatin' out how I'm gonna pay the plumber. I done time and I stood up but I can't take no more chances. Next time, it's gonna be me goin' to Florida."

In *The Brink's Job*, it is safe crackers and bank robbers who populate the shadows of the city in the 1940s and early 1950s. Upon his release from prison the film's protagonist Tony Pino, played by Peter Falk, becomes a sweaty, undershirt-clad counter man at a diner in a downtrodden sector of the city. As a sideline, he fences stolen goods that he keeps in the basement. As he develops his grandiose plan to rob a Brink's depository, much of the planning takes place in this dank, filthy basement that is shot in a succession of close-ups to emphasize the sweat of the planners and the despair of their circumstances. William Friedkin's direction often shows Falk amid dirty laundry and his co-conspirators on a wooden staircase, framed by a decaying and greasy handrail.

Figure 5.2 Our Thieves Survey the Brink's Depot in *The Brink's Job* (1978).

In *The Verdict*, we see the regional class divide from a different perch, as we dwell in the world of the fallen elite and the elite itself (Figure 5.3). In this world of lawyers, Cardinals and Monsignors, and doctors, our working class-hero is a female immigrant and the victims are, while Boston born, of similarly modest means. Frank Galvin, the film's central character, is a down-on-his-luck lawyer who spends more time at the bar that dispenses alcohol than the one that ostensibly dispenses justice. That bar is poorly lit, smoky, and decidedly working class. Galvin's office, a wreck of a space in a clearly pre-gentrification downtown Boston, has potential but is a chaotic mess. Galvin is on a appropriately downward trajectory, and his physical environs confirm this. In contrast to the other two films, *The Verdict* focuses on a character who has seen better days and who accesses worlds of greater status and privilege. But the time when he belonged in such worlds has clearly passed.

All three films emphasize the despair of place and its inhabitants. It is that despair that leads to tragedy, as each figure attempts to strive for a greater wealth, but not necessarily greater status. The films depict work itself as limited in scope and opportunity. Unlike the view of the academic world of *Good Will Hunting* (1997) or that of banking in *The Town* (2010*)*, we see

Figure 5.3 Frank Galvin takes on Boston's elite in *The Verdict* (1982).

the gravel pit where guns are transacted in *Eddie Coyle*, a site on the urban periphery, which is in keeping with the larger geographic orientation of the film; or, in *The Brink's Job*, the thieves rob a gumball factory and a chicken abattoir. These are all small and regional enterprises, also well away from the city center and indicative of a vision of pre–World War Two sprawl, an era that prefigures the rise of interstate highways in the 1950s. Also notable is the fact that these places are not in operation when we encounter them, so we never see actual work being done. In *The Verdict*, the focus is moving toward the emergent orientation of the city—it is focused on the urban core, and it is a matter of professionals. The courtroom drama focuses on the paralysis of a working-class woman who aspirates into her mask as she is being sedated. Her advocates are her sister and brother-in-law, who are marked as working class by their dress, speech, and aspirations; yet, we are never provided even a clue as to the work they do.

This last film points to the fact that the city and region by the early 1980s already possessed the academic and intellectual infrastructure to begin moving toward its ultimate success in the coming postindustrial "information age" in the elaboration of the technological corridor along Route 128, featuring such military-industrial giants as Raytheon, Digital, and General Electric. In the 1980s the burgeoning computer industry would establish itself through the formation of companies like Wang, Lotus, and Prime. By 1990, the regional workforce had morphed into a one that was, in national terms, disproportionately white collar.[15] But the region's spatial orientation as of the 1950s was decidedly away from the urban core and that fact is evident in *Eddie Coyle* and to some degree *The Brink's Job*. Each of these films develops a vision of the city that is substantially centrifugal, a world of roads and cars. Such an "urban" vision and then its undoing in *The Verdict* suggests how these films represent the changing spatial emphases of cities, as they rehearse the emergent postindustrial development of the movement of elite populations *back* to the central cities. Such change is the driving force of gentrification, as inner-cities increasingly house the genteel and educated classes, while the residue of the working class is in suburban locales. This is certainly the case with Boston and the relative absence of a more contemporary sense of space and place dates these first two films.

Race and ethnicity in Boston

It is difficult to talk of Boston historically and representationally without discussing its vexed history of racism. These films touch on that history in ways that mark their chronology. Boston as of 1972 was a spatially segregated city, with its African American population overwhelmingly residing in the neighborhoods to the south of downtown, primarily Roxbury and Mattapan. It also was a city with only a very small percentage of non-white residents, 18 percent, most of whom were African American. But even though that was a fairly small number and distinctly small for a city of that time in the northeast corridor of the United States, that population had doubled over the past ten years, since 1960. Each of these films has a recessed racial commentary that is nevertheless significant and effectively can be brought to the fore and employed as a key interpretive element. Indeed, by picturing the spatial logic that both reifies and reproduces the fact of segregation, the key demographic rationale for court-ordered busing, these films show us a city with virtually no black or brown faces.

Since class and race are easily placed near the center of these films, and since the busing crisis serves as their temporal context, I would like to focus on their depiction of race relations, as well as more broadly blackness and whiteness, and bring that representational focus closer to the center of the three films. Each of the films has at least a moment where considerations of race become pronounced, if not exactly emphasized, and through a noting and of those moments, we may come to see the embedded conception of place that animates these 1970s and 1980s explications of "Boston."

The Friends of Eddie Coyle begins with a kidnapping that is the beginning of a bank robbery. But rather than an ornate downtown depository, this robbery takes place in a nondescript branch, one that is in the inner-ring suburb of Dedham. This introductory scene is a reasonable entree into the decidedly downbeat world of the film. But beyond our plot, spatially the film rehearses the moment just before gentrification becomes an important regional shift, a later time when industrial suburbs like Quincy serve as a fulcrum between the gentrified zones of the inner-city and the wealth of certain bedroom suburbs. Both Dillon, played by Peter Boyle, and Coyle are vestiges of another time, a moment where cities and their immediate environs were the zones of crime of those left behind. But even as we see those spaces, we are provided with a vision of a kind of urban renewal, as we see the ever-ugly but once-new City Hall Plaza with its uninviting brutalist architecture, and which opened in 1968. The ugliness and barrenness of this new landmark suggests the failures of urban renewal as a governmental enterprise. Indeed, it may have the impact of elevating the significance of the past, of the comity of spaces like Quincy Market and Fanueil Hall, as well as the more vibrant and architecturally distinctive Scollay Square, which was razed to build this new enclave. The Plaza stands as a replacement for former public spaces that far more effectively provided a welcoming space for the public. It signifies the demise of that sphere and in effect, heralds the coming of the neoliberal regime.

Ultimately, we see Eddie's demise set up in the parking lot of the Quincy mass transit station, a modern domain of heartlessness akin to the ugly City Hall Plaza, a place of no honor among thieves. And the prelude to the execution takes place in the decaying, rat-infested edifice of the old Boston Garden, a declining space that, due to the vagaries of state and local politics, outlasted its effective usefulness. The Garden was built in 1928 and was, even at its opening, a facility too small for a regulation hockey rink, a significant problem since the Bruins were one of its primary tenants. As *Eddie Coyle* hit the local theaters in the early summer of 1973, there was already a plan, announced by Mayor Kevin White the year before, to replace the undersized and decrepit facility with a gleaming new one, to be built in a site abutting North Station. Some twenty-two years later, a new Boston Garden was built on a parcel abutting its prior location.

Yates employs the grimy, claustrophobic, and crumbling facility as part of his vision of place. The all-white crowd loves its team in an unquestioning way, and is quick to respond to the blood on the ice. In an ironic aside, the beer-addled Coyle stands up and affirms his appreciation for the Hall of Fame player Bobby Orr, commenting on both his talent and his great future—as of 1972, Orr was only twenty-four; however, because of repeated knee injuries, Orr was already hobbled by 1972, and would play his last full season in 1974–5, at the age of twenty-seven. Yates captures the unthinking, vaguely inhuman aspect of the crowd and this crowd in particular, and in his depiction is knowingly space specific. The Eddie Coyle-moment of Boston life is already sliding from the center of the picture when this film is released in 1973, but yet, it remains textually central. This treatment of professional sports and the old Boston Garden stands in contrast to the use of the resonant brand of the Red Sox and Fenway Park in films ranging from *Field Of Dreams* (1989), *Good Will Hunting* (1997), *The Town* (2010), or *Moneyball* (2011).

When Eddie Coyle and Dillon are out and about in Boston, Quincy, or Dedham, the faces we see are only white. This is both historically accurate and elaborative of the terms of spatial segregation in the city. Though by 1970 roughly one in five Bostonians was African American, the city remained largely segregated by region, with most African Americans living in the Roxbury and Mattapan regions south of downtown. When the various banks are robbed in this film, it is instructive that we see neither a black patron nor a black worker at any of those institutions, though the distance from Mattapan, an increasingly African American neighborhood as of the early 1970s, to Dedham is only about five miles. It is notable that Coyle's Quincy would be substantially Vietnamese and Cambodian by the 2000s.

In a key scene in the film, Eddie Coyle, in conversation with his partner in crime and ultimate betrayer Dillon, played by Peter Boyle, confides that he needs one last payday before he goes off to prison, so that his "wife will not have to go on welfare, like a nigger." This comment is captured in a sequence of close-ups and two-shots as Coyle sits on a bar stool and Dillon stands behind the bar. The visual language of the scene provokes its intimate terms and the sincerity of the speaker. This racial and racist language is uttered in passing without embellishment and elicits no comment. This is a world where African Americans are broadly reduced and where assumptions of behavior track very clearly with such prejudice. In ways, this moment, along with the absence of brown and black faces from public spaces, opens out into a world defined by the racial antipathies displayed in the busing crisis. In this manner, then, the accents so carefully elaborated by the various actors, which provide the sound of authenticity to the film, are easily employed in the service of racist utterances. Indeed, such utterances occurred just the other day at Fenway Park, as a player for the visiting team was the object of them.[16]

The Brink's Job is a far more stylized drama, less gritty and less noir. It is set in the late 1930s and mid- to late 1940s, and is a period piece with a sense of nostalgia informed by kitsch. The actual Brink's robbery takes place in January of 1950. The film largely depicts the inter-ethnic alliances conflict between Irish and Italian criminals, including somewhat more established and successful Irish criminals, and including some—apparently by their accents—recent émigrés to the United States. And just as *Eddie Coyle* has its moment of racial elaboration, one with broader implications in the world depicted, so does *The Brink's Job*. About four-fifths of the way through the film, after some of the robbers have been apprehended for profligately spending their ill-got gains, in the very next scene we see our main characters, Jazz and Tony—both Italian American, discussing what has happened to their compatriots and how to stay out of jail. This conversation takes place as they walk through the elevated railway Dudley Station, which is in the center of Roxbury, the center of the city's African American community, both then and now. By 1950, that population had roughly doubled in the previous decade from 5,700 to 11,000. Our historical sense of the district is further enhanced by the memoir of Malcolm X, who called Roxbury home during the 1940s, and wrote:

> I saw and met a hundred black people there whose big-city talk and ways left my mouth hanging open. I couldn't have feigned indifference if I had tried to. I didn't know the world contained as many Negroes as I saw thronging downtown Roxbury at night, especially on Saturdays. Neon lights, nightclubs, poolhalls, bars, the cars they drove! Restaurants made the streets smell—rich, greasy, down-home black cooking! Jukeboxes blared Erskine Hawkins, Duke Ellington, Cootie Williams, dozens of others. If somebody had told me then that some day I'd know them all personally, I'd have found it hard to believe.[17]

Yet, the Dudley Station we see Tony and Jazz walking through is all white. Similarly, when they walk off the station platform there is no sense of an African American presence, though the film IS very aware of period details, such as campaign signs, local products, and the period clothing. In effect, this film erases the African American presence from the city's distinctive African American district.

In the last of these films, *The Verdict*, we have perhaps the most powerful expression of casual racism in any of the three. In this courtroom drama, the case against the archdiocese brought by the Irish lawyer, Frank Galvin—BC law school—depends upon the expert testimony of a doctor, who vanishes just as he's about to take the stand. This leaves Galvin scrambling for another expert witness, and he finally gets a Doctor Thompson to take the train from New York. When he arrives, Galvin lets him walk past, not recognizing him until Thompson introduces himself. The fact that he is African American, a fact Galvin did not previously know, clearly causes a great deal of consternation. Galvin never recovers his equanimity and the court also treats Thompson with minimal respect. Galvin's upset may be a matter of his own racial orientation, but the broader treatment of Thompson suggests a more systemic racism.

The Verdict also emphasizes the connection between the church and other centers of power in the city—all of them monolithically white—in effect making it a political organization more substantially concerned with its own authority and wealth than with any abiding sense of justice. Similarly, the judiciary is also represented as deeply involved with the city's centers of power and less with its role of functioning as a neutral device for the exacting of justice. In this moral positioning, then, *The Verdict*, engages the broadly liberal political dimension of the early 1980s in order to focus on the residue of retrograde reactionary dimensions of the city tagged as "Boston." Such a view is a vital aspect of the film's narrative and one which plays off of broad mass-cultural association of the city with racism and broader reaction.

This broad association of Boston and its often retrograde politics of race are at least implicitly summoned in the later two films the still-recent busing crisis, a historical event of 1974 that would soon be effectively represented in the best-selling work of nonfiction, *Common Ground: A Turbulent Decade in the Lives of Three American Families*, published in 1985 and written by former *New York Times* reporter, J. Anthony Lukas, who had already won both a Pulitzer Prize and a Polk Award. This book is also part of the city's media presence and history. *Common Ground* would also be recognized with a Pulitzer, as well as a National Book Award for nonfiction. It was the source material for a two-part made for television movie in 1990.[18]

Lukas's book, then, affirms the class divides and racial antipathies that are embedded in these films. In looking at these films as the beginning of a relative emphasis on the city in Hollywood films, we can begin to see the extant narratives that crime writers like Robert Parker and Dennis Lehane have built on. They also delineate that which has been so central to the filmmaking of Ben Affleck and Matt Damon: an image of Boston as a place of deep connections forged by both class and space. And though films such as *Good Will Hunting, The Town, Manchester by The Sea*, and *Gone Baby Gone* offer distinct and far more spatially and thematically articulate views of place and region, the distillation that is redolent of place in these earlier films can be heard in their echoes. These earlier productions, then, suggest the ways in which later mass-cultural entertainments have become more assertively place specific in the era of galloping globalization. Such affirmations of place may be seen as dialectically connected to the power of international commerce that leaves a shopping street in Istanbul oddly similar to one in Chicago. Both feature much of same merchandise, the same stores and storefronts, the recurring brands. In such a world, then, a city's distinctiveness may necessarily be elaborated in ways that reach into the past and which accentuate its residual features—often through iconic symbols. Chicago becomes the Cubs, the Wrigley building, the L; Istanbul, the Hagia Sofia, the floating bridge over the Bosphorus, the minarets of its mosques dotting the skyline. In a very contemporary example, the decidedly multicultural and the increasingly neoliberal city of New Orleans is experiencing significant social strife over the city government's decision to raze its monuments to Confederate icons.[19] These symbols are deeply meaningful to those who embrace a version of the city's past that highlights its resistance to integration and incorporation, a past that the neoliberal moment seeks to sanitize and minimize, and replace with a more resolute and anachronistic celebration of the city's multicultural basis. And while this latter version is also "true," it reduces the facts of strife and conflict. While I am fully in support of this action politically, it nevertheless is emblematic of the neoliberal desire to create place in particular terms. In Boston, in lieu of Kevin Lynch's map, we now have working-class regional accents and a reifying of the contours of spatial segregation—three decker houses in South Boston, age old resentments between Catholics and Protestants, a blind fealty to local sports teams, and a default racism. Such embedded signifiers of place are the stuff of historical misunderstanding, or, at best, very limited comprehension, offering nostalgia and not analysis. They are the unthinking rationale behind social intransigence, and thus deserve a thorough analysis and rebuttal.

Notes

1 Kevin Lynch, *The Image of the City* (Cambridge, MA: MIT Press, 1964), 3.

2 Sharon Zukin, *Naked City: The Death and Life of Authentic Urban Places* (New York: Oxford University Press, 2010), 221–222.

3 See Barry Bluestone and Mary Hoff Stevenson, *The Boston Renaissance: Race, Space and Economic Change in an American Metropolis* (New York: Russell Sage, 2000), 1–22; Elihu Rubin, *Insuring the City: The Prudential Center and the Postwar Urban Landscape* (New Haven, CT: Yale University Press, 2012), 205–220.

4 Eric Jay Dolin, *Fur, Fortune, and Empire: The Epic History of the Fur Trade in America* (New York: W. W. Norton, 2011), 145–160: Howard Bodenhorn, *A History of Banking in Antebellum America: Financial Markets and Economic Development in an Era of Nation-Building* (Cambridge: Cambridge University Press, 2000), 30–34.

5 Sharon Zukin, "David Harvey on Cities," in *David Harvey, Critical Reader*, ed. Noel Castree and Derek Gregory (Malden, MA: Blackwell, 2006), 114.

6 David Harvey, *The Condition of Postmodernity: An Enquiry into the Origins of Cultural Change* (New York: Wiley, 1992), 95.

7 See my *Starring New York Filming the Grime and the Glamour of the Long 1970s* (New York: Oxford University Press, 2011) for a discussion of the many films that prominently drew on New York City sites for filming.

8 Bluestone and Stevenson, 6.

9 Thomas H. O'Connor, *Building A New Boston: Politics and Urban Renewal, 1950-1970* (Boston, MA: Northeastern University Press, 1995), 105–107.

10 Ibid., 105.

11 See Rubin, 106–137.

12 See Bluestone and Stevenson, 91–99, 14–17.

13 See Gerald Gamm, Urban Exodus: *Why the Jews Left Boston and the Catholics Stayed* (Cambridge, MA: Harvard University Press, 2001), 222–279.

14 Louis Masur, *The Soiling of Old Glory: The Story of a Photograph That Shocked America* (New York: Bloomsbury Press, 2008), xi.

15 Bluestone and Stevenson, 51–73.

16 Ben Nightengale, "Orioles' Adam Jones Berated by Racist Taunts at Fenway Park," *USA Today*, May 1, 2017, https://www.usatoday.com/story/sports/mlb/2017/05/01/orioles-adam-jones-berated-racist-taunts-fenway-park-peanuts/101187172/.

17 *The Autobiography of Malcolm X, as Told to Alex Haley* (New York: Ballantine Books, 1964), 41.

18 J. Anthony Lukas, *Common Ground: A Turbulent Decade in the Lives of Three American Families* (New York: Knopf, 1985).

19 Richard Fausett, "*Tempers Flare over Removal of Confederate Statues in New Orleans,*" New York Times, May 7, 2017, https://www.nytimes.com/2017/05/07/us/new-orleans-monuments.html?_r=0.

6

Undead Detroit:
Crisis Capitalism and Urban Ruin

Camilla Fojas

Detroit is left for dead. And yet cities, unlike people and other sentient beings, rarely die.

William K. Tabb

There is an ongoing cultural fascination with the ruins of Detroit as a postindustrial landscape riddled with empty lots and abandoned buildings. Several artists, including the photographers Yves Marchand, Romain Meffre, and Camilo Vergara, frame the city for an objectifying tourist gaze as "ruin porn," as an obscene or unseen place that exposes some intimate reality about the US industrial past.[1] These artists provide a visual template and precursor to contemporary cinematic images of the city. Detroit is the sign of an era of rapid economic growth given way to globalization of production, the fall of the housing market, racialized poverty, and white flight suburbanization. In 2008, the city became a symbol of the economic freefall and its deserted factories and abandoned houses a harbinger of doomsday capitalism. Writers and critics describe the city using metaphors of illness and death and urge publics to seek remedies and antidotes against loss of urban identity. Within capitalism, collapse and decline are deemed a natural part of the boom and bust cycles that coincide with the US mythos of regeneration and rebirth. As such, Detroit is the perfect set for a number of dark stories about the city as a place of haunting loss and anxious abandonment by white people. A few recent films engage the city as haunting or horrific Great Recession ruins; these include *Only Lovers Left Alive* (Jim Jarmusch, 2013), *It Follows* (David Robert Mitchell, 2014), and

Lost River (Ryan Gosling, 2015), along with documentaries about the state of the city in decline, most notably *Requiem for Detroit?* (Julien Temple, 2010) and *Detropia* (Heidi Ewing and Rachel Grady, 2012).

Of the recent fictional narratives about Detroit, I focus predominantly on *Only Lovers Left Alive* for the way it offers perhaps the most haunting aesthetic engagement with the deindustrialized past of the city as undead, that is, one that persists after death, despite death and beyond it too. It challenges the prevailing metaphors of urban death by showing how the past might persist in the present. The story features a pair of vampires who bemoan the onslaught of modernity and preserve Detroit's cultural patrimony. They embrace urban decay and ruin as conditions befitting their nocturnal existence. In other horror films of this post–Great Recession urban ruin genre, the past is the stuff of terror and a menacing sign of all that ails the present. For example, *Lost River* tells the fictional story of an eerily haunting spell cast on a group of lone survivors that is broken only through violence. *It Follows* is a horror film about an evil spirit that inhabits white teenagers who, to vanquish it, ultimately dare to cross the symbolic border, the 8 Mile marker, that maintains the racial segregation of city to suburbs. The ruins of Detroit create the ambience, backdrop, and tone in these films about the haunting persistence of the past in the crumbling structure of the city. In contrast, *Only Lovers Left Alive* resists the objectification of ruin for genre-based effects and, in so doing, offers a unique approach to imagining the future of the city beyond the preponderance of spectacles of ruin. Other nonfiction works such as the documentary *Detropia* or the Unreal Estate project expound upon the nonlinear and anti-capitalist approach to the city. For instance, Unreal Estate re-signifies the built environment or "real estate" from capitalist systems of value. Taken together, these works refuse the narrative of crisis capitalism as one of destruction and renewal. These stories imagine another possible storyline and future, one not based on the logic of capitalism and "natural" cycles of ruin and resurgence.

Detroit dramatizes many of the symptoms of the 2008 financial crisis, particularly as they relate to housing and dwelling. While it is known for its car industry, it is also the municipality with the highest rates of home ownership. As a city that led the nation in homeownership and, by 2008, in foreclosures, it is the symbol of the role of housing in the United States. And there is no better example of the spectacle of the economic freefall than the series of crises, occurring over decades, that resulted in the city's bankruptcy. The city experienced a fall from the height of industrial wealth to the depths of racialized poverty. The ruination of the city began in the 1967 race riots that spurred white flight to the suburbs, thereby decimating the tax structure that sustains the services of the urban center. The signing of the North American Free Trade Agreement in 1994 set off another series of disastrous consequences in the hemorrhaging of car manufacturing jobs south of the border, where the Big Three automakers fled unions, enjoyed tax breaks, exploited low-wage labor, and avoided strict environmental regulations. In 2013, Detroit became the largest municipality to file for bankruptcy. Racialized poverty and deindustrialization intensified.

Detroit is a site that reveals the racialization of capitalism, its promise and mythos, its global expansion and the devastation it leaves in its wake. Marginal populations are instrumentalized as totems of national blight. It is also a symbolic center of capitalism's story as one based on the cyclical patterns of nature. Organic metaphors inform and drive the story of capitalism as the natural order of things, subject to the forces of entropy but always renewable. Even without infusions of capital, Detroit's recovery was afoot, not in actual terms, but in the phantom speculations of storyville. Stories of recurrence and return are part of the mythos of capitalism. The boom and bust cycles of capitalism are merely moments in an ongoing and endless cycle of ruin and resurgence and of death and rebirth. This is the mythos of crisis capitalism or the idea that capitalism has natural cycles of birth and economic boom, over-leverage or entropy, and decline into death, followed optimistically by rebirth. The catastrophes of capitalism are merely events of the natural world. Capitalist crisis is inevitable and certain and a precondition for rebirth.[2]

Imperial ruins

Capitalist-driven crisis is indeed not natural or organic but a consequence of the forces of empire and colonialism. And the visual culture of the city exposes this history. Photographer Camilo Vergara documents ruins in Detroit and various cities in the United States over an extended period of time as spectacular signs of lapsed greatness. Other artists fascinated with the decline of the city make explicit reference to empire. In *The Ruins of Detroit*, the French photographers Marchand and Meffre argue that ruin is the consequence of the "fall of empires" and they describe the city as a "contemporary Pompeii."[3] In his introduction to their book, Thomas J. Sugrue notes:

> The abandoned factories, the eerily vacant schools, the rotting houses, and gutted skyscrapers that Yves Marchand and Romain Meffre chronicle in the following pages are the artifacts of Detroit's astonishing rise as a global capital of capitalism and its even more extraordinary descent into ruin, a place where the boundaries between the American dream and the American nightmare, between prosperity and poverty, between the permanent and the ephemeral are powerfully and painfully visible. No place epitomizes the creative and destructive forces of modernity more than Detroit, past and present.[4]

The Ruins of Detroit locates the city within the global historical narrative of the ruins of empire, using Rome and European heritage sites as points of reference.

Camilo Vergara's take on Detroit also signals the fall of empires but is slightly different from other artistic renderings of US ruins. His story of the city begins in the Americas and locates the United States as an imperial presence in the hemisphere. He tacitly absorbs US cities—Detroit and other postindustrial zones—into a trans-American narrative, describing how his provenance in a small town in Chile shapes his aesthetic vision and authorial gaze. Vergara roots his fascination with ruination in the United States in his family's change in circumstance in Chile of the 1950s that left them impoverished. His family sold off their luxury furnishings and depended on extended family to fund private school and for the necessities of daily living. He attributes to this demotion in status his distaste for "objects of value" and an attraction to things that are "shunned, falling apart, and changing."[5] What he omits from his story is the political and cultural climate of the 1950s, particularly for a nation struggling with its relationship to the United States, a place to which Latin American elites would have ready access as part of the dynamics of US imperialism. For the United States, Latin America served as a crucible of empire through military interventions and covert operations, economic coercion through aid and trade agreements, the soft power of popular culture, and collaboration and cooperation between the economic elites of the North and the South.[6]

Significantly, Vergara's vantage is that of a Chilean who, upon arrival to the United States for a university education, finds "an immensely wealthy, self-confident, and energetic nation."[7] And while he does not explicitly state his aim as such, he proceeds to expose the opposite of his original impressions of the colossus of the North. While his work may fall into the genre of "ruin porn," it is also work that tacitly reveals an anti-imperial gaze, one that exposes the failed ambitions of empire and the disregard for racialized populations who are marooned when the tide of industrialization recedes.

In *American Ruins* Vergara insists on Detroit as an "American Acropolis" and proposes preserving the abandoned skyline in its current state as an "urban ruins park" and monument to the US industrial past. He notes that the response to this idea is outrage: "My proposal of keeping twelve square blocks south and west of Grand Circus Park as an American Acropolis—that is, to allow the present skyscraper graveyard to become a park of ripe ruins—is seen by most as at best a misguided and at worse a cruel joke."[8] He finds no support for this idea but continues to elaborate on it:

> Yet I am unable to give up the vision of an American Acropolis ... Why can't the planned rebuilding take place *around* the ruins, as it has in Rome? ... In downtown Detroit, as in Rome, it is still possible to marvel at the crumbling of such essential pieces of urban history. Are these not places where we can meditate on progress?[9]

While he notes the polarized image of the United States as reflected in a city that embodies progress and decay, the two extremes are not directly linked: "While the United States remains a leader in industry and technology, it also now leads the world in the number, size, and degradation of its abandoned structures."[10] Vergara tacitly suggests the larger geopolitical implications in this analogy that would identify the United States as an empire—with Detroit as its Rome at the center—within a critique of ideas of "progress" and "modernity," ideas that were imported wholesale to Latin America at the expense of local and indigenous cultures and histories. Detroit is an archaeological object that signifies both the end of an empire and the repositioning of the United States in the Americas, a reshuffling of the American hierarchy of nations. The display of empire in ruins is a cautionary spectacle. It recasts the modernizing storyline of colonialism as a kind of "chronicle of a death foretold." The decline of the city foretold the end of empire and decline of the capitalist formations structuring the city that inverted the place of the United States in the Americas. Almost a decade prior to Vergara's work on Detroit, Ze'ev Chafet described Detroit as "America's first Third World city."[11] And it is an internally colonized city that is starkly divided along racial lines.

The impact of deindustrialization disproportionately impacted African Americans. These conditions intensified during the Great Recession. Thomas Sugrue argues that after the World War Two postindustrial urban poverty was racialized and spatialized with the flight of whites to the suburbs. Sugrue argues that there is no single explanation for persistent African American impoverishment but a complex set of integrated factors with roots in the historical interrelation of housing segregation, racial discrimination in the workplace, and deindustrialization. Federal subsidies for highway construction created the conditions of communication for suburban development. Whites were incentivized to move to the suburbs with tax credits on new homes and their flight was further inspired by racialized fears. And blacks were violently barred from settling in the suburbs.[12] Post-crisis horror films about Detroit reflect this history to exploit racialized fears by playing up the eeriness and anxiety associated with white residential tenacity within the 8 Mile border or white traversal of black spaces in the city. The characters' refusal of the safety of white entitlements registers as terrifying. For example, in *Only Lovers Left Alive,* the protagonists live in an area of the city that has largely been abandoned, which suits their need for privacy and seems the perfect context for the undead. The white characters of *Lost River* remain even as their neighbors evacuate. And the main characters of *It Follows,* a band of teens, live in the suburbs but cross the 8 Mile border into the city to trap and terminate the spirit that haunts them.

With the exception of these recent films, popular culture tends to instrumentalize Detroit to tell a story about the reanimation of capitalism through ideas about urban renaissance. In post-crisis images, advertisements, and stories the city emblematizes rebirth and renewal in a manner that effaces the past and the conditions that caused and intensified its entropic decline. Conversely, the horror, vampire, and noir films of Great Recession Detroit are about the living past in the present that occupies and refuses to abandon it, that insists on the past, rather than the future, of the city. And of the various tropes of haunting in these films, that of the vampire lends a unique and productive intervention into the preponderance of organic metaphors and symbologies associated with urban death or what George Galston calls the "mortropolis."[13]

A death foretold

Urban scholars and writers use diverse terms to describe the city, some preferring organic metaphors that describe the dynamism of urban space. Peter Eisinger uses the organic metaphors of urban death that have fallen out of favor since Jane Jacobs's work on the life cycle of cities.[14] He argues that the understanding of urban death might be engaged more critically since it is the prevailing trope used to describe Detroit. Urban death doesn't simply mean effacement or being rendered nonexistent, it means a change in status through the loss of characteristics that define a city. These metaphors of illness and death are used in political exhortations to protect and preserve urban identity.

Peter Eisinger considers the distinction between urban and organic forms of death:

> Urban death, of course, is not identical to biological death. In the latter case the organism is eventually extinguished, but even the most distressed places tend to reserve a population made up of people who will not or cannot leave. At some point these places stop being what we call cities. Urban death involves the withering or failure of crucial urban functions involving governance and economic opportunity, as well as the diminution of lesser functions such as cultural preservation and the provision of public spaces... It is quickly becoming hard to call Detroit a living city anymore.[15]

Ultimately, Eisinger argues that the death of organic matter cannot be equated with the death of a built environment. The metaphor is merely an illustrative opening for further analysis.

This idea of imagining the city beyond organic capitalist metaphors of death and renewal is the subject of Andrew Herscher's work on "unreal estates." Under the rubric of "unreal estate," he describes the various projects to occupy Detroit differently in order to re-signify the city and cities in general from the capitalist model of expansion, growth, and economic development. He argues that a city in ruins, one that is contracting, is a site of possibility that opens opportunities not available to cities following a linear plan of development. "Unreal estate" refers to places or built structures that are literally outside of mainstream economies; these places or things have a different system of value, they resist valorization or are deemed without value. Once they no longer participate in a market system of exchange, they might be used for purposes other than the extraction of wealth and typical forms of use value.[16] They are entirely outside of a system motivated by profit. These are spaces in which the dissolution of capitalism is evident, if short-lived.

Herscher's philosophical project The Detroit Unreal Estate Agency imagines how we might oppose the idea of Detroit as a problem to be solved and encourages new ways of inhabiting space in the city. The agency's calling card reads:

> Dear Friend,
> I am not here to capitalize on the value of the real estate that you own, use,
> inhabit, identify with, or dream about.
> Any estates that I wish to capitalize on are wholly unreal.
> Thank you for your understanding.
> Detroit Unreal Estate Agency[17]

The Detroit Unreal Estate Agency "has been unified by an interest in animating valueless or abandoned urban property by new cultural, political and social desires." It is a powerful indictment of an approach to the city energized by the ambition to renovate and renew through capital and corporate investment.

Projects like Unreal Estate and other do-it-yourself (DIY) efforts proliferate throughout the city creating small communities and collectives. Private and individual initiatives step in where public services are defunct or ineffective. The city's low housing costs and low restrictions on business operations draw a class of creatives who might set up small-scale initiatives and create insular communities. This might be interpreted as an instantiation of Richard Florida's promulgation of gentrification through an influx of the (often white) creative classes to poor communities—a colonial settlement strategy that displaces marginalized populations.[18] And these initiatives may not be poised to make a significant impact on local tax revenue. Instead, the story of Detroit has been commandeered by another major figure in the home mortgage business, founder and CEO of Quicken Loans, Dan Gilbert. Like David Siegel, Gilbert made his fortune in the industry that brought the nation to its knees in the financial crisis. And he continues this legacy. Quicken Loans is the parent company of a new mortgage broker, Rocket Mortgage, that promises to deliver an eight-minute mortgage in a manner that recalls the easy lending of the 2008 crisis.[19]

Gilbert is part of the economic elite that guides state policy and represents the imperial power of the United States to shape global economic events. He set up shop in Detroit and has colonized a major part of the downtown with plans for urban revival in his vision and for his corporate and personal gain. His plans include parks and condos and businesses that only deepen the racialized economic divide between city and suburbs, inflecting that divide back into the city. Moreover, Gilbert's development creates a fiefdom organized by and around an industry that continues to assert its power to shape local and national policies.[20] It creates an image of the "rebirth" of the city through capital investment and development, one that is premised on effacing the urban past of decline, ruin, and the historic structures of the city's past.

Undead urbanism

The "death" of Detroit is imagined differently in Jim Jarmusch's film *Only Lovers Left Alive*, a film about a pair of vampires who resist modernity while living in urban decay that befits their need for solitude and nocturnal existence. Vibrant cities are defined as sites of the linear progression of capitalism, places that nurture modernity, industry, and technology. For Jarmusch, the film suggests, capitalist progress—accumulation, industry, planned obsolescence—is a force of death and the work of "zombies," or humans who participate in and perpetuate neoliberal capitalism (e.g., people in the music industry), while historical memory, creativity, literature, and the arts are the domain of the anachronistic vampire protagonists. The "undead" occupy the ruins of Detroit and actively preserve the legacy of the city as the center of creative forces— music, architecture, art, and literature. Unlike the display of Detroit within the visual culture of "ruin porn," *Only Lovers Left Alive* puts the vacant landmarks of Detroit into their historical context and ponders the future of a city within a culture dominated by capitalist "zombies." The vampire is an apt metaphor for the city as undead or beyond the biological cycles of nature—birth, death and rebirth or renewal—and perhaps beyond similar organic notions of the functioning of urban capitalism.

The vampires of *Only Lovers Left Alive,* aptly named Adam and Eve, recall the prelapsarian myth of Eden and graft it onto Detroit. Except in this instance, the fall is not the economic freefall of the city but the threat of its capitalist remake. Adam (Tom Hiddleston) lives in Detroit while Eve, his lover, resides in Tangier, but soon joins him. Adam is a musician who lives in a large dilapidated Victorian house in a desolate area of abandoned and unoccupied buildings, a perfect refuge for a vampire (Figure 6.1).

He surrounds himself with a collection of vintage instruments—Silvertones, Supros, Gibsons, and Gretsches—and what some might call obsolete technology—a Revox reel to reel, amps with tubes, a record player. He records music only for himself, not for profit, but sometimes releases his work to the world to leave his trace upon culture.

These vampires are reminiscent of the creatures of lore. Gregory Waller describes the vampire as variously "Transylvanian aristocrat, seductive siren, anonymous walking dead, superior natural creature, or satanic master-villain,

Figure 6.1 Eve (Tilda Swinton) and Adam (Tom Hiddleston) in *Only Lovers Left Alive* (2013).

even as bumbling anachronism or as cultured, romantic hero or as troubled isolated victim of immortality."[21] In this way, *Only Lovers Left Alive* draws on the mythos of the vampire as cultured and anachronistic romantic hero and "isolated victim of immortality" within the context of the neoliberal version of capitalism. The vampire in its other forms has long been a figure that elicits anxieties about repressed sexuality and sexual perversion that threatens to consume humans. But *Only Lovers Left Alive* is not about the vampire threat to humans. Humans are the real threat as purveyors of capitalism and contaminants of blood, water, and culture. They are totems of capitalist obsolescence and historical amnesia while the vampires preserve and carry global cultural patrimony across generations. *Only Lovers Left Alive* recuperates the history of Detroit as a place of music, art, cultural production, and architecture that, in its ruined state, is liberated from the constraints of market capitalism.

The struggle and tension of the story is not that between vampire and human but between notions of immanence and historical memory. The fear evoked in the story has more to do with the demise of the vampire and what this means for the role of art and cultural production in capitalism. The vampires thematize the presence of art and literature; for example, they use the aliases of Stephen Dedalus, from James Joyce's literary work, and Daisy Buchanan, the elusive female character idealized by Jay Gatsby in F. Scott Fitzgerald's *The Great Gatsby*. They bring forth the living presence of historical literary figures they knew personally, opining that Lord Byron was "a pompous ass" and Mary Shelley, author of *Frankenstein*, was "delicious," while William Shakespeare was a "poseur" and the work ascribed him was really written by Adam's pal and fellow vampire, Christopher Marlowe—a theory that abides in some literary circles. And, significantly, though not broached in the film, in 1819 John William Polidori published the novella *The Vampyre*, which is based on a fragment by Byron, and would ignite fascination with the genre, inspiring, among other works, Bram Stoker's *Dracula*. Adam and Eve are symptoms and signs of an intertextual literary matrix and preservationists of this cultural patrimony. They literally transport their literature as precious cargo and invaluable artifacts, carrying personal archives of books when they travel. They identify with these classic works and their deceased authors more than living humans or other vampires just as they, as kindred spirits, are out of step and marginalized in contemporary neoliberal culture (Figure 6.2).

Adam and Eve's relationship allegorizes the central concept of "spooky action at a distance," referring to Einstein's description of the theory of entanglement in which two correlated particles are separated and any effect upon one will simultaneously impact the other, even at a great distance. This suggests the intimate bond between these vampires while it signals the impact of actions across time and space, synchronically and diachronically or globally and historically. It is a cautioning to act carefully and with forethought—resonant in the case of the many contradictory ideas regarding the future of Detroit.

In *Only Lovers Left Alive*, Adam is suffering a sense of doom and has fallen into an existential depression; he is only able to write dirges, or as he calls it, "funeral music." Eve, intuiting his despair from across the world in Tangier, travels to his side. His crisis emanates from the threat posed by "zombies" or humans and "the way they treat the world," which makes him feel as if "all the sand is at the bottom of the hourglass." He claims they have contaminated blood and water and are causing decline and ruin the world over. Adam has come to the end of his immortality, a crisis that impacts Eve and for which she blames the Romantic poets, Shelley and Byron. She, however, is older and wiser and cautions him that "we've been here before," and reminds him of

Figure 6.2 Adam and Shakespeare in *Only Lovers Left Alive* (2013).

the Middle Ages, the Tartars, the Inquisition, the floods, and the plagues. But the current world order, we are to infer, is much more tied to the conditions plaguing Detroit, ones that emanate from the destructive onslaught of capitalist ventures and that destroy culture for profit leaving ruin in its wake.

Ava, Eve's younger sister, fresh from Los Angeles, represents the invasive force of capitalism upon culture. Ava threatens to expose their protected lair to the human world by indulging the old way of obtaining blood sustenance, through preying on humans. She is a contemporary vampire—like creatures of the vampire series *True Blood* (HBO, 2008–14)—who is wild, self-absorbed, and unpredictable, exhibiting all of the deleterious characteristics of the industrial center of capitalist culture, Hollywood. She is a "tourist vampire" who visits the city but shows no interest in its historical character, its residents, or its culture.

Adam, on the other hand, is aligned and allied with Detroit. His foray into the city at night to retrieve blood from the hospital, the only source of uncontaminated blood, is an evocative and somnolent tour of city history. We see the city from his vantage as he passes the luminous facades of empty buildings adorned with graffiti art. He gives a lamenting tour of the city to Eve at night when it is most looming and ominous in a way that captures the ethos of vampire solitude in a world that privileges the present over the discarded past. He shows her the city before its resurgent turn, before the vultures and zombies realize its lucrative potential—which she notes is its proximity to a vast supply of fresh water. The tour includes singer-musician Jack White's family home—part of the cultural legacy of the city—and the massive and iconic Michigan Theater that was built on the same site upon which Ford built the first automobile prototype and that now, in its lapsed greatness, houses a parking lot. This scene reminds us of the passing of Fordism along with the promise of US industry during the boom in car manufacturing. The car energized the city and indeed the nation's economy and was the symbolic center of the American Dream with its middle-class comforts and entitlements and immersion in consumer culture. As the unionized workers in *Detropia* attest, and that resounds in a constant refrain, workers no longer make the kind of living possible before the intensification of globalization. And the auto industry threatens to move remaining jobs beyond the borders of the United States. Jason Sperb notes that these depictions of empty spaces and decrepit factory buildings are imbued with nostalgia for a mythic time before racial conflict, deindustrialization, and economic decline.[22]

In *Only Lovers Left Alive*, Adam excavates the various historical epochs evident across Detroit, noting the archaeological layers that are often occluded in stories of the city as mere ruins. He points out the Packard plant "where they once built the most beautiful cars in the world." Ever optimistic and contrapuntal, Eve notes, "but this place will rise again." Adam is not so certain. They, like their mythical precursors, are thrown out of their Eden when Ava not only kills a human associate but also destroys Adam's precious vintage 1905 Gibson. Ava's presence signals the final rupture of the protagonists from Detroit. They return to Tangier without a connection to black market blood supply and resort to the old method of obtaining sustenance, feeding on humans. Their future, like that of Detroit, is uncertain. Yet they are highly mobile and have the means to move in and out of the city at will.

While *Only Lovers Left Alive* has its protagonists flee the city, *Detropia* shows what happens when residents of Detroit remain and how they negotiate the depleted landscape of the city under conditions of deindustrialization, economic austerity, and rollback. It is not, like *Requiem for Detroit* and other documentaries about the city, concerned with reviewing the historical circumstances leading up to its current deindustrialized state. Rather, in a manner much more akin to fictional modes, it presents a mood and gives affective resonance to the experience of the city for survivors. Like *Only Lovers Left Alive* the city is conveyed in often dream-like images accompanied by somnolent music and the overall style is observational—we follow subjects in their daily labors—though each subject is also presented through interviews. Crystal Starr, a videographer who documents the city, is reminiscent of Adam and Eve, who move through the city as the unseen undead taking in its lapsed greatness. Starr channels the ghostly residents of abandoned luxury apartments and narrates what she imagines occurred in their confines; she intuits the "memory of when it was bangin'." This is not a story of ruin and renovation, but like Jarmusch's film, a commemoration of the past and of Detroit during the boom years along with the story of the impact of the receding tide of industry. The story does not depend on a mythos of the organic cycles of capitalism, its inevitable rebirth, or the desire to be great again. Rather, from union organizers to individual business owners, *Detropia* documents the individual struggles of residents to survive and to better the city and who, despite the odds, remain. Eschewing the rhetoric of renewal and resurgence, Grady and Ewing dedicate the film to "the many Detroiters who work everyday to make the city a better place."

After the Great Recession, stories and images about the ruins of Detroit were as prevalent as the idea of the city's resurgence. From the art and writing about city ruins by Camilo Vergara and Marchand and Meffre, to autopsies of dead cities by writers and urban scholars, to the optimistic stories of urban renewal in the DIY movement, Detroit allegorizes the story of capitalism and its organic cycles of life, death, and rebirth. Horror films *It Follows* and *Lost River* make use of the city as a site of haunted ruins in which terror lurks in dark, often racialized, spaces (Figures 6.3 and 6.4).

Figure 6.3 Bones (Iain De Caestecker) in *Lost River* (2014).

Figure 6.4 Searching for Answers in *It Follows* (2014).

Jim Jarmusch's *Only Lovers Left Alive* uses the ruins of Detroit to imagine a different storyline and mythos in which the past and obsolete ideas and technologies reside in the present, albeit one populated by white characters making use of racialized aesthetic forms. It is not the capitalist story of supercession and renewal but of a supersaturated and deeply historical present that resists the linear course of progress and renovation. Likewise, the documentary *Detropia* by Rachel Grady and Detroit native Heidi Ewing eschews the language and logic of renewal and rebirth in their account of Detroit residents trying to make their immediate conditions livable. The film documents and visually preserves abandoned spaces and the people who remain after widespread and ongoing flight from the city. *Only Lovers Left Alive*, the Unreal Estate movement, and *Detropia* refuse to accept the "lifecycles" of capitalism that justify the creative destruction of the city and the marginalization of the poor and people of color to make way for new developments.

Ruins demand interpretation. In these cases, they represent a past of greatness and power, the memory of which inspires the rebuilding to return to former glory. *Only Lovers Left Alive*, *Detropia*, and the Unreal Estate movement resist the desire to rebuild the city, for the city to be reborn as a glorified version of its past. Instead, these cultural interventions provide an alternate imaginary of Detroit that eschews regenerative tropes and the organic lifecycles of capitalism. The Unreal Estate movement is the most explicit on this matter, urging the consideration of "real estate" beyond its capitalist framing and turning the built environment, ruins and all, into an imaginative landscape. *Only Lovers Left Alive* gives us a city that revels in its archaeologically layered history, while *Detropia* shows the daily struggle of living in the precarious conditions created by urban ruination. None of these cultural productions ends with a sense of optimistic upswing, revitalization, and renewal, nor do they suggest that ruins are a sign of the death of the city. Post-crisis stories of ruin, failure, and devastation contain imaginaries of new formations, of alternate ways of living in capitalism, of refusing its storylines and rerouting its linear course. These are not stories of life and death, of destruction and renewal, but of what happens when we no longer define urban space on organicist and capitalist terms. They imagine the city through different ideas about progress, futurity, and creative habitation to preserve the past and refuse the deleterious course of capitalist obsolescence and supercession.

Notes

1   Richey Piiparinen, "Are We Unfairly Stigmatizing of Rust Belt Photography?" https://rustwire.com/2012/02/03/are-we-unfairly-stigmatizing-of-rust-belt-photography/ (accessed April 29, 2017).

2   See Camilla Fojas, *Zombies, Migrants, and Queers: Race and Crisis Capitalism in Pop Culture* (Urbana Champaign: University of Illinois Press, 2017), 7.

3   Yves Marchand and Romain Meffre, ed., *The Ruins of Detroit* (Gottingen, Germany: Steidl Publishers, 2010), 16.

4   Thomas Sugrue, "City of Ruins," in *The Ruins of Detroit*, ed. Yves Marchand and Romain Meffre (Göttingen: Steidl, 2010), 15.

5   Camilo Vergara, *The New American Ghetto* (New Brunswick, NJ: Rutgers University Press, 1995), x.

6   See Greg Grandin, *Empire's Workshop: Latin America, the United States, and the Rise of the New Imperialism* (New York: Metropolitan, 2006); Camilla Fojas, *Islands of Empire: Pop Culture and U.S. Power* (Austin: University of Texas Press, 2014); John Mason Hart, *Empire and Revolution: The Americans in Mexico since the Civil War* (Berkeley: University of California Press, 2006).

7   Ibid.

8   Camilo Vergara, *American Ruins* (New York: Monacelli Press, 1999), 205.

9   Ibid., 206.

10 Ibid., 12.

11 Quoted in William K. Tabb, "If Detroit Is Dead, Some Things Need to Be Said at the Funeral," *Journal of Urban Affairs* 37.1 (2015), 1.

12 Sugrue, *The Origins of the Urban Crisis: Race and Inequality in Postwar Detroit* (Princeton, NJ: Princeton University Press, 1996), 8–12.

13 Quoted in Tabb, 1.

14 Peter Eisinger, "Is Detroit Dead?" *Journal of Urban Affairs* 36.1 (2013); Jane Jacobs, *The Death and Life of Great American Cities* (London: Random House, 1961).

15 Eisinger, 9.

16 Andrew Herscher, *The Unreal Estate Guide to Detroit* (Ann Arbor: University of Michigan Press, 2012), 8–9.

17 Geoff Cooper, et al., "Mobile Society? Technology, Distance, and Presence," in *Virtual Society? Technology, Cyberbole, Reality*, ed. Steve Woolgar (Oxford: Oxford University Press, 2002), 296.

18 Richard Florida, *Cities and the Creative Class* (New York: Routledge, 2005).

19 Eisinger, 8.

20 Ibid.

21 Gregory Waller, *The Living and the Undead: Slaying Vampires, Exterminating Zombies* (Urbana: University of Illinois Press, 2010), 3.

22 Jason Sperb, "The End of Detropia: Fordist Nostalgia and the Ambivalence of Poetic Ruins in Visions of Detroit," *Journal of American Culture* 39.2 (2016), 212–227.

7

The Flexible Urban Imaginary: Postindustrial Cities in *Inception, The Adjustment Bureau,* and *Doctor Strange*

Nick Jones

While cities in many ways change organically and even haphazardly, there is a significant history of top-down spatial management projects that have sought to restructure the urban environment according to a master plan. Influenced by what spatial theorist Henri Lefebvre called abstract space—the conceptualization of space as abstract void rather than embedded, historically contingent materiality—this kind of city planning presumes a broad spatial equivalence.[1] This spatial self-sameness allowed Baron Haussmann to raze Paris and impose new geometry upon it, Le Corbusier to propose a "radiant city" masterplan that would dismiss existing urban reality, and Robert Moses to cut through the Bronx with a "meat ax" in the 1950s.[2] Key moments in the history of modernity, these examples nonetheless speak to an idea and even an *ideal* of urban restructuring that remains prevalent today. Postmodernism may have arisen in part as an opposition to this form of abstract planning, and postmodern architecture may in many cases emphasize plurality and openness rather than monomaniacal uniformity,[3] but even so the conception of urban space as something that can be repurposed and intentionally molded in dynamic and even dizzying ways persists. Indeed, responsive restructuring

This work was made possible thanks to a British Academy Postdoctoral Fellowship (pf150084). I'm grateful to the academy for this opportunity. I would also like to thank the book editors, the anonymous peer reviewers, Hollie Price, and Alice Pember for their valuable comments on earlier drafts.

becomes ever more crucial in those postindustrial cities that were forced to remake themselves after the failure of their industrial economic foundations in the 1960s and 1970s.[4] A city's heritage and history may endure in this context, but it is subject to adaptation and commodification, and is in many cases stripped of embedded social meaning. Moreover, as digital technologies and virtual simulations have gained ground as tools of building design and city planning in the 1990s and 2000s, the conception of urban space as abstract, flexible and remixable has only become more pronounced. As a result, if there is today what might be called a dominant spatial imagination, a "unitary code or common language of the city," then it includes flexibility and a certain kind of virtuality as key aspects.[5]

To explore this imagination, I examine the representation of the city across sequences from recent blockbusters *Inception* (Christopher Nolan, 2010), *The Adjustment Bureau* (George Nolfi, 2011), and *Doctor Strange* (Scott Derrickson, 2016). Rather than look at the cinematic representation of narrative scenarios that directly or indirectly intersect with postindustrial urban changes, I focus on how the contours of the postindustrial flexible urban imaginary are visible within the motif of the flexible city in these three science fiction films (and beyond). A nonliteral presentation of postindustrial urban concerns and strategies, this motif crystallizes something of the underlying code of today's neoliberal cities. Engaging with the work of Henri Lefebvre and David Harvey as well as discourses around architecture in the digital age, I show how these films are symptomatic of a broader urban planning rhetoric that stresses the malleability and abstraction of urban space. This form of urbanism is increasingly influenced by digital logics of virtuality, adjustability, and hyper-connectivity; accordingly, these films conceive of the city as a malleable space subject to radical digital re-engineering. Their topological cities scale up the kinds of fractal or algorithmic architecture that is increasingly found in contemporary architectural discourse, and even echo modernism's concerns with abstract planning and highly engineered formal qualities, albeit with a new emphasis on a kind of plastic responsiveness and the potential for spatial remixing. Far from discussing the concrete, problematic, and often controversial realities of the postindustrial city, these films depict imagined zeniths of postindustrial flexible urbanism.

Tuning and remixing

Significant cinematic precursors to these recent visualizations of the flexible urban imaginary can be found in the much-written-about Los Angeles of *Blade Runner* (Ridley Scott, 1982), as well as the later titular environment of *Dark City* (Alex Proyas, 1998). The former depicts an overpopulated, hyperdense Los Angeles, a postmodern bricolage of architectures and technologies in which the boundaries between old and new have broken down alongside those between human and machine, and urban planning has not so much failed as it has quietly withdrawn to the off-world colonies. *Dark City* then amps up the spatial confusion of *Blade Runner* by having the city actually change shape overnight. The setting is an unnamed metropolis that floats unmoored through space, controlled by malevolent aliens seeking a better understanding of the human soul. To do this they endlessly and secretly revise and reorder urban space and the lives of the people within it. The city in both films is gothic, noirish, and mostly overpowering. Protagonist Deckard (Harrison Ford) may know his way around *Blade Runner*'s Los Angeles, but by the time he meets the replicant Roy Batty (Rutger Hauer) he is reduced to fleeing through strange, baroque spaces and across slippery, ornate rooftops. *Dark City*'s man-on-the-run Murdoch (Rufus Sewell), meanwhile, eventually learns how to control the space of the city—referred to as "tuning"—and so wrests command from the aliens and reshapes this urban fabric to his own desires (tilting it to face the sun; building a tranquil shoreline). In this, his character forms a useful bridge toward the films discussed in more detail below.

Meanwhile, a range of contemporary films similarly emphasize the flexibility of their urban terrains, and do so with extensive recourse to digital manipulation. *Elysium* (Neill Blomkamp, 2013) depicts a dystopian future in which the 1 percent have eloped from Planet Earth to the entirely manufactured idyll of an orbiting space station consisting of luxury mansions, panoptic control rooms, and technological superiority. Both *The LEGO Movie* (Phil Lord and Christopher Miller, 2014) and the *Resident Evil* franchise (Paul W.S. Anderson et al., 2002–17) portray highly flexible urban spaces: in the former, a city constructed from the titular brick toy is repeatedly de- and re-constructed by the "master builder" protagonists, while across the latter, material simulations of urban and suburban space are deployed to confuse both the films' heroes and their viewers.[6] Elsewhere, the bricolage cities of the *Dark Knight* franchise (Christopher Nolan, 2005–12), *Her* (Spike Jonze, 2013), and *Big Hero 6* (Don Hall and Chris Williams, 2014) evince a related conception of urban form that pays little attention to specific geography, even as these films also deploy iconic cityscapes for visual pleasure and recognition.[7] This perhaps reaches its pinnacle in a brief moment in *Transformers: Dark of the Moon* (Michael Bay, 2011), in which in the middle of a large-scale battle between alien robots in central Chicago, Beijing's CCTV Building can be glimpsed in the background. There is little reason for this structure to appear in an otherwise highly localized sequence, employing (and naming) as it does Chicago landmarks like Trump Tower, Willis Tower, and Lake Michigan. The CCTV Building (designed by Rem Koolhaas) is an icon in and of itself, part of Beijing's wider embrace of cutting-edge architectural projects of global renown. As such, its appearance in *Dark of the Moon*'s Chicago, marginal as it may be, further underlines the current presence of a digital, postindustrial urban imagination of flexibility and remixing.

These bricolage cities represent a highly intentional erosion of spatial boundaries and urban embeddedness, and implicitly posit that such amalgamated urban forms are best suited to the task of depicting the twenty-first-century city. Of course, films have always engaged in their own forms of "tuning," altering the urban environment in ways creative, expedient, and at times accidental. In the 1920s, Lev Kuleshov fashioned a single urban space from scenes shot in Moscow (with Gogol's monument and the Moscow embankment visible) and Washington (establishing footage of the White House). Playing continuity editing against itself to unify that which was disparate, he called this "creative geography."[8] This composite urban production, while an invention, nonetheless tells us much about cinema's relationship with space and the city, underlining the fluidity, virtuality, and produced nature of cinematic space. In the specific case of Kuleshov's work, what is communicated is the importance of monumental, branded architecture, and the articulation of the United States and the Soviet Union as twinned, mutually coexistent powers. Meanwhile, *Blade Runner* and *Dark City* depict futures in which "the circuits of space-time have been crossed,"[9] and everything from cognitive mapping to a stable subjective identity is lost in their resulting gothic milieux. By contrast,

Inception, The Adjustment Bureau, and *Doctor Strange* find excitement and agency in their contemporary flexible cities. Postindustrial or postmodern urbanism moves from being a source of threat to a site of possibility. In the flexible city sequences of these films, the materiality and fixity of urban space, if not abandoned entirely, is reshaped according to logics of ephemerality, adjustability, and hyper-connectivity, as cities warp, flex, or otherwise redefine their spatiality before our very eyes. In this space, the privileged individual can bend the metropolis to their passing notions. From a folding Paris within a dreamscape, to a hidden network of teleportation doors, to a kaleidoscopic "mirror dimension" of fractal disembedding, the cities in key sequences of these films evoke a post-Fordist ideal of urban flexibility taken to extremes and influenced by computerized planning and architectural design procedures. Operating as fantasies of the kind of flexible space described by geographical and urban theory, these cinematic cities remediate architectural discourses of topological and fractal building design. Furthermore, these films do not just reflect changes in imaginations around urban form, but actively participate in and help constitute a social ideal of urban form that functions in this virtually-but-literally flexible manner.

Postindustrial cityscapes

The roots of this flexibility have a long history, which it is necessary to describe before moving onto the films themselves. Space, as Lefebvre has argued, is culturally produced through action and expectation, and these social processes have long been controlled by capitalist structures.[10] Indeed, he proposes that cities are in many ways incubators where capital can effectively renew and expand itself, and that following the World War Two the reshaping of the city and social life by the "bureaucratic society of controlled consumption" resulted in a more comprehensive consolidation of urbanism as a way of life, meaning that in this period "the urban problematic becomes predominant."[11] Urbanization—a term Lefebvre explicitly prefers to "postindustrial society," although they are very roughly synonymous—is thus not just the physical process by which populations agglomerate in defined areas; it also names a broader social shift in which the entire world effectively becomes urbanized thanks to the importance and inescapability of capital forces that are shaped and managed by and through urban forms.[12]

This urbanized environment relies upon standardization and homogenization: rather than sites of historical, embedded meaning, capital seeks spaces of repeatable, predictable procedure, what Lefebvre calls abstract space.[13] Conceiving of space this way—and propagating this conception to and through the urbanized populations of the world—allows for the contents of space to be effectively reshuffled for the purposes of the market, a process of "creative destruction" in which space is simultaneously invested in and demolished to make room for new investments.[14] The dramatic "restructuring of geographical space" that has occurred from the 1960s onwards thanks to shifts in the global economic order relies upon and expands this abstract imagination.[15] This restructuring, by its nature, presumes the malleability of space: as David Harvey describes, postindustrial capital accumulation is "marked by a startling flexibility with respect to labor processes, labor markets, products, and patterns of consumption."[16] This concept of flexibility recurs in readings of the contemporary city and geographical labor practices. As Edward Soja argues, the "postmetropolis" that has arisen in recent decades is often viewed by economic geographers "primarily as an expression of a new regime of capitalist accumulation that is more flexibly organized than the rigid, hierarchical, mass production/mass consumption systems of the postwar era."[17] Likewise, for Guiseppe Dematteis, the post-1970s city is a less stable, more responsive and malleable entity than that which preceded it: a given city is now only "*one* possible, deliberate construction: a local geographical order born out of the turbulence of global flows and with which it must interact in order to continue to exist."[18] The city is not only more flexible in itself, but must communicate this flexibility to successfully participate in global labor and capital investment markets. No longer a static product of historical process, Dematteis argues that the contemporary city is a dynamic "product of self-organization," an "asset" of "risk capital to be ventured in global competition."[19]

The rise of the postindustrial city from the 1970s onwards, meanwhile, is also linked in much critical theory to another schismatic break, the movement from modernity to postmodernity. Soja is indicative when he describes "the major changes that have taken place in cities during the last quarter of the twentieth century" as a *"postmodern urbanization process."*[20] More generally, across a range of books from the last decade of the twentieth century, Soja and other geographers explored the links between shifting economic realities and experiences of space and time in the postindustrial city.[21] According to this work, the movement to postindustrial modes of labor in the United States (and, with less emphasis, Western Europe) has led to new—or at the very least significantly changed—spatial imaginations, architectural approaches, and urban arrangements.[22]

Cinema, by creating cities that look and function in certain ways, visualizes and propagates such ideas around urban space; as a result, it responds to and helps reveal prevailing spatial imaginations.[23] So, in his reading of *Blade Runner*, Harvey notes that the film's aesthetic of decay and its reliance upon simulacra both visually and narratively explores conditions of flexible accumulation and time–space compression.[24] Cinema, Harvey asserts, can act as a mirror to the postindustrial city of the 1980s (even if it cannot enact an alternative to what is shown to be a torrid, broken urban environment). Here, the term "postindustrial" points specifically to the *difficulties* of deindustrialization and the social, cultural, and economic fallout experienced by cities and people undergoing these changes.[25] Yet, if post-industrialism is defined by conditions of "startling flexibility," then these conditions not only produce ruinous fallout, but also engender an imagination of possibility.

It is this that concerns me here: the *idea* of postindustrialism as a force that frees the contents of space and spatial experience from the strictures of concrete, fixed terrain. An imagination of space as flexible (that is, an imagination of space as a stable, neutral surface with material contents that are re-arrangable upon this surface) may have a long history, but it becomes particularly important to the postindustrial city. As labor markets, production economies and consumption practices are seen to be endowed with a new-found mobility in the postindustrial era, so too space and the city undergo conceptual change. Geographers describe very real restructurings of lived space, but they also point to changes in our imagination of the city and space in an era of globalization, and as such it is necessary to think this flexibility as both material and conceptual, both "hard" and "soft."[26] This spatial shift occurred across the later decades of the twentieth century, and initial cinematic treatments like *Blade Runner* considered its deleterious and alienating effects. However, by the 2010s, and perhaps thanks to the proliferation of mobile devices and their own activation of a digitally enabled consumer-oriented subjectivity, cinema begins to think of this urban flexibility in more individualized terms, considering the contemporary city as a site not only of threat, but also of personalized adaptive remixing.

The flexible cities of *Inception, The Adjustment Bureau,* and *Doctor Strange*

In many ways inaugurating the current motif of flexible cities, *Inception* was a critical and commercial success when it was released in 2010. Its central narrative conceit is a machine that allows characters to enter the dreams of others, a machine used by the film's protagonists to both steal secrets and plant ideas. A team of thieves led by corporate spy Dom Cobb (Leonardo DiCaprio) design and somehow "build" realistic dream environments into which they import their target's sleeping consciousness, who is then tricked into unintended revelations. The spaces the team create are overwhelmingly commercial environments like central business districts, office lobbies, and luxury hotels (although traces of older manufacturing economies still remain in the form of an abandoned warehouse in which the team hides out). For all their illegality, Cobb and his team are corporate presences who adopt the spatial strategies of ruling powers as these have been defined by various spatial theorists.[27] Throughout, they build space to conceal, mystify, and control, designing it not only to prompt revelation but to engender the adoption or purchase of an idea (the inception of the title).

Having established that dreams can be built and occupied, the film then expands upon this by suggesting that dreamspaces can be transformed at will by the dreamer. Noteworthy scenes show Cobb explaining such rules to prospective dream architect Ariadne (Ellen Page) on the streets of Paris. This Paris, it turns out, is actually a dreamspace itself, and once Ariadne has got over the shock of its verisimilitude (she initially did not know she was dreaming), she calmly begins to manipulate her surroundings. She first bends the fabric of the city over on itself, and then creates bridges and other structures from scratch. The possibilities of such dreamspace architecture are further shown in the film's third act, when Cobb and Ariadne visit "limbo," a space of deep dreaming where Cobb and his wife Mal (Marion Cotillard) were previously trapped for many decades of dream time. Earlier glimpses of this period have shown the couple erecting (and demolishing) twenty-story buildings as easily as sand castles, and now we see in more detail the endless grid of skyscrapers they built. Director Christopher Nolan claims to have been inspired here by the work of Le Corbusier, Baron Haussmann, and John Nash, and in particular their utopian urban masterplans which, though well intentioned, could become "alienating and monstrous" in their uniformity.[28] However, dream architects Cobb and Mal embed the highly personal and historical within this corporate expanse: at the heart of the empty metropolis sits a plaza (filmed at the John Ferraro Building, headquarters of the Los Angeles's Department of Water and Power) with several half-submerged and out-of-place houses— one, for instance, is a small dilapidated French cottage. These, Cobb explains, are recreations of his and Mal's earlier domiciles, and he describes it as "our neighbourhood" as he leads Ariadne into the lobby of another modernist skyscraper, the elevator of which leads incongruously to Cobb and Mal's literal dream apartment, a Frank Lloyd Wright-style rural bungalow. Despite the emphasis on modernist and even premodern architecture, then, this limbo offers something of a postmodern urbanism of bricolage and eclecticism. As Cobb explains, while in the real world it would be necessary to choose to live in either a corporate skyscraper or a rural idyll, in this dream world both spaces can be impossibly conflated.[29]

Through its plot device of dream invasion and its special effects sequences of urban remixing, *Inception* offers literally a dream of urban planning. This planning is unhindered by local populations or construction realities, although both appear as echoes of themselves. During Ariadne's training sessions, Paris is filled with wandering pedestrians; projections of his subconscious, Cobb explains, this anonymous public go about their non-business until Ariadne's changes become too overt and noticeable, at which point they sense a threat and attack her. In this way, and in a similar fashion to *Dark City*, the city's body politic is assumed to be docile as they and their spaces are reshuffled, but their quiescence is strained should these spatial changes become overly noticeable and disruptive. Materiality would also seem to be jettisoned in Ariadne's restructuring, but it endures as an imaginative presumption, albeit in a changed form. Ariadne uses her mental will to change Paris outlandishly, but the way the city blocks lift, bend, and fold appeals to rational foundations and physical laws: Ariadne can only picture the city as a spatially extensive blueprint, one that she folds and reworks, but which remains a rigid, solid object undergoing intentional changes (Figure 7.1). The onscreen folding is also accompanied by the mechanical groans of enormous industrial gears, further underscoring the materiality that is imagined to underpin this virtual space (when the city blocks come to rest, inverted, on top of one another, they audibly thud into place). Ariadne may ask "what happens when you start messing with the physics of it all?," but physics and physical processes clearly endure in one way or another.

The Adjustment Bureau, released a year after *Inception*, offers a different but related resculpting of city space. The setting is contemporary New York, albeit a New York which is secretly monitored by a group of otherworldly (perhaps angelic) "agents." These characters carefully intervene in human events, and make sure history moves forward according to the master plan of an unseen Chairman. To accomplish his, they navigate the city in an unorthodox fashion: when wearing their magic hats, they use seemingly ordinary doors to traverse vast spaces instantly. Protagonist David Norris (Matt Damon), a politician destined to be a progressive US President but more interested in finding true love, is given a hat by a sympathetic agent in the finale, and pulls Elise Sellas (Emily Blunt) out of her imminent but ill-advised wedding and through a door that takes them from a New York Courthouse bathroom to Yankee Stadium. Another door at Yankee Stadium reveals a darkened stairwell; climbing this,

Figure 7.1 The streets of Paris folding over in *Inception* (2010).

they arrive above ground at 54th Street and 6th Avenue, where another nearby door takes them to Liberty Island. Through these various linkages, Manhattan changes psychogeographical shape. The materiality of the city remains stable, but the possibilities inherent within its geography increase exponentially.[30]

The locations visited are for the most part touristic—the Museum of Modern Art features early on, then Yankee Stadium, and most obviously Liberty Island—but even the fictional building that the agents call home (and which is only accessible using one of their hats) utilizes significant Manhattan locations like the New York Public Library (for interiors) and the roof of Rockefeller Center (for exteriors). This speaks to director George Nolfi's stated desire to film on location in New York as much as possible; more pertinently, in the context of the multiple teleportations, the city is reorganized from a real urban space into a series of contiguous, almost overlapping key locations. As in Kuleshov's creative geography, space is compressed. Here, the space created is an urban environment consisting solely of that which is noteworthy or architecturally beautiful. That said, the visuals in this film are less overtly spectacular than *Inception*: the city does not warp and bend before our eyes, and digital bedazzlement is restricted for the most part to the incongruity of walking through a door in one part of New York and arriving in a completely different part of the city. Postproduction special effects stitch these spaces together and even create an MC Escher-style shot in which Norris and Elise run onto the roof of Rockefeller Centre, then go back inside and down some stairs, only to run through a door at the bottom of the stairs and find themselves once again at the Top of the Rock. At this moment, coming at the end of the climactic chase, the topological control Norris has briefly exercised fails him, and the spatial flexibility of the city is shown ultimately to serve the agents of fate he has been attempting to outwit.

This film thus offers an intriguing reading of New York as a spatial multiplicity. For much of the narrative, we follow Norris as he tries to connect with Elise against the wishes of the mysterious bureau. At these moments, the city is a vast terrain, one almost impossible to traverse on time and in the ways that one would wish. By contrast, the agents are able to appear seemingly from nowhere thanks to their use of the hats and doors. However, the film still positions this teleportation as rule based and even spatially embedded: specific doors lead to specific places (rather than anywhere desired), and downtown

Manhattan is described as more teleportationally confusing than midtown or uptown thanks to the many layers of historical "substrate" and the build-up of overlapping portals. Such details negotiate between the dream of an entirely convenient and consumer-centric time–space compression, and a lived, concrete reality, albeit one with innovative and fantastic spatial connections. Ultimately, through its location shooting and foregrounded spatial specificity, *The Adjustment Bureau* takes the city as it stands, but makes it flexible through a (retro) science fictional technology associated with a group of characters who seek to plan and manage not just urban space but all of human affairs.

By contrast, the spatial restructurings of *Doctor Strange* bend cities entirely out of shape, but the manner in which this occurs nonetheless evokes similar ideas around the flexibility of urban space. In this superhero film, egotistical surgeon Dr. Stephen Strange (Benedict Cumberbatch) seeks a cure for his crippled hands beyond the bounds of Western medicine; finding a group of benign sorcerers, he learns their ways and quickly becomes proficient in magic. As part of his induction, he is told that Earth is mystically protected by three "sanctums" which together form a sort of magical force field. These sanctums are located in London, New York, and Hong Kong, and as they are attacked by malevolent forces, action sequences unfold in each of these urban centers. Most notable is an extended sequence in New York in which Strange and another sorcerer Mordo (Chiwetel Ejiofor) flee from enemies through Lower Manhattan. In this chase, the city is rendered unstable: the action is taking place in the "mirror dimension," a parallel dimension of irrational possibilities that the villain Kaecilius (Mads Mikkelsen) can bend to his will. To prevent Strange and Mordo from teleporting away from this dimension, Kaecilius waves his hands and makes the streets bend and become vortices, and skyscrapers ripple and split in two. Eventually, through these actions, the city as a whole turns into a literally kaleidoscopic space of suspended, fractalized architectural fragments (Figure 7.2).

The mirror dimension conceit, much like *Inception*'s dreams, allows *Doctor Strange* to visualize fantastical spatial alterations in urban centers. In London, the neoclassical architecture around Whitehall becomes a series of enormous, grinding gears, and a slowly curving street is turned on its side to become a rolling conveyor belt. The more sustained New York sequence, meanwhile, operates on a larger canvas, depicting the city changing in a

Figure 7.2 New York becomes kaleidoscopic and fragmented in *Doctor Strange* (2016).

variety of ways. Finally, a climactic showdown on a generic Kowloon street in Hong Kong (filmed in Longcross Studios outside London) shows various destroyed buildings remaking themselves around the battling central characters, as Strange uses his powers to reverse time. In all these sequences, the city is assertively not destroyed. When space is altered, it bends and folds (or in the case of Hong Kong, re-materializes in its original form). In New York, Kaecilius slams his hands down on the side of a skyscraper upon which Strange and Mordo are running; however, the structure does not buckle and the glass does not break. Instead, a rippling wave rolls across the length of the building in manner that evokes less any actual physical substance and more a kind of abstract, computerized rendering of fluid dynamics. As in *Inception*, sound design again asserts the materiality of the fluctuating structures. Ripples on a building are accompanied by a wobbling sound, like a large, quivering piece of metal board; when Kaecilius twists and splits this same skyscraper, it creaks and clunks.

As the New York sequence goes on, Strange and Mordo find themselves in an even more fragmented and fragmenting milieu, running along fire-escape-like structures which constantly assemble and reassemble under their feet. Meanwhile, around them and in the distance, aspects of the city remain as splinters—shards of sidewalks filled with pedestrians; lines of yellow cabs; sets of traffic lights; the spires of a church. At one point, leaping for a section of road, Strange even tumbles into a hole and slides through an upended subway carriage before landing back on the road. In these later stages of the sequence, even though space is changing constitution in massive and unpredictable ways, the city remains recognizable as such, and even recognizable as New York thanks to iconic elements like yellow cabs.

All of these films, then, depict what Anna Secor calls "topological cities": sites in which space is defined not by distances and fixed points but by "the characteristics that it maintains in the process of distortion and transformation (bending, stretching, and squeezing but not breaking)."[31] Trading in "post-Newtonian, nonmetric space-time," these cities may be radically reshaped but they do not collapse.[32] These are not cities under distress, subject to overwhelming forces that tear them apart or destroy buildings; rather, the remaking of them seems to be embedded within their architectural foundations. Designed to be bent, stretched, and endlessly remade in unpredictable but repeatable patterns, they visualize urban space as a kind of modular, plastic agglomeration of malleable elements. Urban space is here depicted as something simultaneously material (heavy, machinic) but immaterial and virtual in its malleability. The cities change, but they remain the cities they were and are; what we witness are the various geometrical figures that can be made out of the single, apparently relatively stable topological figure of "Paris," "London," or "New York."[33] *Inception* is perhaps most telling in this regard. As Ariadne reshapes Paris, she uncovers the real city: she generates from thin air a footbridge over Avenue du Président Kennedy which exists in real life, and through a play with infinity mirrors she produces the pont de Bir-Hakeim. The way her apparently improvisational interventions bring this initially vague and generally "Parisian" dreamspace closer to the real Paris indicates the inherent validity of her changes—the historical, material urban formation and the imaginative actions of the all-powerful dream architect are made to entirely align with one another.

While the films differ tonally, they all speak less to the experience of those caught at the sharp end of postindustrial changes than they do to those who have benefited from them. A postindustrial city engenders a postindustrial population, a white-collar workforce who can navigate the flexible economy and its global flows. These sequences may not directly concern themselves with gentrification and its reshaping of urban space, but they tap into an imagination of urban space that prepares the ground for this kind of radical demographic and economic restructuring. Just as gentrification pushes out existing residents and businesses that either no longer have the capital to remain or are not desired by the new cultural economy of a given area, so too the cities in these sequences alter according to the desires of an individual who is from a wealthy and/or corporate background. Ariadne, though apparently a diligent student, expresses no qualms about joining an enterprise that is, as Cobb admits, "not strictly speaking legal," and indeed this team of thieves is very much in the Michael Mann mold: professional, well financed, and educated. Norris may ride the bus and connect with blue-collar voters, and his topological navigation of New York may be hard won, but he is nonetheless shown to be entitled to reshape the city according to his desires—his wresting of control from the agents is emotionally endorsed and narratively necessary. And Strange may use up his considerable personal fortune trying to fix the injuries to his hands (suffered while driving dangerously along a coastal road in a sports car), but this concern is jettisoned as he becomes a superhero and takes up the mantle of world protector (and the spacious Greenwich Village residence that comes with it).

These characters wave their hands to reposition space to better serve their goals and moods in any given moment. As if designing or engaging with space on a computer screen, simple gestures enact massive changes in the urban fabric. And indeed, if these films arise from an imagination of space and the city that is influenced by postindustrial flexibility, they also crucially rely on the related spatial presumptions of digital technologies and their aesthetics. Such technologies are instrumental both in creating the digital effects of these films and in, more generally, allowing topology and an excessively flexible materiality to infiltrate architectural planning discourse. This discourse relies to a great extent on virtuality: an imagination of space that is both abstract and utopian, and which discards history and materiality for a blank slate of morphological possibility.

Dreaming flexibility

Topology has become increasingly important to geographers and philosophers across the 2000s and 2010s. Secor cites its importance in the work of Gilles Deleuze and Giorgio Agamben, as well as those human geographers and social scientists that have used the methodologies of these philosophers for analyzing space and experience.[34] Topology speaks to segmentation and connection, to the experience of the city as a divided and compartmentalized extensible space on the one hand, and as a network of connections that reinforce, overcome, and reshape that extensible space on the other. But it is also predicated on both movement and the imagination. As Brian Massumi describes, topological transformation can only be perceived in virtual terms, as that which is imagined as being possible.[35] Even so, Massumi identifies a trend in architectural design toward topological structures, "mutant" buildings which do not connect to the body's lived experience of space.[36] These "blob architectures,"[37] isomorphic architectures, or parametric architectures can only be realized through the use of complex algorithms and digital processing, as outlined by Branko Kolarevic:

> In the conceptual realm, computational, digital architectures of topological, non-Euclidean geometric space, kinetic and dynamic systems, and genetic algorithms, are supplanting technological architectures. [...] The generative and creative potential of digital media, together with manufacturing advances already attained in automotive, aerospace and shipbuilding industries, is opening up new dimensions in architectural design.[38]

The shifts thus enacted in built space are "fundamental and inevitable," as "models of design capable of consistent, continual and dynamic transformation [replace] the static norms of conventional processes."[39]

This use of algorithmic, topological design is most clearly visible at the level of individual buildings; Frank Gehry's Bilbao Museum, Rem Koolhaas's CCTV Building in Beijing, and the work of Zaha Hadid are standout examples. But this design methodology is also being used to reconsider the planning of cities themselves. In his introduction to a special issue of the journal *Architectural Design* (2009), Neil Leach asks, "How might these digital technologies help us to design cities?," and the articles that follow offer various views on the usefulness of algorithmic, parametric, and topological urban design.[40] If the various renderings of redesigned urban space that illustrate Leach's text appear science fictional, they nonetheless expound an influential digital urban imaginary that is sleek, modular, quasi-organic, and fractal. There is nary a brick nor pane of glass in sight; instead, everything in these computer-generated images (CGIs) seems to have been made from a sort of white-ish plastic polymer. Surroundings (roads, horizons) are constructed either from this polymer or rendered as a black void. Such hypothetical architecture seeks to do away with what Greg Lynn has disdainfully called "statics." Outlining the work of his own architectural firm, Form, Lynn's book *Animate Form* (1999) proposes that statics—and their assumption that architecture must be associated with permanence, usefulness, typology, procession, and verticality—need no longer dominate architectural thinking thanks to the rise of digital technologies for building conception and manufacture. He argues instead that "each of these [static] assumptions can be transformed once the virtual space in which architecture is conceptualized is mobilized with both time and force."[41] For Massumi, Lynn's work brings architecture closer to our topological, proprioceptive, and non-Euclidean being-in-the-world: digital algorithms informed by pseudo-organic flux create better buildings than cartographic plans ever could, because they retain dynamism, movement, and cognitive possibility through their logic of "lightness" rather than grounded structure.[42] Digitally inspired, -enabled, and -mediated architecture thus endorses, as Ellen Dunham-Jones puts it, a "future of unlimited possibilities," as the "speed, mobility and malleability of digital, nomadic, post-industrial culture" make obsolete any "traditional preoccupations with matter and substance."[43]

These words speak more to the myth of the digital than to its reality. Konstantina Kalfa rightly takes issue with Lynn's own assumptions and the kind of visual aesthetic he promotes (and Massumi endorses). Kalfa rebuts their rhetoric with the assertion that algorithmic, vitalist, or "organic" architecture is a "spell," "an ideological, mystifying device that relegates life to bare life, to a life that is stripped of culture and simply exists as a biological event."[44] This spell points to a dangerous dream of laborless production: wishing for 3D printed buildings erected at the push of a button disregards not only the labor processes and construction economies this sort of creation would displace, but crucially ignores the actual, material, highly "dirty" labor of 3D printing and its social, economic, and environmental footprints.[45] Sidestepping the existence of such realities, the city itself fades away along with the material production required to produce and maintain it, not to mention those actual biological events that populate it and rely on their surroundings to nurture and sustain them. Outside the realm of topological architecture, Gillian Rose, Monica Degen, and Clare Melhuish have described how digital visualizations of forthcoming urban developments and redevelopments, while they may have a photographic realism, nonetheless offer "a very particular sensory/ aesthetic vision of urban life," one that is "leisured, sunny, attractive," a dream of the future building rather than its lived reality.[46] In much the same way, the 3D virtual simulations of buildings and cities that are found in Leach and Lynn's texts argue for a consumerist space that can be built to order, and so needs to pay little attention to spatial specifics or existing populations. The virtualization process is in all these cases not only a means to an end (a marketing image, a design tool), but a reflection and mobilizer of a highly specific reading of urban space.

If *Inception, The Adjustment Bureau,* and *Doctor Strange* are influenced by an economy of flexible accumulation, then they are equally and unsurprisingly symptomatic of the spatial imagination propagated by these kinds of architectural visualizations and their digital technologies of production. Mark Fisher comments on how *Inception's* folding of Paris is staged as a kind of CGI engineering demonstration,[47] and all three films rely on digital imaging technologies to render their particularly digital urban flexibility. Indeed, Autodesk software like Maya and 3ds Max is used both by architectural firms like Lynn's Form and the companies constructing the visualizations that Rose, Degen and Melhuish speak of, and by film and television special effects houses (not to mention computer game design). So, both *Inception*[48] and *Doctor Strange*[49] relied on Maya to visualize their folding and fractal reshapings of Paris and New York respectively, while a lead architect at Zaha Hadid's architectural firm has written the foreword to a book indicating how useful Maya is for parametric building design.[50] Whether used cinematically or in architectural practice, the software allows designers to build, continually manipulate, and effectively visualize three-dimensional structures that operate in dynamic, visually arresting ways.

Such technological overlaps underscore the importance of computer culture in shaping these visions. This is made overt in *Doctor Strange* when a character describes how the "mystic arts" provide the user access to the "source code that shapes reality," a line which links digital creation, laborless production, and mysticism in a dream of individualized spatial practice familiar from Kalfa's critique. Meanwhile, shots in this film of London's grinding gear-like formations, or New York's wobbling and splitting skyscrapers, directly invoke the digital urbanisms of architectural firms like Form, and more tangentially might be thought to resemble a glitching screen-shot from a *SimCity* game. *Inception*'s dreamspaces are also notably aligned with cyberspace and video games, and offer their onscreen participants (and the viewer) a world that is digitally responsive, multileveled, and goal oriented.[51] The perception of the world as digital entity is no less important to *The Adjustment Bureau*: for all its nostalgic, arcane, or esoteric technologies (the hats the agents wear; a hardback book which maps the direction of fate in real time), the film depicts a city of topological access that could only be coherently imagined in an era of internet hyperlinks and wired connectivity.

This imagination finds cinematic expression beyond just these three films. Near the beginning of this chapter I mentioned several other films from the 2000s and 2010s which treat the city as remixable; further to these, a range of other recent media more specifically visualize ideas of urban flexibility, and similarly rely upon digital effects—and a digital conception of space—in order to do so. In *Ready Player One* (Steven Spielberg, 2018), the real world has become a cluttered and alienating terrain, and a virtual reality world called the Oasis functions as a key escape for a beleaguered US populace. The flexible possibilities of this virtual space are shown early on, as a digital New York unfolds and revises its layout in order to provide the terrain for a frantic car chase. Both *Upside Down* (Juan Diego Solanas, 2012) and *Star Trek: Beyond* (Justin Lin, 2016), meanwhile, depict cities that are bent and folded in gravitationally incomprehensible ways, using digital imaging to produce urban vistas that are at once novel (inverted cities in the sky; ribbons of skyscrapers scything through space) and entirely recognizable in their spatial presumptions (Figure 7.3). Finally, the Ariana Grande music video *No Tears Left to Cry* (Dave Meyers, 2018) finds the singer performing in the hallways, rooftops, and fire escapes of a spiraling, endless, multidimensional city that could only have been rendered—or indeed imagined—in an era of digital technologies. This proliferation of flexible, fractal metropolises demonstrates the potency of this digitally enabled urban imagination, and its apparent purchase as a municipal ideal.

Figure 7.3 Gravitationally flexible urban space: Starbase Yorktown in *Star Trek Beyond* (2016).

But as much as these examples are visualized using digital effects tools, the postindustrial cities they visualize have corollaries in the real world, such as the newly built Songdo in South Korea. A self-proclaimed "smart city" or "ubiquitous city," Songdo was completed in 2015 at a cost of around $40bn on land reclaimed from the Yellow Sea. It is structured around digital technology and automation: telecommunications company Cisco has wired the city so that it will harvest data on the movements, activities, even glances of its millions of inhabitants.[52] These people themselves benefit from a city with unparalleled connectivity—screens and other interfaces are built into seemingly every wall and surface—and Orit Halpern describes how the city indexes "a historical change in how we apply ideas of cognition, intelligence, feedback, and communication into our built environment, economies, and politics."[53] In the context of this chapter, Songdo operates as the virtual urban imagination made material: a site intentionally manufactured from scratch (on land that is itself human made), existing within segregated and specialized economic terrain (it is part of the Incheon Free Economic Zone) and ordered by and through digital mediation. As Halpern puts it, this city is "an elastic and plastic territory, infinitely mobile, networked to the information economy."[54] The city itself is not virtual in the same sense as a digital effect, but it points purposefully toward this virtuality as an ideal. For all its tangible concreteness, Songdo is explicitly an experiment as much as a holistic project: it is an example of the new urban epistemology of the "test bed" with which smart cities are frequently associated, an epistemology that presumes vast future rollout of similar but updated environments.[55] While Songdo does not have the overt malleability of, say, *Inception*'s Paris, it is an example of an urbanism that encodes flexibility and virtuality at its core, a site that seeks to concretize the abstract appeal of the visualizations discussed above. Songdo puts digital, postindustrial urbanism into practice on a clean slate and in the material world, and so highlights how important this conceptual lens is to contemporary urbanism.

Conclusion: virtuality and the postcinematic city

Just as Songdo is recognizable as a city even as it simultaneously rethinks what a city is through the concrete use and affective appeal of digital technologies, so too the shifting, remixing cinematic cities explored in this chapter combine familiar urban representations with virtualized understandings of space and time. These cities extend Lynn's argument that the "cinematic model" of architecture—one based on "the multiplication and sequencing of static snapshots" to simulate movement—is no longer tenable in a digital age, and should now be replaced by a dynamic understanding of architecture as immersing its occupants "within dynamic flows."[56] So while the city of *The Adjustment Bureau* may be edited together like Kuleshov's montage, this is not the most appropriate cinematic metaphor for the urban spaces of the above films. Montage or continuity editing relies on blocks of connotation or denotation which are assembled in particular ways in order to generate meaning. Space is in this way made stable, fixed as a coherent container for narrative action. By contrast, what the films examined here articulate is closer to a kind of "post-cinematic" register of space and perception. As Steven Shaviro has argued, "Digital technologies, together with neoliberal economic relations, have given birth to radically new ways of manufacturing and articulating lived experience."[57] This, for Shaviro, is a "new media regime" with a "different mode of production"—all of which he argues can be principally identified in the way in which new audiovisual media function expressively and the ways they generate affect.[58] In the case of *Inception, The Adjustment Bureau,* and *Doctor Strange,* we are provided an affective map of a kind of presumed utopian experience of the contemporary city. Rather than the more difficult and complex articulations of today's computerized financial economy that Shaviro explores in his case studies, the more mainstream entertainments explored here all admire the new media regime of personalized screens and digital flexibility. Linking Shaviro's "post-cinematic" media and a broader structure of feeling permeating contemporary urbanism, the cities in these films are both reflections of prevailing ideas and metaphors of postindustrial urbanism, and propagations of this urbanism and its digital contours.

This imagination of digital urbanism must be approached as an imagination, a conception of hypothetical possibility. Lefebvre has claimed that the urban should be defined "not as an accomplished reality, [...] but rather as a horizon, an illuminating virtuality."[59] The urban is never achieved, but it is thought and perpetually planned. Following this, all of these films offer us a glimpse of what the concept "urban" looks like today: these are not accomplished literal manifestations of the urban, they are instead visualizations of its horizons of potential, expectation, and intention. In this, they operate both as an "illuminating virtuality" in Lefebvre's terms and also themselves illuminate the very amplified virtuality that lies at the heart of contemporary urbanism. This is a digital virtuality which, as I have shown, is influenced by computer technologies and regimes of postindustrial flexible accumulation. Bringing the master planning of modernity and the bricolage of postmodernity together, the films analyzed in detail here literalize the flexibility imagined by the postindustrial urban planner.

The films even to an extent highlight this virtuality in their narratives and through their use of digital effects tools: the "plastic and elastic" malleability of the city is in each case strongly delineated as an alternative realm, be it a dreamspace, hidden mystical connections, or an alternative dimension, and the digital spectacle of the sequences demarcates and amplifies their unreality. So, for all that these films literalize and make material what Halpern calls the "infinite mobility" of today's postindustrial urbanism, they also accentuate that this mobility is a possibility more than a reality. In this, they ultimately reaffirm the logic of virtuality used to construct these sequences and which operates as a key aesthetic determinant and visual pleasure. In the terms introduced above, the cities function according to the epistemology of the test bed: these are imaginative realms in which to experiment and hone the way the city is organized. As a result, they also further a particular urban imagination which views the very material city itself as a site of instant, digitally influenced, and -imagined reorganization. For all that these urban remixings are materially lived by onscreen characters who navigate the shifting spaces in an embodied, tactile manner, the use of digital effects and the post-cinematic register in which they operate keep these cities within the realms of the utopian and imaginary. Far from creating distance between these outlandish urban environments and our actual postindustrial present, this actually bonds fact and fiction together all the more overtly, powerfully demonstrating the presence of a flexible urban imaginary that overoptimistically illuminates the contemporary city.

Notes

1   Henri Lefebvre, *The Production of Space*, trans. Donald Nicholson-Smith (Oxford: Blackwell, 1991).

2   On Robert Moses, see Marshall Berman, *All That Is Solid Melts into Air: The Experience of Modernity* (London and New York: Verso, 1983), 294.

3   Charles Jencks, *Critical Modernism: Where Is Post-Modernism Going?* (Chichester: Wiley-Academy, 2007).

4   See Lawrence Webb, *The Cinema of Urban Crisis: Seventies Film and the Reinvention of the City* (Amsterdam: Amsterdam University Press, 2014).

5   Lefebvre, *Production*, 73.

6   For more on the spatial dissembling of the *Resident Evil* franchise, see my "This Is My World: Spatial Representation in the *Resident Evil* Films," *Continuum* 45.1 (2016).

7   In the *Dark Knight* franchise, Gotham City is built from often recognizable portions of Chicago and New York. *Her* is set in Los Angeles but has been filmed in both that city and Shanghai to create a composite urban space—for a detailed reading of this mixing, see Lawrence Webb, "When Harry Met Siri: Digital Romcom and the Global City in Spike Jonze's *Her*," in *Global Cinematic Cities: New Landscapes of Film and Media*, ed. Johan Andersson and Lawrence Webb (London and New York: Wallflower, 2016), 95–118. In another example of United States–Asian fusion, *Big Hero 6* is set in San Fransokyo, a city with the geography of San Francisco but with Japanese urban mise-en-scene (the Golden Gate Bridge is adorned with torii-style detailing, for instance).

8 Lev Kuleshov, "Art of the Cinema," in *Kuleshov on Film: Writings by Lev Kuleshov*, ed. and trans. Ronald Levaco (Berkeley, Los Angeles, and London: University of California Press, 1974), 52.

9 Marcus A. Doel, and David B. Clarke, "From Ramble City to the Screening of the Eye: *Blade Runner*, Death and Symbolic Exchange," in *The Cinematic City*, ed. David B. Clarke (London and New York: Routledge, 1997), 142.

10 Lefebvre, *Production of Space*, 73.

11 Ibid., 277–278; Henri Lefebvre, *The Urban Revolution*, trans. Robert Bononno (Minneapolis: University of Minnesota Press, 2003), 163–164, 5, 31.

12 Ibid., 2, 4.

13 Lefebvre, *Production of Space*, 229–291.

14 See David Harvey, *The Condition of Postmodernity* (Cambridge, MA and Oxford: Blackwell, 1990), 16–18, 106–107; and David Harvey, "Neoliberalism as Creative Destruction," *Geografiska Annaler* B 88.2 (2006).

15 Neil Smith, *Uneven Development: Nature, Capital, and the Production of Space* (Athens: University of Georgia Press, 1984), 1.

16 David Harvey, *The Urban Experience* (Baltimore, MD: Johns Hopkins University Press, 1989), 256.

17 Edward Soja, "Exploring the Postmetropolis," in *Postmodern Geography: Theory and Praxis*, ed. Claudio Minca (Oxford and Malden, MA: Blackwell, 2001), 42.

18 Giuseppe Dematteis, "Shifting Cities," in *Postmodern Geography: Theory and Praxis*, ed. Claudio Minca (Oxford and Malden, MA: Blackwell, 2001), 113.

19 Ibid., 118.

20 Edward Soja, "Postmodern Urbanization: The Six Restructurings of Los Angeles," in *Postmodern Cities and Spaces*, ed. Sophie Watson and Katherine Gibson (Oxford and Cambridge, MA: Blackwell, 1995), 125.

21 See, for instance, Michael J. Dear, *The Postmodern Urban Condition* (Oxford: Blackwell, 2000); Harvey, *Condition of Postmodernity;* Claudio Minca, ed., *Postmodern Geography: Theory and Praxis* (Oxford and Malden, MA: Blackwell, 2001); Edward Soja, *Postmodern Geographies* (London and New York: Verso, 1989); Sophie Watson and Katherine Gibson, eds., *Postmodern Cities and Spaces* (Oxford and Cambridge, MA: Blackwell, 1995).

22 For Fred Block, postindustrialism is defined above all by three trends that work against long-standing industrial frameworks, all of which shore up previously static or fixed structures: first, the growth of the service economy in size and importance; secondly, computerization and automation; and thirdly, a less linear and rigorously structured "life course" (the labor force now consisting of both

men and women who may change labor roles several times in their lives). Block, *Postindustrial Possibilities: A Critique of Economic Discourse* (Berkeley, Los Angeles, and Oxford: University of California Press, 1990), 10–11.

23 For more on this, see my "The Visual Production of Urban Space: Lefebvre, the City and Cinema," in *Routledge Handbook of Henri Lefebvre, the City and Urban Society*, ed. Michael E. Leary-Owhin and John P. McCarthy (London and New York: Routledge, forthcoming).

24 Harvey, *Condition of Postmodernity*, 313.

25 In this, the postindustrial is perhaps intuitively posited as a counter term to the postmodern in the context of urban form. The latter, as Michael Dear describes in *The Postmodern Urban Condition*, is all "glittering surfaces" (64), while the former is more embedded in concrete spatial changes and the systemic modifications that have engendered them. ("Postindustrialism," when the term is employed today, also benefits from an implicit economical-spatial emphasis, one which happily escapes the millennial fervor with which the postmodern is often loaded.)

26 Jonathan Raban, *Soft City* (New York: E.P. Dutton, 1974).

27 See my *Hollywood Action Films and Spatial Theory* (London and New York: Routledge, 2015), which draws on texts such as Lefebvre's *Production of Space*.

28 Quoted in Joe Fordham, "In Dreams," *Cinefex* 123 (2010), 66.

29 These comments highlight the audacious double standard of Cobb and Mal's architectural and planning ideology: seeing the value of memory, history, and personalization, they have nonetheless built a city purposefully lacking these (except in their own private enclave).

30 Elsewhere, I have written about sequences from *Sherlock Jr.* (1924), *Jumper* (2008), and *Thor: The Dark World* (2013) which teleportationally compress global or multidimensional spaces in similar ways: see *Hollywood Action Films*, 50–54.

31 Anna Secor, "Topological City (2012 Urban Geography Plenary Lecture)," *Urban Geography* 34.4 (2013), 431.

32 Ibid., 433.

33 Brian Massumi, *Parables of the Virtual: Movement, Affect, Sensation* (Durham, NC and London: Duke University Press, 2002), 134.

34 Secor, 435–436.

35 Massumi, 134–135.

36 Ibid., 177.

37 Luciana Parisi, *Contagious Architecture: Computation, Aesthetics, and Space* (Cambridge, MA and London: MIT Press, 2013), xi.

38 Branko Kolarevic, "Designing and Manufacturing Architecture in the Digital Age," *Architectural Information Management* 5 (2001), 117.

39 Ibid., 123.

40 Neil Leach, 'Introduction," *Architectural Design*, special issue on *Digital Cities* 79.4 (2009), 8.

41 Greg Lynn, *Animate Form* (Princeton, NJ: Princeton Architectural Press, 1999), 13.

42 Ibid., 290 n. 29; see also 183.

43 Ellen Dunham-Jones, "New Urbanism as a Counter-Project to Post-Industrialism," *Places* 13.2 (2000), 26; see also Rem Koolhaas, *S M L XL* (New York: Monacelli, 1995).

44 Kalfa, Konstantina, "Where the Spell Is Chanted (Fallacies of Contemporary Architectural Discourses)," *Architecture and Culture* 3.3 (2015), 317.

45 Ibid., 318.

46 Gillian Rose, Monica Degen, and Clare Melhuish, "Dimming the Scintillating Glow of Unwork: Looking at Digital Visualisations of Urban Redevelopment Projects," in *Cities Interrupted: Visual Culture and Urban Space*, ed. Shirley Jordan and Christoph Lindner (London and New York: Bloomsbury, 2016), 109.

47 Mark Fisher, "The Lost Unconscious: Delusions and Dreams in *Inception*," *Film Quarterly* 64.3 (2011), 40.

48 See Fordham, 48.

49 Mike Seymour, "Doctor Strange's Magical Mystery Tour in Time," *fxguide*, November 14, 2016, https://www.fxguide.com/featured/dr-stranges-magical-mystery-tour-in-time/ (accessed July 20, 2017).

50 Fulvio Wirz, "Foreword," in *Parametric Building Design Using Autodesk Maya* (Abingdon and New York: Routledge). It is not always the case that Maya is used for architectural design, since there are other packages that specialize in this (such as Autodesk's 3ds Max and Dessault Systèmes's CATIA) which do not have Maya's emphasis on moving-image rendering and real-world texturing. For a full account of the use of Maya in creating animations, see Aylish Wood, *Software, Animation and the Moving Image: What's in the Box?* (Basingstoke and New York: Palgrave, 2015).

51 Elizabeth Tan, "The Only Way You Can Dream: Interfaces and Intolerable Spaces in Christopher Nolan's *Inception*," *Continuum* 30.4 (2016), 409.

52 Orit Halpern, *Beautiful Data: A History of Vision and Reason since 1945* (Durham, NC and London: Duke University Press, 2015), 3.

53 Ibid., 4.

54 Ibid., 33.

55 Nerea Calvillo, Orit Halpern, Jesse LeCavalier, and Wolfgang Pietsch, "Test Bed as Urban Epistemology," in *Smart Urbanism: Utopian Vision or False Dawn?* ed. Simon Marvin, Andrés Luque-Ayala and Colin McFarlane (London and New York: Routledge, 2016).

56 Lynn, 11.

57 Steven Shaviro, *Post-Cinematic Affect* (Winchester and Washington: Zero Books, 2002), 2.

58 Ibid., 2–3.

59 Lefebvre, *Revolution*, 16–17.

8

A Networked Life:
Representations of Connectivity and Structural Inequalities in *Fruitvale Station*

Amy Corbin

Fruitvale Station, a feature film directed by Ryan Coogler in 2012, was released just as the issue of police and vigilante violence against African American men was reaching a new prominence in the United States. The film is based on the story of Oscar Grant, who was killed by a transit officer in Oakland, California in 2009. But it entered movie theaters just as George Zimmerman was on trial for the killing of Trayvon Martin in July 2013, creating a parallel between film and reality. Since then, killings of black men or boys, usually by police officers, continue to make headlines. And like some of these, the shooting of Grant was captured on cell phone video, marking another convergence of social issue and moving images.

Fruitvale Station is a fictional version of a true story, and includes some video footage from the shooting at the beginning of the film and from a rally held in Oakland after Grant's death at the film's end. Its complex interplay between reality and dramatization makes it a unique intervention into public discourse not only on police shootings, but also on the broader issues of systemic injustices facing young African American men and their representation in fiction film. Starting with an analysis of the narrative structure and techniques of filming locations and mobility, this chapter then explores how the film situates the specificity of Grant's life within broader structures of racialization, economics, and policing. I argue that the film's ability to keep both the individual and his social context in sharp focus is accomplished through a nuanced depiction of what can be called a "networked" life. Coogler delivers a narrative that documents Grant's physical and digital connections to people in different locations and of different social positions, and at the same time insists that these connections were not enough to allow Grant to transcend economic constraints and racialized violence.

Shaping reality into fiction

While this chapter is about a fictional film, it is essential to give a brief account of what happened to the real Oscar Grant, both to honor his memory and because the way that Coogler shaped real events into a feature film is important to understanding the film's power. I will refer to the real Oscar Grant by his last name and to the fictionalized character by his first name. Grant was a 22-year-old man from Hayward, California, located in the East Bay of San Francisco. He was heading back from New Year's Eve festivities in San Francisco when he and his friends were pulled off a Bay Area Rapid Transit (BART) train car onto the Fruitvale Station platform by BART officers who were looking for the people involved in a fight that had been reported on the train. Tensions rose as Grant and his friends were questioned without being charged and taunts were exchanged. Grant was forced to lie on the platform face down and resisted being cuffed, at which point Officer Johannes Mehserle shot him in the back. Grant died a few hours later at a hospital. Officer Mehserle, who claimed he was reaching for his taser instead of his gun, was found guilty of involuntary manslaughter, instead of the more substantial charges of second-degree murder or voluntary manslaughter. He was sentenced to two years, of which he served eleven months. Cell phone video footage was key to the way the public understood the incident—within days, hundreds of thousands of people watched several videos that bystanders posted online. There were protests around the Bay Area for what was considered a light sentence and continue to be yearly vigils.[1]

When asked about making Grant's story into a fiction film, Coogler said:

> I personally believe that narrative filmmaking, when done right, can get you closer to a character than a documentary can. In this story, I wanted the audience to be as close to Oscar as possible, without the barrier of the character knowing that he is being filmed ...[2]

I wanted the audience to get to know this guy, to get attached … so that when the situation that happens to him happens, it's not just like you read it in the paper, you know what I mean? When you know somebody as a human being, you know that life means something.[3]

Coogler here distinguishes between fiction and nonfiction such as documentary or journalism—a significant choice when one is dealing with a true event and one that represents urgent political and social problems of the moment. His priority was getting the audience "close" to Oscar, which appears to mean emotional attachment and intimacy. His means to accomplish this goal was to create a compressed narrative structured around the details of Oscar's last day of life, rather than a more expansive narrative in terms of temporality or character point of view. In this way, Coogler "attaches" the audience to Oscar, allowing *Fruitvale Station* to contribute to an ongoing project of African American filmmaking: creating young, black male characters that defy the still-pervasive stereotypes of violence and criminality, and placing them in emotionally intense situations intended to move viewers of all different backgrounds.

Much of the narrative is taken up by the mundane routines of Oscar's day, with little dramatic tension—except that the audience watches knowing what will happen at the end, since the film begins with some of the real cell phone video footage taken in the moments of the shooting. So viewers are split between what we might call a neorealist attention to small details, in which we closely follow our main character's largely unremarkable daily activities, and a retrospective narrative point of view that distances us from Oscar because we know his fate and he, of course, does not. The spectator's greater range of knowledge is one element of a didactic mode that is found in many films about young African Americans coming of age in the city, from the "hood" films of the early 1990s, such as *Boyz N the Hood* (John Singleton, 1991), *Menace II Society* (Allen and Albert Hughes, 1993), to later examples like *ATL* (Chris Robinson, 2006) and *Dope* (Rick Famuyiwa, 2015). Such films often use a short narrative time frame and an emphasis on everyday life, but combine these narrative choices with overt addresses to the audience via voiceover or text printed on the screen. The text or voice may instruct the audience on the crime and poverty in the neighborhood, introduce the fictional characters, or foreshadow the ending. The result is to give the audience a sense of studying the diegetic world from a sociological perspective, seeing the narrative as a representation of social forces and positions. So through the very precise attention to small-scale actions, the audience is meant to understand that the individual characters' lives represent thousands of real people. Further, the blending of the realist and the didactic modes means that such films can address both viewers who share these life experiences and those who are "outsiders," whom the films assume a mission to educate.[4]

In *Fruitvale Station*, Coogler invents minor incidents and condenses them into a 24-hour timeframe in order to convey the texture of life in low-income areas of the East Bay as well as how lives there are connected to broader social phenomena, including mass incarceration and the limited options available to ex-felons, income inequality, and racially biased policing. Elements of the film are specific to the San Francisco Bay Area, including the architecture of neighborhoods and the wealth gaps made more pronounced by the new technology economy. Other key elements, including the near-constant use of cellular phones, are experienced by a broad swath of the US population. Oscar's loving and joking interactions with his family members—such as when he buys a greeting card with a wholesome-looking white family on it to playfully jab at his sister—present ordinary interactions many people can relate to. The variety of narrative scenarios that arise from a day in Oscar's life allows Coogler to blend elements that are specific to geography, race, and class with more generalizable experiences.

Urban itineraries: Oscar's mobility and senses of place

These goals of the specific and the broad are accomplished largely through a thematic emphasis on Oscar's physical mobility and digital connectivity. The "day-in-the-life" narrative focuses on Oscar's travel, encounters in various parts of the Bay Area, and his cellular communication with a variety of people. The film starts with the time stamp "Hayward California; New Year's Eve 2008; 12:10 am," evoking the rhetoric of documentary as well as attention to minute detail. Oscar and his girlfriend Sophina are in bed when their daughter Tatiana interrupts them because she cannot sleep. The family then resettles in bed and when Oscar notices it is December 31, he sends a quick "Happy Birthday" text message to his mother, Wanda, before going to sleep. A brief montage follows: an establishing shot of the skyline of San Francisco with a swath of the East Bay in the foreground, a long shot of a BART train on elevated tracks running through a neighborhood at dawn, and thirdly a close-up of a shower head. The montage signals the interconnection of the metropolitan, the neighborhood, and the domestic home, three geographic scales that all shape Oscar's life. It also foreshadows the narrative, in which Oscar will traverse several cities in the Bay Area and then get fatally shot outside of a train.

The film's attention to the granular details of place and of a daily routine can be seen by recounting the narrative as if it were a personalized "map" of the San Francisco area. Such a narrative map replaces the common definition of a map—an abstract and unchanging representation of locations in relation to each other—with an experiential and time-based map, charting the itinerary of one individual and how his journey connects one place to another in a manner specific to his own social position and personal relationships. Such a dynamic conception of mapping has been employed by Allan Pred, among other geographers. Pred mapped daily paths of individuals and, by assembling them, could create a complex "time-geography" of a city that depicted "the interplay between individual behavior and experience, the everyday and place-specific workings of society, and particular forms of social and spatial transformation."[5]

So after the prologue described above we observe Oscar, Sophina, and Tatiana as they get ready in the morning, and Oscar drives Tatiana to day care and Sophina to work. He then heads north from Hayward to Oakland, entering Farmer Joe's, a real natural foods market in the Dimond district of Oakland, where he buys food for his mother Wanda's birthday dinner and pleads with his former boss to get his job. He then goes back to his house in Hayward, worries over rent that is due as well as helping his sister with her rent, goes to another store to get his mother a birthday card, and heads to the western edge of Oakland, right by the Bay, to fill his gas tank and meet Marcus, a drug-dealing acquaintance to discuss a sale. At the end of the work day, he returns to Hayward to pick up Sophina and Tatiana, spend some time at Sophina's grandmother's house, attend Wanda's birthday party, and finally drop Tatiana off at Sophina's sister's house to go to bed, while he and Sophina head to the South Hayward BART station to join their friends and travel into

San Francisco for New Year's Eve festivities. It is on the return train from San Francisco to Hayward, which passes through Oakland's Fruitvale BART station, that Oscar is shot.

The choice to document Oscar's activities on this micro-level, including inserting enough place markers that someone who knows the Bay Area can, in fact, "map out" Oscar's last day by watching the film, aligns the film with traditions of neorealism, including shooting on location (for example, on the actual Fruitvale Station train platform) and attending to the mundane details of life.[6] The diversity of locales and activities has a particular function when working in conversation with African American representations in popular culture, and that is to insist that Oscar is a young man with multiple identities and connections. Oscar is not reduced to a one-dimensional category like "ex-felon" or "shooting victim," but is all these things plus job-seeker, part-time drug dealer, father, son, and participant in an extended family network that includes his African American family and Sophina's Latinx family.[7] Additionally, Oscar is not confined to one neighborhood, but instead his social and economic networks take him all around the San Francisco Bay Area, from neighborhoods that are fairly segregated to those that are inhabited and traversed by people of different races and income levels.

This episodic narrative also gives the audience a near-experiential sense of what it might have felt like to be Oscar Grant moving through the Bay Area. There are numerous medium close-ups of Oscar in the car followed by point of view shots of what he sees looking out the window (Figures 8.1 and 8.2).

Sequences like these call out the reality of their location through featuring recognizable street signs and architecture. This is a long tradition in African American city films, including "race" films of the 1920s and '30s, 1970s black action ("Blaxploitation") films, some films of the LA Rebellion movement, and 1990s coming-of-age ("hood") films.[8] These techniques of documenting real spaces contrast with other approaches to filming the African American city that are more subjective (such as the emphasis on interior spaces in *Killer of Sheep* [Charles Burnett, 1978]) or stylized (such as the vibrant colors and unnatural lighting of *Do the Right Thing* [Spike Lee, 1989]).[9] *Fruitvale Station*'s approach is more similar to the films that rely strongly on a rhetoric and aesthetic of authenticity.[10] Its time stamps and extensive documentation of Oscar's movements contextualized within the urban environment continually

Figure 8.1 Oscar driving in *Fruitvale Station*.

Figure 8.2 Oscar's view from the car in *Fruitvale Station*.

remind viewers of the physical and social realities that underlie the fictional cinematic narrative.

Other choices go beyond a rhetoric of authenticity to create embodied sensations for the viewer. One is the use of handheld camera placed behind

Oscar, following him as he walks into and through various locations. This cinematographic choice evokes the feeling of a human body moving through space and encourages the viewer to imagine inhabiting the streets, homes, and stores.[11] Another similar effect comes from the glare on the car window, which results in a superimposition of Oscar's reflection and what he sees outside the window. There is a sense of the materiality of the vehicle, not just the unimpeded visual display of a cinematic backdrop.[12] This visual effect, combined with the loud music Oscar plays in the car that blocks out external sounds from the street, suggests that the viewer is traveling in the car with Oscar in his personal "environmental bubble."[13] Such driving scenes, as well as others when Oscar is alone, increase the intimacy a viewer may feel with Oscar, because they reveal his thoughtfulness and how he acts when he is not conforming to others' expectations.[14] And the variety of locations—from the isolated West Oakland waterfront where Oscar sits on a rocky outcropping and gazes at the water, to the busy Fruitvale commercial district and packed train cars—further flesh out the variety of sensations available to someone moving through this complex metropolitan area. Both the detailed itinerary Oscar follows and the simulation of embodied movements through space are key ways in which viewers are encouraged to feel "attached" to Oscar, as though they have traveled alongside this character.

The emphasis on Oscar's mobility complicates the image of the hyper-segregated "ghetto" resident that has been created by other fiction films and news media.[15] The cycle of films from the early 1990s directed by African American directors (including *Boyz N the Hood* and *Menace II Society*) developed a rhetoric of immobility and isolation in the way that they depicted low-income urban African American neighborhoods.[16] Films from this era contrast an overall sense of entrapment with the protagonist's efforts to control his own life, which is often equated with a freedom to leave the neighborhood. While true to many people's experiences, these films arguably contributed to an exaggerated image of these neighborhoods as completely cut off from the rest of America—an image that persists in popular media, despite the fact that many people's lives are more complicated, working in both legal and illegal economies, and alongside people of different races and classes.

The early 1990s films formed such a cohesive statement about urban African American life that films since then have sought different approaches to avoid what quickly became a dominant trope and, for some, a stereotype. Films like *ATL* and *Roll Bounce* (Malcolm D. Lee, 2005) take an optimistic approach by following a group of friends who largely succeed in overcoming social constraints, while films like *Precious* (Lee Daniels, 2009) and *Moonlight* (Barry Jenkins, 2016) take an introspective approach that explores the subjective experiences of a young woman and a gay man, expanding the previous focus on young, straight men. *Fruitvale Station* returns to a narrative more closely aligned with the earlier films—that of a young man constrained by his environment—but takes its own nuanced approach to the question of entrapment versus mobility in the city.

Digital connectivity and networks

The nuanced exploration of mobility in *Fruitvale Station* means that scenes of Oscar's physical movements through urban space are accompanied by a depiction of his frequent transcending of location via cellular phone usage. In early twenty-first-century societies such as the United States that are saturated with digital technology, we must think of mobility as not only physical but also virtual, where devices such as phones and the internet allow instant communication to multiple locations.[17] Throughout his day driving and taking public transit to disparate locations, Oscar is also in constant communication with family and friends via phone calls and text messages. The emphasis on voice and text communication is more than just a gimmick, as some reviewers suggested.[18] It emphasizes the way that Oscar is in constant contact with multiple locations and people, while he physically travels.

Depictions of cellular phone calling, texting, and data usage have appeared in many films and television shows of the 2000s; those using cell phones prominently and as key to the narrative include *Disconnect* (Henry Alex Rubin, 2012), *LOL* (Lisa Azuelos, 2012), *Cell* (Tod Williams, 2016), *Sherlock* (BBC, 2010–17), and *House of Cards* (Netflix, 2013–17).[19] There has been little scholarship on the aesthetics or representation of cell phone technology in fictional narratives, however.[20] Scholars of the television show *The Wire* (HBO, 2002–8) have noted the omnipresence and symbolic value of cell phones and pagers in that show's plotlines of urban poverty and crime. Most of it has to do with the theme of police surveillance,[21] but one character's use of his cell phone anticipates the way that *Fruitvale Station* uses cellular technology to show how one individual's network spans different sectors of society. The drug kingpin Stringer Bell uses his phone to direct his subordinates in the drug trade, buy and sell stock, and plan his real estate purchases—and these diverse roles are performed in equally diverse settings, including cars, the copy shop Stringer runs as a cover for his organization, and housing projects.[22] Not restricted to any single location, Stringer maintains simultaneous multiple connections to other individuals who participate in governmental, corporate, and drug networks.

Depicting the networked quality of social experience, in which each individual is a "node" with multiple connections to others in various social spheres, as opposed to existing in an enclosed sphere, is not dependent on the presence of cellular technology. Parallel editing has long been used to depict simultaneous events occurring in multiple places and imply similarity or connection. Increasingly complex "multi-thread" or "network narratives" depict large casts of characters meeting in different locations with interconnected storylines, and these narratives are often associated with urban life, due to its density and variety of human experience.[23] In *The Wire*, along with other network narratives to varying degrees, such narrative complexity allows for "examinations from a variety of perspectives of the way societal contexts shape characters and their arcs."[24] But the incorporation of cellular technology shows the way that networked existences have been amplified by the ability to be in constant and simultaneous communication with individuals in a variety of locations, rather than older network narratives that depended on individuals having to meet in shared physical space or remaining unaware of the connections that are obvious to the spectator through parallel editing.

The concept of a networked existence and its literalization through cellular phone technology has a particular importance in the context of depictions of African American urban life, with its traditional (and in many senses, accurate) emphasis on entrapment. Cellular technology is often described as a means to minimize the importance of physical proximity: a cell phone is attached to a user rather than a location, so the user may be reached no matter where he or she is.[25] This technology further extends the collapsing of space enabled by twentieth-century technologies, such as the car and telephone. As noted by Steven Bruhm, the cell phone user may even choose to hide his or her location, talking as a disembodied figure:

> Cell phone users manufacture a ghostly, dematerialized presence as an interlocutor ... while we may no longer be fixed in space to communicate, across distance, with an other, we now inhabit an amorphous plane somewhere between connectedness to the world at large and social insularity, and between the embodiedness of speaking subjects and their discorporeality.[26]

So, for instance, Oscar is filling his gas tank, on his way to meet Marcus, when he texts Sophina to ask if they might meet on her lunch break. Because this exchange occurs via a cell phone and not a land line, Sophina has no idea of Oscar's whereabouts or this particular activity that she disapproves of, and Oscar's electronic interaction with her functions independently from the location he is in and the other in-person interaction he is about to have. The virtual space of the text exchange is represented through a translucent blue box superimposed over the photographic image of Oscar holding his phone. Within the blue box, bright white letters appear as Oscar types his message to her (Figure 8.3).

Figure 8.3 Oscar texting in *Fruitvale Station*.

The blue box simulates the sense that Oscar is immersed in a space distinct from the physical location he is standing in. As he is typing, he looks down at the phone, in that moment disconnected from the gas station. For the purposes of communication with Sophina, he is disembodied and place-less, even while he remains a physical body in a particular location accomplishing other tasks. The simultaneity of his virtual exchange and his bodily presence is aptly visualized through the translucence of the blue box, which superimposes two "locations" over each other.

This depiction of place-less communication and the anonymity of disembodiment has a particular resonance for representations of African American young men, who in real life are subject to heightened surveillance and in screen narratives are often depicted as trapped in neighborhoods and narrowly proscribed roles. Just as Stringer in *The Wire* benefits from the cell phone's ability to hide his location—so that he might be in the housing projects and not lose any credibility when making a phone call to a wealthy real estate developer—Oscar uses the cell phone to virtually shift locations, to reveal only the information he chooses to those with whom he communicates, and to fulfill multiple social roles at once.

In this and other scenes of Oscar using his phone to call or text, we can see the way that cell phone use in public creates a layering of interactions, combining interactions that are "co-present" (individuals in the same physical space) with those that are "tele-present" (individuals on either end of a phone call or text message exchange).[27] Public space can be infused with private interactions, blurring these spheres, and an individual may be multitasking by communicating with a family member or close friend while engaging in a commercial transaction or more superficial interaction with a stranger. Thus individuals may experience a "'simultaneity of place': a physical space and a virtual space of conversational interaction. It can also be said that there has been an extension of physical space, through the creation and juxtaposition of a mobile 'social space.'"[28]

A more complex example of "simultaneity of place" occurs in *Fruitvale Station*'s grocery store scene. It is here that Coogler invents a character, Katie, though she seems to be based on a similar incident Grant's grandmother remembered in the past.[29] When Oscar arrives at the store to buy crabs for Wanda's birthday party and to ask for his job back, he is talking with a friend and former co-worker behind the seafood counter, and a young white woman asks for advice about how to fry fish. Oscar spontaneously calls his grandmother, who gives Katie cooking tips over the phone. The barriers to public interaction with strangers break down slightly through Oscar's evident pleasure in helping her and his pride in his grandmother's skills; his conversation with Katie ends with a friendly "happy new year." While Katie is on the phone with his grandmother, Oscar goes to the grocery store manager to ask for his job back, but is unsuccessful; the manager had fired Oscar for being late when, as Oscar puts it, he was "going through some s*** before, trying to get back on my feet." So in this scene, we observe how Oscar simultaneously occupies multiple roles of aspiring job-seeker, helpful stranger, and grandson. We understand the way urban life enables connections between those of different identities, at the same time as those with certain social identities are constrained in their ambitions. The phone enables Oscar to be simultaneously in two places (the commercial place of the grocery store and a familial place via talking with his grandmother) and in fact he merges these places by putting Katie on the phone with his grandmother. The overlapping of co-present and tele-present interactions also ensures that Oscar, as a representative of young African American men in the media, is not seen in one dimension, but rather as possessing multiple coexisting identities.

As most of Oscar's calls and texts are to his family and girlfriend, the emphasis on his use of this technology also underscores the close bonds he has with these individuals. This representation parallels research by Roderick Graham and Kyungsub Stephen Choi that documents higher rates of cell phone use for voice and texting among African Americans compared to white Americans.[30] These authors, in agreement with other studies of cell phone use, assert that cell phones do not create new social networks but strengthen those that already exist, and serve to maintain ties across time and space.[31] In the particular context of African Americans, cell phones are a technology that facilitates already high expectations for communication within extended families, including frequent interactions between family members not living in the same household, parents juggling changing work schedules, and desires to support extended family members or close friends in need.[32] In addition, access to cell phones can keep individuals in touch with work opportunities and other appointments, thus ensuring that these individuals are not cut out of communication networks, even as the "digital divide" exists in other realms of information technology.[33]

This social science work on African American cell phone use contrasts sharply to one study of representations of pagers and cell phones in popular African American cultural products. Analyzing rap lyrics and comedy and thriller films, Davin Heckman finds that wireless communication devices are either used to facilitate morally questionable behavior or as means of state surveillance—in either case, their representation in popular culture appears negative.[34] So even in this rather niche topic of cell phone representations, *Fruitvale Station* offers a more nuanced and accurate view of the social function of communications technology, which is in keeping with its overall important contribution to representations of African American urban life.

Coogler's own comments on the subject show that the film's use of cell phones was very much about social connection:

> The role of cell phones and video cameras in the case inspired us to explore the use of cell phones throughout the film. It made us think about how we use them. Though it was four years ago, Oscar connected with his loved ones often through his cell phone, even on the last day of his life.[35]

Coogler's intent here echoes the social science research, which emphasizes the role of cell phones in maintaining family connections. While, on the one hand, the cell phone allows Oscar to be "present" in multiple locations and interactions, Geoff Cooper et al. remind us that this device also allows an individual to maintain a constant, multifaceted identity no matter where he is:

> The fact that the mobile allows people to be reached anywhere can, paradoxically, contribute to a kind of stasis of identity for practical purposes; retention of the same mobile number means that moving office or house, being stationary or on the move, are not significant from the perspective of the caller.[36]

Reconciling the ideas of interactions with multiple types of people and a stable identity enabled by the cell phone, we might say that, depending on his location and interactions, one facet of Oscar's identity is emphasized over others. At the grocery store asking for his job back, his identity as a young man with a spotty job record comes to the forefront, but his identity as a family member is still present through the phone call he makes to his grandmother, and his other identities have not disappeared either. He simultaneously holds many identities and the overlapping of physical and digital spaces emphasizes this—yet at any given moment, some identities predominate.

Rather than being confined to a "ghetto," Oscar's reality is more comparable to a networked existence, which many scholars have deemed the defining metaphor of the early twenty-first century. In brief, each individual can be seen as a "node" that is connected to many other "nodes" through both personal interactions and flows of communication, and these networks transcend the confines of physical locations, making interactions through electronic communication as defining of individuals' experiences as the people they share a locality with, or even more so. Scholars differ as to what extent digital networks truly supersede physical communities or augment them, which is a key question for understanding the depiction of a networked existence in *Fruitvale Station*. Here, I am emphasizing both in-person and digital networks as ways in which Oscar's social position is understood. As the preceding film analysis shows, Oscar's participation in various networks brings him in contact with people of different races and socioeconomic status, as well as centering his most significant network around his family and friends. In-person interactions are the core of his family and friend network, but are strengthened by his ability to stay in touch electronically. Physical and digital mobility allows him to engage in a variety of encounters, both social and economic, sometimes simultaneously.

The limitations of the network

And yet, as "networked" as Oscar is, his connections and his mobility do not eliminate the social and economic constraints put on his life, nor protect him from death at the hands of law enforcement. Coogler's use of two invented white, middle-class characters—the young woman Katie and an unnamed man in San Francisco—is a key tactic in reminding the audience of Oscar's structured race and class position.

During their evening in San Francisco, Oscar and his friends are standing outside a closed store, having just persuaded the manager to let the two women with them go inside to use the bathroom. A young white couple approaches and when Oscar sees the woman is pregnant and also urgently needs the bathroom, he persuades the manager to let her in as well. While she is inside, Oscar and the white man talk about marriage, and the man reveals that he stole money through credit card fraud in order to afford a wedding ring. But, he says, they got through that dark time and he now has a successful web design company. He cheerfully gives Oscar his business card "if you ever need anything."

This unnamed character's success through a web design company is a direct reference to the technology boom that has shaped the San Francisco Bay Area in the last few decades. Enormous wealth has been created through internet companies such as Google, and that wealth has displaced many long-time residents of the Bay Area due to skyrocketing housing costs. These changes have increased the number of whites and decreased the number of African American and Latinx people who live in the area, first in San Francisco proper, but at the time of the film's making, these shifts were spreading to Oakland and the rest of the East Bay.

The exchange between these two characters further contrasts racial disparities in the consequences of criminal activity. While this man's "white collar" crime apparently had no lasting effects on his life, Oscar's previous stint in jail for selling drugs sets in motion a chain of events that ultimately leads to his death. The fight on the train that resulted in transit officers coming to Fruitvale Station and pulling Oscar and his friends off the train was between Oscar and a man with whom he had served time in San Quentin State Prison and had an old dispute (this episode appears to be based on witness testimony, even if some details are unknown).[37] So Oscar's prison past triggers the fight, and the racialized identities of Oscar and his friends cause the transit officers, who did not witness the fight themselves, to assume they were likely participants in the fight and to pull them off the train. The viewer is thus able to contrast Oscar's fate, which was set in motion by his prison past and by racial profiling, with that of the white man who was able to transcend his illegal activity and become financially successful.

Katie, whom Oscar first met at the grocery store in Oakland, reappears on the train heading back from San Francisco, recognizing and greeting Oscar. The coincidence of her being on the same train is a storytelling choice that seems implausible and has no grounding in accounts of Grant's last hours—yet it effectively dramatizes the geographical concept that the same literal place is experienced differently by individuals dependent on social position. Oscar and Katie's first encounter likely conjures in audiences their own memories of fleeting but warm encounters with strangers—those brief connections that make our experiences in public spaces more meaningful. To bring Katie back during Oscar's final moments, however, is to make a more political point about how Oscar and his friends experience public spaces—specifically the train— differently from Katie due to their racialized and gendered identities.

When Oscar and Sophina plan their night out, Coogler inserts a comment from Wanda, advising them to take the train instead of drive into San Francisco on the grounds that it will be safer on New Year's Eve. On their way into San Francisco, Oscar and the other passengers find themselves stuck on a stalled train as the clock turns to midnight, so there is a spontaneous countdown to the new year and a sense of celebration unifying the crowd. This moment represents the possibilities for community that exist when people of diverse backgrounds share a confined public space. And yet, on the train ride back, this public space becomes one in which African American men are automatically seen by law enforcement as targets for discipline, while passengers that outwardly exhibit other identities (white, female, middle class) are safe from this harassment. The train, for some citizens, transforms from the "safe" option into a space of danger.

As the train pulls into Fruitvale Station, Oscar and his friends get off to avoid further fighting, only to see officers approaching. Sophina and Oscar agree that she will exit the station and meet him at the Hayward station, while he gets back on the train to try to blend into the crowd. But the officers pull Oscar and his friends off the train, and line them up against the platform wall. Verbal taunts between the friends and the officers, triggered by long-held suspicion between the two groups and the fact that the officers are holding the young men without evidence, escalate when the officers handcuff them, still without making any charges. Oscar is assaulted (though the details are unclear since Coogler shoots these actions from a distanced position to reflect the point of view of the onlookers), held face-down on the platform, and then shot. Katie and many other passengers look on in horror, several of them recording with their phones. The camera cuts from a medium frontal shot of the passengers looking to an over-the-shoulder shot of Katie recording the incident on her

Figure 8.4 Katie shooting video in *Fruitvale Station*.

phone camera, its bright (though blurry) screen and the violent actions both centered in the frame and competing for the viewer's attention (Figure 8.4).

Similar to the way that the superimposition of text messages over photographic images in earlier scenes emphasized two simultaneous locations, the composition of these shots holds two realities in conversation with each other: the simultaneous assault on a body and the mediated gazes of others.

The moment of human connection Oscar and Katie experienced earlier in the grocery store is now eclipsed by the fact that these two characters are cast into socially proscribed roles. Katie and those who look like her are much less likely to be victims of police violence. While Oscar himself takes a cell phone photo of the officer's badge number and asks on what basis he and his friends are being held, the long history of policing the African American community renders his attempt to stick up for his rights futile. It is instead Katie who is able to document the civil rights abuses and then the shooting itself. She is structured into the role of bystander who is safe, and a visual witness.

To return to the concept of a networked society, then, we can see that *Fruitvale Station* both dramatizes the way that African Americans participate in social and digital networks just as other Americans do, and underscores the fact that these networks do not liberate them from the realities of their places.

And places should be understood to mean both the geographic locales they inhabit and the socially and economically proscribed roles in which they are embedded. Scholarship on networks and on postmodern transcending of time and space can, as Darin David Barney explains, sometimes suggest that digital flows of information have greatly diminished the influence of place, so that

> localized experience of time and place—the constraint of place—no longer limits the growing volume of increasingly significant human activity expressed in the communication of information via global network media ... It is in this sense that the [sic] human beings experience time in the network society as timeless, and space as placeless.[38]

But *Fruitvale Station* argues that locality still matters a great deal. Oscar's experience in a particular moment and place shape his destiny despite his participation in diverse networks. His place is radically different from the other people he encounters in his last day, and is structured by his access to employment, by a criminal record, and by the way that his body is read in public as a danger.

A close look at the way that *Fruitvale Station* dramatizes Oscar's use of cellular technology reveals that, despite the mobile phone's seeming ability to "render location insignificant," the particular ways in which phones are used are quite locally variable.[39] *Fruitvale Station* visualizes this contrast through images of Oscar's phone lying on the train platform, as Sophina calls but he is unable to answer, and of Katie's recording the police assault on Oscar (and our extra-diegetic knowledge that real bystanders like Katie were then able to upload this footage onto YouTube). Cell phone usage enables each user to construct his or her own experience of a given location, blending as it does a physical presence in one location, that individual's social positioning, and connections to people in that individual's social network who are currently in other locations. In this way, Oscar's experience throughout his last day is both singular and connected, and while he shares public space with some characters and communicates digitally with others, his own fate is distinct, the unique combination of his physical movements and his social and digital networks.

One way to think about the tension between Oscar's networked existence and his structural places is to return to the idea of simultaneous "presences" enabled by cellular phone communication. If, prior to twentieth-century technologies, one's community lined up closely with one's physical presence, and then digital technologies have caused theorists to claim that virtual or digital communities have overtaken physical locations—we might instead understand through *Fruitvale Station* and specifically Oscar's cell phone use that Oscar inhabits multiple communities at once but that they are differentiated in terms of their significance to Oscar's life and death. The phone enables Oscar's close contact with family members no matter his physical location, and when he is doing things that are either mundane or things that run counter to his family responsibilities. A secondary sense of community arises from his interactions with strangers in public spaces, often simultaneous to his more emotionally central interactions with those on the phone. And then in his last hours, he is in communication with Sophina when she calls to ask where he is and he tells her he is being held by the officers, but that tele-present interaction is unable to prevent what is happening to him in his physical location. So in various moments, co-present or tele-present interactions fluctuate in their prominence, and which networks Oscar is participating in shift in their determinative power.

The rhetoric of universality versus the specificity of police killings

Understanding the way Coogler balances Oscar's co-present and tele-present interactions, his mobility and structural limitations, helps to address a critique that has been made of *Fruitvale Station*'s marketing. Like many other fiction films about so-called minority experiences, *Fruitvale Station* was promoted using a rhetoric of "humanizing" Oscar Grant. Mark Cunningham writes:

> I detect a form of pacification or politeness in Ryan Coogler's revelation [in *Entertainment Weekly*] that he made his film *Fruitvale Station* (2013) about "human beings and how we treat each other [,] ... how we treat the people we love and how we treat the people we don't know," especially when juxtaposed to the candor of his comments in the *Los Angeles Times* that filmmaking is "my outlet for my fears, for the things that make me angry or frustrated, for messages I want to get out. I was terrified, shocked, angry. I felt this was the film I was born to make."[40]

Here, Mark Cunningham expresses his concern that Coogler's universalist rhetoric minimizes the specific horrors and injustices African American are subject to. And to say that a film is needed to "humanize" Grant is outrageous in a sense: he was inherently human, just as inherently "black lives matter." Yet as the backlash against that phrase has shown us, such a basic assertion of humanity needs to be made because of the thousands of ways that African American have been, and continue to be, dehumanized in popular culture and in news media.

On one level, the rhetoric of humanizing and relatability is a reflection of the dominance of Hollywood-style narrative even in American independent filmmaking. Films with aspirations toward wide audiences, which are made independently but seek to be picked up by a major distributor as *Fruitvale Station* was, often mimic Hollywood's limited capacity to imagine that audiences with identities other than African American would want to see a black-centered film unless they are told the characters are "just like them." On another level, however, we can see this idea of humanizing as related to Coogler's goal of getting the audience to feel "attached" and "close" to Oscar, as quoted earlier. By experiencing locations in which Oscar was present and by observing his social and economic networks, viewers are invited to understand both the specificity of his experience and the ways that his experience is networked into the wider fabric of American society. In other words, there is a combination of understanding that Oscar's experiences are structured by his specific social identities—that much of what happened to him was made more probable by being a low-income African American young man—but also a relational element evoked by seeing his family ties and his intersections with people of other races and occupations, such as a Latino grocery store manager, an Asian American drug dealer, and a white technology entrepreneur.

What finally insists that Oscar's socially proscribed positions override the experiences that he shares with Americans of other identities is, of course, his fatal shooting at the hands of a police officer. Coogler's staging of Oscar's death combined with his use of real cell phone footage of the shooting inserts *Fruitvale Station* into a public conversation about the viewing of extrajudicial killings of African Americans via videos that are shared on social media and by traditional media. The debate over whether watching these videos will ignite social change or merely render the broader society numb to black suffering only became more relevant after *Fruitvale Station*'s release, as the number of shootings captured on video increased, including Eric Garner (July 17, 2014), Laquan McDonald (October 20, 2014), Tamir Rice (November 22, 2014), and Walter Scott (April 4, 2015).[41]

While police abuse of minority, especially African American, communities is nothing new, the documentation of such acts is. Several writers have noted that the widespread access to two technologies—cellular phones with cameras and internet sites such as YouTube which allow the immediate upload and dissemination of video to a wide public—has led to a marked increase in public dialogue and concern over this issue.[42] Older structures of surveillance, in which a few centers of power can watch many citizens, are now challenged by a system of "sousveillance," "in which citizens wield cellphones such that they have the potential to influence public opinion and potentially inform state decisions about police in ways that have not been achieved before."[43]

In the years since Grant's killing, as video footage of other shootings have repeatedly circulated on the internet and on TV, news sites and blogs have published reflections on what it means to watch videos of real people dying. A main theme in these writings is the pull to "witness" versus the push against passively "watching" and thereby succumbing to further exploitation of black suffering.[44] If excessive watching is propelled by entertainment or profit-generation, the videos only "further normalize the commodification of black death."[45] Others point to the power of visual evidence to energize collective outrage, going back to the role of photographs of Emmett Till's battered body in adding momentum to the civil rights movement.[46]

Such concerns over the circulation of cell phone or police camera videos in journalism and social media are addressed by the recreation of video witnessing in *Fruitvale Station*, thereby asking the film's viewers to critically reflect on the purpose and the ethics of watching real shootings. The return of the fictional character Katie at the moment of Oscar's shooting stands for the many Americans who watch such incidents without direct experience of police violence. On the one hand, she clearly represents the social divide that makes Oscar the target of violence and those who look like her able to merely stand and watch. Yet, if one distinguishes between passively "watching" and "witnessing" as an act of activism, Katie's physical presence and ability to upload her video to the internet, thus making the incident visible to those who are not physically present, does allow her to contribute to a fight for social justice. Coogler's invention of this narrative episode, then, asks viewers who are not African American, or who do not personally fear law enforcement as an instrument of surveillance and violence, to "watch" their on-screen surrogate "witnessing"—potentially considering if there is a way that their own watching could become witnessing.

But then, Coogler moves the focus away from the outsider witness to the final moments of private grief that Wanda, Sophina, and his friends experience as they wait inside the hospital, praying that the doctors can save Oscar. The devastating moment of watching Oscar shot is emotionally matched by observing the devastation of those left behind when they learn that Oscar has not survived the bullet wound. Yet these are moments that are not caught on video and circulated in the media. They are one element that a fictionalization of police shootings can add to journalistic or documentary accounts. And they directly speak to those viewers who have had (or who fear) personal experience with police violence, by dramatizing intimate moments with the survivors. When juxtaposing the public shooting with the private vigil over Oscar's last moments, it is clear that Coogler has found a cinematic means to represent two different experiences: those who are not likely to experience police violence, but who may witness it, and those whose social positioning makes it more likely they will encounter such violence. And, regarding the intimacy the film has encouraged between its viewers and Oscar's character, viewers leave the distanced spatial perspective Coogler uses to film Oscar's shooting and enter a private space of grief alongside Oscar's family and friends, vicariously unifying with those characters because the viewers have also "lost" the person with whom they have been traveling through the film.

Finally, the film prods its viewers toward action with its final images: documentary footage of protests outside the Fruitvale BART station that followed on New Year's Day several years after Grant's death. In this way, the film takes its audience out of the immersive fiction it has created, and back into reality. It also puts Grant's last day back into the broader context of life in the so-called inner city, with its connotations of entrapment and enclosure. *Fruitvale Station* documents the way that Grant's death, via video footage, contributed to a growing public awareness of police shootings, rather than remaining sealed within local knowledge (bystanders and the immediate community around them) and invisible to the broader public. More broadly, *Fruitvale Station* updates earlier dramatizations of young African American men in their neighborhoods, with a fully twenty-first-century portrait of a networked urban existence, characterized by encounters with those of different social groups and constant digital communication. Yet—crucially—the film ensures that a thoughtful viewer will not conclude that the networked life of Grant and those like him will lead to a utopian collapsing of space and a subsequent liberation from social positioning. He, and those who died after him, are just connected enough to have their oppression witnessed.

Acknowledgment

I dedicate this chapter to the Oakland-based artists and activists whose work gives visibility to lives like Oscar Grant's. And I thank Beth Corzo-Duchardt and an anonymous reviewer for perceptive feedback that helped improve this chapter.

Notes

1   Overviews of these events can be found in Katherine Blaisdell, et al., "Race, Place, and Police," *Harvard Journal of African American Public Policy* 21 (2015), 65–72; Mary Grace Antony, "'This Is Citizen Journalism at Its Finest': YouTube and the Public Sphere in the Oscar Grant Shooting Incident," *New Media & Society* 12.8 (2010), 1280–1296; Joe Rhodes, "A Man's Death, a Career's Birth: A Bay Area Killing Inspires 'Fruitvale Station'", *New York Times*, June 28, 2013.

2   "Fruitvale Station Production Notes" (The Weinstein Company, 2013), 6, twcpublicity.com.

3   Rhodes.

4   Paula J. Massood, *Black City Cinema: African American Urban Experiences in Film* (Philadelphia, PA: Temple University Press, 2003), 165.

5   Allan Pred, *Making Histories and Constructing Human Geographies: The Local Transformation of Practice, Power Relations, and Consciousness* (Boulder, CO: Westview Press, 1990), 108.

6   For overviews of narrative and style in Italian neorealism, see Christopher Wagstaff, *Italian Neorealist Cinema: An Aesthetic Approach* (Toronto: University of Toronto Press, 2007); Mark Shiel, *Italian Neorealism: Rebuilding the Cinematic City* (London: Wallflower Press, 2006); Laura E. Ruberto and Kristi M. Wilson, "Introduction," in *Italian Neorealism and Global Cinema*, ed. Laura E. Ruberto and Kristi M. Wilson (Detroit, MI: Wayne State University Press, 2007), 1–24, Table of contents http://catdir.loc.gov/catdir/toc/ecip072/2006033483.html.

7   On this point, see also Robin M. Boylorn, "From Boys to Men: Hip-Hop, Hood Films, and the Performance of Contemporary Black Masculinity," *Black Camera* 8.2 (2017): 146–164.

8   Massood, *Black City Cinema*, 85.

9   This is not to say that films like *Killer of Sheep* and *Do the Right Thing* are unrelated to their specific cities and neighborhoods; both these films have clear markers of life in South Central Los Angeles and in the Bed-Stuy neighborhood of Brooklyn. However, they take some of these specific geographical properties and blend them with a poetic or allegorical approach. Some key works that discuss the way place is represented in those two films are Clifford Thompson, "Good Moments in a Tough World," *Cineaste* 33.2 (Spring 2008), 32–34; Paula J. Massood, "An Aesthetic Appropriate to Conditions: Killer of Sheep, (Neo) Realism, and the Documentary Impulse," *Wide Angle* 21.4 (July 9, 2004), 20–41; Catherine Pouzoulet, "The Cinema of Spike Lee: Images of a Mosaic City," in *Spike Lee's Do the Right Thing*, ed. Mark Reid (Cambridge: Cambridge University Press, 1999), 31–49; Massood, *Black City Cinema*; Ed Guerrero, *Do the Right Thing* (London: British Film Institute, 2001).

10 See Valerie Smith, "The Documentary Impulse in Contemporary African American Film," in *Black Popular Culture*, ed. Gina Dent (Seattle, WA: Bay Press, 1992), 56–64; Saverio Giovacchini, "'Shoot the Right Thing': African American Filmmakers and the American Public Discourse," in *Towards a New American Nation? Redefinitions and Reconstruction*, ed. Anna Maria Martellone (Staffordshire: Keele University Press, 1995), 207–221; Sharon Willis, *High Contrast: Race and Gender in Contemporary Hollywood Film* (Durham, NC: Duke University Press, 1997); S. Craig Watkins, *Representing: Hip Hop Culture and the Production of Black Cinema* (Chicago, IL: University of Chicago Press, 1998); Amy Lynn Corbin, *Cinematic Geographies and Multicultural Spectatorship in America* (New York: Palgrave Macmillan, 2015).

11 On film simulations of movement, see Anne Friedberg, *Window Shopping: Cinema and the Postmodern* (Berkeley: University of California Press, 1993).

12　On materiality and embodiment in film, see Laura U. Marks, *The Skin of the Film: Intercultural Cinema, Embodiment, and the Senses* (Durham, NC: Duke University Press, 2000); Vivian Carol Sobchack, *Carnal Thoughts: Embodiment and Moving Image Culture* (Berkeley: University of California Press, 2004).

13　John Urry, "Automobility, Car Culture and Weightless Travel: A Discussion Paper," n.d., http://www.comp.lancs.ac.uk/sociology/008ju.html; Ellen Strain, *Public Places, Private Journeys: Ethnography, Entertainment, and the Tourist Gaze* (New Brunswick, NJ: Rutgers University Press, 2003).

14　Boylorn, 158.

15　Robert A. Beauregard, *Voices of Decline: The Postwar Fate of US Cities* (Oxford and Cambridge, MA: B. Blackwell, 1993).

16　For sources on this cycle of films, see Massood, *Black City Cinema*; Watkins; ed. Guerrero, *Framing Blackness: The African American Image in Film* (Philadelphia, PA: Temple University Press, 1993). On showing the ghetto as an enclosed space, see Mark Reid, *Black Lenses, Black Voices: African American Film Now* (Lanham, MD: Rowman and Littlefield, 2005), 56 and Corbin, *Cinematic Geographies and Multicultural Spectatorship in America*. For sources on the limited mobility experienced by inner city residents, see Douglas S. Massey and Nancy A. Denton, *American Apartheid: Segregation and the Making of the Underclass* (Cambridge, MA: Harvard University Press, 1993); Linda McDowell, *Gender, Identity and Place: Understanding Feminist Geographies* (Minneapolis: University of Minnesota Press, 1999); Elisabeth Mahoney, "'The People in Parentheses': Space under Pressure in the Post-Modern City," in *The Cinematic City*, ed. David B. Clarke (London and New York: Routledge, 1997), 168–185.

17　Geoff Cooper, et al., "Mobile Society? Technology, Distance, and Presence," in *Virtual Society? Technology, Cyberbole, Reality*, ed. Steve Woolgar (Oxford: Oxford University Press, 2002), 296.

18　For one example, in an otherwise positive commentary, see Roxane Gay, *Bad Feminist: Essays* (New York: Harper Perennial, 2014), 246.

19　Rachel Dodes, "From Talkies to Texties," *Wall Street Journal*, April 4, 2013, https://www.wsj.com/news/articles/SB100014241278873232965045783984311 79979920; "First Use of On-Screen Text Messages," *Movies & TV Stack Exchange* (blog), n.d., https://movies.stackexchange.com/questions/9879/first-use-of-on-screen-text-messages-like-in-sherlock-and-house-of-cards.

20　Two essays focus on the horror film: Steven Bruhm, "Cell Phones from Hell," *The South Atlantic Quarterly* 110.3 (Summer 2011), 601–620; Allison Whitney, "Can You Fear Me Now? Cell Phones and the American Horror Film," in *The*

Cell Phone Reader: Essays in Social Transformation, ed. Anandam P. Kavoori (New York: Peter Lang, 2006), 125–138. A brief meditation on the way that cellular phones represent freedom, individualism, and the erasure of distance in European film is found in Graeme Harper and Owen Evans, "Editorial: Who You Gonna Call?," *Studies in European Cinema*, May 2016, 87–88.

21 Scholarship on surveillance in *The Wire* includes: Ryan Brooks, "The Narrative Production of 'Real Police,'" in *The Wire: Urban Decay and American Television*, ed. Tiffany Potter and C.W. Marshall (New York: Continuum, 2009), 64–77; Linda Williams, *On The Wire* (Durham, NC: Duke University Press, 2014); Stanley Corkin, *Connecting The Wire: Race, Space, and Postindustrial Baltimore*, First edition, Texas Film and Media Studies Series (Austin: University of Texas Press, 2017).

22 Stephen Lucasi, "Networks of Affiliation: Familialism and Anticorporatism in Black and White," in *The Wire: Urban Decay and American Television*, ed. Tiffany Potter and C.W. Marshall (New York: Continuum, 2009), 141.

23 On urban network narratives, see Hsuan L. Hsu, "Racial Privacy, the L.A. Ensemble Film, and Paul Haggis's *Crash*," *Film Criticism* 31.1–2 (Fall/Winter 2006), 132–156; Sebastian Thies, "Crystal Frontiers: Ethnicity, Filmic Space, and Diasporic Optic in Traffic, Crash, and Babel," in *E Pluribus Unum? National and Transnational Identities in the Americas*, ed. Sebastian Thies and Josef Raab (Berlin: Lit Verlag, 2009), 205–226; Amy Corbin, "Map-Making through Multi-Thread Urban Film and Television Narratives," *Studies in the Humanities* 42.1–2 (December 2015), 60–81.

24 Ted Nannicelli, "It's All Connected: Televisual Narrative Complexity," in *The Wire: Urban Decay and American Television*, ed. Tiffany Potter and C.W. Marshall (New York: Continuum, 2009), 200.

25 Anthony M. Townsend, "Life in the Real-Time City: Mobile Telephones and Urban Metabolism," *Journal of Urban Technology* 7. 2 (2000), 85–104; Bruhm.

26 Bruhm, 617.

27 Nicola Green, "On the Move: Technology, Mobility, and the Mediation of Social Time and Space," *The Information Society* 18 (2002), 281–292; Cooper, et al.

28 Lana Srivastava, "Mobile Phones and the Evolution of Social Behaviour," *Behaviour & Information Technology* 24.2 (April 2005), 123. Srivastava cites the phrase "simultaneity of place" from Sadie Plant, *On the Mobile: The Effects of Mobile Telephones on Social and Individual Life*. Motorola. Retrieved from: http://classes.dma.ucla.edu/Winter03/104/docs/splant.pdf.

29 Aisha Harris, "How Accurate Is Fruitvale Station?" *Slate*, July 12, 2013.

30 Roderick Graham and Kyungsub Stephen Choi, "Explaining African-American Cell Phone Usage through the Social Shaping of Technology Approach," *Journal of African American Studies* 20 (2016), 21–22; Roderick Graham, *The Digital Practices of African Americans: An Approach to Studying Cultural Change in the Information Society* (New York: Peter Lang, 2014).

31 Richard Seyler Ling, *New Tech, New Ties: How Mobile Communication Is Reshaping Social Cohesion* (Cambridge, MA: MIT Press, 2008); Manuel Castells, et al., *Mobile Communication and Society: A Global Perspective: A Project of the Annenberg Research Network on International Communication* (Cambridge, MA: MIT Press, 2007), 87–89.

32 Graham, *The Digital Practices of African Americans*, 74, 76.

33 Davin Heckman, "'Do You Know the Importance of a Skypager?': Telecommunications, African Americans, and Popular Culture," in *The Cell Phone Reader: Essays in Social Transformation*, ed. Anandam P. Kavoori (New York: Peter Lang, 2006), 179–180; Graham, *The Digital Practices of African Americans*, 73–74.

34 Heckman.

35 "Fruitvale Station Production Notes," 6.

36 Cooper, et al., 298.

37 Harris.

38 Darin David Barney, *The Network Society* (Cambridge: Polity, 2004), 29.

39 Cooper, et al., 288. See also Green; Townsend.

40 Mark Cunningham, "No Getting around the Black," *Cinema Journal* 53.4 (Summer 2014), 140.

41 Kirk Miller, "Watching the Watchers: Theorizing Cops, Cameras, and Police Legitimacy in the 21st Century," in *The Politics of Policing: Between Force and Legitimacy*, ed. Mathieu Deflem, vol. 21, Sociology of Crime, Law and Deviance (Bingley: Emerald Group Publishing Limited, 2016), 263–265.

42 Miller; Victor Oguejiofor Okafor, "Trayvon Martin, Michael Brown, Eric Garner, Et Al.: A Survey of Emergent Grassroots Protests & Public Perceptions of Justice," *The Journal of Pan African Studies* 7.8 (March 2015), 43–63. Work on the role of social media in igniting activism and public concern includes n.d.; Sarah J. Jackson and Brooke Foucault Welles, "#Ferguson Is Everywhere: Initiators in Emerging Counterpublic Networks," *Information, Communication & Society* 19.3 (2016), 397–418.

43 Miller, 259.

44 James Poniewozik, "A Killing. A Pointed Gun. And Two Black Lives, Witnessing," *New York Times*, July 7, 2016.

45 Armond R. Towns, "That Camera Won't Save You! The Spectacular Consumption of Police Violence," *Present Tense* 5.2 (2015), 1.

46 Renee Graham, "Why We Must Watch the Video of Alton Sterling's Killing by Police," *The Boston Globe*, July 6, 2016.

Part Three

Cinema and Gentrification

9

For Whom Are the Movies?
The Landscape of Movie Exhibition
in the Gentrified City

Brendan Kredell

The existence of this volume bespeaks an underlying truth: for a long time now, the discourse around gentrification has been bound up in questions of culture, and scholars looking for an entry point into this relationship have often looked to media as a means of observing the cultural work of gentrification in situ. Of course, gentrification was about culture in the first instance; when Ruth Glass wrote of changes to the "social character" of gentrified neighborhoods, she was explicitly talking in cultural terms.[1] But here, I mean to more explicitly invoke the term in the sense of cultural production and the cultural industries; as the research agenda on gentrification has expanded and diversified in the decades since Glass's seminal work, considerable attention has focused on the intersecting issues of mediation and gentrification.

Sharon Zukin's work on the "loft lifestyle" was foundational in this regard. Among her many contributions to the discourse, her argument concerning the "aesthetic conjuncture" that drove demand for urban loft spaces in 1970s Manhattan is most relevant here; she emphasizes the extent to which "taste-setting mass media" is responsible for "a heightened sense of art and history, space and time" that helps drive demand for a particular reconfiguration of urban space.[2] Julie Podmore's work on Montreal—which follows from Zukin and focuses in particular on questions of media—is equally productive. Borrowing from Zukin, Podmore describes the "loft living" habitus thusly:

The spatial configuration of this relationship between local actors, landscapes and media representations illustrates the role of media imagery in building relationships between distant landscapes and social practices.[3]

At least within the field of media studies, we have tended to approach this "conjuncture" from the direction of what Podmore calls "media representations": the notion that there is something to be gained by identifying particular media texts as significant to the study of gentrification, and then reading those films against the existing critical literature. To cite but a few recent examples, consider Philip Lawton's work on the films of Woody Allen, Johan Andersson's research on 1980s New York City-set films, or my own writing on Wes Anderson and Martin Scorsese.[4]

However, I want to submit here that this tradition of research, productive though it is, also limits our capacity to appreciate the scope of the cultural changes wrought by gentrification. While the emphasis on "media representations" and "media imagery"—on reading media texts against the cultural and geographical backdrop of gentrification—presents some fascinating and provocative scholarship, in this chapter I propose an approach rooted outside this tradition. Given the abundance of work on these urban representations—some of which is contained within the pages of this very book—it seems to me that our responsibility is to consider what we are missing by focusing so much attention on the work of the film text.

In an oft-quoted analogy making the case for what he calls the "new cinema history," Richard Maltby observed that "the history of the American cinema is not the history of its products any more than the history of railroads is the history of locomotives."[5] His argument is that a history that is too "product"-centered "denies the contextual significance of the material conditions under which movies were produced and consumed." Likewise, it constrains our ability to perceive media functioning as a system; in short, when we use the term "cinema," we are signifying something far broader and more potent than the exhaustive catalogue of all the films ever released.

Here I contend that if we want to understand cinema's role in the gentrification of cities, we ought to focus our attention on questions of consumption, rather than reproduction. Paying careful attention to the way that films are screened in cities—which films are screened where, by whom, and for which audiences—is the key to understanding how cinema functions both to facilitate and to reify the social divisions of urban life. In what follows, I propose a different tack. Rather than attempting to locate the gentrifying impulse in media texts, I suggest that there is a more proximate and equally productive way to talk about media and its relationship to gentrification: through a careful examination of the sites of media consumption. When we talk about the spatiality of media, the potency of cinematic urban imaginaries almost demands that we focus our attention on the diegetic space of the city within the films that we watch. But we have much to gain by stepping back from the film text, and considering where theaters are sited, who attends them, and what kinds of audiences are imagined by those in the business of marketing and selling cinema to the public.

I frame this argument specifically with an eye toward recent efforts within sociology to navigate the seeming binary of supply- and demand-side explanations of gentrification. This debate has been framed differently over time—perhaps the most oft-cited being the exchange between David Ley and Neil Smith over the "rent gap"[6]—but at root the argument concerns questions of structure and agency. On the one hand, proponents of the structural (or "production") argument describe urban gentrification as a symptom of broader forces acting upon the city: capitalism, postindustrialism, structural racism, etc. On the other, proponents of the "consumption" argument contend that gentrification is a function of changes in consumption habits, the reflection of what Ley called a "pro-urban" worldview of in-movers.[7] More recently, scholars have attempted to shift the debate beyond this binary; Schlichtman and colleagues observe a "huge 'reality gap'" in the discourse, arguing that the inability to reconcile these two positions has stymied our efforts to properly understand gentrification.[8]

From this I draw a simple but powerful conclusion: our understanding of the city is at once shaped by the stories we tell about it (the aforementioned "media representations"), but also by the ways those stories are themselves structured by the social, cultural, and industrial forces that produce and constrain them. With this in mind, I hope to demonstrate in this chapter how we might understand recent developments in American cinema in light of the raced and classed conflicts produced by gentrification.

Christopher Nolan, Ava DuVernay, and the space–time of moviegoing

By way of an entrée, consider the remarks of Christopher Nolan in a July 2017 interview with *Indiewire* preceding the release of his film *Dunkirk*. Training his view on the state of the industry-at-large, he lambasted the release strategy adopted by Netflix for films that they distribute:

> I think the investment that Netflix is putting into interesting filmmakers and interesting projects would be more admirable if it weren't being used as some kind of bizarre leverage against shutting down theaters. It's so pointless. I don't really get it.[9]

With these comments, Nolan inserted himself into one of the ongoing debates in a film industry beset by technological change. As modes of distribution and exhibition have rapidly shifted in the 2010s, with streaming services moving from the fringes to the center, the role of media companies like Netflix and Amazon has become ever more contentious. Especially as those streaming services have expanded their portfolio, producing and acquiring films for exclusive distribution on their platforms, their place within the broader media ecosystem has become a matter of much debate.[10]

On its face, it would seem that the willingness of streaming services to invest in their projects is an unqualified good; just as the American independents of the 1980s flourished at a time when home video money flooded the industry, streaming services have provided an influx of capital for a segment of the industry that sorely needed it. With that said, Nolan's comments bespeak a lingering frustration in some quarters; only a few months earlier, Bong Joon-ho's *Okja* opened to boos at the Cannes film festival when the Netflix logo appeared during the film's title sequence.[11] To date, most Netflix "originals" have received streaming-only releases, with the firm opting to release select high-profile films theatrically in order to garner awards consideration. (In addition to *Okja*, this list includes films like *Beasts of No Nation* [Cary Joji Fukanaga, 2015], *The Little Prince* [Mark Osborne, 2015], and *First They Killed My Father* [Angelina Jolie, 2017].) Even when it has arranged for theatrical distribution, Netflix has steadfastly pushed for day-and-date releases, meaning that films are available for streaming on the same day as their theatrical release.

Thus the crux of the issue would seem to concern temporality: when Nolan accuses Netflix of undermining the theatrical experience, he is taking up arms with a generation's worth of filmmakers and exhibitors who have pushed back against distributors' efforts to shorten or eliminate the theatrical "window." By this reckoning, there is something unique about the experience of viewing a film in a cinema, and for Nolan, the Cannes critics, and others, the threat that Netflix represents is a gradual eradication of the theatrical market itself. Notably, Netflix's chief competitor in the United States—Amazon—has adopted a much more conciliatory posture toward the exhibition industry. Amazon Studios executive Jason Ropell spoke at CinemaCon, the exhibition industry's trade show, in 2017, promising the audience that "we believe in the theatrical window fully for our releases ... [our] customers want to see great movies, and great movies play in theaters."[12] (Perhaps unsurprisingly, then, it was Amazon and not Netflix that claimed glory at the Academy Awards that year, when Amazon-distributed features won three Oscars, the first ever awarded to films released by streaming services.[13])

But the temporal question Nolan asks—that is, how can we preserve the moviegoing experience by maintaining the importance of the theatrical window—elides a separate question about cinemagoing that is fundamentally spatial. Fellow filmmaker Ava DuVernay phrased it succinctly in a tweet responding to Nolan's *Indiewire* interview: "But, what if there's no movie theater in your neighborhood?"[14] This, in so many words, is the question that animates this chapter: Who gets to have theaters in their neighborhoods, and who does not? And what broader lessons can we learn from the location (or absence) of those theaters; that is, to what extent are the sites of consumption correlated with patterns of consumption? The technological upheavals of motion picture distribution and exhibition wrought by the entrance of Netflix and Amazon into the movie business have certainly precipitated considerable change to our cinema culture, and scholars are racing to develop new models for understanding the media industries that can more fully take into account the transformational impact of these new players. But there is a seductiveness to such an industrial-focused history to which we should resist falling prey. After all, while the way audiences watch films may have changed considerably over the prior decade, the audiences themselves have changed much more slowly. In moments of profound technological change such as these, we would do well to recall Robert C. Allen and Douglas Gomery's definition of history as the explanation of "change and stasis over time,"[15] a useful reminder that in our haste to make sense of disruption, we risk understating the constancy of the social forces that shape technology.

Theaters in the neighborhood

For generations, the American cinematic landscape was firmly anchored around the institution DuVernay references in her tweet, the movie theater. In its many incarnations—the nickelodeon, the movie palace, the neighborhood theater, the multiplex—the theatrical experience was synonymous with the movie experience. Of course, that arc of exhibition history was permanently disrupted by the introduction and evolution of home video technologies. But focusing our attention on that rupture masks a more gradual change to the geography of the theatrical experience, a history lurking just underneath the surface of DuVernay's question. By asking "where are the movies?," we implicitly answer the question "for whom are the movies?"

Perhaps the clearest way to focus on this is to consider a former institution of the American urban landscape, the neighborhood theater. Once a fixture of cultural life, the single- and double-screen theaters that once dotted the map in every city around the country were a casualty of a number of diverse-yet-interrelated trends: postwar suburbanization and the flight of capital from cities; consolidation in the exhibition industry and the trend toward multiplexing; and the rise of home video (and later streaming services) as a competitor to theatrical exhibition.

As a general trend, the decline of the neighborhood theater and consolidation in the exhibition industry seems inexorable. As recently as 1995, there were 7,744 theatrical sites in the United States, according to the National Association of Theatre Owners' statistics; these represented 27,843 screens. By 2016, the number of sites had declined by 30 percent (to 5,472), but the number of screens crossed the 40,000 threshold, an increase of 44 percent. The average number of screens per site more than doubled in the space of twenty years, from 3.59 in 1995 to 7.34 in 2016.[16] In the name of economies of scale, "bigger and fewer" have become the watchwords for the film exhibition industry in the United States; certainly this is true over the past two decades, but it traces its roots to the 1970s boom in suburban shopping mall construction and the attendant growth in the exhibition business, what William Paul has described as the "mall movie" phenomenon.[17]

Not coincidentally, the consolidation on the exhibition side mirrors the overall decline in films receiving wide theatrical release from the major studios. In 1995, the Big Six studios distributed 110 films in wide release, a figure that would fluctuate but stay more or less constant throughout the next decade.[18] But 2009 marked a turning point for Hollywood in the theatrical market; since then, major studios have reduced the number of films they distribute, to a new low of seventy-nine in 2017. To some extent, this gap has been filled by other distributors who have stepped into the breach; for 2016, the last year for which complete data are available, Disney and Paramount each released fewer films than prolific independent distributors Lionsgate and A24.[19] But even accounting for this, the overall trend toward consolidation is indisputable: judged by the number of films in wide release in a given year, the five most paltry years in modern Hollywood history have all come since 2010.[20]

What to make of all this? The conclusion seems inescapable: the Hollywood model in recent years has been to show fewer films on more screens, concentrating marketing and advertising budgets on an increasingly smaller number of films and driving audiences toward so-called tentpole films. The consequences of such a strategic shift are numerous, and have been explored at much greater length and detail by others.[21] The overall trends are clear: toward consolidation of sites, fewer releases showing on more screens, and the final and complete victory of what Douglas Gomery calls the "industry business strategy" of the blockbuster. Against this backdrop, the war of words between directors DuVernay and Nolan makes more sense in context: Nolan, arguably more so than any other filmmaker, represents the trend toward large-scale, high-concept films as the primary output of the Hollywood studios. His film *The Dark Knight* became just the second film to earn $500 million in domestic box office receipts (after *Titanic*), and the continued commercial success of his films has made Nolan one of the highest-grossing filmmakers in Hollywood history. He is, to put it lightly, heavily invested in the ongoing success of the theatrical model of film exhibition.

DuVernay, on the other hand, has been at the forefront of a new generation of filmmakers working hand-in-hand with streaming services like Netflix and Amazon to navigate around the traditional distribution–exhibition bottleneck represented by the major studios and dominant exhibition chains. Despite her success within Hollywood, DuVernay has been just as influential for developing distribution structures for other filmmakers with an eye toward diversifying the kinds of stories told in American cinema.[22] As a distributor, then, she is well aware of the implicit "centrisms" of theatrical consolidation: fewer theatrical sites means less diversity, more focus by major studios on dominant cultural norms, and less attention to marginal and subaltern audiences. It is through this process of centering that cinema constructs its others; the wager made by DuVernay and others is that new technological shifts in film distribution can bypass these constraints and facilitate a new era of cultural specificity in cinema.

Urban exhibition

With what I hope is a clearer picture of the urban audience in mind, we can turn to consider what I regard as the crux of DuVernay's question—its theoretical implication. Her response to Nolan represents a shift in perspective that I argue is critical: rather than talking in ontological terms about cinema—that the "movieness" of *Dunkirk* is in some way bound up in its theatrical exhibition—DuVernay orients us toward a phenomenological perspective: that theaters represent a structuring experience in our understanding of cinema. By this way of thinking, for a community to "have" a theater is a precondition of its participation within cinema culture, an instance of literally being "on the map." By extension, this line of thought explains DuVernay's investment in streaming services like Netflix: by erasing the line between the formerly discrete categories of theatrical film and direct-to-video, Netflix is attempting to redefine the category "movie screen" in such a way as to include every internet-connected device in service. (Her reasons for taking up sides with Netflix should be all the more clear considering the discussion in the prior section of the cultural geography of urban cinema.)

It is clear that the present and the future of cinema is bound up in the answer to this experiential question concerning changing habits of cinema consumption. But to better understand the cultural impacts of gentrification on the cinema, it is important that we not lose sight of important micro-level developments amid the sea of macro-level trends in the film business. By way of framing this, I would return to DuVernay's question and invert it: What if there *is* a movie theater in your neighborhood? Answering that question can help us to better understand the unevenness of urban development in recent decades, and the consequent impacts that this unevenness has had on the film industry. In short, the construction and maintenance of critical cinema infrastructure—most notably, movie theaters—in certain urban areas has allowed for the promulgation of what I have called elsewhere the "cinema of gentrification."[23] By this, I mean to say that it is possible for film producers and distributors to target niche audiences within cities with films that affirm the cultural agenda of gentrification, enabling a process of distinction and self-perpetuation. In Sarah Schulman's elegant phrase, "gentrification is a process that hides the apparatus of domination from the dominant themselves."[24] Echoing Schulman, I submit that cinema represents one of the most potent forces of ideological domination, insofar as it simultaneously serves a mythmaking function by narrativizing and aestheticizing the process of gentrification, while at the same time participating in the material process of gentrification by virtue of the transforming the economies of entertainment in urban areas.

As I have previously indicated, the prior function of cinema—that of narrativization and aestheticization, or, in other terms, the textual basis of gentrification—is outside the scope of this argument, but well documented elsewhere in this text and in other scholarship. It is this latter function, cinema's material role in transforming the politics and economics of culture, that most interests me here. As an infrastructural matter, the presence or absence of movie theaters in urban areas is as close as we have to a mapping of the constituencies of the film industry. By paying attention to where theaters are sited, we learn about the implicit valuations that the industry makes about different audiences. In light of this, the presence of a theater in a gentrifying/gentrified neighborhood not only serves as an affirmative indicator of the changing "social character" of a district (to return to Ruth Glass's phrase), but it also functions as an important tool for drawing and policing social boundaries, for creating group identity and maintaining social cohesion. To understand why is to consider the essential difference between the act of viewing a film in a theater versus in the home setting: it is a question of publicity and privacy, projecting the cinema into the public square, so to speak.

At root, the claim made by DuVernay is that there is latent demand for different kinds of cinema, a demand that remains untapped by the cinema industry. I would go further and suggest that there is an inherent unevenness to the way that the film industry addresses its urban audiences. Though data on these questions are not abundant (at least for those outside of the industry itself), what scarce information we can gather helps explain how demand changes across the urban landscape. Considering that in light of the underlying question—how the business of film exhibition helps us understand the gentrification of American cities—we are able to better understand how the loci and lacunae of urban exhibition tell us something more profound about agency and participation in American popular culture. Theatrical box office has always proved an imperfect barometer of audience demand, for exactly the reasons discussed above: selling tickets to movies is first and foremost a retail business, and like any other retail business, the location of stores structures the composition of the market. The collective decision by big exhibition chains to largely abandon cities and focus their expansion efforts on suburban retail complexes during the 1970s and 1980s not only redefined the contours of the film business, but it also privileged the taste preferences of an ascendant suburban middle class.

The failure of the film industry to adequately service audiences of color should not be dismissed with so anodyne a term as "market failure," then; instead, we ought to consider it for what it is: a business strategy designed to reify the cultural dominance of one group—suburban, middle-class, largely white viewers—over others. The metrics of success used to describe the movie business adopt the same cultural assumptions baked into this model of exhibition. As an example, consider the degree to which the wide openings and high box office receipts of blockbuster films are designed with an imaginary, homogeneous national market for cinema in mind. Flattening out cultural difference—or strategically casting and writing films in such a way as to facilitate marketing them to different audience segments—serves as a way of feeding what Manohla Dargis terms the fundamental "myth" of Hollywood:

The ideal of one nation under a movie theater has obvious appeal, but the dream that American movies are for everybody has always been a self-serving myth of what historically has been a white, male-dominated industry. The industry still leans on that myth, including at that nostalgia-wreathed testament to self-love known as the Academy Awards. But the movies didn't conquer the mass audience once upon a time by incidentally ignoring and demeaning swaths of humanity; it partly conquered that audience specifically because of what it ignored and who it demeaned. I'm talking about movies, but this myth didn't originate in Hollywood.[25]

Beginning with the assumption of *e pluribus unum* has obvious appeal for the film industry, justifying the approach of producing fewer and more expensive films to be shown on more screens (but in fewer places). Consequently, producers of "niche" cinema find themselves at a comparative disadvantage: without adequate infrastructure in place to exhibit their films, and with the terms of success defined in such a way as to ensure the continued domination of mall multiplexes and the blockbuster movies that dominate their screens, the long-term viability of niche cinema would seem grim.

Despite the deck being stacked in this way, however, there is considerable evidence to suggest that unevenness and difference remain defining qualities of the American (urban) market. This is important to recognize as a precursor to consider the ramifications of gentrification on urban exhibition, because the success of the cinema of gentrification has often come at the expense of other urban niche cinemas that have struggled to keep pace. By way of illustrating the uneven topography of audience demand across the American theatrical market, let us briefly consider the example afforded by Chicago, one of America's largest and most segregated cities, and in particular of the fate of the city's Inner City Entertainment (ICE) exhibition chain. Now closed, ICE was a small exhibitor operating several multiplexes across the South Side of Chicago during the 1990s and 2000s, serving largely black and—to a lesser extent—Latina/o audiences. Following the success of the initial Magic Johnson Theatres location in Los Angeles, the proprietors of ICE were able to attract funding and municipal support to build three theaters, beginning in 1997. By operating in partnership with Cineplex Odeon, these theaters were able to compete

Table 9.1 National box office compared with ICE box office, 2005–2007

	National Box Office, 2005–7	Inner City Entertainment Box Office, 2005–7
1	*Pirates of the Caribbean: Dead Man's Chest*	*Madea's Family Reunion* (#44, 2006)
2	*Star Wars Episode III: Return of the Sith*	*Four Brothers* (#31, 2005)
3	*Spiderman 3*	***Big Momma's House 2*** (#39, 2006)
4	*Shrek the Third*	***Spiderman 3***
5	*Transformers*	Norbit (#30, 2007)
6	*Pirates of the Caribbean: At World's End*	***X-Men: The Last Stand***
7	*Harry Potter and the Order of the Phoenix*	*Stomp the Yard* (#42, 2007)
8	*The Chronicles of Narnia: The Lion, the Witch and the Wardrobe*	*Daddy's Little Girls* (#85, 2007)
9	*Harry Potter and the Goblet of Fire*	*Roll Bounce* (#122, 2005)
10	*I Am Legend*	*Little Man* (#53, 2006)
11	*Night at the Museum*	*Get Rich or Die Tryin'* (#90, 2005)
12	*Cars*	*Fantastic Four* (#13, 2005)
13	*X-Men: Last Stand*	***Shrek the Third***
14	*War of the Worlds*	*Final Destination 3* (#60, 2006)
15	*The Bourne Ultimatum*	*Akeelah and the Bee* (#119, 2006)
16	*King Kong*	*Waist Deep* (#113, 2006)
17	*The DaVinci Code*	*Hustle and Flow* (#110, 2005)
18	*National Treasure: The Book of Secrets*	***Transformers***
19	*Alvin and the Chipmunks*	***King Kong***
20	*300*	*The Gospel* (#131, 2005)
21	*Wedding Crashers*	*ATL* (#114, 2006)
22	*Charlie and the Chocolate Factory*	***War of the Worlds***
23	*Ratatouille*	*Dreamgirls* (#19, 2006)
24	*Batman Begins*	*Chicken Little* (#14, 2005)
25	*Superman Returns*	***Batman Begins***
26	*Happy Feet*	*Are We Done Yet?* (#53, 2007)
27	*Ice Age: The Meltdown*	***The Chronicles of Narnia: The Lion, the Witch and the Wardrobe***
28	*Madagascar*	*Scary Movie 4* (#20, 2006)
29	*Mr. and Mrs. Smith*	***Cars***
30	*The Simpsons Movie*	*Saw II* (#21, 2005)

Source: Boxofficemojo.com   Source: Inner City Entertainment Theaters

against the national exhibition chains that dominated the Chicago theatrical landscape for sought-after films.

Their initial success was owed in large part to the radically uneven distribution of theatrical sites around the city of Chicago. More than a quarter of the city's 2.7 million people live on Chicago's South Side, and yet by the mid-2000s, the three ICE theaters were the area's only remaining exhibitors. By way of context, according to the 2002 Economic Census of the United States, movie exhibition was a $58 million business in the city of Chicago, with twenty-three motion picture theaters located in the city.[26] Given their market position as exhibitor-by-default to an underserved region with over 750,000 people—one that is more than 90 percent African American—the ICE theaters served to illustrate the inverse of Ava DuVernay's question: What if the neighborhoods that do not have access to movie houses did? What would the film industry look like then? Comparing the highest grossing films at the ICE locations against nationwide box office over a three-year time period (2005–7), one is struck by the lack of commonalities. Only 30 percent of the films from the national list appear on the ICE list. (These are the films in bold in Table 9.1. For films that played well at ICE but not nationally, their overall position in the domestic box office charts for the year of their release is listed in parentheses after the film title.)[27]

Likewise, eight of the top ten grossing films at ICE theaters are nowhere to be found on the national list. While there are of course limitations on how much we can generalize from such specific data, the implication is clear: to DuVernay's point, when communities have access to a theater, their film-viewing habits shift accordingly. Here, Tyler Perry is cinema's highest grossing filmmaker, and *Fantastic Four*—directed by Tim Story, the first African American filmmaker to helm a Marvel film—outgrosses blockbusters such as *Transformers, Batman Begins*, and *King Kong*.

Gentrification, "indieplexes," and symbolic boundaries

Eventually, the ICE chain met its demise; its owners were forced to close two of its three locations, and the third and most profitable location was sold to new management. Nonetheless, the lessons it teaches us about the cultural specificity of film audiences are important to bear in mind. Above all else, the

ICE example demonstrates that the movie theater is never a culturally neutral site; instead, when considering the spatiality of film exhibition, we must also attend to the questions of geography and demography that inform our understanding of cinema audiences. Turning to consider gentrification itself, the implication is clear: as new residents arrived in cities, the composition of the urban audience itself changed. At or about the same time that chains like ICE and Magic Johnson Theatres were building out a national circuit of multiplexes in urban neighborhoods that marketed to African American audiences, we also observe the growth of what Michael Z. Newman has termed "indieplexes."[28] Chains like Landmark Theatres and Angelika Film Center grew out of the arthouse and repertory cinema world of the 1970s, but began in the 1990s to expand nationally, proliferating in precisely the kinds of urban neighborhoods transformed by gentrification: Baltimore's Inner Harbor, Washington DC's Chinatown, New York's Lower East Side, and Chicago's Lakeview, to name but a few examples. Along with other players like the Alamo Drafthouse and Sundance Cinemas (since acquired by AMC), these chains share an important lineage with the traditional arthouses of yesteryear, but their business operations look much more like the other national chains they program against.[29]

Why were the indieplexes able to grow so quickly, when and where they did, considering that the macro trends discussed at the outset of this chapter would seem to be countervailing? Gentrification is not only a process of economic but also cultural transformation, and these theaters not only indicate but participate within that process. To harken back to Ruth Glass, she was aware from the outset of how culturally destructive gentrification could be: the initial wave of in-movers might arrive in a neighborhood for a variety of reasons—low rents, proximity to transit lines, heritage architecture, etc.—but as that group grows, the commercial and cultural infrastructure of the area—what Glass termed the "character of a district"—changes to accommodate the taste preferences of in-movers. The movie theater is perhaps the *ne plus ultra* of this transformation. Certainly we can think of other examples of businesses and cultural institutions that signify the process of gentrification at work; the coffeeshop has become an especially potent symbol of gentrification in recent years, for example.[30] But by virtue of the significant capital expense of opening a new theater, and its high operating costs, the construction of a new movie theater in a neighborhood marks what I have elsewhere described as the "capstone of gentrification."[31] Given the square footage requirements and the expense, proprietors have to err on the side of caution when identifying prospective new locations for urban theaters; consequently, the arrival of a new theater should be understood to mark a turning point in the process of gentrification, an indication that the "character" of the neighborhood, to again use Glass's term, has changed to the point that a new taste public exists, the theater's imagined audience. Understood in this way, the movie theater has the effect of cultivating some audiences and excluding others—by its location, by its programming, and through its marketing, it serves as a concrete answer to Ava DuVernay's question of who the movies are for—and who they exclude.

This is an uncomfortable conclusion for many cultural observers to make, because the truth is that they—we—are over-indexed among the groups participating in the very gentrification that we write about. (It is from this position of self-awareness that Schlichtman and colleagues begin, recognizing that those most concerned with the cultural processes of gentrification are also themselves participants within those processes.[32]) In that way, the gentrification of America's cities stands in marked contrast to many previous waves of migration to urban areas, in which in-moving residents shared a common ethnic, linguistic, racial, or religious heritage. Gentrification represents a very different cultural formation; instead of the ethnic ghettos that characterized industrial-era cities, it produces pockets of urban affluence in which communities form around a set of shared taste preferences. While the norms of migrant and immigrant communities in previous generations were themselves the result of a complex process of cultural negotiation, the work required to cohere gentrifying migrants into distinct communities represents a much different kind of cultural labor. Absent a shared language or common ethnic heritage, "community" becomes a much more elusive concept; to the extent that we can speak of a unifying force among the in-movers of gentrification, it would be a shared set of aesthetic and lifestyle preferences, which are reproduced and to some extent policed by the cultural institutions of the gentrified neighborhood.

At the outset of the postindustrial era, during a period otherwise marked by a flight of capital from cities across the country, affluent—and largely white—elites sequestered themselves into preexisting enclaves of privilege, in neighborhoods like Chicago's Gold Coast and New York's Upper East Side. And as Lawton argues, a sort of feedback loop existed between the upper-class urban habitus and its representation on screen. He quotes Woody Allen describing the logic of the gauzy version of urban life accessible only to the wealthy on offer in his films:

> I wanted people to be able to go to the theater at 8:40 and then to a supper club, and to be able to walk home through Central Park. I didn't want them to have to fear for their lives. So I pushed my idea of it, and people always used to say to me, "Oh, you look at New York through rose-colored glasses." And that's fine, but I got my idea of New York from Hollywood.[33]

Of course, the theater figures not only as a place of consumption but as a textual site in Allen's films, a public square for the denizens of his particular version of New York, most famously, in the Marshall McLuhan scene from *Annie Hall* (1977). Allen's films are among the clearest examples the cinema offers of urban retrenchment: not only were the characters in these films fortified into bastions of affluence, but as Allen's quote above suggests, there is a self-conscious effort to construct a cinematic imaginary that allowed for the existence of such rarified precincts. In the retrenched city, cultural institutions like arthouse theaters occupied an important role in the reproduction and maintenance of what Michèle Lamont termed "symbolic boundaries":

> They are tools by which individuals and groups struggle over and come to agree upon definitions of reality ... Symbolic boundaries also separate people into groups and generate feelings of similarity and group membership. They are an essential medium through which people acquire status and monopolize resources.[34]

Of course, the notion of the community in cities is never fixed or stable; the durability of the palimpsest metaphor in urban studies attests to the potency of the city's many pasts, and the transience of its particular present.[35] As we observe—and, for some of us, participate in—the gentrification of America's cities, we see the "rose-colored" urbanism of Allen's films spilling out beyond the rarified precincts to which it had previously been constrained, leading to a new round of pitched battles over the symbolic boundaries that define urban communities. As Vanessa Mathews argues, art is an important tool in the discursive construction of community within the city: the same mean streets of SoHo that Scorsese films in *After Hours* (1985) are re-presented, twenty years later, as the stomping grounds of the bourgeoisie in *Sex and the City* (HBO, 1998–2004).[36] But here I have argued that *where* the movies are—that is, the physical place where we watch them—is a proxy statement of *who* the movies are for: as the geography of consumption changes, so too do the audiences for these urban representations. Consequently, the stories we tell ourselves about the places we live change to reflect the audiences for those stories. More than any single film, it is this structural transformation that reflects the powerful cultural work of gentrification.

Notes

1   I invoke here the foundational work of sociologist Ruth Glass, widely credited with coining the term "gentrification" in her study of cultural transformation in the central London neighborhoods like Islington and Notting Hill. The term first appears in the introduction she wrote to a book issued by the research center she chaired, the Centre for Urban Studies at University College London. Ruth Lazarus Glass and Centre for Urban Studies, *London: Aspects of Change* (London: MacGibbon & Kee, 1964).

2   Sharon Zukin, *Loft Living: Culture and Capital in Urban Change*, Second Edition. (New Brunswick, NJ: Rutgers University Press, 1989), 15.

3   Julie Podmore, "(Re)reading the 'Loft Living' Habitus in Montréal's Inner City," *International Journal of Urban and Regional Research* 22.2 (1998), 287.

4   Philip Lawton, "Culture, Capital and the Big Screen: Tracing the Changing Dynamics of Gentrification in the Films of Woody Allen," *Urban Geography* 39.3 (2017), 367–387; Johan Andersson, "Landscape and Gentrification: The Picturesque and Pastoral in 1980s New York Cinema," *Antipode* 49.3 (2017) 539–556; Brendan Kredell, "Border Lines: Boundaries and Transgression in the City Films of Martin Scorsese," in *A Companion to Martin Scorsese*, ed. Aaron Baker (Malden, MA: Wiley-Blackwell, 2014); "Wes Anderson and the City Spaces of Indie Cinema," *New Review of Film and Television Studies* 10.1 (2011), 83–96. Notably, all of these articles reflect a New York-centricity within the discourse; just as the city can be said to be the birthplace of American

gentrification studies, via the writing of Jane Jacobs and later Sharon Zukin, so too has it occupied a central place within the imagination of filmmakers depicting stories of gentrification, and of scholars researching the histories of those representations.

5   Richard Maltby, "How Can Cinema History Matter More?" *Screening the Past* 22 (2007), http://www.screeningthepast.com/2015/01/how-can-cinema-history-matter-more/.

6   Neil Smith, "Commentary: Gentrification and the Rent Gap," *Annals of the Association of American Geographers* 77.3 (September 1987), 462–478; David Ley, "Reply: The Rent Gap Revisited," *Annals of the Association of American Geographers* 77.3 (September 1987), 465–468.

7   David Ley, *The New Middle Class and the Remaking of the Central City* (Oxford: Oxford University Press, 1996).

8   John Joe Schlichtman, Jason Patch, and Marc Lamont Hill, *Gentrifier* (Toronto: University of Toronto Press, 2017).

9   Eric Kohn, "Christopher Nolan: I Won't Work with Netflix Because Their Film Strategy Is 'Pointless'" *indieWIRE*, July 19, 2017, http://www.indiewire.com/2017/07/christopher-nolan-interview-dunkirk-netflix-1201857101/.

10   The issues attending this conversion have become a growing part of the contemporary literature on the media industries; consider, for example, Kevin Sanson, *Distribution Revolution: Conversations about the Digital Future of Film and Television* (Oakland: University of California Press, 2014).

11   "Cannes: Netflix Film *Okja* Stopped after Technical Glitch," *BBC*, May 19, 2017, http://www.bbc.com/news/entertainment-arts-39972987.

12   Anita Busch and Anthony D'Alessandro, "Amazon Studios Execs: 'We Believe in the Theatrical Window Fully for Our Releases' – CinemaCon," *Deadline Hollywood*, March 30, 2017.

13   The Amazon-distributed *Manchester by the Sea* (Kenneth Lonergan, 2016) won Best Actor and Best Original Screenplay, while the Academy Award for Best Foreign Language Film went to *The Salesman* (Asghar Farhadi, 2016). It should be noted that the Netflix-distributed *The White Helmets* (Orlando von Einsiedel, 2016) won the Academy Award for Best Documentary (Short Subject); Netflix documentaries have consistently earned Academy nominations going back to 2013.

14   This being Twitter, it should also be noted that her tweet concluded with the side-eye emoji; it should also be noted that DuVernay's 2016 documentary *13th* was

distributed by Netflix; she is presently in development on a mini-series on the Central Park Five to be produced by Netflix, and the streaming service also hosts films distributed by DuVernay's ARRAY Now collective. https://twitter.com/ava/status/887721737898475520.

15 Robert C. Allen, and Douglas Gomery, *Film History: Theory and Practice* (New York: Alfred A. Knopf, 1985).

16 All exhibitor data collected from the National Association of Theatre Owners, available at http://www.natoonline.org/data/.

17 William Paul, "The K-Mart Audience at the Mall Movies," *Film History* 6 (1994).

18 Indeed, Hollywood reached its recent peak in 2006, when the major studios distributed 128 films in wide release. I use "major studios" and "Big Six" interchangeably here to refer to Columbia, Disney, Fox, Paramount, Universal, Warner Bros., and their respective affiliates.

19 Data here are cited from Nash Information Services' site *The Numbers* (http://www.the-numbers.com/market/). There is some discrepancy in publicly reported data as a result of methodological differences in its collection; for example, Nash reports that Disney released twelve films in wide release in 2016, while competitor Box Office Mojo (http://www.boxofficemojo.com/studio/?view=parent&view2=yearly&yr=2016) tracked thirteen films. But the overall trend lines are identical.

20 Perhaps coincidentally, there were seventy theaters across the United States for every one film released by a major studio in 1995; despite the ever-shrinking release slate of the majors in the intervening years, the corresponding consolidation in the exhibition industry means that this ratio remains virtually unchanged today.

21 A useful jumping off point here is Julian Stringer, ed., *Movie Blockbusters* (London and New York: Routledge, 2003).

22 Her initial effort in this regard, the African-American Film Festival Releasing Movement (AFFRM), reorganized itself as ARRAY in 2015, with a broader mandate to also release films directed by women.

23 Kredell, "Wes Anderson and the City Spaces of Indie Cinema."

24 Sarah Schulman, *The Gentrification of the Mind: Witness to a Lost Imagination* (Berkeley: University of California Press, 2012), 27. To the reader steeped in film theory, this is an especially potent and productive framing, of course, given the centrality of ideology and "the apparatus" to the history of film theory; I refer here, of course, to writers like Jean-Louis Baudry, Christian Metz, Laura Mulvey, and Peter Wollen, inter al.

25 Manohla Dargis and A.O. Scott, "One Nation under a Movie Theater? It's a Myth," *New York Times*, September 7, 2017.

26 These data are culled from information reported in the 2002 Economic Census for North American Industry Classification System (NAICS) code 512131, "Motion Picture Theaters (except Drive-Ins)." This data set is not without its issues; notably, the Economic Census defines NAICS 512131 to include "establishments primarily engaged in operating motion picture theaters (except drive-ins) and/or exhibiting motion pictures at film festivals, and so forth." In practice, most film festivals are either structured as non-profit organizations or hosted by a larger entity with a separate NAICS classification; as examples, the Chicago International Film Festival is classified as a Civic/Social Organization (813410), while the Chicago International Children's Film Festival is produced by Facets Multi-Media and is thus shares its parent organization's classification as "Other Motion Picture and Video Industries" (512199). So while it is difficult to conclude with certainty that the Economic Census measurement does not include any itinerant or seasonal exhibitors within its scope, it appears to be as precise a measurement as is available of historical exhibition activity at the city level.

27 ICE data were provided to the author directly by its proprietor, Alisa Starks, in private correspondence dated July 1, 2014.

28 Michael Z. Newman, *Indie: An American Film Culture* (New York: Columbia University Press, 2011).

29 Barbara Wilinsky, *Sure Seaters: The Emergence of Art House Cinema* (Minneapolis: University of Minnesota Press, 2001).

30 Emily Nonko, "'Do or Die' Bed-Stuy Is Definitely Gentrifying," *New York Post*, January 7, 2016, https://nypost.com/2016/01/07/gritty-bed-stuy-is-starting-to-show-its-softer-side/; Julie Turkewitz, "Denver Cafe 'Happily Gentrifying'? Neighbors Aren't So Happy," *New York Times*, November 27, 2017, https://www.nytimes.com/2017/11/27/us/denver-cafe-gentrification.html.

31 Brendan Kredell, *Redeveloping the City, Redeveloping the Cinema: Film and Urban Culture at the Turn of the Twenty-First Century*, PhD diss., Northwestern University, 2011.

32 Schlichtman, Patch, and Hill.

33 Lawton, 5.

34 Michèle Lamont and Virág Molnár, "The Study of Boundaries in the Social Sciences," *Annual Review of Sociology* 28.1 (2002).

35 Among many others who have invoked this metaphor, I think particularly here of the work of Michel de Certeau, particularly regarding the "spatial practices" of urban life. See Michel de Certeau, *The Practice of Everyday Life, Volume 1* (Berkeley: University of California Press, 1988).

36 Vanessa Mathews, "Artcetera: Narrativising Gentrification in Yorkville, Toronto," *Urban Studies* 45.13 (December 2008), 2849–2876.

10

Ebbets Field and Other Monuments: Outer Borough Neighborhoods and Revanchism in 1990s Cinema

Erica Stein

Postindustrial New York is often defined in terms of loss: of economic security, a manufacturing economy, spatial coherence, the right to public space, and above all, the coherent individual and collective identity they once authored.[1] Especially in film, this amalgam of undoing is indexed through one additional loss, that of a city easily imaged by its populace. This nexus of loss and image—of image as what has been lost—has in turn fueled a fetish for industrial New York as a socio-spatial ideal in which the itineraries of residents, the characteristics of neighborhoods and public spaces, and the identities of the citizens they mutually constitute are all visible, legible, and unified. This "nostalgia for modernity"[2] is evident in many independent films of the 1980s and 1990s. These films helped codify the representation of New York as a postindustrial city still rich in (counter)cultural capital as it emerged from the urban crisis while anxiously insuring this capital with references to earlier urban forms. This trend surfaces in the costuming and soundtrack of *Stranger than Paradise* (Jim Jarmusch, 1984), the specter of Brooklyn's racially integrated past in *Do the Right Thing* (Spike Lee, 1989), and elegiac period pieces like *A Bronx Tale* (Robert De Niro, 1993). An idealized vision of industrial New York is also used to justify many contemporary new urbanism projects, including the public–private partnerships, business improvement districts, and tax increment financing schemes that intensify the postindustrial city's uneven development.[3]

New York's independent cinema of the late 1980s and early 1990s participates in, extends, and nuances what Michael Dwyer has described as the general tendency of Reagan-era culture to produce nostalgic imagery of the mid-century, especially of the 1950s. Dwyer is largely concerned with 1980s blockbusters and their use of nostalgia to obscure and elide late twentieth-century national tensions, particularly as regards race.[4] The early 1990s independent films discussed in this chapter, by contrast, take the local, specific, and authentic rather than the national and generic as the objects of their nostalgia. They do not so much avoid the problems of the present as they celebrate what they take to be vestiges of a superior past obtruding into this present. In doing so, these films oscillate between what Svetlana Boym has identified as two key modes of nostalgia, the prefabricated and the reflective. The former forecloses the future in favor of the hermetically sealed world of the lost past, while the latter acknowledges the past's subjective and incomplete nature, making dialogue with the present and future possible.[5]

The postindustrial city itself is constituted by a prefabricated nostalgia structured by the logic of revanchism. This chapter discusses Abel Ferrara's *King of New York* (1990) and Wayne Wang/Paul Auster's *Smoke* and *Blue in the Face* (both 1995). By analyzing the films' depiction of urban space, their thematization of criminality, and their relationship to urban history, I show how these films place the prefabricated nostalgia of revanchism in conversation with reflective nostalgia and illuminate the ways in which the postindustrial city's longing for the past is the longing for straight white men to regain/retain their mastery of the urban environment. At the same time, because these films visualize and concretize their nostalgia for the industrial city in the form of monuments in particular and imageability in general, they reveal the extent to which the longing for a transparent, legible urban environment is itself bound up in the logic of revanchism.

Neil Smith associates revanchism with a discourse of loss, and locates its origins in the increasingly uneven development and economic stratification that followed the first wave of gentrification in the late 1970s. Revanchist rhetoric undergirds urban policies that recover the city from an "invasion" by the poor and people of color that has removed it from its "true form." Revanchism positions the postindustrial city as an historical aberration that can only be addressed by "re-taking" public and residential urban spaces through the just workings of the market and the police.[6] Revanchism justifies itself by gesturing to crime statistics and other modes of discourse that invoke a "frontier" mentality.

The films this chapter considers were made between 1990 and 1995, a short span that marks the moment when New York City's economic fortunes reversed and the last vestige of the urban crisis—high crime rates—fell away, setting the city on the track of super-gentrification and starkly uneven development it maintains to this day.[7] The year 1990 saw the city's yearly murders peak at 2,245, falling to 1,550 by 1995, a trajectory that continues today, with 352 murders in 2015, and a continued decline through 2017.[8] New York City's real estate value began its meteoric rise at the same time, jumping by 10.8 percent in early 1990, despite the common belief that crime rates and property values are mutually opposed. This financial shift was matched by the beginning of civic, as well as public–private, investment in multiple landmarks and public spaces long subject to official neglect.[9] This transitional moment, and in particular the role revanchism played in it, is often discussed through quality films concerned either with the white upper-middle class in Manhattan enclaves or with popular genre films that center on violent, civilian-targeted crime and dystopian cityscapes.[10]

By contrast, *King of New York, Smoke*, and *Blue in the Face* present a view of postindustrial New York in which crime is a tool of socio-spatial construction and connection, linking multiple classes and races together in generally successful neighborhood cohabitations. Like many of the other New York-based independent films of the period, they are set in the outer boroughs, which may suggest an automatic temporal displacement from—or a traditional center–periphery relationship with—the Manhattan epicenter of postindustrial conditions. But unlike their contemporaries, these films' nostalgia for the industrial city is not explicit in setting, mise-en-scène, or theme. *King of New York, Smoke*, and *Blue in the Face* potentially articulate a kind of reflective nostalgia that is anti-revanchist and an alternative to the narrative of the postindustrial city as loss. Yet their narrative structures and treatment of space deny that their respective diegeses occur within the postindustrial city at all, instead claiming their outer borough neighborhoods as anachronistic extrusions of, or monuments to, the industrial city. This construction of the neighborhood as monument, a kind of embodied (prefabricated) nostalgic object, both demonstrates these films' veneration of the industrial city as the imaged city and distorts a key element of imageability, the landmark. *King of New York, Smoke,* and *Blue in the Face* demonstrate the extent to which revanchism co-opts other, seemingly progressive urban narratives for its own ends.

The image of the city/the lost city

David Harvey argues that the landmark was key to industrial New York's preeminence. Landmarks gave the city its iconic skyline, and what Edward Dimendberg has called its sense of "photodocumentary cliché," by increasing the scale of debt-financed public spaces and the absorption of surplus capital into a built environment soon studded with bridges, tunnels, parks, stadiums, and other outsized structures.[11] These landmarks also helped give industrial New York what Kevin Lynch—writing just before the onset of deindustrialization— has described as "an especially clear image." Sharon Zukin has more recently associated this image with the production of since-lost authentic experience and public intimacy.[12] While the iconic skyline and many of the individual buildings the era produced survived intact in the postindustrial city, they were also divested of the itineraries and spatial practices that once produced them as spaces, leaving them as vacant monuments to a much-diminished territory. Just as the capital they once absorbed has moved on to spaces much larger and more ephemeral, the embodied urban experience they once produced has long since dissipated. Moreover, some landmarks—such as Pennsylvania Station and Ebbets Field—*were* demolished, and thereafter became discursive monuments.

Kevin Lynch's canonic urban studies work *The Image of the City* suggests landmarks like Pennsylvania Station as crucial to an urban inhabitant's ability to formulate a clear image of both a city's overall structure and their own place within that structure.[13] New York's landmarks helped establish it as an especially legible city: "One whose districts or landmarks or pathways are easily identifiable and are easily grouped into an overall pattern."[14] Lynch's description of the social effects of this clear image is sharply reminiscent of the qualities Zukin suggests as most fleeting, yet sought after, in the postindustrial city:

Such a structure gives an individual a possibility of choice and a starting-point for the acquisition of further information. A clear image of the surroundings is thus a useful basis for individual growth. A vivid and integrated physical setting, capable of producing a sharp image, plays a social role as well. It can furnish the raw material for the symbols and collective memories of group communication.[15]

When this structure is strong enough to "frame" the entire city, then the city as a whole may take on the status of landmark—a situation Lynch suggests obtains in industrial Manhattan—especially when it produces a continuous fluctuation in scale as well as a series of sharply hierarchical pathways.[16] New York's grid system, coupled with its especially sharp edges and framing by waterways, produces the city itself, as well as its distinctly individuated neighborhoods, as landmarks. Works like *Smoke, King of New York*, and *Blue in the Face* prominently feature iconic landmarks, such as Ebbets Field and the Triborough Bridge. They also utilize the fluctuation of scale and hard edges to cast the neighborhoods at their center as a kind of collective landmark. However, these structures and neighborhoods produce a navigable image of the city only to the extent that they replicate the industrial city; they are not landmarks, because landmarks are mutually constitutive with spatial practices in the present and help to produce itineraries. Landmarks are for the living. The edifices and areas in these films, by contrast, attest to the impassable nature of the postindustrial city. They exist only as a taxidermy of the industrial city that mourns its death: they are monuments.[17]

Moreover, the transformation of landmark into monument speaks to the danger of continually mourning and valorizing not only industrial New York per se, but also the ideal of the image of the city in general, especially when that image is rendered unifocal. As Lynch himself notes, the city is comprised of multiple images, not just one, and within the images that dominate policy, planning, or representation not all neighborhoods are accorded equal status— just as not all images, or the identities they compose, are equal within the socio-spatial order. "The loss of New York" amounts to the loss of a secure "starting-point" for socio-politically dominant identities.

In her treatment of *Taxi Driver* (1976) and Martin Scorsese's other 1970s New York cityscapes, Sabine Haenni argues that "the decline of the city seems to engender the decline of the male hero—Travis's inability to function in individual, collective, or heteronormative terms."[18] Haenni couples this decline with a loss of control over public space, the ability both to correctly read the landmark (or are they already monuments?) "hieroglyphics" that constitute New York as a socio-spatial structure and to secure the borders, integrity, and unified images that produce specific neighborhoods as the bastions of a racially and sexually homogeneous territory. This erosion of control, boundary, identity, and image—of self and of city—results in "a fascinatingly underdetermined social space with as yet illegible rules."[19] The nostalgia for industrial New York and the fantasy of the recovery of that city-as-monument in the guise of an anachronistic postindustrial neighborhood is the desire for the return to dominance of one particular image of the city and the identity it helped constitute. When the image of the city becomes a fetish, it is instrumental to the discourse of revanchism.[20] *Smoke*, *King of New York*, and *Blue in the Face* retain the preoccupation with crime and masculinity that mark Scorsese's films, and they intertwine these themes with a discourse of authenticity and authority that rests on control of the city reverting to its rightful owners.

The neighborhoods on which the films focus are at once paradoxically frozen in their industrial identity and yet undergoing a highly compressed experience of deindustrialization, crisis, and gentrification. *Smoke* takes place in Park Slope, with several scenes set in the nearby neighborhoods of Boerum Hill and Greenpoint and a few outside the city upstate in Peekskill; *Blue in the Face* is set solely on 16th Street between 7th and 8th Avenues at the southern boundary of Park Slope; and *King of New York* takes place in Harlem, the South Bronx, and Ridgewood, Queens, with some scenes set in midtown Manhattan near Central Park. These neighborhoods have distinct functions in New York's cultural imaginary and played extremely diverse roles in the urban crisis and onset of postindustrialization. Moreover, each, with the exception of Ridgewood, has always fallen outside the territory claimed by bourgeois and working-class heterosexual white male identities.

Most notably, Harlem and the South Bronx are African American and Latino neighborhoods that, in the former case, functioned as "the capital of the black world" in the industrial era, and, in the latter, symbolized the nadir of New York's ability to perform basic civic services at the height of the urban crisis.[21] Moreover, both spaces have experienced belated gentrification, with Harlem not seeing a drastic shift in demographics, closure of established retailers, and sharp rise in the rental market until the early 2000s.[22] For its part, the South Bronx is today engaged in widespread local resistance to the early stages of cultural capital-driven gentrification.[23] Conversely, Park Slope was one of the first neighborhoods to serve as a non-suburban outpost for middle-class, white Manhattanites. Suleiman Osman argues that its image as the platonic ideal of the "human-scale" cityscape emerged out of its evolution from a 1950s-era slum and had solidified by the late 1970s.[24] Yet Park Slope, like Harlem and the South Bronx, is historically affiliated with an image of the city other than the dominant one, in this case that of lesbian and bisexual women. Queer women have constituted a large presence in the neighborhood since the dawn of the postindustrial era, and began moving to the neighborhood in the 1940s.[25]

Despite these neighborhoods' divergent histories and identities, *Smoke*, *Blue in the Face*, and *King of New York* represent them in remarkably similar thematic terms, using clearly related visual language, and in the end recreate them as bastions of heterosexual white male urban identity. The films accomplish this by focusing on monumental structures of transit and communal performance—such as the Brooklyn, Triborough, and Queensboro Bridges, and Ebbets Field—that are also closely associated with the individual neighborhoods that serve as the films' main settings. These locations help the films produce the neighborhoods as metonymies for the "authentic" (industrial) city while also suggesting that the collective communal identity produced in and by the neighborhood is a comparable, and comparably limited, monument to this fetishized epoch.

Misplacing the Triborough Bridge:
King of New York's encoded city

Abel Ferrara's *King of New York* initially suggests an anti-revanchist position by valorizing the neighborhoods of Harlem and the South Bronx. The film explicitly claims these areas for their current inhabitants while establishing moral and economic equivalences among the city's organized crime syndicates, its police force, and its power brokers. Yet, when the film depicts the efforts of recently released drug dealer Frank White (Christopher Walken) to take over and unify all drug trafficking within the five boroughs and, in so doing, save them, it portrays him as saving the city from the depredations of too-traditional, overly territorial, indiscriminately violent African American, Chinese, and Latino gangsters. In fact, White explicitly condemns his fellow criminals for not supporting their own neighborhoods and for exploiting members of their own ethnic groups.[26] In her study of Ferrara, Nicole Brenez argues that, while his criminal adversaries are highly territorial "monarchs" of closely limited and guarded ethnic turfs, Frank explicitly sets out to save the city and its under/working class as a whole.[27] Frank prevents *King of New York* from articulating a critique of revanchism because he is the embodiment of the revanchist city.

King of New York also enunciates a prefabricated nostalgia by figuring the city's salvation as the construction of monumental public works—the restoration of an "art deco" hospital in the South Bronx and the reopening of the "Harlem Ballroom." The film aligns these fictional projects with the new urbanism of postindustrial New York through Frank's pronouncement that only "private money" can restore these structures, the glowing testimonials of doctors and community members in their defense, and the presence of city councilmen at private fundraising galas. These resonances are only strengthened by the fates of the buildings on which Frank's projects are based. *King of New York*'s dank, underfunded, overworked "Bronx Memorial" hospital resembles the Norwood, Bronx-based Montefiore Hospital, which was revitalized by a series of grants in the mid-2000s. The "Harlem Ballroom" appears to be a conflation of the Savoy Ballroom and the Apollo Theater, both premiere uptown entertainment venues associated with the center of Harlem's cultural life during the industrial era.[28] While the Savoy was demolished in 1959 to make way for the Delano Village low-income homes, the Apollo survived a later decline during the 1970s to see initial small-scale reinvestment by private parties in the mid-1980s. Purchased by New York State in 1991, the Apollo regained its reputation as a premiere venue for both live music and comedy specials following architectural rehabilitation in 2001. The film's assessment of which redevelopment projects in the postindustrial city could and should be undertaken was nothing if not prescient, yet this prescience amounts to a prefabricated nostalgia that preserves the built structures while precluding future community transformations of or claims to them.

King of New York presents the fictional versions of these projects as altruistic actions on Frank's part that produce unalloyed good for New Yorkers. However, the film's own logic of doubling, boundary crossing, and redefinition of criminal behavior cannot erase the specter of artifice, questionable accumulation, and violence that haunts Frank's investments. The real-life history of the Apollo and Montefiore attest to the role that the new urbanist approach pursued by multiple mayoral administrations has played in the shaping of today's postindustrial New York, and the extent to which that approach transforms landmarks into monuments. These projects bear out Zukin's claim that the super-gentrified city both fetishizes the "authenticity" of the industrial city and attempts to superficially restore the sharpness and stability of its image.[29] They also illustrate Smith's charge that gentrification generates spatial practices that ensure only capital, not the citizenry, have a right to the spaces produced, and that this right is enforced by the stringent policing of which people may use the space.[30]

Despite their clear analogues in New York's postindustrial landscape, "Bronx Memorial" and the "Harlem Ballroom" also point out *King of New York*'s absurd treatment of the city's physical geography and history. Both Ferrara's work in general and this film in particular are closely associated with authenticity. In an interview in *Film Comment*, Ferrara, actor Laurence Fishburne, and interviewer Gavin Smith all invoke this quality as a justification for the film's violence.[31] Yet *King of New York* produces a completely mapped, totally imaged city that is simultaneously composed of fictional landmarks like the Harlem Ballroom and historically impossible geographies that return it to revanchist discourse. Frank's image of a redeemed postindustrial New York and his simultaneous capital extraction from and introjections of monuments into the South Bronx and Harlem are predicated on the reproduction of the "secure base" of individual and collective social identity centered on heterosexual white masculinity otherwise disrupted by the loss of the industrial image of the city.

In this film, New York remains suspended in and between two distinct historical moments, neither of which correspond to the postindustrial city in which the film was produced and set. While the murder rate peaked in 1990, in that same year the tax base had largely stabilized, the financial sector had begun recovering from the late 1980s crash, and city services were restored. Yet

King of New York portrays only a single act of civilian-targeted violence, and a relatively low civilian body count (on Frank's part, at least, the police being less discriminate), as only rival criminals are murdered. At the same time, the film's image of postindustrial New York is still mired in the socioeconomic nadir of the late 1970s' bankrupt city, as represented in the breakdown of infrastructure and social services combined with a "rival gang" police department modeled on the ultra-corrupt NYPD of *Serpico* (Sidney Lumet, 1973) fame. The film also maps a highly legible New York of discrete neighborhood "turfs" each ruled over by ethnically differentiated mafias, offering a fantasy of postwar industrial New York perhaps most familiar from the nostalgic gangster films of the 1970s. In *King of New York*, Puerto Ricans live in East Harlem, Italians in Little Italy, and Chinese in Manhattan's Chinatown—no matter that by the 1990s the borders of these areas and the demographics of their inhabitants had shifted, or that Ferrara himself had made such changes central to *China Girl* (1987). White himself, improbably, represents and speaks for Harlem and the South Bronx, just as he comfortably leads a predominantly black gang, his captaincy of the latter apparently giving him rights to the former. *King of New York* offers a prefabricated nostalgic, revanchist fantasy in which everyone is in their right place: ethnic minorities are restricted to historical ghettos, rendering them safe for the same kind of cinematic slumming gaze that characterized images of industrial New York, while Frank White lays claim both to those individual neighborhoods that best represent the "incursion" of the poor and the non-white *and* to those public spaces where the losses inflicted by that incursion are most felt.

Frank's claim to all of New York is evident from the film's opening sequence, which is punctuated by landmark structures that once allowed for the production of the unified image of the city and identity that Frank strives to restore, which the film produces as monuments. The sequence intercuts Frank's journey back to the city from Sing Sing Prison in Ossining to a luxurious shower at the Plaza Hotel with his lieutenants assassinating the heads of rival Latino gangs (Figure 10.1).

Frank's return trip is both highly specific and geographically ludicrous. The east side of midtown Manhattan is easily accessible from Ossining via the Major Deegan Expressway, the Harlem River Span of the Triborough Bridge, and the FDR Drive. By contrast, Frank's route finds him leaving the Expressway

Figure 10.1 Frank overlooks Manhattan from his suite at the Plaza, his trip through the outer boroughs delivering him to a traditional seat of power. *King of New York* (1990).

and driving through the South Bronx on surface streets, the descending, subterranean nature of his detour emphasized by the car passing underneath elevated portions of the 4 and D trains in a series of hard cuts. In the next shot, the Queens-Manhattan span of the Triborough Bridge is visible, which would imply that Frank has already traversed the Bridge and is now on the FDR Drive going south while the camera looks east. However, the next shot finds Frank looking south and traveling west as the limo crosses the Queensboro Bridge to Manhattan from Long Island City in Queens. The sequence ends as Frank showers in his suite at the Plaza Hotel, just south of Central Park. The choice of surface streets/elevated train, the Triborough Bridge, and the Queensboro Bridge encapsulate *King of New York*'s thematic use and differentiation of space within the five boroughs, as well as Frank's symbolic mastery of New York City reduced to a monument as a whole.

One of the largest debt-financed infrastructure projects of the industrial city, the Triborough Bridge links the Bronx, Queens, and Manhattan, respectively associated with the urban underclass, white ethnic suburbia, and the city as iconic product of capital. The film returns to the location multiple times, often juxtaposing the blasted landscape of the South Bronx on which it is built with the skyline gathered at its back. The South Bronx, in turn, gives the lie to

Berenz's assertion that Frank, unlike the other gangsters, lacks a territory and a territorial instinct. The South Bronx is the only space in the opening sequence viewed from street level and with any kind of attention to socioeconomic or spatial detail. Frank is literally on the same level as the neighborhood, and moves through it like a royal tour, taking stock of his individual subjects. In contrast, Queens is not only associated with white ethnic suburbia in general, but, in this film, with the territory of the police as a rival gang in particular, whose social and ritual spaces are all clearly placed within the borough. The rivalry between the South Bronx and Queens, Frank's gang and the police, is echoed by the disparate treatment of the two spaces. Queens is never visible in the sequence; the Queensboro Bridge stands for the borough as a whole, and ensures that Frank always relates to it from a place of distanced physical and geographic mastery. If the Queensboro Bridge reduces Queens to an inference and Midtown Manhattan to a silhouetted text, then the South Bronx becomes a clubhouse, nearly empty but for Frank's gang, who turns its burnt out buildings into communal spaces of sex, drugs, and music as they effortlessly negotiate the labyrinthine streets under its bridges and trains. Frank moves smoothly between the two spaces, almost always using the subway.

A symbol of the danger and unruliness of public space in New York since the mid-1960s,[32] the subway evidences Frank's mastery of public space. As Johan Andersson has pointed out, while Frank is confronted by several would-be African American muggers on the subway in a repetition of a scenario familiar from 1970s to 1980s vigilante films, the scene ends not in physical violence but in Frank's making, and the muggers accepting, a job offer.[33] Through Frank's movements and his expansive habitus—equally useful in negotiating the corridors of midtown power and money, "foreign" ethnic ghettos, and crime-blasted but mutually supportive neighborhoods—*King of New York* represents the uneven development of the postindustrial city while subsuming the spaces that constitute it in a narrative of white professionalism and mastery. These spaces of crisis and of gentrification are elided in the fantasy of the hyper-imageable industrial city that Frank has always already recovered. Whatever the socio-spatial truth of industrial New York might have been, *King of New York*'s resurrection of it as monument suggests that a fully encoded, imageable city is not what postindustrial New York should be, or has lost. Rather, this ideal is the tool by which both heterosexual white masculinity and the capital with which it is bound up continually asserts its right to the city's past, present, and future, while foreclosing any other image of the city as one that might be livable.

Nostalgia and archive in *Smoke* and *Blue in the Face*

Like *King of New York, Smoke* and, to a lesser extent, *Blue in the Face* depict crime as a means of social engagement and fellowship that benefits neighborhoods while illuminating the social networks and territorial lines that establish neighborhoods as monuments to the industrial city and as resistant to postindustrial characteristics. In all three films, crime maps community and helps produce an artificial image of the city from which an individual can imagine a stable identity that aligns with the revanchist city. In *Smoke* and *Blue in the Face*, however, reflective nostalgia makes temporality more complex and contradictory.

Both films are co-directed by Wayne Wang and Paul Auster, the latter of whom wrote the short fiction piece on which the films are based. Filmed nearly concurrently in 1995, the companion films narrate everyday vignettes in the life of Park Slope between 1990 and 1991. Many of these scenes and sketches explicitly invoke the question of the neighborhood's future, the challenges and opportunities associated with its present, and the glories of its past. However, while that past is both historically and spatially exact—tied to Ebbets Field and the Jackie Robinson-era Dodgers—the present seems to retain traces of that same era in terms of identity and image formation as well as an uncanny lack of connection to the defining elements of the postindustrial city. In Ferarra's film, the entire city appears to be frozen in the same socio-spatial clichés of industrial New York. Here, only Park Slope seems to occupy that anachronism, with other nearby neighborhoods displaying affiliations with the urban crisis (DUMBO) and the postindustrial, unevenly developed city (Boerum Hill). Moreover, the narratives of both films detail the threat of these other, more recent times and spaces to Park Slope. In *Smoke* and *Blue in the Face* the only safe place is in the past.

Given this preoccupation, it is not surprising that most of the critical literature on the films approaches them in terms of the politics of nostalgia.

Most notably, this underpins bell hooks's elucidation of *Smoke*'s racist politics.[34] It also acts as the basis for Paul Frosch's hesitations about the valorization of both auteurism and mechanization at the base of the film's aesthetics.[35] *Smoke*, following hooks's influential reading, is often criticized for its nostalgic invocation of homosocial space, paternal and artistic authority vested in middle-aged white male figures, and the mirror image of violent criminality as blackness. Conversely, as with Mark Brown and Wilbert Turner's accounts, *Blue in the Face* is lauded for its harnessing of this nostalgia as a kind of guarantor of the authenticity and longevity of today's multiethnic, polyphonic Park Slope.[36] hooks herself posits *Blue in the Face* as reparative of the white supremacist politics and spatial restrictions of *Smoke*.[37]

However, I argue that both films utilize similar strategies to establish Park Slope as a nostalgic monument to the industrial city, an authentic space of human-scaled community within the de-personalized, illegible, and dangerous postindustrial city. Park Slope's authenticity arises from its identity as an imageable territory mutually constitutive with white masculinity. The films' politics rest on the ways in which prefabricated nostalgia invariably intimates that the only city worth missing, the only city worth living in, is inimical to the postindustrial age. In the films' diegetic present, by contrast, Park Slope is threatened by the presence of people of color and the violence the films associate with them, as well as by the potential osmosis between Park Slope and the rest of Brooklyn.

Smoke takes pains to establish Park Slope as exceptional within Brooklyn.[38] In *Blue in the Face*, this uniqueness is then, paradoxically, used to establish Park Slope as a metonymy of Brooklyn, and the borough itself—referred to as "the people's republic of Brooklyn" in the film's promotional materials and much of Auster's other work—as the last vestige of pre-lapsarian New York, a pristine monument-image held separate from a degraded postindustrial Manhattan. While cultural contrasts between Manhattan and the outer boroughs couched in terms of temporality are familiar from many other postindustrial texts, urban crisis films, and even earlier studio-era movies,[39] the Auster/Wang films are unique in the range of oppositions Park Slope organizes.

Smoke details the interconnected adventures of Auggie Wren (Harvey Keitel), Paul Benjamin (William Hurt), and Rashid Cole (Harold Perrineau). Auggie manages the local cigar/candy/news store, The Brooklyn Cigar Co., and plans to supplement his income by selling illegal Cuban cigars. Rashid, a runaway from the nearby Boerum Hill projects, has been taken in by Auggie's customer, novelist Paul Benjamin, who has prevailed on Auggie to employ Rashid in the store. Rashid promptly ruins the cigars, but makes restitution with the proceeds from the robbery he witnessed in Boerum Hill, which precipitated his own flight to Park Slope. Auggie then takes the money to his ex-girlfriend, Ruby (Stockard Channing), to help her enroll their daughter, currently living in a DUMBO shooting gallery, in rehab. All of Brooklyn is open to Park Slope, and the film's structure produces a pretense of equality through this porousness, especially in the circulation and transformation of the stolen money. The narration of this circulation helps to compose an image of the city much like Lynch's. The landmark of Brooklyn Cigar Co., the edge of the Brooklyn-Queens Expressway (BQE), the paths between Boerum Hill and Park Slope are all locked into a clear, hierarchical, and navigable image that provides a "starting point" and a "basis for individual growth" for each of the three main characters. Perhaps more important, the circulation of the money and the image it produces align Paul and Rashid in a familial and artistic relationship that crosses racial lines, strengthens companionate ties between Paul and Auggie across class lines, and also romantically reunites Auggie with Ruby. This image of the city allows Rashid, whose real name is Thomas, to spin a new identity for himself. It helps Auggie to recognize the lynchpin-like role he plays in the neighborhood and to reaffirm his loyalty to it. Finally, Paul's mentorship of Rashid enables him to reconnect with others and to share his love of literature after the death of his wife. Park Slope apparently stands at the center of an image of the postindustrial city that "can furnish the raw material for the symbols and collective memories of group communication."

This image is limited, however, in two crucial ways. First, while *Smoke* appears to narrate an egalitarian map of New York (or more accurately, Brooklyn) as a clearly imaged city, the symbols and spaces it uses to do so limit this "city" to Park Slope, defining its virtues in large part against all other areas of the city. Second, Park Slope's virtues are expressly tied to its apparent anachronistic identity; *Smoke* continually focuses on aspects of culture and identity associated with the industrial city. In doing so, the film excludes Park Slope's actual inhabitants, as well as the image of the postindustrial city their history produces. While *Smoke* narrates the circulation of affection and money throughout the borough, this movement is not an equitable one. Help and assistance of all kinds flow from Park Slope to DUMBO and Boerum Hill. The former is never named as a neighborhood at all, and takes its character from the deserted streets, dead ends, and retaining wall separating it from the BQE as it approaches the Manhattan Bridge. The dilapidated space matches Felicity (Ashley Judd), who can only be redeemed by her acceptance of Auggie's Park Slope money and her physical removal from DUMBO. Boerum Hill, generally referred to as "the projects," is not glimpsed until the film's end credits, and exists only as a place for Rashid to flee, and a criminal incursion into otherwise law-abiding—and as hooks notes, largely white—Park Slope. In fact, the stripping of capital from Boerum Hill provides the other characters with their happy endings. Rashid notes that the money came from a robbery at "a check-cashing place" in his own neighborhood. The stolen funds represent his own neighbors' paychecks, but the money only enables communal support, *neighborliness*, when it is removed to, and circulates within, Park Slope's economy—and only after Rashid gives up all claim to it as the price for remaining there. As this summary and hooks's analysis suggest, *Smoke's* nostalgic racial politics are clearly aligned with the revanchist city. Yet *Smoke* cannot quite erase revanchism's dependence on the removal of capital from poor people of color.

The financial and spatial walls erected between Park Slope and the rest of Brooklyn echo the temporal ones that remove Park Slope into its own imagined history. It is no accident that Rashid's Aunt and Uncle are named Emily and Henry, or that Rashid continually refers to Park Slope as "another world"; *Smoke's* central neighborhood plays Oz to the rest of Brooklyn's Kansas, and seems to have escaped the confines of history all together. This is especially evident in Park Slope's apparent exemption from the postindustrial troubles of DUMBO and Boerum Hill, especially given the real-life fears of crime and unemployment displayed in census data and media coverage of Park Slope at the time. *Smoke* also downplays Park Slope's racial diversity and status as an enclave for queer women.[40] Moreover, *Smoke's* Park Slope is littered with signifiers of the industrial city. In the all-male spaces of the Brooklyn Cigar Co. and the local bar, relations with customers and the sawdust on the floor recall much of the "authenticity" and sense of community that Zukin argues has been so fleeting, and so sought after, for inhabitants of the postindustrial city. This association of the past with the authentic appears throughout the set design and characterization, from Auggie's vintage Cadillac to Paul's use of a typewriter and lack of a television (when he eventually gets one, it's only to watch baseball). These symbols and spaces coalesce to produce Park Slope as a monument to the industrial city and a re-inscription of that city as white, heterosexual, and male. *Smoke*'s Park Slope is at odds with the real neighborhood's history, demographics, and the image of the city they produce.[41] This history and these images of the city are comprehensively erased in *Smoke*, to the extent that this neighborhood often characterized as the "lesbian Castro" features nearly no women.[42]

Blue in the Face intensifies, rather than mitigates, the revanchist stance articulated by *Smoke*. The possible sale of The Brooklyn Cigar Co. provides the framework for *Blue in the Face*, and it is narrated in near-apocalyptic terms. As Auggie tells store owner Vinnie (Victor Argo):

> It's just a dumpy neighborhood store, but everybody comes in here ... Mrs. Arthur for her soap opera magazines, Frank Diaz for his *El Diario*, fat Mr. Chen for his crossword. And it helps to keep the neighborhood together, cause twenty blocks from here, 12-year-old kids are shooting each other for their sneakers. You close this store, and it'll be like one more nail in the coffin. You'll be helping to kill off this neighborhood.

Auggie's impassioned plea doesn't save the store. As Vinnie explains, the offer from the buyer, who wants to open a health food store in the space, is too good. Vinnie's rationale for selling and Auggie's warnings produce an ill-fitting historical coupling. Park Slope remains in the undisturbed anachronism that *Smoke* established for the neighborhood, while all around it swirls the uneven development characteristic of the postindustrial city—which includes both the homicidal 12-year-old and the health food store—attempting to infiltrate and "kill off" the neighborhood. Park Slope has both remained frozen in time, yet to experience all the tumult of the twenty-five years since the onset of the postindustrial city, and still unmercifully exposed to all the forces of that city, all compacted into one instant.

Reinforcing Park Slope's affiliation with the industrial city, the Brooklyn Cigar Co. is eventually saved by the ghost of Jackie Robinson (Keith David), who reminds Vinnie that the Dodgers left Brooklyn—and, implicitly, damaged the borough—over a similar matter of "dollars and cents." Auggie's appeal to the neighborhood's future cannot save the store, but Robinson's invocation of the past does, turning yet another landmark into a monument. Peter Brooker claims that this invocation of the Dodgers amounts to a positive "politicization of memory," which helps to produce a laudatory image of Park Slope as "mixed and heterogeneous, without a unitary history or identity."[43] Contrary to Brooker, I argue that *Blue in the Face* uses the Dodgers to fuse industrial Brooklyn into a prefabricated nostalgic monument, unifying memory and identity into the same figure of the heterosexual white male elite at the center of *Smoke*.

This occurs despite *Blue in the Face*'s multivocal structure, which features improvised sketches, found footage, interviews, the presentation of (generally accurate) statistics, and the loosely scripted drama of the Brooklyn Cigar Co's close shave. Although the film celebrates the multiracial complexity, geographic diversity, and historical density of Brooklyn in its documentary footage, it does so through the recitation of demographic facts—by a variety of non-actors who are suggested to be the ethnically varied clientele of Brooklyn Cigar Co.— that lack context or detail. The more emotionally inflected memories, larger set pieces, and full interviews are nearly without exception reserved for the middle-aged, white cultural elites that Zukin identifies as the face of first-wave gentrification.[44] These scenes, populated by celebrities like Lou Reed and Jim Jarmusch, narrow the definition of and emotional investment in Brooklyn not only to the industrial city, but also to an especially white and male experience of it.

Although both Reed and Jarmusch are primarily associated with Lower Manhattan and postindustrial New York, their scenes focus repeatedly on the iconicity of Brooklyn and the industrial city. Reed's scene, in addition to touching on several clichés of Brooklyn and greater New York in general (egg creams, the street grid, misanthropy), focuses on the trauma of the Dodgers' 1958 departure to Los Angeles. Notably, Reed claims that, because "you can't be a Mets fan and you're certainly not going to root for the Yankees, baseball is removed from your life." The use of the second person shifts the loss of the Dodgers from a historically localizable wound to one suffered eternally by all New Yorkers. It cannot be closed by substituting another team or avoided by those born after the event.

This sense of the Dodgers and their loss as a constitutive historical trauma, a nostalgic talisman, is amplified by an interview with a memorabilia collector, who says of the day the team left "there never was a worse day." The collector goes on to describe Ebbets Field as "a social club," where "neighborhood guys" went to see each other, or even participate in the team as members of the Field's volunteer orchestra. This communal sense extended to the street life around the team, as the collector describes meetings with the players, who "all lived around the neighborhood." The sequence is intercut with historical footage of the 1962 destruction of Ebbets Field, and leads directly into the threatened sale, and then salvation, of Brooklyn Cigar Co. What goes unmentioned in between is the fate of the area around Ebbets Field, which was not located in Park Slope but rather in Flatbush (the stadium's address is in today's Crown Heights), a Jewish and African American neighborhood that experienced the full brunt of the urban crisis and was, in fact, the kind of area denigrated in the revanchist discourse Auggie gestures to in his invocation of deadly struggles for sneakers. Thus, Park Slope supplants Crown Heights as the inheritor of the Dodgers' spirit, the location of "authentic" Brooklyn is tied irreversibly to the industrial city, and the only authentic urban experience is one of unending grief that recognizes as worth saving only that which resonates with its prefabricated nostalgic gaze. This is not the politicization of memory; it is the recruitment of memory for the revanchist claim to the city through the figure of the monument.

Conclusion: my spot

Neil Smith has characterized New York's gentrification in the late 1970s–'80s, and the revanchism that followed it, as the return of capital, rather than people, to the city.[45] This return manifests itself in the policing of central public spaces, the transferal of ownership to public–private partnerships, and the association of outer borough neighborhoods with authenticity and the industrial city as narrated in *King of New York*, *Smoke*, and *Blue in the Face*. These examples suggest that revanchism amounts to capital's assertion of its right to the postindustrial city. Henri Lefebvre's concept of the right to the city holds that no meaningful social change can proceed except if first through the appropriation and production of urban space as a collective work to which the masses have a right. It is the opposite of the revanchist city.[46] Such a city would, to a certain extent, be imageable, but it would be a multifaceted image, and one that admitted for landmarks, not monuments, neighborhoods, not territory, and reflective, rather than prefabricated, nostalgia. *King of New York, Smoke,* and *Blue in the Face* demonstrate both how the fetish of the imageable city drives revanchism and how this iteration of capital's right to the postindustrial city is cloaked by an idealization of the neighborhood that removes any notion of the livable city to the past, and reduces it to a monument.

Despite its revanchist characteristics, *Smoke* also suggests how the valorization of neighborhood and/as landmark could instead be recruited to reflective nostalgia and produce the city as a collective work. One of *Smoke's* most remarked on aspects is Auggie's "project," an archive of over 4,000 photographs (Figure 10.2).

Taken each morning at 8:00 a.m. on the corner of 3rd Street and 7th Avenue, the photographs chronicle the façade of the Brooklyn Cigar Co. from 1977 to 1990. The photographs produce the store as a landmark rather than as a monument. Taken each day at the same time, capturing the intersection in front of the store and the storefront, they are "all the same, but each one's different." The photographs contain the repeated itineraries that constitute the urban

Figure 10.2 A photograph of Paul's late wife, Ellen, from Auggie's archive, which offers an alternative view of the neighborhood's history from the film's usual nostalgia. *Smoke* (1995).

everyday, but they also inspire viewers first to pattern recognition—giving meaning to runs of rainy or sunny days, trends in clothing, the presence and absence of regulars, the progress of relationships—and then to a *connaissance*, rather than proprietary knowledge (*savoir*), of the space and the people with whom it is mutually constitutive.[47] This construction of pattern ensures that Brooklyn Cigar Co. is not fixed in time and significance like Ebbets Field; it is not a monument. Rather, it is defined by the actions of its users, and changes with its environment, just as Lynch suggests a landmark does. The photographs affirm Auggie's appropriation of the store as "my spot," overriding his managerial and tenant status.[48] Yet the assemblage of the photographs and the terms of their legibility also affirms Brooklyn Cigar Co. as "our spot," as a local landmark that is an archive for a sense of nearness, of closeness to home, of neighborliness, and of collective ownership of the postindustrial city, one that points to the future as well as to the past.[49]

Notes

1   Stanley Corkin, *Starring New York: Filming the Grime and the Glamour of the Long 1970s* (Oxford and New York: Oxford University Press, 2011); Rem Koolhaas, *Delirious New York: A Retroactive Manifesto for Manhattan* (New York: The Monacelli Press, 1997 [20th anniversary edition]); Mark Shiel, "A Nostalgia for Modernity: New York, Los Angeles, and American Cinema in the 1970s," in *Screening the City*, ed. Mark Shiel and Tony Fitzmaurice (London: Verso, 2003), 160–179; Lawrence Webb, *The Cinema of Urban Crisis: Seventies Film and the Reinvention of the City* (Amsterdam: Amsterdam University Press, 2014); Sharon Zukin, *Naked City: The Death and Life of Authentic Urban Places* (Oxford: Oxford University Press, 2010).

2   Shiel, 160–162.

3   Neil Smith, *The New Urban Frontier: Gentrification and the Revanchist City* (New York: Routledge, 1996).

4   Michael D. Dwyer, *Back to the Fifties: Nostalgia, Hollywood Film, and Popular Music of the Seventies and Eighties* (Oxford and New York: Oxford University Press, 2015), 18–23.

5   Svetlana Boym, *The Future of Nostalgia* (New York: Basic, 2002), 49–52; 351–353.

6   Smith, 210–227.

7   I use "crisis" here to refer specifically to the vacant housing stock, outward flow of capital, and erosion of the tax base that marked deindustrialization, rather than the rhetoric of crisis, tied first to revanchist fears of "superpredators" and later to neoliberal cries for austerity, that have subsequently marked the city.

8   George James, "New York Killings Set a Record, While Other Crimes Fell in 1990," *New York Times*, April 23, 1991 (New York); "NYPD Compliant Historical Data (2006–2015)," https://data.cityofnewyork.us (accessed August 21, 2018).

9   See Smith, 72–90; Zukin, 18–35.

10 Jennifer England, "Disciplining Subjectivity and Space: Representation, Film and Its Material Effects," *Antipode* 36.2 (2004), 295–321; Vanessa Mathews, "Set Appeal: Film Space and Urban Redevelopment," *Social & Cultural Geography* 11.2 (2010), 171–190.

11 David Harvey, *Rebel Cities: From the Right to the City to the Urban Revolution* (London: Verso, 2011), 9–12; Edward Dimendberg, *Film Noir and the Spaces of Modernity* (Cambridge, MA: Harvard University Press, 2004), 85–120.

12 Kevin Lynch, *The Image of the City* (Cambridge, MA: The MIT Press, 1960), 81.

13 Ibid., 8–9, 26; Zukin, 15–22.

14 Lynch, 3.

15 Ibid., 4.

16 Ibid., 67.

17 M. Christine Boyer, *The City of Collective Memory: Its Historical Imagery and Architectural Entertainments* (Cambridge, MA: The MIT Press, 1996), 281–302.

18 Sabine Haenni, "Geographies of Desire: Postsocial Urban Space and Historical Revision in the Films of Martin Scorsese," *Journal of Film and Video* 62.1–2 (Spring/Summer 2010), 67.

19 Ibid., 69.

20 Smith, xvi, 45.

21 Paula Massood, *Making a Promised Land: Harlem in Twentieth Century Photography and Film* (New Brunswick, NJ: Rutgers University Press, 2013), 5–11.

22 Smith also notes early attempts in the late 1980s and early 1990s, as well as their limited scope and success, 143–167; Zukin, 72–85.

23 Michael Kamber, "Bracing for Gentrification in the South Bronx," *New York Times*, October 4, 2015; David Goodman, "De Blasio Expands Affordable Housing, but Results Aren't Always Visible," *New York Times*, October 6, 2017.

24 Suleiman Osman, *The Invention of Brownstone Brooklyn: Gentrification and the Search for Authenticity in Postwar New York* (Oxford and New York: Oxford University Press, 2012), 101, 277.

25 Jen Jack Gieseking, "Queering the Meaning of Neighborhood: Reinterpreting the Lesbian-Queer Experience of Park Slope, Brooklyn, 1983–2008," in *Queer Presences and Absences*, ed. M. Addison and Y. Taylor (New York: Palgrave Macmillan, 2013), 178–200. "New York City Demographic Shifts, 2000–2010," *Center for Urban Research*, http://www.urbanresearchmaps.org/plurality/ (accessed December 30, 2014).

26 Philippe Met, "Abel Ferrara: Filming (on) the Wild Side (of New York)," *Senses of Cinema* 68 (September 2013).

27 Nicole Brenez, *Abel Ferrara* (Urbana and Chicago: University of Illinois Press, 2007), 38–41.

28 The name also suggests The Harlem Renaissance Ballroom, or Rennie, a 1920s reception hall.

29 Zukin, 130–137, 220–223.

30 Smith, xvi, 70.

31 Gavin Smith, "Moon in the Gutter," *Film Comment* 26.4 (July/August 1990), 40–46.

32 Johan Andersson, "Variations of an Archetypal Scene: The Paris Métro Confrontation in Michael Haneke's *Code Unknown*," *Environment and Planning D: Society and Space* 31.4 (2013), 694.

33 Ibid., 697.

34 Bell hooks, *Reel to Real: Race, Sex, and Class in the Movies* (New York: Routledge, 2008), 155–177.

35 Paul Frosh, "Filling the Sight by Force: *Smoke*, Photography, and the Rhetoric of Immobilization," *Textual Practice* 12.2 (1998), 323–340.

36 Wilbert Turner, Jr., "Tony, Auggie, and the Mook: Race Relations in Cinematic Brooklyn," in *The Brooklyn Film*, ed. John Manbeck and Robert Singer (London: McFarland & Company, 2003), 71–82; Mark Brown, "We Don't Go by Numbers: Brooklyn and Baseball in the Films of Paul Auster," in *The Brooklyn Film*, 127–147.

37 Hooks, 155–156, 163–167.

38 Ibid., 159; Turner, 78–79.

39 For accounts of this dynamic as it shifts and re-inscribes itself across various historical periods in film, see James Sanders, *Celluloid Skyline: New York and the Movies* (New York: Knopf, 2003); Merrill Schleier, *Skyscraper Cinema: Architecture and Gender in American Film* (Minneapolis: University of Minnesota Press, 2009), as well as many of the chapters in *The Brooklyn Film*. For accounts of how this relates to urban planning and self-fashioning, see Zukin, Osman, and Rothenberg.

40 Zukin, 8; "Brooklyn Community District 6 Census Track Data 1990," *New York City Government Planning*, http://www.nyc.gov/html/dcp/pdf/lucds/bk6profile.pdf; "Population Growth and Race/Hispanic Composition," *New York City Government Planning*, http://www.nyc.gov/html/dcp/pdf/census/nyc20001.pdf; "Fighting Crime Main Issue in Election: Park Slope," *New York Times*, August 5, 1989.

41 Tamar Rothenberg, "And She Told Two Friends: Lesbians Creating Urban Social Space," in *Mapping Desire: Geographies of Sexualities*, ed. David Bell and Gill Valentine (London: Routledge Press, 1995), 150–165.

42 Ibid., 152.

43 Peter Brooker, "The Brooklyn Cigar Co. as Dialogic Public Sphere: Community and Postmodernism in Paul Auster and Wayne Wang's *Smoke* and *Blue in the Face*," in *Urban Space and Representation*, ed. Maria Balshaw and Liam Kennedy (London: Pluto Press, 2000), 108–112.

44 The sole exception is an interview with an eighteen-year-old African American girl who is savoring the early moments of her birthday on a bench near the Coney Island boardwalk. Interestingly, this is also the only interview visibly filmed outside of the neighborhood.

45 Smith, *New Urban Frontier*, 70.

46 Henri Lefebvre, "The Right to the City [1968]," in *Writings on Cities*, trans. Eleonore Kofman and Elizabeth Lebas (London: Wiley Blackwell, 1996), 63–185.

47 Henri Lefebvre, *The Production of Space*, trans. Donald Nicholson-Smith (London: Blackwell, 1991), 10.

48 Frosh, 336.

49 Lynch, 83.

11

Gentrification by Genre:
Desperately Seeking Susan and the 1980s Screwball

Johan Andersson

By the early 1980s, film scholars had begun to note how the aesthetic eclecticism and self-reflexivity of some American cinema could be understood as an economic diversification strategy appealing to several subsections of the market simultaneously. In an influential essay, Noël Carroll identified a "boom of allusionism" in Hollywood cinema from the 1970s and beyond, which he attributed to both auteurism in the industry and connoisseurship among subsections of the audience. According to Carroll, Hollywood directors with auteurist aspirations utilized the form of old genres to reach large audiences while simultaneously filling them with allusions aimed at critics and moviegoing aficionados. Thus he argued: "The film-historically conscious director can deftly manipulate the old forms, satisfying the adolescent clientele while also conveniently pitching allusions to the inveterate film gnostics in the front rows."[1]

In this chapter, I discuss Susan Seidelman's second feature film *Desperately Seeking Susan* (1985) as an example of this "two-tiered system of communication": a cinema that grapples with its dual status as corporate commodity and auteurist work of art. Aimed at consolidating Seidelman's reputation as one of the United States' most promising young directors— her independent debut *Smithereens* (1982) had competed for the Palme d'Or at Cannes in 1982 and in Wim Wenders's documentary *Room 666* (1982) about the festival, she features among the likes of Godard, Fassbinder, and Antonioni—*Susan* is at the same time an attempt to reach large audiences. In contrast with the meagre budget of *Smithereens* ($80,000), *Susan* cost $5 million, was backed by the "mini-major" Orion, and proceeded to make over $27 million at the US box office. In interviews promoting the film, however, Seidelman is clearly uncomfortable with her incorporation into mainstream Hollywood and tries to remain in the newfound company of European auteurs. A typical promotional feature (for the appropriately countercultural *High Times*) describes how "the idea of becoming a slick Hollywood director makes Seidelman fidget" and proceeds to point out that her use of "improvised scenes, natural lighting, handheld cameras and a jagged, elliptical style of editing" has more in common with the French New Wave than contemporary Hollywood.[2]

In truth, this stylistic repertoire describes *Smithereens* better than *Susan*: the principal way the latter tries to distinguish itself from the "mainstream" is instead through intertextual references decipherable mainly for a cinephile audience. The existing literature on *Susan* has tended to view the film within this context of postmodern pastiche with David Shumway highlighting how it self-consciously uses the historical form of the screwball comedy and "acknowledges its debt to the classical films ... by means of several striking allusions." In different contexts, Jackie Stacey (1987) and Laura Mulvey (1998) have deployed comparative approaches to analyze the film's relationship with *All About Eve* (Joseph L. Mankiewicz, 1950) and *Céline and Julie Go Boating* (Jacques Rivette, 1974).[3] In this chapter, I want to add to these earlier arguments by including in the film's dual address its settings in the East Village and SoHo, where both Seidelman and the film's main star, Madonna, lived and worked at the time. Cinephile allusions apart, the film includes various "edgy" locations and subcultural landmarks such as the vintage shop Love Saves the Day, the Bleecker Street Cinema, and "alternative" local celebrities in minor roles, which authenticate the film's subcultural aura. Yet, simultaneously, these references incorporate downtown Manhattan's bohemia into mass culture: while the similar Lower Manhattan settings in *Smithereens* were packaged in a punky Nouvelle Vaguesque form, the screwball format of *Susan* turns subculture into mass commodity in a process we might call *gentrification by genre*.

The basic plot of the film is a "back to the city" narrative in which suburban housewife Roberta (Rosanna Arquette) follows mystery woman Susan (Madonna) into SoHo and the East Village, which already at the time were case studies in the literature on arts-led gentrification.[4] While there has been a long-standing focus on art and artists in the gentrification in this part of New York, the role of cinema has until recently been neglected. An analysis of the romantic comedy, in particular, however, can bring the frequently downplayed libidinous aspect of gentrification to the fore: the genre invested erotic capital into particular urban locations and participated in a process whereby gradually the symbolic perception of the Lower East Side "shifted from fear and repulsion to curiosity and desire."[5] Unusually for a romcom from this period, sexual desire in *Susan* is not straightforwardly heterosexual and to conclude this chapter, I will read the film's queerness intertextually by focusing on the multilayered references in an early scene in which Susan leaves her belongings in a Port Authority locker. Similar to a number of films, but in particular a scene in *Marnie* (Alfred Hitchcock, 1964), the symbolism of the locker—or *closet* rather—accentuates the queer quality of *Susan*, which is indeed another aspect of its two-tiered communication. Before looking specifically at *Susan*, however, the ways in which it deploys New York's geography can be placed within a broader trend in 1980s cinema.

The screwball and its geographical binaries

After losing more than 10 percent of its population in the 1970s, New York began to grow again in the following decade. Between the early 1980s recession and the stock market crash of 1987, real estate values increased rapidly and earlier debates over "planned shrinkage" receded in favor of a new emphasis on gentrification, which had previously been localized, but now started to impact large parts of the city. While several films set in different boroughs centered on resistance to gentrification—the South Bronx in *Wolfen* (Michael Wadleigh, 1981), the Lower East Side in *batteries not included* (Matthew Robbins, 1987), or Bed-Stuy in *Do the Right Thing* (Spike Lee, 1989), for example—the return of the romcom as a popular genre in the 1980s is instead emblematic of the phenomenon itself. Illustrating shifting perceptions of public space, the genre celebrates New York as a romantic playground and deploys Manhattan's diverse public spaces as the setting in which previously unknown characters first "meet cute."[6] However, while the settings are diverse, the protagonists are almost exclusively white and relatively youthful, overlapping with the key image of the so-called "pioneering" gentrifiers who were often seen to embrace urban difference without necessarily interacting with it.

In an often-discussed article written at the end of the 1970s, after a decade or more of shrinking industrial cities, Brian Henderson had boldly predicted the demise of the romantic comedy, which he viewed as characterized by smug urban superiority. Furthermore, the dramatic tensions of the romantic comedy, he argued, had been dependent on a "condition of non-fucking" under the self-censorship of the classical Hollywood-era, which was no longer possible after the sexual liberation movements and simultaneous disintegration of the Production Code in the late 1960s.[7] Yet Henderson was writing this at exactly the time when the romantic comedy was making a comeback with Woody Allen's late 1970s "nervous romances" and later in the 1980s with a cycle of films that Stephen Neale has dubbed "new romances." Neale's genre analysis is not spatial, but many of his examples of "new romance" films—*Splash* (Ron Howard, 1984), *Something Wild* (Jonathan Demme, 1986), *Moonstruck* (Norman Jewison, 1987), *Working Girl* (Mike Nichols, 1988), *Big* (Penny Marshall, 1988), and *When Harry Met Sally* (Rob Reiner, 1989)—are set in New York, illustrating the city's preeminence as setting for the 1980s romcom. Manhattan, in particular, is central to "aspirational" narratives about white-collar work and the renegotiation of romance and gender roles in the city's restructured economy. According to Neale the "new romance" cycle is often characterized by a gendered narrative pattern in which an "eccentric woman" tries to liberate "a highly conventional man." In this context, eccentric tends to mean flirtatious and sexually assertive while the conventionality attributed to the male characters, at least partly, refers to materialistic values. Ultimately, however, Neale concludes in a discussion of *Something Wild*, the "new romance" film "eventually manoeuvres its couple, and its heroine in particular, into an 'old-fashioned', 'traditional' and ideologically conventional position."[8]

This narrative arc from adventure back to tradition connects the "new romance" film with the screwball cycle from the 1930s to 1940s—in particular the "comedies of remarriage"—in which the Production Code dictated that marriage, ultimately, was reaffirmed.[9] While not all 1980s romcoms end in a traditional position, a striking number of them pay homage to screwball comedies by deploying similar plot structures and eccentric characters. In the New York context, *Who's That Girl* (James Foley, 1987) is a remake of *Bringing*

Up Baby (Howard Hawks, 1938) while *Arthur* (Steve Gordon, 1981), *Susan* and *After Hours* (Martin Scorsese, 1985) have all been discussed as screwballs in genre literature and *Married to the Mob* (Jonathan Demme, 1988) was received as such in the media. The revival of the screwball is perhaps best understood in relation to Carroll's argument about two-tiered allusionism insofar that the genre had broad commercial appeal yet at the same time arguably more status among the cognoscenti than any other form of romantic comedy. In contrast with New Hollywood experiments such as *What's Up, Doc?* (Peter Bogdanovich, 1972), and *The Fortune* (Mike Nichols, 1975), however, 1980s screwballs tend to use the historical form to say something contemporary about both shifting gender conventions and the economic restructuring of New York.

The genre's ideological ambiguity with its simultaneous celebration of "eccentricity" and traditional values was perhaps well-equipped to deal with some of the contradictions of the Reagan era: while the US divorce rate hit an all-time high in the early 1980s (it has since gone down in parallel with declining marriage rates), the period is also associated with a conservative backlash against the sexual liberation of the preceding decades. Moreover, the AIDS epidemic, of which New York was one of the epicenters, created anxieties that suited the genre's narrative structure of repeatedly cancelled or postponed sexual opportunities (Andrew Sarris has aptly described the screwball as a "sex comedy without the sex").[10] The 1980s variations are not quite as chaste, but their tendency to pay homage to the genre means that they often refrain from explicit sex scenes. However, in common with some of the decade's kinky thrillers that have been linked to AIDS—*Fatal Attraction* (Adrian Lyne, 1987) and *Sea of Love* (Harold Becker, 1989) for example[11]—sexual danger tends to be mapped onto risqué female characters. The men, in contrast, and in line with the gendered tropes of the original cycle from the 1930s, often come across as juvenile.

Writing on the classical screwball films, Wes D. Gehring noted "the childlike quality of the male" and how "a toyshop *mise-en-scène* frequently surfaces in the genre."[12] Similar settings and characters feature, above all, perhaps, in the 1980s "baby romcom" subgenre: in *Three Men and a Baby* (Leonard Nimoy, 1987) and *Look Who's Talking* (Amy Heckerling, 1989) the juvenility of some of the male characters is symbolized by various toys and jukeboxes in their apartments and offices, whereas in *Baby Boom* (Charles Shyer, 1987) premature ejaculation is the signifier of a kind of adolescent masculinity. Broadly speaking, the emasculation of men of letters and absent-minded professors in the original screwballs "seem[s] to have been displaced on to yuppie values and lifestyle" in romcoms from the 1980s and '90s.[13] Thus in contrast with the testosterone-filled trading floors and phallic skyscrapers of financial dramas such as *Wall Street* (Oliver Stone, 1987), the yuppie milieu including neighborhoods and apartments associated with these professions is frequently infantilized. Characters who want to escape this arrested development for more "adult" adventures leave the materialistic comfort of the suburbs or affluent neighborhoods for the fashionable bohemia downtown in what can also be understood as a gentrifying move.

Contrary to the dominance of high-society settings in the screwball films of the 1930s, which have been understood as a form of escapism from the economic depression, the class journeys in the films from the booming 1980s often go in the opposite direction with characters "slumming" it downtown.[14] The Upper versus Lower Manhattan binary on which many of these journeys rest had been established much earlier: in her analysis of "apartment plots" between the mid-1940s and mid-1970s, Pamela Robertson Wojcik highlights how Greenwich Village locations have tended to signify "bohemian culture, relative poverty, and often youth," whereas "the Upper East Side and Upper West Side feature characters who operate within commercial artistic or intellectual professions, such as advertising or publishing."[15] However, from the late 1970s onwards, the Lower East Side and in particular SoHo appears to have replaced Greenwich Village, which at this point perhaps was perceived as too bookishly bourgeois, as Manhattan's erogenous zone.

This spatial trope of SoHo as sexy features across genres ranging from erotic thrillers to romcoms and is firmly founded by 1978 through the pornographic themes of *The Eyes of Laura Mars* (Irvin Kershner, 1978), the group sex scene in *Fingers* (James Toback, 1978), and as the site of emancipation for female characters in *Girlfriends* (Claudia Weill, 1978), and *An Unmarried Woman* (Paul Mazursky, 1978). In particular the latter, which was critically and commercially acclaimed, can be seen to have started a mini-trend by contrasting SoHo's artistic bohemia with the materialistic conformity embodied by the protagonist's former stockbroker husband. Variations of this theme were recycled in a string of films from the mid-1980s—*Susan, After Hours, Hannah and Her Sisters* (Woody Allen, 1986), *Parting Glances* (Bill Sherwood, 1986), *9 ½ Weeks* (Adrian Lyne, 1986), *Something Wild* (Jonathan Demme, 1986), and *Legal Eagles* (Ivan Reitman, 1986)—which vary significantly in tone and genre, but tend to celebrate the area's eccentric or arty inhabitants as a source of escape for more conventional protagonists (or in some instances warn against their seductive appeal). Through the narrative device of the urban encounter, these films analogize the experiences of romance/sex, discovering an edgy neighborhood and, ultimately, (re)discovering oneself in a gentrification trope.

In a reading of *After Hours* as a postmodern screwball, Cynthia Willett has highlighted how the classic Hollywood binary of rationality and eroticism is mapped geographically onto Upper and Lower Manhattan when office worker Paul Hackett (Griffin Dunne) pursues a seductive blond (Rosanna Arquette) during one chaotic night in SoHo. According to Willett, the screwball comedy was historically structured around this "comic dialectic" in which a rational and a transgressive character eventually achieve mutual transformation through moderation. Unlike in the original screwball, however, there is no resolution in *After Hours*, but instead "a nightmare of repetitions and reversals without dialectical advance until Dunne is by chance returned home (for the yuppie, work is home) exactly on time for work."[16] For Willett, this lack of reconciliation is indicative of the postmodern condition yet the return to the narrative space of origin she maps out in *After Hours* is by no means compulsory in the 1980s screwball.

In films which dichotomize the suburbs with Lower Manhattan, such as *Married to the Mob* and *Susan*, the female protagonists who have "escaped" ultimately stay downtown. Thus while the screwball has been influentially understood as a genre of "indeterminate space"—in contrast with "determinate space" genres such as the Western in which the hero enters and eventually leaves a contested setting[17]—the endings of the 1980s films are determined spatially by whether the main characters persist in the flight from their suburban or Upper Manhattan malaise or eventually return to where they came from. Moreover, if we accept Neil Smith's influential gentrification metaphor of the "urban frontier,"[18] the 1980s screwball variations in common with the Western take place in a contested space of displacement and conflict. This conflict, however, is rarely (if ever) the main focus of the plot, which instead centers on the fulfillment and romantic self-realization of the white protagonists.

Susan as gentrification cinema

Illustrating many of the genre developments sketched out above, *Susan* can be read as a gentrification narrative centered on housewife Roberta who is bored in the burbs and romantically unsatisfied with her husband—a home spa retailer who exhibits all the childlike and materialistic values typical of the male in the 1980s romcom. After coming across Susan in a personal ad, Roberta embarks on a series of adventures in Manhattan where she becomes romantically involved with Dez, a film projectionist at the Bleecker Street Cinema and temporarily moves into his loft. At this point, the arts-led gentrification Sharon Zukin analyzed in *Loft Living* has been replaced with yuppification: Dez's girlfriend runs off with a man in a Porsche while Roberta brings with her the restoration ethic of the gentrifying classes ("You could do a lot with this space. There's a lot of light"). Ambiguously positioned in relation to the transformation of the area, *Susan* celebrates the semi-bohemian subculture under threat from displacement yet by romanticizing it in the accessible form of the screwball also gentrifies by genre.

As Shumway has argued, *Susan* deploys the screwball "as a historical form to be self-consciously used as needed: transformed, parodied, played off against" yet in contrast with the "comedies of remarriage," ultimately, affirms "independence and divorce as potentially positive choices."[19] This choice between marriage and divorce is mapped onto a clear geographical binary between the heteronormative suburban ideal of Fort Lee, New Jersey, and Lower Manhattan—in particular the East Village and SoHo—which function as spaces of escape from the accumulative and reproductive norms of the suburban couple. Furthermore, the geographical binary is accentuated in Edward Lachman's colorful cinematography which depicts Roberta's suburban world in claustrophobic pastel colors, while the downtown settings associated with Susan are glamorized in neon. The bold palette and the use of Madonna's music—"Into the Groove" was recorded for the soundtrack and the accompanying music video is based on the film—suggest perhaps an affinity with MTV aesthetics, yet *Susan*'s style is less obtrusive. In contrast with the sometimes disparaged "tendency of films since the early 1980s to privilege gloss, atmospherics, and camerawork" and "manic editing that often features flash-cuts, jump-cuts, and the stirring together of varies film stocks, colors, and speeds,"[20] it has a distinct local flavor: indeed, the film is not merely a depiction of the downtown scene, but also an expression of its visual culture. Seidelman (2009) has described how in *Smithereens* this style was achieved in DIY-fashion (through clothing, paint, and posters), whereas the experimentation with color in *Susan* is bolder: a form of "hyperrealism" with a "gritty but ... slightly romanticized edge."[21] Similarly, its vintage ethos—fashion items drive the narrative and a couple of scenes are set in the now closed East Village store Love Saves the Day—is not merely a plot device, but informs the look of the film as many props and outfits were bought in the area's second-hand shops.

Much of the comedy in *Susan* derives from a wide-eyed outsider being confronted with this colorful world. In some ways, it is an "out-of-downtowner" film—an intra-city variation of the popular "out-of-towner"-motif—in which Roberta, the ditzy suburban housewife, is "out of place" in Lower Manhattan's youth culture.[22] While much of the confusion is caused by an episode of amnesia, the theme of mistaken identity around which the narrative revolves connects the film with one of the recurring plot devices of the screwball genre. While the screwball—and the romcom generally—typically depends on an initial "meet cute" between the main characters, the whole narrative in *Susan* is structured around random urban encounters and in his review, Roger Ebert praised "the cheerful way it bopped around New York, introducing us to unforgettable characters, played by good actors."[23] Similar to *After Hours*, this narrative structure becomes a vehicle for celebrating the quirky eccentricity of various "types" associated with downtown Manhattan in an episodic form which has sometimes been understood almost in semi-anthropological terms. Michael Ballhaus—the cinematographer on *After Hours*—has suggested that the film simply "showed all the different characters, the clubs and everything, and all the weirdness that happened in that area"[24] while Mulvey's essay on *Susan* concludes that new equipment such as faster film stocks, sharper lenses, and mobile equipment had "transformed 35mm location work in the 1980s, opening up narrative itself."[25] The lively sense of place and narrative structure facilitated by this technology, however, should not be mistaken for spontaneous depictions of street life "as it is": the inclusive portrayal of public space in *After Hours*, but especially in *Susan* crams in as many demographic types as possible into the exterior street scenes in what are clearly carefully staged tableaux.

Thus *Susan* deploys similar backdrops to the contemporary *Something Wild* in which Cameron Bailey noted how, in spite of an all-white lead and supporting cast, the film "strews black faces across the background of the film, providing a literal local colour that adds to the film's hip credibility."[26] Similarly, in *Selling the Lower East Side*, Christopher Mele argues that the East Village's minorities, homeless, and prostitutes were instrumental in attracting trend-sensitive creative industries to the area for whom these populations "function as a cast of background players in an abstracted environment themed around carefully managed representations of dysfunction and difference."[27] In *Susan*, street hustlers and drunks often feature in the street scenes in a colorful repackaging of the Lower East Side tradition of both reformist and exploitative representations of destitution. In their early critique of the arts-led gentrification of the East Village, Cara Ryan and Rosalyn Deutsche highlighted how "the figure of the bum provides the requisite identification with marginal figures and social outcasts by which avant-garde and bohemian glamour accrues to the East Village scene despite its embrace of conventional values."[28] Or as Martha Rosler forcefully had put it in an earlier critique of so-called Bowery photography: "The buried text of photographs of drunks is not a treatise on political economy."[29] Neither of course can the carefully staged mise-en-scène in *Susan* be seen as a treatise on pluralist democracy when the minority characters so rarely get to speak.

The most conspicuous of these minority silences concerns the AIDS crisis, which by the mid-1980s enfolded downtown Manhattan and as Sarah Schulman has argued, accelerated gentrification when those who died of AIDS turned "over their apartments *literally* to market rate at an unnatural speed" (a process further exacerbated by the lack of legal protections for gay people whose "surviving partners or roommates were not allowed to inherit leases that has been in the dead person's name").[30] The first US feature film about AIDS—Bill Sherwood's *Parting Glances*, which was filmed in 1984 and released in 1986—deployed a similar downtown geography of lofts and nightclubs as *Susan* and *After Hours* yet was safely compartmentalized and marketed as a "gay film." In cinema with broader target audiences, AIDS was rarely mentioned—*Hannah and Her Sisters* includes an ill-judged joke about dentists and gay patients—in spite of a clear tendency to recognize the presence of gay men in this milieu. Among the potpourri of "diverse types" in *Susan*, the flamboyant store attendant in the vintage shop scenes is clearly a representative of sexual diversity much like the butch leather queens and the street cruiser are in *After Hours*. Thus gay male culture and some of its most stereotypical representatives feature as quirky examples of liberal pluralism at exactly the moment when these types had come to signify death. While President Reagan has been criticized with justification for refusing to publicly use the word AIDS until 1985, his silence, it seems, was mirrored in the arts where the first dramatizations of the health crisis—*An Early Frost* (John Erman, 1985) on TV, the theater-production of *The Normal Heart* (Larry Kramer, 1985), and *Parting Glances*—appear mid-decade after an initial period of traumatic aphasia.

The current status of *Susan* and some of the other mid-1980s films mentioned here as cult classics rests perhaps on this aphasia. Novelist Edmund White (2015) recently identified "an intense yearning for a specific five-year period in New York City, those years between the blackout in 1977, and 1982, when AIDS was finally named by the Center for Disease Control." Yet since AIDS was never mentioned in the dramatic arts until several years after the outbreak,[31] cinema from beyond these five years continues to shape an idealized notion of the 1980s. While the silence on AIDS in *Susan* is revisionist, the carefree sexuality embodied by Madonna can simultaneously be viewed as a form of resistance to the conservative backlash that had already begun. Even the sexual ambiguity between Roberta and Susan, which earlier scholarship has commented on, has a queer quality insofar that it resists homonormative temptations for "happy endings."

In the final section of this chapter, I want to add to earlier readings of *Susan* as a homoerotic film by highlighting how intertextual references reinforce its queer status. The postclassical tendency toward allusions is here deployed to distance and disrupt in subtle ways the heteronormative assumptions of the genre. Indeed, the two-tiered allusionism Carroll identified as characteristic of American cinema from the 1970s onwards serves not only to appeal to cinephiles, but also to address different sexual demographics simultaneously.

Queering *Susan*

While some 1980s romcoms played with non-normative sexualities and lifestyles—"interspecies" romance in *Splash*, pedophilia/intergenerational love in *Big*, same-sex parenting in *Three Men and a Baby* and cross-dressing in *Tootsie* (Sydney Pollack, 1982)—Neale's analysis written in the early 1990s stated categorically that the genre is always heterosexual. Attempts to read individual films queerly, for example, by analyzing "male homosocial desire" in *Something Wild* have therefore tended to focus on overarching narrative structures such as the love triangle.[32] On a literal level the narrative in *Susan* is heterosexual although the basic premise of the plot in which Roberta first identifies Susan through a personal ad and follows her through Manhattan clearly flirts with the lesbian market. Moreover, the narrative dynamic between an eccentric woman and a conventional man that Neale identified in the "new romance" films of the 1980s takes place here primarily between Susan and Roberta with the former liberating the latter. The fact that the implicit homoeroticism of their relationship is never allowed to fully blossom led Teresa De Lauretis, in an overview of 1980s "women's cinema," to place the film within the broader context of homophobia, while others have viewed the film's sexual politics in more emancipatory terms.[33]

Certainly, the unspoken and unconsummated homoeroticism between the protagonists means that, contrary to genre expectations, *Susan* resists "settling down" into a traditional pattern of monogamy and domesticity. As Robin Wood (1986: 229) noted in relation to the male buddy films of the 1970s, the "surreptitious gay texts" of these narratives often had more radical potential than later "male lovers" films, which mimicked and adopted the liberal ideals of family. A key characteristic of the buddy film, Wood (1986: 228) noted, was "the absence of home"—a theme adopted in *Susan* through Roberta's rejection of her suburban life in New Jersey and embodied in Susan's nomadic persona. In a broad sense, then, *Susan* is a queer text insofar that a stable home and the accumulative and reproductive logic of property and family are rejected in favor of playfulness; joie de vivre ultimately triumphs over the yuppie values typically associated with the male characters of the genre in the 1980s.

However, in more specific terms, the homoerotic subtext in *Susan* is multilayered and expressed through narrative structure (the whole film is basically about Roberta stalking Susan through Manhattan), iconography (Roberta erotically draws a circle with red lipstick around Susan's personal ad), point-of-view shots (the camera mimics Roberta's longing gaze on Susan), and match cuts.[34] In addition, paratextual material such as an alternative ending available on the DVD in which Susan and Roberta are seen riding a camel together in Egypt suggests that they have left their male suitors behind. The rejection of this scene by test audiences in favor of a heteronormative ending in which they instead appear to start dating the male characters perhaps illustrates the limits to sexual ambiguity in a studio-backed film at the time. Finally, the film's queerness resides in its multiple references to other films, which I will illustrate by focusing on one scene alone in which Susan arrives from Atlantic City to the Port Authority Terminal in New York.

This early arrival scene intertextually flags up the film's central thematic concerns with the fluid relationship between appearance and identity and more concretely, feminist and queer politics in urban space. When Susan leaves her bag in a storage locker including various eccentric fashion items around which the film's theme of mistaken identity revolves, this appears to be a reference to a similar early scene in *Marnie* (Alfred Hitchcock, 1964), where the protagonist changes appearance and leaves her belongings in a locker in a railway station (Figures 11.1a, 11.1b, and 11.1c). If this "quote" seems oblique, it is followed immediately by a cut to *Rebecca* (Alfred Hitchcock, 1940), which Roberta is watching on TV in her suburban house. Now *Rebecca* and *Marnie* are not just any Hitchcock references, but the two most obvious examples of films with "lesbian" characters: in the former, Mrs. Danvers is erotically obsessed with Rebecca, the dead wife of her employer, while the protagonist of the latter—

Figure 11.1a Lockers in *Marnie* (Alfred Hitchcock, 1964).

Figure 11.1b *Ms. 45* (Abel Ferrara, 1981).

Figure 11.1c *Desperately Seeking Susan* (Susan Seidelman, 1985).

who is disgusted by physical contact with men—has also been understood as queer.[35] The thematic similarities between *Susan* and *Marnie*, in particular, are striking: both films are concerned with masquerade, kleptomania, unspoken same-sex desire, and use Atlantic City as a geographical marker of the liminal status of their heroines. (Susan is introduced there stealing from the man she slept with the previous night while Marnie is identified as a thief at the racetracks by a man from her dubious past.) Both characters deploy their sex appeal to steal from patriarchy and the lockers/closets in which they keep information about their identity can be read as symbols of their nomadism and refusal to settle down in heteronormative domesticity.

More site-specifically, Susan's arrival scene at the Port Authority Terminal quotes Abel Ferrara's rape and revenge film *Ms. 45* (1981) in which the misandrist vigilante protagonist Thana places the body parts of one of her victims in the same lockers. Crudely applied to the Feminist Sex Wars, which had divided activists in New York in the early 1980s, Thana is an anti-porn warrior of the Andrea Dworkin/Catharine MacKinnon-variety. To begin with she only kills men who have sexually assaulted her, but eventually—in line with the "all heterosexual intercourse is rape"—maxim often attributed to Dworkin/MacKinnon—starts to pursue men in general that she has seen together with women. The anti-porn theme is transferred to the world of fashion in which the film is set and one of Thana's sleaziest victims is a fashion photographer. In contrast, Susan—not unlike Madonna's real-life persona—is a pro-sex feminist more in tune with Gayle Rubin and Pat Califia of the 1982 Barnard Conference-school-of-thought. Like Thana, she is constantly the object of the male gaze in the streets yet skillfully navigates and manipulates it to her advantage. Inhabiting New York's public spaces effortlessly, she "transgresses conventional forms of feminine behaviour by appropriating public space for herself."[36]

In his *New York Times* review, Vincent Canby (1985) even drew a vivid analogy between the film's popular accessibility as a "genial farce" and the inclusivity of some of Manhattan's most iconic public spaces describing it as "a New York movie that, like Times Square at 4 A.M. or Central Park at high noon, is available to everyone." However, Times Square at 4 a.m. is an unusual example of urban inclusivity: as New York's center for porn exhibition, it was a contested space in the 1980s and the target for Take Back the Night-marches whose anti-porn feminism had been influenced by Mulvey's work on the male gaze in Hollywood cinema. In an otherwise critical comment on Mulvey, Marshall Berman acknowledges that "her lurid vision of the world was a perfect fit for a street that had collapsed into 'the dirty boulevard,'" namely 42nd Street around Times Square where "the male gaze turned aggressively nasty."[37] Commenting on Allan Moyle's *Times Square* (1980), a similarly homoerotic film about two young women who appropriate public space for themselves (they live on a pier and hang out in Times Square), Berman (2006: 185) disparagingly refers to its "pastoral vision." Yet in both *Times Square* and *Susan*, it seems, the politics of the gaze have moved beyond the anti-porn logic of Take-Back-The-Night marches and Mulvey's critique of gendered spectatorship in Hollywood cinema from the 1970s. Reflecting some of the sex-positive ethos that emerged from the Feminist Sex Wars in the early 1980s, *to-be-looked-at-ness* for these female characters is no longer viewed merely in oppressive terms, but also as a way of navigating and accessing parts of the city.

Finally, the arrival scene resonates intertextually with a famous arrival in the same part of Manhattan, namely that of Joe Buck in *Midnight Cowboy* (John Schlesinger, 1969), another homoerotic love story in which the relationship between Joe and "Ratso" is never allowed to become fully visible. When Susan gets off the bus, she is wearing a feminized version of a cowboy hat and, in effect, becomes a female version of Joe although her postmodern understanding of the semiotics of fashion is vastly superior to his. Buck believes that his Texan cowboy outfit is an authentic signifier of heterosexual virility, but is quickly confronted with the realization that in Times Square this look attracts the attention of the gay male gaze. In a reading of *Midnight Cowboy*, Kevin Floyd has suggested that the changing meaning of Joe's mass-produced Texan cowboy outfit is about the crisis of Fordism itself while the film as a commercial product aimed at a countercultural niche audience marks the transition into a post-Fordist society.[38] Yet while *Midnight Cowboy* may have been aimed at a specific market segment, the film's box office success and multiple Academy Awards instead point ahead to a new logic of audience maximization. While Joe is *to-be-looked-at* by a queer cinema audience, the decision to merely hint at a love story between him and "Ratso" ensured that the film remained within the acceptable moral boundaries of the "mainstream" at the time. In this respect, *Midnight Cowboy* illustrates how the two-tiered allusions Carroll had identified as characteristic of American cinema from New Hollywood onwards were not merely deployed to distinguish between high-brow and popular audiences, but also to address minorities within films with mass appeal. By the 1980s this dual address had been fully developed in films such as *Susan* which combined the accessible form of romantic comedy with a plethora of references lending it both subcultural and queer credibility.

Conclusion

In this chapter, I have highlighted how the screwball-inspired romcom of the 1980s frequently structured its narrative around geographical binaries in which affluent parts of New York and its suburbs were contrasted with semi-bohemian settings in downtown Manhattan. Thus, in many instances, the genre's historical and gendered emphasis on eccentric characters was mapped geographically onto arty neighborhoods such as SoHo with a perceived capacity for both individual and urban rejuvenation. In particular, the romcom's narrative emphasis on personal satisfaction through romance intersected with the ongoing gentrification of lower Manhattan when locations previously associated with dereliction and crime became imbued with desire and emancipatory potential. Often the screwball's narrative dialectic between rationality and erotic–transgressive eccentricity was dramatized as romance between a yuppie and a bohemian, yet as I have argued specifically in a reading of *Susan*, this narrative duality can also be understood in relation to the films' dual address that targeted different audience segments simultaneously. Combining subcultural allusions—including hip urban locations—with the widely accessible genre tropes of the romcom, these films literally opened up new parts of the city to mass audiences.

Since the bifurcation of the American film industry in the late 1980s and 1990s, the dual address has arguably been replaced with a more consolidated split between "mainstream" and "indie." In the context of the New York romcom, the tendency toward allusions first identified in 1970s cinema as well as remnants of the "smarter" sensibilities of the 1990s now feature mainly in indie romcoms, such as *Frances Ha* (Noah Baumbach, 2012) and *Maggie's Plan* (Rebecca Miller, 2015).[39] While these films are partly set on the rapidly shifting gentrification "frontier" in Brooklyn, broad-based examples of the genre have typically remained in Manhattan where the interconnections between urban and personal change no longer tend to define the romantic scenarios. The 1980s formula of "meet cutes" between one bohemian and one yuppie, for example, has largely been replaced with romance between professionals and with the bohemian or arty character gone, the intellectualism of the two-tiered allusions has also been replaced with a more homogeneous address. If the earlier "opposites attract" formula typically involved compromise through the moderation of both materialistic and "eccentric" values—in the form of a trade-off between money and savoir-faire, financial and subcultural capital—the intra-professional affair is less likely to question or moderate the link between materialism and life satisfaction.

Arguably, this ideological homogenization also includes the sexual politics of the studio romcom. While queer updates of other historical genres have gained commercial and critical acclaim, such as the western motifs of *Brokeback Mountain* (Ang Lee, 2005), the biopic of *Milk* (Gus Van Sant, 2008), the melodrama of *Carol* (Todd Haynes, 2015), or coming-of-age drama of *Moonlight* (Barry Jenkins, 2016), there are no examples of similar stature in the case of the romantic comedy. Instead, the bifurcation of the genre has segregated same-sex romance into niche indie films for the queer film festival circuit, while studio romcoms have become unambiguously heterosexual with the dual address now made redundant. In that respect, the homophobic climate that relegated same-sex desire to the realm of subtexts and allusions in some instances produced queerer romcoms than the supposedly affirmative period that succeeded it.

Notes

1   Noël Carroll, "The Future of Allusion: Hollywood in the Seventies (and beyond)," *October* 20 (1982), 56.

2   "Desperately Seeking Susan (Seidelman)," *High Times*, May 1985, https://allaboutmadonna.com/madonna-library/desperately-seeking-susan-seidelman-high-times-may-1985.

3   David R. Shumway, "Screwball Comedies: Constructing Romance, Mystifying Marriage," *Cinema Journal* 30.4 (1991), 19; Jackie Stacey, "Desperately Seeking Difference," *Screen* 28.1 (1987), 48–61; Laura Mulvey, "'New Wave' Interchanges: *Céline and Julie* and *Desperately Seeking Susan*," G. Nowell-Smith and S. Ricci, eds., *Hollywood and Europe: Economics, Culture, National Identity 1945–95* (London: BFI Publishing, 1998).

4   Sharon Zukin, *Loft Living: Culture and Capital in Urban Change* (Baltimore, MD: Johns Hopkins University Press, 1982), 212; Rosalyn Deutsche and Cara Gendel Ryan, "The Fine Art of Gentrification," *October* 31 (1984), 91–111.

5   Christopher Mele, *Selling the Lower East Side: Culture, Real Estate, and Resistance in New York, 1880–2000* (Minneapolis: University of Minnesota Press, 2003), 233.

6   Deborah Jermyn, "I ❤ NY: The Rom-Com's Love Affair with New York City," in *Falling in Love Again: Romantic Comedy in Contemporary Cinema*, ed. Stacey Abbott and Deborah Jermyn (London and New York: IB Tauris, 2008), 12.

7   Brian Henderson, "Romantic Comedy Today: Semi-Tough or Impossible?" *Film Quarterly* 31.4 (1978), 11–23.

8   Steve Neale, "The Big Romance or Something Wild?: Romantic Comedy Today," *Screen* 33.3 (1992), 294–297.

9   Stanley Cavell, *Pursuits of Happiness: The Hollywood Comedy of Remarriage* (Cambridge, MA: Harvard University Press, 1981).

10 Andrew Sarris, "Sex Comedy without Sex + Movies," *American Film* 3.5 (1978), 8–15.

11 Frank Krutnik, "The Faint Aroma of Performing Seals: The "Nervous" Romance and the Comedy of the Sexes," *The Velvet Light Trap* 56 (1990), 72.

12 Wes D. Gehring, "Screwball Comedy: An Overview," *Journal of Popular Film and Television* 13.4 (1986), 182.

13 Constanza del Río, "*Something Wild*: Take a Walk on the Wild Side (but Be Home before Midnight)," Peter William Evans and Celestino Deleyto, eds., *Terms of Endearment: Hollywood Romantic Comedy of the 1980s and 1990s* (Edinburgh: Edinburgh University Press, 1998), 91.

14 There are occasional slumming narratives in the original screwball cycle too, not least in *It Happened One Night* (Frank Capra, 1934), which is the film *Susan* most directly references.

15 Pamela Robertson Wojcik, *The Apartment Plot: Urban Living in American Film and Popular Culture, 1945 to 1975* (Durham, NC: Duke University Press, 2010), 66–67.

16 Cynthia Willett, "Baudrillard, *After Hours*, and the Postmodern Suppression of Socio-Sexual Conflict," *Cultural Critique* 34 (1996), 150.

17 Thomas Schatz, *Old Hollywood/New Hollywood: Ritual, Art, and Industry* (Ann Arbor, MI: UMI Research Press, 1983).

18 Neil Smith, *The New Urban Frontier: Gentrification and the Revanchist City* (London: Psychology Press, 1996).

19 Shumway, 19.

20 Marco Calavita, "'MTV Aesthetics' at the Movies: Interrogating a Film Criticism Fallacy," *Journal of Film and Video* 59.3 (2007), 15–16.

21   Janet Maslin, "At the Movies," *New York Times*, March 22, 1985, http://www.
     nytimes.com/movie/review?res=9D06E4DF1738F931A15750C0A963948260.

22   The "out-of-downtowner" narrative can be thought of as an intra-city variation
     of the out-of-towner motif mainly associated with Arthur Hiller's *The Out-of-
     Towners* (1970) and Sam Weisman's 1999 remake with the same name. In the
     original, a couple from Ohio is confronted with crime and other perils of New
     York life yet in the 1980s, the basic premise of this film was frequently redeployed
     as a vehicle for romantic stories between *one* out-of-towner and *one* local. The
     creativity with which this motif was treated can be exemplified with titles such
     as *Splash* (Ron Howard, 1984), *Moscow on the Hudson* (Paul Mazursky, 1984),
     Crocodile Dundee (Peter Faiman, 1986), *Big* (Penny Marshall, 1988), and *Coming
     to America* (John Landis, 1988) in which respectively a mermaid, a Soviet circus
     musician, an Australian crocodile hunter, a suburban child in an adult body, and
     an African prince get romantically involved with locals while struggling in the
     big city. These blockbusters, which aimed for the family market, cannot, perhaps,
     be considered in the same vein as the subculturally more hip out-of-downtowner
     narratives centered on SoHo yet all of them deploy geographical stereotypes
     for their "opposites attract" scenarios. Moreover, all of them seem to reject a
     particular type of materialistic masculinity either in favor of something more
     bohemian downtown or, in the family films, typically for a man from abroad not
     yet contaminated by Manhattan's materialism.

23   Roger Ebert, "*Desperately Seeking Susan*," March 29, 1985, http://www.rogerebert.
     com/reviews/desperately-seeking-susan-1985.

24   James Sanders, *Scenes From the City: Filmmaking in New York, 1966–2006* (New
     York: Rizzoli International Publications, 2006), 154.

25   Mulvey, 122.

26   Cameron Bailey, "Nigger/Lover: The Thin Sheen of Race in *Something Wild*,"
     Screen 29.4 (1988), 32–33.

27   Mele, 292.

28   Deutsche and Ryan, 110.

29   Martha Rosler, "In, around, and Afterthoughts (on Documentary Photography),"
     in *The Contest of Meaning: Critical Histories of Photography*, ed. R. Bolton
     (Cambridge, MA: MIT Press, 1989), 304.

30   Sarah Schulman, *The Gentrification of the Mind: Witness to a Lost Imagination*
     (Berkeley: University of California Press, 2012), 27; 36.

31   Edmund White, "Why Can't We Stop Talking about New York in the Late 70s?,"
     New York Times, September 10, 2015.

32 del Río, 86.

33 Teresa de Lauretis, "Guerrilla in the Midst: Women's Cinema in the 80s," *Screen* 31.1 (1990), 19. Both Stacey and Shumway view the film's implicit homoeroticism in more positive ways.

34 See Stacey, 58 on point-of-view shots and Shumway, 20 on match cuts which "by replacing one woman with the other who is not in the scene, disrupts expected shot/reverse shot sequences and the process of suture."

35 Lucretia Knapp, "The Queer Voice in *Marnie*," *Cinema Journal* 32.4 (1993), 6–23.

36 Stacey, 60.

37 Marshall Berman, *On the Town: One Hundred Years of Spectacle in Times Square*, Random House Incorporated, (2006), 176.

38 Kevin Floyd, *The Reification of Desire: Toward a Queer Marxism* (Minneapolis and London: University of Minnesota Press, 2009), 156.

39 On smart cinema in the 1990s, see Jeffrey Sconce, "Irony, Nihilism and the New American 'Smart' Film," *Screen* 43.4 (2002), 349–369.

12

Frances Doesn't Live Here Anymore: Gender, Crisis, and the Creative City in *Frances Ha* and *The Giant Mechanical Man*

Martha Shearer

In her 2007 book on romantic comedy, Tamar Jeffers McDonald notes that "rote use of the city as iconography in the neo-traditional romantic comedy seems another sign that this type of film has exhausted its inspirations."[1] Cinematic romantic comedy has long had an urban bias, arguably a means of rendering the crowd a source of pleasure rather than peril. But the wave of romcoms made since the huge success of *Pretty Woman* (Garry Marshall, 1990) that Jeffers McDonald refers to have often relied on a particular mode of representing the city, emphasizing iconicity, affluence, consumerism, ease, and a professional world, a city that enables both meet-cutes and shopping montages. These films often work through anxieties about the pressures of professional life (and perhaps implicitly the global city) frequently displaced onto female characters, positing a postfeminist conflict between romance and work, between femininity and the demands of the work ethic. Yet with the exception of films like *Kate and Leopold* (James Mangold, 2001) and *Two Weeks Notice* (Marc Lawrence, 2002) that Diane Negra argues foreground issues of real estate and architecture to express post-9/11 anxiety about New York, neo-traditional romantic comedies rarely express anxiety about the city itself. As Negra argues, "Romantic comedies are notable for a shared dedication to the view that the couple and the city stand in particular relation to one another, that the union of one is somehow bound up with the unity of the other."[2]

Lately, however, the status of the romcom has changed. A number of journalists and bloggers, noting declining numbers of films released as well as the genre's apparently declining commercial fortunes, have suggested that the romantic comedy is dead or, at best, alive only in TV sitcoms.³ This death-of-the-romcom narrative relies on a restrictive definition of the romcom and a narrow emphasis on Hollywood cinema and the North American market.⁴ But if the romantic comedy has not "died," in the American context it has undergone some fundamental shifts; in the wake of the 2008 financial crisis, the conflation of consumerism, glamorous femininity, and romanticized, iconic cities has been destabilized. Lauren Berlant has influentially argued that the post-2008 period has been marked by a pervasive experience of crisis:

> The current recession congeals decades of class bifurcation, downward mobility, and environmental, political, and social brittleness that have increased progressively since the Reagan era. The intensification of these processes, which reshapes conventions of racial, gendered, sexual, economic, and nation-based subordination, has also increased the probability that structural contingency will create manifest crisis situations in ordinary existence for more kinds of people.⁵

Berlant suggests that crisis situations reshape both conventions of identity and modes of representation. So how might the crisis affect forms like the romantic comedy, and the (interrelated) conceptions of both urban space and gender it constructs?

In recent years, there has been a shift toward indie romcoms, such as *In a World ...* (Lake Bell, 2013), *Laggies* (Lynn Shelton, 2014) and *Sleeping with Other People* (Leslye Headland, 2015), as well as what I will call "post-romcoms." Whereas neo-traditional romcoms, Jeffers McDonald argues, deploy allusion to earlier romance films and self-reflexivity for nostalgic purposes, to invoke a notion of "old-fashioned" romance, post-romcoms extend the genre's reflexivity into sustained critical reflections on both the romcom as a form and dominant cultural conceptions of romance.⁶ This tendency can be seen in television shows like *The Mindy Project* (CBS/Hulu, 2012–), *Crazy Ex-Girlfriend* (The CW, 2015–), and *Love* (Netflix, 2016–), studio romcoms like *Friends with Benefits* (Will Gluck, 2011) and *How to Be Single* (Christian Ditter, 2016), and indie films like *(500) Days of Summer* (Marc Webb, 2009), *Celeste and Jesse Forever* (Lee Toland Krieger, 2012), and *Don Jon* (Joseph Gordon-Levitt, 2014). These texts approach this post-romcom project in a variety of ways, with some (*Crazy Ex-Girlfriend*, for example) clear examples of what

Todd Berliner, writing about 1970s genre revisionism, calls a "genre breaker," a text which "loudly broadcasts its violation of tradition." Others, however, do not necessarily withhold or deny the pleasures and conventions of the genre: see, for example, the perhaps unexpectedly clichéd unions of heterosexual couples at the conclusions of *Friends with Benefits* and *Ruby Sparks* (Jonathan Dayton and Valerie Faris, 2012). While Berliner contrasts genre breakers with the "genre bender," which "violates conventions without advertising the fact" thereby "misleading [viewers] to expect a more conventional outcome," these films often effectively do the reverse, misleading viewers to expect a significantly less conventional outcome than they actually provide.[7]

While recent scholarship has considered the gendered contours of post-crisis media—notably Negra and Yvonne Tasker's collection *Gendering the Recession*—I argue that these post-romcoms and indie romcoms also reframe the urban contexts in which romcoms have been situated, and that anxieties about those urban contexts are crucial to how such texts operate.[8] Crucially, such texts frequently displace the romcom from its pre-crisis urban settings to the urban contexts that most preoccupy indie culture. Michael Z. Newman suggests that indie cinema "has the potential to be counter-hegemonic," but tends instead to reproduce class stratification through an emphasis on an indie taste culture.[9] Brendan Kredell has extended this argument to claim that indie cinema is marked by an impulse to "selectively reappropriate the city as an aesthetic object," constituting a "cinema of gentrification" by obscuring the historical and cultural specificity of its settings.[10] But in addition to gentrifying neighborhoods, another major context for indie cinema is the so-called creative city. Indeed, Newman describes indie culture as "comparatively urbane, sophisticated, and 'creative class,'" and indie romcoms and indie post-romcoms tend to depict cities largely populated by artists and people working in creative industries.[11]

Off-screen, indie cinema has been thoroughly shaped by the industrial and urban policy effects of the "creative city" as propagated by figures such as Charles Landry and, especially, Richard Florida: interurban competition for industry and labor evident in rankings, the development of creative industries, gentrification, and the amenities presumed to appeal to a "creative class." For Florida, "creative centers" are those cities that can attract the creative class, both those working in creative industries and "creative professionals," those roles in, say, tech and finance that entail "creative problem-solving."[12] The creative city, then, has been a key point of contact between creative industries, including cinema, and the postindustrial city. Michael Curtin and Kevin Sanson argue that popular culture is the "most charismatic sector" of a new "global postindustrial hierarchy" that has fueled global competition between cities for media production, "a race to the bottom as conglomerates hopscotch the globe, playing each place against the others, in large part by exacting concessions from workers."[13] Indie films in particular rely on measures such as local agencies and production incentive schemes (largely at the state level, but often with an urban emphasis). While a Marvel film might be shot in Ohio or overseas locations like Seoul and Norwich, the locations available to the typical low-budget independent production are far more constrained. And the rankings of creative cities regularly produced by Florida or *Forbes* magazine are mirrored in the rankings of the best city to be an indie filmmaker produced annually since 2003 by *MovieMaker* magazine, foregrounding factors like availability of crew and equipment, as well as "pro-business" policies like incentive schemes.[14]

Florida's conception and promotion of the "creative class" had provoked serious criticism before the crisis, as a neoliberal quick fix, fuzzy and meretricious.[15] To a certain extent, the crisis has accelerated interest in the creative city as a means of recovery in an uncertain climate, what Jamie Peck refers to as "placebo dependency."[16] Florida himself has argued that the crisis constitutes an opportunity for the emergence of a new geography of creative cities within innovative mega-regions, with large swathes of the country effectively abandoned.[17] Yet for others, the creative city has come to seem like a "symbolic marker of a now defunct era of economic optimism."[18] Reactions have been felt against production incentive schemes, for example, on the Left as welfare for corporations and on the Right as a waste of state money and needless government intervention.[19] In addition, in his 2015 book *Culture Crash: The Killing of the Creative Class*, arts writer Scott Timberg argues that the combination of recession and the impact of the internet has meant the creative class—which he deliberately defines much more narrowly than Florida to exclude, for example, finance—is "melting."[20] The post-2008 period, then, is a period of flux for the creative city, flux that indie films that are so closely engaged with the creative city in terms of both production and representation have a stake in exploring.

In this chapter, I examine the ways in which that flux is managed in two films, one indie post-romcom—*Frances Ha* (Noah Baumbach, 2012)—and one indie romcom—*The Giant Mechanical Man* (Lee Kirk, 2012)—both of which focus on young white women in precarious employment whose lives are thrown into crisis, and each set in cities with distinct experiences of crisis: New York and Detroit, respectively. In so doing, I argue that indie cinema has reframed the romcom in terms of crisis, expressing anxieties about urban conditions, yet also reconstituting the romcom's concerns with professional life through an embrace of creative femininity and evading any meaningful critique through valorization of the creative city.

Magic: *Frances Ha*

Frances Ha, about an apprentice dancer (Greta Gerwig) in New York who loses her place in her company at roughly the same time as she and her best friend start to drift apart, sending her into a tailspin, is perhaps less explicitly post-romcom than the examples listed above. Yet there are definite connections. In its depiction of Frances's struggles to survive, the film denies core aspects of the pre-crisis romcom urban experience—affluence, consumerism—and its filming of New York conspicuously avoids landmarks, in stark contrast to its sequences in Paris and Sacramento. It also self-consciously minimizes any possible romantic narrative: it starts with Frances breaking up with her boyfriend; her friend Benji (Michael Zegen) repeatedly calls her "undateable"; and Frances seems oblivious to his attempts to flirt with her until the very end of the film. Instead, the film is preoccupied with female friendship, with Frances and Sophie's (Mickey Sumner) friendship repeatedly compared to a romantic relationship—Frances tells Sophie, "We are like a lesbian couple that doesn't have sex anymore"—to the extent that it could be regarded as a romcom about female friendship.

The other narrative line that displaces romance is career. Angela McRobbie argues that such displacements are typical for female creative workers:

> The idea of "romance" has been deflected away from the sphere of love and intimacy and instead projected into the idea of a fulfilling career. No longer looking for a husband as a sole breadwinner, young women romanticize the

idea of career. They want to find work about which they can feel passionate. Passionate work in turn becomes a mark of feminine intelligibility and success.[21]

We see Frances struggling in her career, but the film is much less concerned with the iniquities of work as such than with Frances's passionate attachment to her career as a dancer, despite it being increasingly apparent that that career path is no longer viable. In that respect, what truly marks *Frances Ha* as a post-romcom is the disappointment it expresses at the inaccessibility of the glamorous careers that characters of earlier romcoms might have had. In an early sequence, Frances asks Sophie to tell "the story of us," their fantasy of a shared future with successful careers, lovers, no children, and "so many honorary degrees." Sophie's dream job, an "awesomely bitchy publishing mogul," is not only a fairly typical romcom job, but also more specifically a perfect description of Sandra Bullock's role in *The Proposal* (Anne Fletcher, 2009), the highest-grossing romcom of the last ten years.[22] The "story of us" sequence is the film's clearest expression of its concern with what Berlant calls "fantasies that are fraying": "upward mobility, job security, political and social equality, and lively, durable intimacy."[23] This post-romcom has two love objects: Sophie and the life of an artist in New York. In its depiction of Frances's anxious attempts to cling onto her desired career and meaningful friendship in the face of a lack of secure work and the city's housing crisis (Sophie tells her, "The only people who can afford to be artists in New York are rich."), the film expresses frustration at the inaccessibility of those fantasies.[24]

Crucially, housing is key in both the friendship and career narrative threads. Frances and Sophie's friendship becomes strained when Sophie moves out of their apartment in Prospect Heights to Tribeca, while Frances had earlier broken up with her boyfriend after he had asked her to move in with him. The narrative progresses as a series of house moves: from her apartment with Sophie to an apartment in Chinatown that she shares with Lev (Adam Driver) and Benji, to putting her stuff in storage before going to her parents' in Sacramento over the holidays, to staying on her friend Rachel (Grace Gummer)'s couch, to dorms at Vassar, to, finally, her own apartment in Washington Heights. The significance of these moves is spelled out when street addresses appear as intertitles throughout the film. And at one stage Frances goes to Paris, paid for on a credit card, because a couple she met a dinner party have an apartment there. Jamie Peck argues that the "creative class" has been defined in part by hypermobility:

The idealized subjects of this new urban economy, a hypermobile elite of high-tech hipsters, allegedly crave opportunity to maximize their innate talents in the context of 24/7 experiential intensity. The now-storied creative class inhabits a socially and economically liberalized world, in which the barriers to sociospatial mobility are progressively removed. And its members are the objects of accelerating "talent wars," among both corporations and cities.[25]

Rather than the delicious mobility of a creative class that thrives in insecurity, Frances is mobile because she is continually forced out. In this respect, the film bears the mark of new urban conditions of instability and insecurity, at worst what Saskia Sassen calls "expulsions," where the gradual generalizing of extreme conditions leads to people being pushed out of systems, including evictions and the impoverishment of the middle class.[26]

By the end of the film, however, the housing crisis the film has intimated becomes ultimately unimportant. Frances takes an office job with her dance company and does choreography on the side (which we see in a final dance performance). The romantic narrative reasserts itself and Frances gets her own apartment in gentrifying Washington Heights. Each of the problems that has provoked so much anxiety is nicely resolved, allowing her to look around her new apartment as the camera zooms in on her smiling face. The overwhelming feeling of this moment is relief precisely because the film up to that point has so effectively mined Frances's anxiety.

The film's concern with anxiety, however, is never turned outwards to empathy with other people in similar circumstances. In a telling sequence, continuities with a wider experience of precarity and poverty are raised, when Benji tells Frances that he and Lev have been considering getting a maid for the apartment the three of them share:

Benji:	Yeah. It's not that expensive. It's like $400 a month.
Frances:	Do you know that I'm actually poor?
Benji:	You aren't poor. There are poor people. You aren't one of them.
Frances:	You'd feel poor if you had as little money as I do.
Benji:	But you're not poor. It's offensive to actual poor people.
Frances:	Yeah. I guess that's true …

These "actual poor people" remain an abstraction; *Frances Ha* is far more concerned with a terror of downward mobility. The film makes it clear that

Frances's challenges are fundamentally personal: earlier in the film, she had been offered the office job she later takes and places to stay but turned both down, insistent that she would still be able to make a living as a dancer. The life she has at the end of the film was set up for her all along; she needed to become flexible. The film therefore reinforces Negra and Tasker's argument that "recessionary media culture implies that management of the self can effect positive change" and Catherine Rottenberg's argument that neoliberal feminism positions gender inequality as individual rather than structural, forming a feminist subject that is both individualized and entrepreneurial.[27]

This evasion of the structural for the individual plays into indie cinema's long-standing emphasis on the personal. At an early screening questions were raised about the whether the film "had any sort of larger social context … besides only being about middle- to upper-class white people," to which Gerwig responded that it was a "very specific story."[28] Gerwig's use of ideas of the personal to deflect criticism of the film's exclusions read as strained. The film's whiteness is foregrounded by its black-and-white cinematography, compared by its DP to both a 35mm print struck from a 16mm negative (due to the image noise of the camera used) and films of the 1930s (due to the silver tone brought forward in color mastering): many of the film's most visually striking images are of pale white faces set against murky backgrounds, arguably replicating cinematographic practices that Richard Dyer argues "assume, privilege and construct whiteness."[29] Dylan Marron's project *Every Single Word*, which edits films down to every word spoken by a person of color, produced a 30-second video for *Frances Ha*, with dialogue spoken by four peripheral characters, none of whom are named.[30] Prominent indie film site *IndieWire* responded to reactions against the film with a column entitled "In Defense of 'Frances Ha': Why Middle-Class White Angst Is Angst, Too," rather starkly indicating the obliviousness of dominant strands of indie culture to any critique of its hegemonic whiteness, critiques that have been made of other contemporary indie filmmakers like regular Baumbach-collaborator Wes Anderson.[31] But this response is fitting for a film that, despite its emphasis on financial insecurity and rising rents, ultimately evades structural crises.

Frances's personal crisis is framed as a case of arrested development rather than a product of increasing systemic precarity. When her credit card is declined, Frances declares, "I'm not a real person yet." Her return to her college and (developmentally inappropriate) attachment to her friendship with Sophie is contrasted with Sophie's engagement. Negra has argued that postfeminist culture is marked by "time crisis," the pressure to achieve certain milestones by certain ages, with the effect that "women who cannot be recuperated into one of these life-stage paradigms generally lose representability within a popular culture landscape dominated by postfeminist definitions of femininity."[32] Frances's defining feature, however, is her girlishness, not in the sense of an exaggerated youthful femininity, but her romanticization of college friendships and apparent inability to make responsible decisions. She repeatedly describes things as "magic," and sequences where she spells out her desires—the "story of us" sequence and another when she describes the relationships she wants—are accompanied by an extract from Georges Delerue's score for *King of Hearts* (Philippe de Broca, 1966), a twinkly, music box-esque score that frames Frances's desires as charming, if child-like, dreams.

But in the qualities of her experience of crisis—fantasy, spontaneous decisions, emotional intensity, lack of polish—also lies her creativity. In its unpolished exuberance, the film's famous tracking shot of Frances dancing down a street soundtracked by David Bowie's "Modern Love" is the flipside of an earlier tracking shot in which Frances falls down while running to find an ATM (Figure 12.1). When Sophie calls her "messy," Frances responds

Figure 12.1 Messy creativity in *Frances Ha* as Frances runs/dances down the street.

"I'm not messy. I'm busy." But Sophie tells her she likes her messiness, and it is in embracing that messiness that Frances is able to triumph. After the performance she has choreographed at the end of the film, she tells Benji, "I like things that look like mistakes." Even the film's title is a mistake. At the end of the film, Frances finds that her full name, Frances Halliday, will not fit in her mailbox at her new apartment, so leaves it as "Frances Ha." James Zborowski contrasts the emphasis on "flow" in the film's opening montage, setting up Frances and Sophie's friendship, with subsequent scenes that emphasize social awkwardness.[33] The film's final sequence of Frances in her new apartment, half-unpacked, replicates that flow, along with the Delerue soundtrack, granting Frances an ending that requires her to be newly flexible but retain her messiness. The emphasis on messiness as the heart of Frances's creativity is neatly echoed by recent discourse on creativity that foregrounds precisely such qualities.[34] And a connection between creativity and messy spontaneity is echoed in the discourses of "creative freedom" that surround the film.[35] While any apparent onscreen spontaneity was produced by an average of thirty-five takes per setup—as Amy Taubin notes, "far removed from the directorial technique of the French New Wave," which the film repeatedly references— Nicole Armour, for example, claims the film had "the air of having been created hastily and on the fly," assuming that the messiness the film celebrates applies to its own production practices.[36]

In her messiness and chaotic qualities, Frances has common ground with Kathleen Rowe's "unruly woman." Rebecca Wanzo has argued that a recent evolution of the unruly woman is "precarious-girl comedy"—her examples are *Girls* (HBO, 2012–17) and Issa Rae's web series *The Misadventures of Awkward Black Girl* (2011–13)—where recession-induced arrested development leads to an "abjection aesthetic" where "women's bodies become a site of the modern mire of economic and intimate abjection" that relies on their remaining immobile.[37] *Frances Ha* differs from these texts, however, in that Frances does change as her messiness is channeled into a productive creative spirit that renders her undisruptive. Unlike the unruly woman, therefore, she poses no threat to "social and symbolic systems that would keep women in their place."[38] Instead, her unruliness grants her a secure place in a social–spatial order.

That space is not the city of the pre-crisis romcom, but one that invokes cinematic traditions of creative urban spontaneity and, in the film's style, replicates Frances's unruliness and ebullience. The film emphasizes street-level tracking shots, with camera movement matching characters, so as to express affinity. It's also clear that Frances's ability to thrive in the end is due to her networks (that provide her with places to stay in New York and Paris and, finally, a job). Anxieties about the city's crises and instability are displaced by the cinematic equivalent of what Peck sees Florida celebrating: "the buzzing, trendy neighborhood, a place where everyday innovation occurs through spontaneous interaction."[39] Furthermore, as Rosalind Galt and Karl Schoonover note, the film's "indie, lo-fi style" allows the film to "garner cultural capital by referencing cinephile histories" through its black-and-white cinematography, Delerue on the soundtrack and other French New Wave references.[40] So the film is interested in constructing a creative city in aesthetic terms, expressed through such references as well as a fit between style and character. And thematically, creativity is presented as the resolution of crisis, as in public policy. Frances's crisis is a temporary halt, rather than a fundamental disruption, that once resolved allows for both a fulfilling creative working life and romance, enabling her to secure her place in the creative city.

Absurdity: *The Giant Mechanical Man*

While *Frances Ha* was a reasonably widely distributed film for its low budget, generating intense public discussion and awards nominations, buoyed by the draw of its star and director, *The Giant Mechanical Man* is little known, but in many ways a far more representative product, made on a micro budget and littered with actors best known for television, playing at Tribeca then briefly opening in one theater before going straight to VOD. The two films do, however, have much in common: depictions of young white women going through personal crises with recessionary resonances and an infatuation with creativity. *The Giant Mechanical Man* focuses on Janice (Jenna Fischer) who gets fired from her temp agency and when subsequently evicted, moves in with younger sister Jill (Malin Akerman). She then gets a job working on a concessions stand at a zoo where she meets Tim (Chris Messina) who works there as a cleaner and has just been dumped by his long-term girlfriend Pauline (Lucy Punch), ostensibly because of his street art, performing as the titular giant mechanical man, essentially a robotic man on stilts in a business suit. *The Giant Mechanical Man* shares with *Frances Ha* a sense of crisis experienced through precarious employment, forced mobility, and a lack of a place in a spatial order.

Where *The Giant Mechanical Man* differs from *Frances Ha*, however, is in its setting: a generic any-city, but clearly shot in Detroit. *Frances Ha* was supported by New York's Made in NY scheme and clearly draws on the city's status as a creative capital. Detroit, meanwhile, has a far more fraught relationship to creative city policies. Faring poorly in creative city rankings and serving as a metaphor for urban and industrial failure in public discourse (including pessimistic accounts of the state of Hollywood), Detroit turned decisively to the creative city model in 2003, with various city agencies collaborating to launch a CreateDetroit brand, including a "creative corridor" along Woodward Avenue, leading to the city hosting the 2008 Creative Cities Summit 2.0.[41] In 2004, Michigan's governor Jennifer Granholm launched the state's "Cool Cities" program that, despite severe spending cuts in other areas, provided grants to encourage, as Peck puts it, "creative gentrification."[42] In 2008 Michigan also introduced aggressive film production incentives: a 40 percent tax credit on Michigan expenditures with an extra 2 percent if produced in one of the state's "core communities," with efforts to encourage film production in Detroit specifically supported by the local agency Film Detroit.[43] A *Huffington Post* article noted the effort to address "two of Michigan's biggest labor-market concerns: how to keep the young creative class from leaving the state and how to keep members of the large industrial workforce employed."[44] Yet amid criticism of such schemes as incompatible with austerity or as having limited impact on the local economy, the state's incentive program was capped in 2011.[45]

The Giant Mechanical Man was written to be set in Chicago, but moved to Detroit to take advantage of Michigan's production incentives and was shot in late 2010, during the three-year window before the cap.[46] Instead of tailoring the film to Detroit, director Lee Kirk chose to present the city as generic: "I had to find a way to make Detroit look like any city—Chicago, Philadelphia, wherever—to just sort of add to the fairy-tale nature of the film."[47] Clear efforts are made to avoid Detroit-specificity: Tim and Janice see job ads in a paper called *The Town Daily Read*; they go to "the art house cinema"; there are references to the Southside, which does not make sense for Detroit; and Tim's apartment is rent controlled, prohibited in Michigan since 1988. The film has little in common with other contemporary Detroit films like *Only Lovers Left Alive* (Jim Jarmusch, 2013) or *It Follows* (David Robert Mitchell, 2014), and in the muted blues and grays of its color palette and its emphasis on loneliness and public transit systems, the film it most closely resembles is the Chicago-set romcom *While You Were Sleeping* (Jon Turteltaub, 1995).

Yet the film is also preoccupied with distinctive qualities of Detroit's architecture. It opens with a montage of downtown Detroit, dwelling on sites of architectural interest such as the Detroit Institute of Arts and the art deco Penobscot Building. We see Tim painting himself up and going out as the giant mechanical man, and then a cut to a shot of the top of the Chicago School skyscraper Grand Park Centre, which the camera lingers on before panning left to show Janice arriving at the Grand Circus Park People Mover station. This sequence uses the urban environment to link its two protagonists visually while also granting the cityscape a narrative prominence. Recognizable place markers and names appear throughout, sometimes quite strikingly, as in the words "Royal Oak" in large white letters on the supposedly generic art house cinema or the numerous scenes at the Grand Circus Park station, with the station name clearly visible in the background (Figure 12.2). There seems to be an assumption that Detroit is inherently anonymous or that an emphasis on the

Figure 12.2 Detroit's Grand Circus Park Station in *The Giant Mechanical Man*.

skyline and cultural landmarks is so out of step with dominant representations of the city as to render it unrecognizable.[48]

There is, however, something resonant about the film's simultaneously obvious and generic use of Detroit. Commentators picked up on its setting (and the film was retitled *Love in Detroit* for its Scandinavian DVD release), linking the film's depiction of precarity to Detroit's own crisis and relying on Detroit's place in post-crisis visual culture.[49] Focusing on Detroit's status as two cities— "the real one with all its complexities and histories, and the one fashioned through ruin images"—Dora Apel argues that Detroit has come to serve as "a central locus for the anxiety of decline." Such representations allow "the real agents of decline—the corporations and the state—to evade responsibility" and justify austerity measures, ultimately serving as "disciplinary warnings" to other declining cities.[50] Creativity has had a central place in narratives of Detroit's revitalization, as an opportunity for young, white creatives to move in and reinvent the city, often prompting comparisons to Brooklyn.[51] By 2014, *Forbes* had declared Detroit the ninth most creative city in America, much to the amusement of local magazine *The Metropolitan*, whose editor noted that only a year earlier *Forbes* had described the city as the most miserable in America.[52] As a filming location, then, Detroit, unlike New York, brings to the forefront both conflicts between the creative city and austerity urbanism and the place of the creative city in narratives of urban revitalization.

The core of *The Giant Mechanical Man*'s project is an alienation from what it presents as conventional urban living. When Tim is interviewed on local television, he explains that the idea behind his art is that "modern life can be alienating. It can be like you're mindlessly walking through it, like a robot, and you can feel lost." The film is preoccupied with a sense of the absurdity of work and routine. Janice has a temp job that entails guarding a door with a broken lock in an art gallery, but the room is empty and in a rarely visited area. At several points, characters go to extremes to claim that necessities such as work and rent are natural or eternal, rendering the notion ridiculous through overstatement. This is most obvious in a speech Pauline's brother Mark (Bob Odenkirk) gives Tim early in the film:

> You're 30-something. You're poor. My sister's leaving you. You got no real
> future to speak of. You know why that is? Look, I'll tell you why that is. It's
> because people weren't meant to live like this, painted up like a metal guy.

There's a reason the entire population gets up in the morning and clogs the freeways: 'cause they gotta go to *work*. That's part of life and always has been. You're a farmer, you know. Whether you like it or not, you're a farmer, and you have got to plough the fields.

Tim skeptically responds, "What fields?" Mark's speech echoes an earlier moment when Janice's landlord appeared at her door to complain that she is consistently late with her rent, telling her that paying rent on the first of the month is a fact of life: "Someone invented months, and then someone invented rent, and then someone decided that rent is due on the first day of the month." One of the film's projects, then, is to resist the reification of work, the fact, as Kathi Weeks puts in her book on anti-work politics, "that at present one must work to 'earn a living' is taken as part of the natural order rather than as a social convention."[53]

But the film also resists expectations of life targets; it might be read as an implicit critique of the kinds of "time crisis" narratives that Negra identifies. As in *Frances Ha*, the film conflates Janice's various struggles into a generalized sense of arrested development, and Jill points out Janice's lack of both a career and romantic experience, yet it suggests that a bigger problem for Janice is that people around her are trying to force her to remold her personality to make herself more employable and socially appealing. Jill, married and comfortably off, tells Janice, "Your life has been on pause for so many years," and concocts various schemes to encourage Janice to get "a new attitude." Several people tell Janice she is lacking something: a new attitude, "a sense of accomplishment," "positive thinking," or, according to her recruitment consultant, being personable. Jill and her husband Brian (Rich Sommer) set Janice up with odious motivational speaker Doug (Topher Grace), whose self-help book is on "the art of small talk" despite his own lack of social graces ("What are your hobbies? One of my hobbies is helping blind kids to build a church."), so that he can teach Janice "how to talk," make her personable. To an extent, then, the film resists and satirizes the idea of the management of the self.

What does enable Janice to find her place in the world is romance. Whereas her sister berates her for being "weird," Tim tells her that he likes her because she does not "pretend to have it all figured out, like everyone else." That recognition is what enables Janice to discover her own agency and autonomy, to resist her sister's efforts to reshape her life, leading to a climactic moment where Janice, frustrated at Jill's attempts to instruct her on how to change her life, exclaims, "Do I have to know what I want? Why do I have to be something?" After she has slept with Tim and found a new sense of self, she tells her line manager that she wants a job where she can "think and make decisions" and is promoted to Assistant Habitat Coordinator, working on the zoo's design based on an earlier moment where she had identified a flaw that allowed visitors to poke sleeping monkeys. Janice's transformation entails a new-found creative impulse that relies on a close link between her romantic and professional lives. Just as *Frances Ha* identifies a gap that enables cathartic expressions of frustration and the potential for resistance only to close that gap through a valorization of creativity, *The Giant Mechanical Man* renders the reification of work absurd only to devote itself more forcefully to what Weeks characterizes as a new postindustrial work ethic, which brings to the foreground a less stressed element of the earlier industrial work ethic: "an element that characterized work as a path to individual self-expression, self-development, and creativity."[54]

The film closes that gap even more forcefully through its gender politics. Tim also struggles financially. When offered the job at the zoo and told it will involve cleaning toilets, he responds, "It's all cleaning toilets at this point." But he also has a rent-controlled loft apartment that he is in no danger of losing. While Janice goes through considerable turmoil in her efforts to achieve agency in the face of a dismissive family and difficult economic conditions, Tim's primary struggle is being accepted for his art. Similarly, in *Frances Ha*, Benji is also drifting, but is able to take loans from his family, and his attempts to write a *Gremlins* script are presented as absurd rather than a problem he urgently needs to resolve. And while it is her relationship with Tim that leads to Janice's transformation, *The Giant Mechanical Man* does not present creativity as masculine. In an early sequence, Pauline takes Tim to her work party where he encounters two men discussing watching porn on $3,000 plasma TVs, to which Tim interjects, "There's a lady right here," before they notice some silver paint on his neck and exclaim, "Dude's wearing makeup!" This moment clearly situates Tim's art as feminine and differentiates him from dominant forms of masculinity, precisely the kind of conformity that his art is intended to highlight. Janice's discovery of fulfilling creative work emphasizes not only her creativity but also her flexibility and adaptability. In short, it is entirely consistent with Rosalind Gill's contention that "the ideal disciplinary subject of neoliberalism is feminine."[55]

The emphasis on Tim's difference from the corporate men he meets, as well as his critique, is significant because ultimately Tim and Janice's relationship indicates their distinction from those around them, rather than their opposition. The resolution of Janice's narrative comes when Jill is able to accept her as she is, just as Tim has found someone who accepts his street art, which itself is critical of a notion of mainstream conformity without being actively oppositional. These threads are tied together at the film's conclusion, where we see Janice on the phone with Jill making theater plans, then spotting Tim performing, surrounded by a crowd, as a concluding shot/reverse shot unites the couple across Grand Circus Park. Indeed, the film's use of its romantic narrative to evade structural questions it raises is especially evident in its urbanism. Through its emphasis on Tim as a street artist, the film foregrounds both street culture and walkable streets, while other scenes in the film show off aspects of the city's culture (an art house cinema) or tourist attractions (the zoo). Kirk found the streets too deserted and brought in extras to "kind of fill in the street scenes so they would look like a bustling downtown that a street performer would be in."[56] The film therefore replicates the efforts of city mayors to, as Ann Markusen argues, "[wave] the banner of creativity use it to showcase their anchor arts institutions and to make claims about urban amenities—mostly directed at tourists," or as Peck suggests, stress "'authentic' historical buildings, converted lofts, walkable streets, plenty of coffeeshops, art and livemusic spaces, 'organic and indigenous street culture', and a range of other typical features of gentrifying, mixed-use, inner-urban neighborhoods."[57]

Furthermore, Kirk's reference to the film's "fairy-tale nature," when combined with the film's avoidance of local specificity, is a familiar strategy to evade acknowledging its overwhelming whiteness.[58] Not only is the city we see here near uniformly white—of course, entirely implausible for Detroit—but also, even entry-level, low-paid jobs are entirely taken up by down-on-their-luck middle-class white people; there is no acknowledgment of any kind of local working-class population. The film in this respect foregrounds a deep-rooted problem with contemporary indie film: the mobility of film production echoes the presumed hypermobility of the creative class, and that mobility not only encourages gentrification but also an obliviousness to the specificity of local populations and struggles. As with *Frances Ha*, the film's endorsement of the creative city not only sidesteps the concerns it raises about precarity, but also depicts such concerns purely as they affect white people. Both films, above all, claim urban space for a creative white middle class.

Conclusion

While both films self-consciously distance themselves from the affluent professional worlds of the pre-crisis romcom and foreground the challenges of living in neoliberal cities, at their conclusions they reconstitute desirable urban spaces that enable romantic narratives. Generic transformations lead to narratives of adjustment that allow the romcom to be reworked so that white middle-class people can once again feel at home in the neoliberal city. Whether difference from the pre-crisis romcom is produced purely by a shift to indie culture or through post-romcom strategies, the project is distinction rather than critique. The creative cities these films construct are, I would suggest, an example of what Christoph Lindner calls "palliative urbanism," dependent on an element of critique of, or release from, the neoliberal city, yet embracing creative gentrification that would exacerbate the problems they raise, ultimately reinforcing the status quo.[59]

A connection between creativity femininity and the romcom's love plots is what produces these narratives of adjustment. While love rescues Janice by awakening her creativity, Frances's embrace of her creativity grants her access to love plots, both romantic and her now rebalanced friendship with Sophie. Both Janice and Frances are then rewarded with a space in cities at one with their creativity, cities that exclude other kinds of narrative (and other kinds of people) that might challenge that sense of unity. Weeks argues that the work ethic serves disciplinary functions: "beyond manufacturing common meanings, it constructs docile subjects."[60] For all the charm each film has—the exuberance and empathy for its protagonist of *Frances Ha*, the quiet melancholy and sincere performances of *The Giant Mechanical Man*—a self-serving emphasis on the magical, life-transforming romance of creative work in a model creative city also leads to docile film-making, complicit in gentrification and at least implicitly racist.

Notes

1   Tamar Jeffers McDonald, *Romantic Comedy: Boy Meets Girl Meets Genre* (London: Wallflower, 2007), 89–90.

2   Diane Negra, "Structural Integrity, Historical Reversion, and the Post-9/11 Chick Flick," *Feminist Media Studies* 8.1 (March 2008), 51–52.

3   See, for example, Claude Brodesser-Akner, "Can the Romantic Comedy Be Saved?," *Vulture*, December 27, 2012, http://www.vulture.com/2012/12/can-the-romantic-comedy-be-saved.html (accessed December 29, 2016); Andy Greenwald, "Where Has the Love Gone?," *Grantland*, February 14, 2013, http://grantland.com/features/new-girl-mindy-rise-romantic-sitcom/ (accessed December 29, 2016); Amy Nicholson, "Who Killed the Romantic Comedy?" *L.A. Weekly*, February 27, 2014, http://www.laweekly.com/news/who-killed-the-romantic-comedy-4464884 (accessed December 29, 2016).

4   There are at least two romantic comedies in the 2016 global box office top 15: romcom/superhero hybrid *Deadpool* (Tim Miller, 2016) and Chinese mega-hit *The Mermaid/Mei ren yu* (Stephen Chow, 2016). "2016 Yearly Box Office Results," *Box Office Mojo*, http://www.boxofficemojo.com/yearly/chart/?view2=worldwide &yr=2016 (accessed January 2, 2017).

5   Lauren Berlant, *Cruel Optimism* (Durham, NC and London: Duke University Press, 2011), 11.

6   McDonald, 92.

7   Todd Berliner, "The Genre Film as Booby Trap: 1970s Genre Bending and *The French Connection*," *Cinema Journal* 40.3 (Spring 2001), 25.

8   Diane Negra and Yvonne Tasker, eds., *Gendering the Recession: Media and Culture in an Age of Austerity* (Durham, NC and London: Duke University Press, 2014).

9   Michael Z. Newman, *Indie: An American Film Culture* (New York: Columbia University Press, 2011), 2.

10 Brendan Kredell, "Wes Anderson and the City Spaces of Indie Cinema," *New Review of Film and Television Studies* 10.1 (March 2012), 86.

11 Newman, 15.

12 Richard Florida, "Cities and the Creative Class," *City & Community* 2.1 (March 2003), 8.

13 Michael Curtin and Kevin Sanson, "Precarious Creativity: Global Media, Local Labor," in *Precarious Creativity: Global Media, Local Labor*, ed. Michael Curtin and Kevin Sanson (Oakland: University of California Press, 2016), 7.

14 See, for example, Richard Florida, *The Rise of the Creative Class, Revisited* (New York: Basic Books, 2012), 411; Erin Carlyle, "America's Most Creative Cities in

2014," *Forbes*, July 15, 2014, http://www.forbes.com/sites/erincarlyle/2014/07/15/
americas-most-creative-cities/#4b078b105073 (accessed January 2, 2017). For
the 2012 *MovieMaker* rankings, see Jennifer M. Wood, "Top 10 Cities to Be a
Moviemaker: 2012," *MovieMaker*, January 16, 2012, http://www.moviemaker.
com/articles-moviemaking/2012-top-10-cities-indie-moviemakers-new-orleans-
austin-albuquerque-new-yor/ (accessed January 2, 2017).

15   Jamie Peck, "Struggling with the Creative Class," *International Journal of Urban
and Regional Research* 29.4 (December 2005), 740–770; Ann Markusen, "Urban
Development and the Politics of a Creative Class: Evidence from a Study of
Artists," *Environment and Planning A* 38.10 (2006), 1921–1940; Allen J. Scott,
"Creative Cities: Conceptual Issues and Policy Questions," *Journal of Urban
Affairs* 28.1 (2006), 1–17.

16   Jamie Peck, "Austerity Urbanism," *City: Analysis of Urban Trends, Culture, Theory,
Practice, Action* 16.6 (December 2012), 648.

17   Richard Florida, *The Great Reset: How New Ways of Living and Working Drive
Post-Crash Prosperity* (New York: HarperCollins, 2010).

18   Jonathan Vickery, *Beyond the Creative City – Cultural Policy in an Age of Scarcity*
(Birmingham: MADE: a centre for place-making, 2011), 2.

19   I discuss debates about Michigan's production incentive scheme below.

20   Scott Timberg, *Culture Crash: The Killing of the Creative Class* (New Haven,
CT: Yale University Press, 2015), 15. Nuanced academic reflections on the
ramifications of the recession for the creative city include Betsy Donald, Meric
S. Gertler, and Peter Tyler, "Creatives after the Crash," *Cambridge Journal of
Regions, Economy and Society* 6.1 (2013), 3–21; Michael Indergaard, Andy C.
Pratt, and Thomas A. Hutton, eds., special issue on "Creative Cities after the Fall
of Finance," *Cities* 33 (August 2013).

21   Angela McRobbie, *Be Creative: Making a Living in the New Culture Industries*
(Cambridge: Polity Press, 2016), 81–82.

22   "Romantic Comedy Movies at the Box Office," *Box Office Mojo*, http://www.
boxofficemojo.com/genres/chart/?id=romanticcomedy.htm (accessed December
30, 2016).

23   Berlant, 3.

24   From 2000 to 2012 median apartment rents had risen by 75 percent with housing
affordability decreasing for all income brackets, with the harshest consequences
for those with the lowest incomes. Scott M. Stringer, *The Growing Gap: New York
City's Housing Affordability Challenge* (New York: Office of the New York City
Comptroller, April 2014), 1.

25 Jamie Peck, "Creative Moments: Working Culture, through Municipal Socialism and Neoliberal Urbanism," in *Mobile Urbanism: Cities and Policymaking in the Global Age*, ed. Eugene McCann and Kevin Ward (Minneapolis: University of Minnesota Press, 2011), 41.

26 Saskia Sassen, *Expulsions: Brutality and Complexity in the Global Economy* (Cambridge, MA and London: Belknap Press of Harvard University Press, 2014).

27 Diane Negra and Yvonne Tasker, "Gender and Recessionary Culture," in *Gendering the Recession*, 2; Catherine Rottenberg, "The Rise of Neoliberal Feminism," *Cultural Studies* 28.3 (2014), 418–437.

28 Royal Young, "'Frances Ha' Greeted with Cynical Debate from Crowd," *The Lo-Down: News from the Lower East Side*, May 15, 2013, http://www.thelodownny.com/leslog/2013/05/frances-ha-greeted-with-cynical-debate-from-rooftop-films-crowd.html (accessed December 31, 2016).

29 Richard Dyer, *White* (London and New York: Routledge, 1997), 89. On *Frances Ha*'s cinematography, see David Heuring, "The Beauty of Noah Baumbach's Black-and-White New York: Using the Canon 5D to Capture 'Frances Ha,'" *Creative Planet Network*, June 20, 2013, http://www.creativeplanetnetwork.com/news/orphaned-articles/beauty-noah-baumbach-s-black-and-white-new-york-using-canon-5d-capture-frances-ha/605680 (accessed March 16, 2017).

30 Dylan Marron, "Every Single Word Spoken by a Person of Color in *Frances Ha*," June 24, 2015, https://www.youtube.com/watch?v=SOHaJizzjdg (accessed March 16, 2017).

31 Anthony Kaufman, "In Defense of 'Frances Ha': Why Middle-Class White Angst Is Angst, Too," *IndieWire*, May 17, 2013, http://www.indiewire.com/2013/05/in-defense-of-frances-ha-why-middle-class-white-angst-is-angst-too-134254/ (accessed January 2, 2017); Rachel Dean-Ruzicka, "Themes of Privilege and Whiteness in the Films of Wes Anderson," *Quarterly Review of Film and Video* 30.1 (2013), 25–40.

32 Diane Negra, *What a Girl Wants? Fantasizing the Reclamation of the Self in Postfeminism* (London and New York: Routledge, 2009), 47.

33 James Zborowski, "Passing Time in *Frances Ha*," *Movie: A Journal of Film Criticism* 6 (2015), 47.

34 See, for example, Jennifer Rosner, ed., *The Messy Self* (Boulder and London: Paradigm Publishers, 2007); Tim Harford, *Messy: How to Be Creative and Resilient in a Tidy-Minded World* (London: Little Brown, 2016).

35 Scott Foundas, "Noah Baumbach's New York State of Mind," *Variety*, April 23, 2013, http://variety.com/2013/film/news/noah-baumbachs-new-york-state-of-mind-1200409933/ (accessed December 31, 2016).

36 Nicole Armour, "Making Connections: The Pleasures and Perils of Free-Thinking Your Way through Life," *Film Comment* 48.6 (December 2012), 64; Amy Taubin, "Emotional Pratfalls," *Film Comment* 49.3 (June 2013), 27.

37 Rebecca Wanzo, "Precarious-Girl Comedy: Issa Rae, Lena Dunham, and Abjection Aesthetics," *Camera Obscura* 31.2 (2016), 33.

38 Kathleen Rowe, *The Unruly Woman: Gender and the Genres of Laughter* (Austin: University of Texas Press, 1995), 3.

39 Peck, "Struggling with the Creative Class," 741.

40 Rosalind Galt and Karl Schoonover, "Hypotheses on the Queer Middlebrow," in *Middlebrow Cinema*, ed. Sally Faulkner (London and New York: Routledge, 2016), 204.

41 Peck, "Creative Moments," 52–62. On Detroit as film industry metaphor, see, for example, Alex Ben Block, "Exec Gives Dim Industry Forecast," *The Hollywood Reporter*, September 29, 2009, http://www.hollywoodreporter.com/news/exec-dim-industry-forecast-89455 (accessed January 10, 2017); John T. Caldwell, "Spec World, Craft World, Brand World," in *Precarious Creativity: Global Media, Local Labor*, ed. Michael Curtin and Kevin Sanson (Oakland: University of California Press, 2016), 33.

42 Peck, "Struggling with the Creative Class," 751–752.

43 Lou Harry, "Michigan Touts Aggressive Incentives," *Variety*, August 26, 2008, http://variety.com/2008/film/features/michigan-touts-aggressive-incentives-1117991123/ (accessed January 10, 2017); *Variety* Staff, "Lockwood Locks up Productions," *Variety*, August 28, 2009, http://variety.com/2009/film/features/lockwood-locks-up-productions-1118007839/ (accessed January 10, 2017).

44 Alexander Eichler, "With Film Incentive Capped, Michigan's Movie Jobs Face an Uncertain Future," *Huffington Post*, November 17, 2011, http://www.huffingtonpost.com/2011/11/17/michigan-film-incentive-jobs_n_1098247.html (accessed January 10, 2017).

45 Todd Longwell, "Made in America," *The Hollywood Reporter*, November 17, 2009, http://www.hollywoodreporter.com/news/america-91459 (accessed January 3, 2017); Alex Ben Block, "Threat to Film Subsidies," *The Hollywood Reporter*, March 21, 2011, http://www.hollywoodreporter.com/news/threat-film-subsidies-169825 (accessed January 3, 2017); Eichler.

46 Zach Johnson, "Jenna Fischer's Son Weston Is 'Starting to Crawl,'" *Us Weekly*, April 25, 2012, http://www.usmagazine.com/celebrity-moms/news/jenna-fischers-son-weston-is-starting-to-crawl-2012254 (accessed January 3, 2017).

47 Patrick Dunn, "Making a Mechanical Man," *Real Detroit Weekly*, accessed August 24, 2014, http://www.realdetroitweekly.com/detroit/making-a-mechanical-man/Content?oid=1544405 (accessed January 3, 2017).

48 The *Variety* review concluded, "The establishing shots, suggesting Lower Manhattan, don't mesh with the rest of the Detroit-shot production." John Anderson, "Review: 'The Giant Mechanical Man,'" *Variety*, April 26, 2012, http://variety.com/2012/film/markets-festivals/the-giant-mechanical-man-1117947443/ (accessed January 10, 2017).

49 Jordan Zakarin, "Tribeca 2012: Jenna Fischer on the Long Road and Love Story behind 'The Giant Mechanical Man' (Q&A)," *The Hollywood Reporter*, April 24, 2012, //www.hollywoodreporter.com/news/tribeca-2012-jenna-fischer-giant-mechanical-man-office-315540 (accessed January 10, 2017); Perry Seibert, "The Giant Mechanical Man," *TVGuide.com*, http://www.tvguide.com/movies/the-giant-mechanical-man/review/375182 (accessed January 10, 2017).

50 Dora Apel, *Beautiful Terrible Ruins: Detroit and the Anxiety of Decline* (New Brunswick, NJ and London: Rutgers University Press, 2015), 4–5.

51 Mark Binelli, *The Last Days of Detroit: Motor Cars, Motown and the Collapse of an Industrial Giant* (London: Birdley Head, 2013), 357; Apel, 35–37.

52 Anthony Brancaleone, "Letter from the Editor," *The Metropolitan*, September 2014, 4.

53 Kathi Weeks, *The Problem with Work: Feminism, Marxism, Antiwork Politics, and Postwork Imaginaries* (Durham, NC and London: Duke University Press, 2011), 3.

54 Ibid., 46.

55 Rosalind Gill, *Gender and the Media* (Cambridge and Malden, MA: Polity Press, 2007), 256.

56 Dunn.

57 Markusen, "Urban Development," 1924; Peck, "Struggling with the Creative Class," 745.

58 Robert Murphy defends the whiteness of 1990s British romcoms by calling them "urban fairytales." Robert Murphy, "Citylife: Urban Fairytales in Late 90s British Cinema," in *The British Cinema Book*, ed. Robert Murphy, rev. edition (London: BFI, 2001), 292–300.

59 Christoph Lindner, "Interrupting New York: Slowness and the High Line," in *Cities Interrupted: Visual Culture and Urban Space*, ed. Shirley Jordan and Christoph Lindner (London and New York: Bloomsbury Academic, 2016), 64.

60 Weeks, 53.

Index

CPSIA information can be obtained
at www.ICGtesting.com
Printed in the USA
LVHW010350060221
678492LV00009B/54